THE LAST OF THE WINDJAMMERS

"HOUGOMONT"

Topical Press Photo

[*Frontispiece*

THE LAST OF
THE WINDJAMMERS

VOLUME II

BY

BASIL LUBBOCK

WITH ILLUSTRATIONS AND PLANS

GLASGOW
BROWN, SON & FERGUSON, LTD., NAUTICAL PUBLISHERS
52 DARNLEY STREET

First Edition   –   1929
Reprinted – – 1960
Reprinted – – 1976

ISBN 0 85174 114 2

© 1976 BROWN, SON & FERGUSON, LTD., GLASGOW, G41 2SG
Printed and Made in Great Britain

FOREWORD

AWAY back before the 1914-18 war I started to gather information with the idea of giving an account of the many beautiful sailing ships which were sailing the seas during the past fifty years. At first I proposed to call the result of my labours "The Last Days of Sail," but this title soon went by the board for fear that the careless or casual reader might confuse "sail" and "sale", and my efforts thus be mistaken for the reduced price catalogue of some fashionable dress emporium.

The book itself has grown and grown as material has come in from all parts of the world so that it has become impossible to compress it within the covers of two such bulky volumes as Volume I. and Volume II. of *The Last of the Windjammers.* I had hoped that this Volume II. would have made an end of it, but I was very much out in my calculations.

For instance, I had planned out an average length chapter for the famous American "round the Horn" clippers and carriers of the seventies, eighties, and nineties, which were known throughout the shipping world as the "Down Easters." This chapter has become a fair sized book, and will follow the present volume off my publishers' launching slips.

Then I have written chapters on the coolie ships, the nitrate traders, and the oil sailers, which between them will, I think, make up still another volume in my attempt to cover the history of the sailing ship during the last half century.

If I attempted to give a list of all those to whom I owe thanks for information and help, as well as for illustrations and plans, it would make yet another volume; but if there is any value in this book from the historical point of view, or any interest in it to those who love ships, it is entirely due to those kind helpers.

Note.—As in all my other books, when I write "mile" I mean the sea mile or 6080 feet, not the statute or land mile of 5280 feet.

Note.—The war referred to in this book, unless otherwise stated, is that of 1914-18

CONTENTS

CHAPTER I.—THE LAST BOOM IN SAIL.

CHAPTER II.—THE LIMEJUICERS OF 1888-9.

vii

CONTENTS

CONTENTS

x   *CONTENTS*

APPENDIX.

ILLUSTRATIONS

LIST OF PLANS

THE LAST OF THE WINDJAMMERS

VOLUME II.

CHAPTER I.—THE LAST BOOM IN SAIL.

Lay her before the wind, up with your canvas,
And let her work, the wind begins to whistle;
Clap all her streamers on, and let her dance
As if she were the minion of the Ocean.

(BEAUMONT and FLETCHER.)

The Age of Change.

THOSE of us who have lived through the past half century have had the luck to take part in perhaps the most important epoch in the world's development.

On land and at sea the changes in our habit of living, in our methods of communication, and in our ways of thought and outlook on life have been truly stupendous. This progress has in some ways been a blessing, but in others a curse, for we have gained much that we could well do without and lost much that we could ill afford to lose.

We have experienced all the horrors and heroisms of war, all the luxuries and laxities of peace, the marvels and mistakes of science and the delights and dangers of sport.

We have fought, as our grandfathers did before us, like gentlemen with cold steel, hand to hand, with grace and courtesy, sword and dagger, bayonet and bludgeon, battle-axe and boarding-pike; but we have also fought like fiends with the horrible new weapons of the mechanic and the chemist.

We have seen the sudden scattering death of bomb and mine and high-velocity, armour-piercing shell, the slow, choking death from poison gas, and the sizzling, stinging death from "flammen werfer."

With the lightning chained to our needs, our hearts braced by dynamite, our wheels turned by oil which has been pumped from the bowels of the earth, we have charted the last dark corners from the Equator to the Poles, adventuring with as desperate a courage as the boldest of our ancestors.

We have faced the blizzard and thawed the frozen ground for gold; sought the orchid in the deadly swamp and steaming jungle; dived with bursting lungs for the pearl in the atoll lagoon and even dug with catching breath for the blue poppy on the crest of the Himalayan Pass. With rifle at the ready we have watched the kill from an Indian machan, and we have shared the long grass with a lion during the evening soiree at an African water hole.

In all this adventuring every kind of transport has been used from shanks' mare to skis, from the saddle horse to the flying machine.

We have galloped the six-horse stage on a Rocky Mountains trail; mushed a team of tired huskies over the Yukon snow, run rock-studded rapids in a birch-bark canoe, crossed donga and drift in a many-spanned bullock wagon and even roamed the desert on a donkey.

The earth has been covered at every speed from a mile an hour to a mile a minute. And at sea our experience has been equally varied. We have run the Easting down at 15 knots with a white-faced helmsman sweating blood, and we have fisted the frozen canvas, hove down and drifting to leeward, in the grip of a Cape Horn snorter. We have breasted the short Channel seas, sprays flying and scuppers under, in a dainty schooner yacht, and rolled with crashing blocks in a Mediterranean calm; and we have watched the creaming wake of a floating palace as she ploughed her 20-knot path through the deep Atlantic blue.

Lastly, we have seen art give way before science, the ancient crafts overcome by the new industries and, alas, the beauty of the countryside blasted and blackened by factory and furnace, by mine dump and polluting duct.

Even the seascape has lost much of its charm since masts and yards have been replaced by funnels and derricks.

The Art of Handling Sail.

There is no time in these days for the leisurely contemplation of natural beauty, nor patience for the study of an out-of-date craft.

The younger generation seem to be entirely absorbed in four overmastering interests—speed, mechanics, vibrations, and the flying ball.

Under the head of speed can be listed every kind of competitive racing; under mechanics all the grubby delights of the oilcan, the sweat rag and the tool bag; under vibrations all the pleasures of song and dance; and under the flying ball all those games of skill from cricket to croquet, from football to fives, which the British race has introduced to the world.

The young man of to-day will grow enthusiastic over a new valve or a new alloy, but he cannot realise the delight of his forebears in juggling with those irresponsible forces, wind and wave, which is the art of handling sail.

In the good old days the Briton valued two great arts above all else, and these were the arts of the shipmaster and the horse-master.

Art can be taught up to a certain point but no further, and that is where it differs from science. No cleverness of brain or dexterity of finger can make a great painter or musician, and it is the same when you come to deal with the ship and the horse. Whether you are handling a fiddle or a tiller, a bridle or a paint brush, you need certain almost indefinable qualities of character to be really successful; and if you lack these qualities you remain a piano thumper, a paint dauber, a wrecker of ships and a spoiler of horses.

Though the man who controls the engine-room telegraph of a modern leviathan navigating in narrow waters must needs be a superb judge of speed, the supreme art of the old-time master mariner has been lost to the world. With the mechanising of cavalry and field artillery, with the motor car jostling the horse in every hunt, and the rising popularity of the mechanical hare it seems possible that the art of the horse-master may be lost likewise before very long.

The Most Beautiful Work of Man.

There have been many discussions as to which of Nature's beauties should be awarded the palm. Some have lauded the snow-capped mountain peak; others the giant forest tree; others again the glories of sunrise or sunset; the charm of running water or the grandeur of the breaking wave. But as regards the works of man, all old-time votes were invariably given to the sailing ship.

An old sportsman who hunted his own hounds in winter and handled his own yacht in summer used to declare:—"The most beautiful work of God is a thoroughbred horse, and of man the 38-gun frigate."

Another ancient saying was:—"God made the forest oak, the living glory of the hills and dales. Man cut it down, but out of its trunk and limbs he built the line-of-battle ship, the glory of the seas."

A sea captain who had sailed to every part of the world was once asked: "In all your voyaging what is the most beautiful sight you have ever seen?" Without a moment's hesitation, he replied: "My own ship a-rolling down to St. Helena under stunsails in the South-East Trade."

This reminds one of Kipling:

> There be triple ways to take, of the eagle **or** the snake,
>   Or the way of a man with a maid,
> But the sweetest way to me is a ship's upon the sea,
>   In the heel of the North-East Trade.

The First Windjammer on the Solent.

The first sail was spread to the wind away back in prehistoric times, and we shall never know whether priority should be given to the square sail of Northern Europe, the lateen sail of the Mediterranean or the mat sail of the Far East.

No doubt in an era when man mostly lived and died within a stone's throw of where he was born, each fishing hamlet had, perforce, to make its own improvements in boat design and methods of propulsion. We can well imagine the excitement of a seafaring community when the local genius first spread a sail. Only those who have long and often over-wearied their muscles in paddling coracles or dugouts against a river ebb or foul tide could appreciate the immense boon this new means of propulsion offered.

I will attempt to visualise the event as it happened to members of my own village of Hamebrise on Hamel Creek in Happy Hampshire, where the Homelea running through the country of the West Saxons falls into the Solent.

Before the days of the West Saxons, before those also of the Jutes, of the Britons, of the Celts and possibly even of the Iberians, a sail was used in Southampton Water: but at any rate we will imagine that the event occurred somewhere about the Neolithic age, when the wild moorland of South Hampshire, long afterwards made a "mickle deer-frith" by William the Conqueror, was chiefly composed of reedy marshes, bounded here and there with osier beds, thickets of withies and tangled brakes of thorn and holly, at the back of which stood clumps of "Dormast" oak, the pride of the forest, whilst in the folds of the higher ground to the northward extended park-like chases of beech, forests of dark green spruce and great open spaces of heather and bracken where the red deer shared his feed with the wild boar, and shaggy unbroken ponies frisked amongst the heavy-shouldered, fly-tormented bison.

Out of this land of marsh and moor, of copse and grove and woodland, came two sturdy hunters, clad in leather jerkins and raw hide leggings. Over the back of the strongest lay a haunch of venison, whilst the other carried a newly flayed deerskin and a couple of long-shafted, stone-headed spears.

Presently the men fell into single file along a narrow beaten track which led past the hamlet of Fawley to the hard at the head of Ower's Leak. The tide was at a little more than half ebb, whilst the wind blew fresh and keen from the sou'-sou'-west. Along the shingle-covered hard, which stabbed its way through the blue-grey mud to the low water mark and was on the south side of the Leak not far from where some thousands of years later a Tudor king built Calshot Castle, was a round-sided coracle, made of sinew-sewn ox-hide stretched over ribs of withy. In this rude ferry boat sat a man of the sea, who had evidently been waiting anxiously for the hunters and whose eyes lit up greedily at the sight of the venison.

With great care the tired hunters stepped into the swaying boat, and squatted down, one in the bow and the other in the stern, whilst the seaman, kneeling amidships, shoved off with a long-handled paddle and began to propel his craft out into the water with the object of crossing to the hamlet of Hamebrise on the other shore.

As soon as the rude craft felt the strength of the ebb, in spite of the vigorous sweeping strokes of the ferry man, she began to drift towards the broken water where the tide was falling over the shingle beds of the spit to south-east of the Ower's Leak. The matter was serious and the weary hunters were compelled to supplement the paddle with their spears. But even this had very little effect, and the coracle was fast being swept into the overfalls when the paddler had his inspiration. Seizing the deerskin, he thrust the two spears through its four corners and held it up to the wind. The effect was seen in a moment. The two hunters next held up the spears in order to allow the seaman to use his paddle and steer the boat.

Then with many guttural exclamations of wonder and delight the Iberians watched their frail craft, under the influence of the strong wind, push its way across the tide towards the haven mouth. And so the first sailing ship ever seen in Southampton Water made her port.

Tall Ships.

From this lurching coracle with its spear-held deerskin curving in the wind it is a far cry to the tall full-rigged ship, the lordly four-master and the mighty five-master with their acres of canvas.

The wood and composite built full-riggers came to their perfection in the eighteen fifties and sixties; the iron clipper had an innings for some twenty years between 1865 and 1885; and finally there came during the short boom of the early nineties the great steel carrier.

I believe that sail and rigging plans reached the summit of their development along with the beautiful wood and composite ships. The need for economy in material and man power spoilt many of the sail plans of more modern days. But during the fifties, when trade was booming, money was plentiful and ships were never stinted as regards their gear, sail plans were very lofty, whilst width was gained by stunsails spread at fore and main from the skysail down.

Racing ships even carried large and small sets of these additional sails, which as late as the days of Nelson were still called "steering sails." I have never seen any explanation of the name "steering sail," nor any reason for its change to "studding sail." My own idea is that they were called "steering sails" because they gave a ship steerage way, when all plain sail, as it was called, was not sufficient to do so.

Sky-Scrapers and Moon-Rakers.

Sailors, in the old days, were very fond of disputing as to which was the tallest ship ever rigged; and as it was the rule for one man to cap the other's yarn, these stories of tall Sou-Spainers or lofty packets were more than even a horse-marine could swallow.

Personally I believe that the *James Baines* of the Black Ball Line crossed the highest yard under Heaven when she mast-headed her famous moonsail at the main. But there is an anecdote in Paul Eve Stevenson's *By Way of Cape Horn*, which, if only it could be verified, would undoubtedly give the palm to a British man-of-war. He writes as follows:—

"Mr. Rarx told me the other day that he spent two years on the West African coast, between Sierra Leone and Lagos, aboard of an English supply steamer: and that while there he saw what, in his estimation, was the loftiest-rigged vessel that ever floated. 'You can talk about your talkabouts,' said he, 'but that English man-o'-war had four yards above her main-royal. I'm tellin' you a fact," he added.

I have not yet succeeded in identifying this vessel, but many of the corvettes and gun brigs employed in the suppression of the slave trade sent up sliding gunter masts, which extended some 15 to 20 feet above their trucks.

On this mast either a raffee, a Bermuda sail or balance lug was set and tacked and sheeted to the skysail yardarms.

The name given to such a sail in the Royal Navy was "lateen moon-raker." It may well be asked what were the recognised names of square sails set above the skysail. In the *Naval Sketch Book*, published in 1835, there is the following passage:—"That was the craft for caperin'-kites—let's see, we used to set ring-tails—water-sails—studden-sails without studden-sails—sky-scrapers—moon-rakers—star-gazers—and heaven-disturbers—never ship could carry such a crowd o' canvas."

"Slieve Roe's" Butterfly Sails.

In a most interesting letter to the *Dolphin and Guild Gazette*, Captain W. H. Clements calls the raffees set by the *Slieve Roe* from truck to royal yardarm "butterfly sails."

He wrote:—"In September, 1926, *Dolphin*, I read with pleasure of my old ship, the *Slieve Roe*. I note what Captain D. G. Ball says; he is quite right in stating that the *Slieve Roe* did $16\frac{1}{2}$ knots per hour. For three days running on our homeward trip we did 350 miles per day, at times she was doing over 16 miles, but the greatest distance I ever saw her do was 400 miles, running the Easting down the voyage Captain Campbell had her, and just a little after noon we lost the fore and mizen topgallant yards and sails. I had the pleasure of being second officer of her at the time, this was the trip before Captain Ball joined us. I was three voyages in her, one with Captain Campbell, and two with Captain McMullan. Captain Campbell left us to join the *Slieve Donard*.

"It was a happy trip, for all the crew were young men—I think I was the oldest man and I was only 24 years old—and I can tell you I was a proud young man, proud of my ship and position. It used to be my greatest pleasure when I was driving her into it to see the white foam flying, and knowing all my watch were ready and willing to jump once an order was given. I look on the *Slieve Roe* to be one of the fastest ships afloat at her time, in fact during the three East India voyages I never saw a ship pass us either with a fair wind or beating. I have a painting of her at home now, and I often tell people she would and did pass mail boats, but, not being sailors, they laugh. We had on that ship what few sailors have seen, and that was—butterfly sails; they set from the truck

"BARON ABERDARE"

Lent by Captain L. R. W. Beavis

See Page 9

"CITY OF HANKOW"

Lent by Captain L. R. W. Beavis

[See Page 16

to the royal yardarm, and can only be set with a fair wind when the yards are off the backstays."

These jib-headed sails did not require a yard; the square sail set above a skysail was always called the "moonsail." This was regularly set on the main in the famous Black Ballers, *Lightning* and *James Baines*, but the moonsails which were set by the Aberdeen clipper *Star of Peace* and the Sunderland tea clipper *Maitland* were really raffees or butterfly sails, as Captain Clements calls them.

Old "tarpaulins" used to delight in letting their imagination go when enumerating their ships' flying kites, and besides the names already mentioned "sailor's delight" and "angel's footstool" were both in common use for more or less mythical sails.

The topmast of all sails on a really tall ship was named the "curse o' God." The reefer who was sent aloft to take in this sail was warned to take his rations with him, for it was more than a day's climb to reach this bit of gossamer, which was usually hidden from sight in the clouds. He also had to take his heavy watch coat, for it was freezing cold on those lofty footropes and the yard was often white with hoar frost.

The greatest number of yards ever crossed by an iron ship was seven on one mast, namely—lower yard, upper and lower topsail yards, upper and lower topgallant yards, royal and skysail yards.

One may imagine the weight and leverage aloft when these yards as well as the masts were all of iron; no wonder dismastings occurred in spite of doubled backstays.

With the advent of steel came the hideous bald-header with her tremendously square topgallant yards and long doublings.

Clipper Lines versus Full Bottoms.

In the eighties with the ever-increasing competition of steam, sailing ship owners had to decide whether it paid best to make slow passages with big cargoes or quick passages with small cargoes.

James McCunn used to declare that his fine-lined "Barons" were a voyage ahead of their full-built rivals in four years.

For a time the canny British owner tried to compromise matters by combining full mid sections with fine ends, and the medium clippers of the eighties were the result.

But by the end of the eighties the fight with the steam tramp had become so bitter, and low freights could only be made to pay by means of big cargoes, that the mid section gradually was made to extend further and further forward and further and further aft, with the result that the bow lines had to swell out and the fine runs had to be shortened up.

There was another good reason for the neglect of speed in favour of carrying power, and that was that it was often cheaper to let grain remain in a ship's hold rather than store it in a warehouse; and this explains the length of time that ships were often kept waiting at the ports of call, Falmouth and Queenstown, before getting orders.

It will thus be seen that although no man who ever possessed an interest in sail ever preferred a slow ship to a fast one, competition, expediency, and possibly a want of courage forced owners to fight steam with box-shaped arks rather than go for speed and clipper-lined vessels of medium size.

Old-time sailors will argue to the end of time on the question as to which was the sharpest ship ever built. Very often a white-headed "know-all" would bring up the name of a vessel no one had ever heard of and tell some very tall yarn of her extraordinary speed, and very few shellbacks of mature years were content to allow the palm for sharp lines to be awarded to any ship in which they themselves had not made a voyage.

Thus the first American clipper ship, the *Rainbow*, or the still more speedy *Sea Witch*, or even the *Lightning* with her long hollow bow, received little support from old seamen; and even *Thermopylae* and *Cutty Sark* were only most grudgingly given credit for their beauty and sharpness of form. In this matter one cannot do better than go by the builders' half-model or the designers' lines.

The Extreme Clipper "Cairnsmore."

Before turning to the full-built ships of the nineties, I propose, by way of contrast, to give an account of some out and out clipper ships, and I will take for my subject one or two which I believe would have rivalled any of the well-known champions if they had not been lost almost at once.

I will take the *Cairnsmore* first of all. This ship was a long way ahead of her time. She was built at Port Glasgow by John Reid & Co., for Nicholson & McGill, and was launched in February, 1854. She registered 1211 tons (old measurement) and her dimensions were:—Length 223 feet; breadth 33 feet 6 ins., and depth of hold 20 feet 6 ins.

She was flush-decked and like a wedge forward, being described at her launch as one of the sharpest sailing ships ever built. Her sail plan was a moderate one with a 72-ft. mainyard, but very lofty with long stunsails booms. She was planned for skysails, but they are not shown on the builders' sail plan, though it is quite possible that they were sent up at sea.

The *Cairnsmore* is remembered for a wonderful maiden passage to Bombay. Captain Crosbie called his record 70 days from Land's End to Bombay. The actual dates from his abstract are as follows:

> April 3—2 a.m.—Dropped pilot.
> April 7—4 p.m.—Achill Head bore East.
> April 17.—Passed Madeira.
> April 25.—Crossed the Equator.
> May 8.—Lat. 35° 55′ S., long. 8° 50′ W. Lost main topmast and mizen topgallant mast and fore topgallant yard.
> May 16.—Crossed Meridian of the Cape.
> May 29.—Off Mauritius.
> June 5.—Crossed the Equator.
> June 13.—Arrived Bombay.
> Average day's run 198 miles. Best run 320 miles.

On her second voyage the *Cairnsmore* was wrecked on an uncharted rock in the China Sea.

"The Caliph"—Hall's Masterpiece.

It is a thousand pities that the tea clipper *The Caliph* disappeared on her second voyage, for she was undoubtedly Hall's masterpiece, being the most advanced of all the China clippers as regards design. She was built like the *Cutty Sark* with the special object of vanquishing the peerless *Thermopylae*; and there is no doubt that she would have been a worthy antagonist both of

Thermopylae and *Cutty Sark* had she survived. She owed her unusual name to the fact that her owner had lived many years in Bagdad.

Captain Henderson, who sailed her down from Scotland, used to declare that she was the fastest ship he had ever had anything to do with, and as he commanded the *Thermopylae* for some years, and others of the green clippers, his opinion should carry weight.

Captain Chapman, who wrote *All about Ships*, after observing her lines in dry dock and noting her tremendous sail plan, gave it out that she would be "one of the fastest ships afloat, if not the fastest, and if care were taken of her she would be a sound ship fifty years hence."

There has always been a good deal of mystery about this ship, and I have heard some very false statements made about her. I have therefore reproduced her lines and sail plan, and given Messrs. Hall's account of her building, as quoted by Captain Chapman, in an Appendix.

The Caliph was Hall's 263rd ship. She was built under a water-tight shed and classed 17 years A1 at Lloyd's. Her registered tonnage was as follows:—Under deck 888; gross 963; crew space 47; net register 914 tons; builders' measurement 1330 tons; length between perpendiculars 213 ft. 3 ins.; breadth 36 ft.; and depth 20 ft. 4 ins.

She sailed from Aberdeen under Captain Henderson on September 19, 1869, and after six hours of head wind came romping south with a nice beam breeze, arriving in the Thames only 36 hours out.

After loading a good general cargo with plenty of liquids, the new flyer left London on October 13 under the command of a Captain Ritson, and bound for Shanghai. She was spoken on November 15 in 2° 50' N., 25° W., so her passage to the Equator was a lengthy one. On February 1, 1870, she arrived at Shanghai, 111 days out, after a close race with the *Titania*, which left London the day after *The Caliph* and arrived at Shanghai on the same day.

The new *Norman Court*, which sailed from the Thames five days behind *The Caliph*, arrived at Hongkong on January 31, 1870, and I believe the two ships were in the Java Straits together.

The Caliph's passage did not altogether come up to expectations, but this was put down to the inexperience of her master, who, it was said, had never been in a racing ship before and was unac-

quainted with the China Coast. She made the usual intermediate
passages, first round to Bangkok, where rice was loaded for Yokohama at 45 cents. per picul. She then went to load tea at Foochow,
but failed to gain a place amongst the cracks, and finally was
compelled to load a cargo in the N.E. monsoon for New York,
where she arrived on March 3, 1871, after a good passage of 88 days.

She left New York on April 1, and arrived in the Thames on
April 22, but it is claimed for her that she made the passage pilot
to pilot in 12 days.

Leaving London again for Shanghai, she passed Anjer on
August 15, 1871, after which she was never heard of again, nor
has the remotest trace of her ever been found. As there had been
no typhoons or bad weather in the China seas, it was suggested
that the *Caliph* had been captured by pirates. But as a rule when
ships were taken by Chinese pirates the loot in the shape of gear,
navigating instruments, etc., generally turned up before very long
in the purlieus of Hongkong, but nothing of the *Caliph's* has ever
come to light.

Dry Decks versus Half-Tide Rocks.

Though ships of clipper lines were often shunned by old
seamen for their wetness, and often cursed as workhouses where
no one ever had a chance to keep a dry skin, they were not, as a
matter of fact, ever so heavily swept by green water as the later
iron and steel carriers. Besides the superior buoyancy of wood,
the clippers were better shaped for contending with rough water,
the length, the lack of beam, and the wall-sidedness of the carriers
being all against dry decks. Sprays in sheets flew across the tea
clippers when they were being driven into a head sea, and the lee
scuppers were probably boiling with white water right up to the
hatch coamings, but this was nothing to the Niagara-like rapids
which filled the maindeck of a steel four-master to the rails when
she was running before the Westerlies in the Southern Ocean.
The difference between a wood and an iron ship in heavy weather
was well shown in the case of the Blackwaller *Newcastle* and the
big iron ship *Oneida*. On March 12, 1876, in lat. 43° S., long.
115° 59' E., the *Newcastle* ran 279 miles before a tremendous N.W.

to S.W. gale, with as usual, for her, the wash deck buckets on the quarter galleries.   She, of course, shipped water but received no damage from the heavy seas, whilst the *Oneida*, commanded by the well-known Captain Clyma, which was in close company, very nearly foundered.   Besides being terribly knocked about, so that she was a wreck on deck, with binnacle and compass, skylights and boats all gone by the board, the *Oneida* lost several of her crew and one of her passengers.

There were, of course, no drier ships than the little Blackwall frigates, and nothing wetter than the heavily rigged, thick-plated, narrow iron ships of the seventies and eighties.

The Unique " City of Hankow."

When steel came in a few ships were built which were registered as being constructed of iron and steel, just as when iron came in iron and wood combined in the composite ships.   The well-known City Line clipper *City of Hankow* was the only vessel ever built with iron topsides over a teak bottom.

Of 1195 tons register the *City of Hankow* was called a composite ship.   Her frames were of iron, and were planked with teak up to a couple of feet above the deep load line, and this planking was sheathed with yellow metal.   Above the teak she had iron topsides and bulwarks to the main rail, then topgallant bulwarks of wood. The upper strake of the teak planking was protected where it jutted out beyond the metal plating by an angle iron, which ran the whole length of the ship.

One would have thought that there must have been severe corrosion between the iron plates, the angle irons, and the copper beneath, but according to those who served in the *City of Hankow* there was no corrosion.

The City liners had to be well built, for they were hard worked and hard sailed.   The *City of Hankow* was classed A1 at Lloyd's for 17 years.

A few words about her sail plan may be of interest.   When at sea she used to send up a sliding gunter skysail mast and yard at the main.   She also had a full suit of stunsails from the royals down, her square lower stunsails being specially big, and sheeted out to the end of a huge swinging boom (passaree boom it was generally called) which was boomed out from a gooseneck on the topgallant rail. Under this lower stunsail a water sail was spread. The *City of Hankow* was provided with a large ringtail, which also had a water sail underneath it, the sheets of which led into the cabin through the stern ports. In addition to these kites she sported a "Jimmy Green" under the jibboom.

Her first captain, Napier, was a very fine shipmaster who never spared himself, being continually on deck day and night, for he was a hard sail carrier who never hesitated to set every possible sail, even if it could only be carried for an hour or two. Though a strict disciplinarian, like all real seamen, he was popular with his crew.

The *City of Hankow* carried 36 hands all told, and when reefing topsails could man all three at once, the port watch going up on the fore, the starboard watch at the main, whilst the apprentices, carpenter, and sailmaker took charge of the mizen, which was a single topsail.

Captain Napier was very proud of the *City of Hankow*, and although the Smiths offered him the command of their first steamer he preferred to stick to the sailing ship and under him she made some of her best passages.

When she was launched the City Line consisted of over 40 ships, all first class and all noted clippers. A regular fortnightly service was maintained to Calcutta, and a monthly service to Bombay, the ships leaving Glasgow on their advertised dates as punctually as any steamship service of the present day. With the *City of Hankow* the Smiths meant to have a cut in at the China tea trade, but as a matter of fact she only made one tea voyage, as we shall see.

On her maiden voyage she took her place on the Calcutta run. Her outward passage was made in 95 days. This was nothing remarkable for such a fast ship, but on her homeward Captain Napier found himself on soundings at the mouth of the English Channel when only 71 days out from Calcutta. Then unfortunately a hard nor'easter came on to blow, and the ship was kept head-reaching under lower topsails for three weeks. A short let-up, during which the wind hauled to the nor'west, allowed the City liner to reach London 93 days out; and then the wind again backed to the N.E. and blew harder than ever. She was one of perhaps half a dozen out of a large fleet held up in the chops of the Channel which succeeded in reaching port. As the easterly wind continued blowing week after week many of the held up ships ran out of food, and steamers had to be sent out to them with provisions.

On her second voyage the *City of Hankow* loaded in the Victoria Dock on the Shanghai berth, where she succeeded the composite barque *Jungfrau.* The voyage out was uneventful until the entrance to the Straits of Gaspar, which were reached at nightfall. Captain Napier anchored for the night, and at daybreak next morning the composite ship *Northampton* of London was seen at anchor close to.

The *Northampton* was a well-known China clipper belonging to the Merchant Shipping Company. Registering 1174 tons she was composite built by Connell in 1866, and was particularly fast in light winds. She also had a very expert commander in Captain W. Barclay. She had left London a fortnight ahead of the *City of Hankow*, and if the latter could only beat her in the race up the China Sea to Shanghai her reputation in the East as a crack sailer would be assured. There was a rush on the two ships as to which should have her anchor up first, and in this the *Northampton* proved the smarter. However, the pair of them had not gone far, with the *Northampton* leading, when the *City of Hankow* bumped on to a reef and stopped there. The *Northampton*, drawing a few less inches of water, got over without touching.

In those days Gaspar Strait was very imperfectly charted, and a number of fine sailing ships, including John Company's East Indiamen, opium clippers, tea clippers, and local traders, came to grief on the numerous coral teeth which studded the Straits.

The strength of the *City of Hankow* was tested severely. For some time she bumped heavily, and when a piece of her false keel about 8 feet long floated up alongside her crew began to grow alarmed, but the carpenter continued to report no water in the well. The two quarter-boats were lowered, and the stream anchor taken away astern to the full length of the ship's towing hawser and dropped. The slack was then hove as tight as possible by means of the hand winches (*City of Hankow* had no steam.)

"MARIA RICKMERS"

Lent by Jas. Randall

"FRANCE": built by D. & W. Henderson, 1890

Photo Adamson

[*See Page* 21

"OLD KENSINGTON"

Lent by Captain L. R. W. Beavis   [*See Page* 23

"PETER RICKMERS" ASHORE, MAY, 1908

[*See Page* 27

Whilst this was going on the *Jungfrau*, which had sailed from London three weeks ahead of the *City of Hankow*, appeared on the scene. Her offer of assistance was refused as there was nothing to do but await the flood. However, the *Jungfrau* stood by. Early in the afternoon the *City of Hankow* began to bump again as the swell lifted her on the rising tide. The tackles were then manned and she was soon afloat.

A few days later the *Northampton* was sighted ahead, and the *City of Hankow* was fast overhauling her when the breeze fell and the light weather flyer went away again. This happened two or three times, and each time the *City of Hankow* failed to get by. At last, on the day before they made Woosung, the breeze held up well. The *City of Hankow* got up to and passed her rival, and keeping ahead reached the anchorage several hours before the *Northampton*.

Captain Napier, however, was not satisfied with the sailing of his ship, and considered that the damage to her bottom had severely interfered with her sailing in light winds.

The *City of Hankow* was dry-docked, repaired and remetalled at Shanghai, and loading 1,626,567 lbs. of tea, sailed from Shanghai on September 14, 1870, in company with the *Northampton*. However, the ships parted outside, and did not see each other again until the London River was reached. The *City of Hankow* passed Anjer on October 17, and reached London on January 12, 1871, 122 days out, having again succeeded in beating the *Northampton*.

On her third voyage she loaded at Glasgow for Calcutta, and made the run out in 74 days; then, leaving Calcutta on July 16, 1871, reached London 89 days out. This was perhaps the smartest voyage of her career, the crew being paid off with six months and nine days.

Her fourth voyage was the round of London, Melbourne, Calcutta, Demerara, New Orleans and Liverpool. On the passage to Demerara Captain Napier was lost overboard near Ascension, and the mate took the ship on.

Her next commander was Captain G. Muir, another very well-known master in the City Line, and under him the *City of Hankow* continued to distinguish herself by her smart passages. In my *Log*

C

of the Cutty Sark I have described how in the winter of 1873-4 she raced the *Thermopylae* out to Melbourne, and in 1874-5 sailed level with the *Cutty Sark* and the *Thomas Stephens* on the same run, her passages being 78 and 70 days respectively.

In 1874 the *City of Hankow* crossed from Australia to India and came home from Tuticorin. In 1875 she crossed the Pacific from Sydney to San Francisco for a grain cargo home.

On the run between San Francisco and the United Kingdom her best passage was 96 days, made in the early eighties.

Captain Muir was succeeded by Captain J. King in 1888, and the latter remained in the ship until she was sold to G. J. Robertson of Sydney at the beginning of the twentieth century. One of his best passages was 106 days from San Francisco to Queenstown in 1894.

In 1903 the *City of Hankow* was converted into a hulk at Thursday Island, where she remained until 1927, when she was brought down the coast to do duty at the new port of Gladstone, Queensland. According to the *Harbour* of Sydney, the old ship proved the strength of her build by the way in which she stood the severe buffeting from very bad weather on this the last passage of her career.

Amongst the ships which were constructed of iron and steel were the four-mast ship *Peter Iredale*, built by Ritson of Maryport, and the *Mayhill*, a four-mast barque built by A. Stephen & Sons, both launched in 1890.

The Last Spurt in Building Sail.

The windjammer boom, which started in 1888 and lasted for five years, was due to many causes besides the advent of steel in ship construction; it was the last desperate fight put up by the sailing ship owners against the attack of the cheaply-run, jerry-built, over-insured tramp steamer.

The great Clyde building firm of Russell & Co. was the largest contributor towards this boom. I have not their official figures, but for four years, from 1890 to 1893, their annual output of large sailing ships was nearer 30 than 20 vessels. Indeed, as many windjammers came off the stocks in Russell yards during that period as from all the other builders put together. I am told that this enterprising firm were always ready to take shares in part payment, but at the same time the firm had built up a wonderful reputation for producing successful sailers, good carriers, and well behaved vessels in a seaway.

It has been contended that the square-riggers, which were sent to sea in the early nineties, were jerry-built steel-boxes, cut off in lengths and so unhandy and ill-balanced that not even the cleverest of sail-trained masters could be sure of any manoeuvre.

This accusation is, of course, a great exaggeration of the facts. No doubt some of the huge steel arks of from two to three thousand tons were very difficult to steer and others, perhaps, were very balky in stays, but amongst the hundreds of ships sent afloat in these boom years there were many splendid vessels which were fit to be compared in every way with their predecessors.

The "Soukar" Won't Steer.

There have always been ships that steered badly and there always will be. One of the most notorious cases was the iron full-rigger *Soukar*, built in 1864 and well known in the New Zealand trade.

The *Soukar* besides being a vile ship to steer was as slow as time. When the wind was right aft not the finest helmsman in the world could keep her near her course; and under such conditions it became the custom to run her with the wind well on one quarter, then to jibe-oh and run an equal distance with the wind on the other quarter. This is practised by the big American staysail schooner yachts when racing, and is called tacking to leeward. But the schooners, like many square-riggers, did this to keep all their sails drawing, not in order to keep a straight wake.

Of the 1890 boom ships the *Crown of Austria* came to grief on her maiden voyage through bad steering. Refusing to answer her helm she went ashore on the coast of Brazil and became a total loss. This ship was a big four-poster of 3137 tons.

The Balky "Babcock."

The well-known Down-Easter *William F. Babcock* had a very curious habit of refusing to obey the helm on occasions.

The notorious "Shot-gun" Murphy, her first captain, used to declare that if you once let her fall off into the trough of the sea no trick of seamanship could get her out of it until she chose to recover her temper; in fact, she balked like a South Georgia mule.

During the late eighties there was often a large fleet of ships all within sight of one another off the pitch of the Horn; and it was on one such occasion that the "Babcock" chose to slide off a sea into the trough and sulk. There happened to be a fair slant of wind for rounding the corner, but the "Babcock" just stayed there, and rolled and rolled.

One ship after another came sailing by whilst the impotent captain and crew of the big full-rigger hauled her yards about and cursed in every known language.

We may imagine the scene! Jim Murphy swearing by all the saints in the Irish Calendar, and his mates by all the devils from Ballyhooley to the bottomless pit, whilst the oldest hand aboard shook his head knowingly and declared that it was the case of the Flying Dutchman over again.

No doubt the best helmsman was sent to the wheel; and after an ineffectual attempt to get the feel of the ship, he probably started to whirl the spokes hard up and then hard down in a vain effort to rouse the sulky Down-Easter, only to give it up with a muttered "Strike me, but the goldarned ship's hoodooed."

Perhaps the exasperated skipper overheard this remark, and promptly belted him over the head with a hard wood belaying-pin. Anyway, one can see all kinds of trouble aboard that ship until she came out of her fit of sulks.

Monster Sailing Ships.

With the introduction of steel came the giant sailing ships. Though unhandiness was the chief complaint of their masters, the most frequent cause of disaster amongst these huge four-masters and the few five-masters that were built was want of stability. The danger came when these heavily rigged ships were under way in ballast, the natural tendency of their captains being to cut down the stiffening to the finest point in order to save their owners' money. The bigger the ship the more careful one has to be to

watch her trim and check her stability tables. It is practically
certain that two of the biggest and finest sailing ships ever launched
from British yards were lost through the margin of safety being
neglected. I refer to the first *France* and the *Maria Rickmers.*

"France" and "Maria Rickmers."

It is true that the *France* was over ten years afloat before
she came to grief, but she was always noted as a tender ship. The
Maria Rickmers gave her crew some nasty thrills on her maiden
outward passage, and disappeared on her way home.

The *France* was launched from Henderson's yard at Partick
on September 2, 1890.

Russell & Co. considered that they were going one better when
they built the *Maria Rickmers* at Port Glasgow in 1891.

It will therefore be of interest to compare the measurements of
these two giant five-masters.

	Tons Gross	Length	Beam	Depth	Deadweight Capacity	Sail Area
France	3784	361 ft.	48·8 ft.	25·9 ft.	6200 tons	49,000 sq. ft
Maria Rickmers	3813	375 „	48 „	25 „	5700 „	57,000 „

The *France* had a cellular double-bottom with a capacity
for 2000 tons of water ballast. She had two steel decks, but only
the usual collision bulkhead forward. She was rigged as a five-mast
barque, and her sail plan was by no means excessive, her masts
being 160 feet from deck to truck; skysail yards were not crossed,
the royal yards being 48 feet long as compared with lower yards
of 85 feet.

The *France* was built for A. D. Bordes, and was fitted for the
handling of nitrate cargoes. In order to ensure quick loading and
discharging she was given four steam winches to each hatch, and
on one occasion she discharged 5000 tons of coal and loaded 5500
tons of nitrate at Iquique in 11 days. The drainings from the
nitrate cargo were allowed to run into the ballast tanks and in this
way were saved instead of having to be pumped overboard. Her
windlass was worked by steam, her braces were of wire and all
her standing rigging was set up by screws instead of deadeyes
and lanyards.

She was found to be tender, when loading coal before her maiden voyage, and she had to be kept well ballasted.

The *France* had a good turn of speed, and on her maiden trip with 5900 tons of Barry coal went from the Channel to Rio in 32 days, which was within one day of the record.

In 1892 she sailed from Prawle Point to Valparaiso in 73 days. In 1896-7 she came home from Iquique to the Channel in 79 days with 6000 tons of nitrate. On the night of Monday, January 25, 1897, she was lying at anchor in Dungeness Roads on her way to Dunkerque, her discharging port. The night was clear, and she had the usual anchor light, and also a bright light showing astern. Suddenly her crew noticed a steamer heading so as to strike the *France* amidships. This was H.M.S. *Blenheim* proceeding up Channel, and steaming at the rate of 13 knots. She mistook the two lights showing from the *France* for those of two fishing boats, and headed to pass between them. The wild shouts from the crew of the French vessel and the sudden loom of the giant ship's hull showed the officer of the watch on the man-o'-war the great mistake he had made. However, he just had time to order the helm of the *Blenheim* to be put hard over, and to set her starboard engine full speed astern, and the handiness of the *Blenheim* saved the *France* from being sunk.

The *Blenheim*, however, struck the *France* a severe though glancing blow on the starboard quarter, causing considerable damage. Some of the latter's upper plates were stove in and even ripped off, the rails, bulwarks, and stanchions being carried away. The stem of the *Blenheim* also cut its way into the captain's cabin of the *France*. No one, however, was hurt. When the case came into the Admiralty Court, Lord Esher ruled that "the riding light forward was necessary and sufficient, and the stern light a source of error, which might cause, or contribute to, an accident." The Admiralty took a similar view, and decided that there was no need to court-martial the officers of the *Blenheim*.

The *France* after this unpleasant accident was repaired and proceeded to make the best passage of her career. This was from Prawle Point to Valparaiso in 63 days.

In 1900 she sailed from Prawle Point to Iquique in 76 days, and in 1900-1 she came home from Iquique to Prawle Point in 78 days. On her next outward passage she loaded 5108 tons of coal from the Tyne for Valparaiso, sailing on March 14. Just two months later she was passed by the barque *Josepha*, which reported the great five-master as being on her beam ends, deserted, and with her decks swept by every sea. This was the last seen of the *France*.

The *Maria Rickmers* was much more heavily rigged than the *France*, crossing double topgallant yards on all four masts, with royals above them, and skysails on fore, main and mizen. She was one of those auxiliaries which promised more than they could ever perform; her engines were triple expansion, capable of 7 knots in a calm sea, and with a feathering propeller.

She was specially adapted for the rice trade between the East and Germany, and the firm of Rickmers expected to get something very remarkable out of her in the way of a maiden passage. Coals were loaded at Barry for Singapore, and when the *Maria Rickmers* took 82 days on the passage her owners cabled out a very plain-spoken reprimand to her captain who, on reading it, fell dead on the spot. The mate took the ship on to Saigon, and sailed for Bremen with a full cargo of rice on July 14, 1892. The *Maria Rickmers* passed Anjer on July 24, but was never heard of again— the supposition being advanced that her crew of 40 men were not sufficient to handle her.

Stability—The "Old Kensington" and the "Undine."

This matter of stability is not always solved by mathematical calculations; some ships were notably tender, others stiff almost to a fault, however loaded or ballasted. For instance, take the two well-known sister ships *Loch Carron* and *Loch Broom*; though they were built from the same model, the first was always tender and generally sent down her royal yards when in port, whilst the latter was perfectly normal, and neither too tender nor too stiff; and, strange to say, the tender ship was undoubtedly the faster of the two.

I have only heard of two heavily rigged ships that were considered safe in a seaway with a swept hold; these were the beautiful little tea clipper *Undine* and the *Old Kensington*; the latter's owners were so pleased with her ability to stand up without a pound of ballast that they declared she was the finest ship afloat. She was almost the first vessel to appear in the Thames with a spike—or as it was sometimes called, a horn—bowsprit.

Fernie's *Cleomene* was built to the plans of the *Old Kensington*, but according to old Captain Langlois, the London surveyor, there was a slight alteration in the bending of her frames, and this made all the difference, for the *Cleomene* always required a certain amount of ballast.

The Capsizing of "Lodore" and "Blairmore."

This ability to stand up without ballast was sometimes a source of danger. Facing page 16 in Vol. I., I give an illustration of Peter Iredale & Porter's *Lodore* in November, 1901, lying on her side in the harbour at Newcastle, N.S.W. This vessel was another very stable ship. After having swung on an anchor without ballast for two months awaiting her turn to load, she happened to take a sheer in a thunderstorm and touched the bottom; it was this in conjunction with the squall right abeam that capsized her. Her master, Captain McMurtry, took it greatly to heart. Though the *Lodore* was righted again without much difficulty, he went home and died shortly afterwards.

The tragic capsizing of the *Blairmore*, mentioned on page 15 in Vol. I., was another case of the same sort. The *Blairmore* was also one of those proud ships which were supposed to be able to stand up without ballast. As a matter of fact, she had a small quantity of stiffening aboard on this occasion; she was lying at anchor in Mission Bay waiting to load grain; the wind was fresh and against the tide, the *Blairmore* was blown athwart the tide in a violent squall, and with the leverage of the tide on her bottom and the wind in her rigging, she was blown clean over on her beam ends. Amongst those caught in her hold and drowned were the second mate and some of her apprentices.

The Naming of Masts.

Though no square-rigged five-masted sailing ship has ever been built for British owners, the French had a second *France*,

"LIVERPOOL" ON THE ROCKS

Lent by A. Darling, Esq.

"LIVERPOOL" ASHORE ON SARK

[*See Page* 25

"PARSEE"

[See Page 28

"FORFARSHIRE"

[See Page 33

built at Bordeaux, and the Germans have built the *Potosi*, *Preussen* and *R. C. Rickmers*, not to mention the queer-rigged *Vinnens*.

There were three famous five-masted iron-clads commissioned under the White Ensign in the sixties. These were the *Minotaur*, launched in 1863; the *Agincourt*, launched in 1865; and the *Northumberland*, launched in 1866.

Though the *Minotaur* began her career with yards on four masts, these three 400 ft. fighting ships were really only jury-rigged with fore and aft sails on their short after masts.

The question of naming five masts has never been settled satisfactorily, and the captains of these men-of-war each adopted a nomenclature of his own.

The first captain of the *Minotaur* called his masts bow, fore, main, mizen and after. Her second captain tried to improve on this with fore, main, mizen, after and jigger.

The ill-fated Captain Burgoyne, when in command of the *Agincourt*, called his masts bow, fore, main, after and jigger. Another captain of the *Agincourt* was content to number his masts 1, 2, 3, 4 and 5, whilst the *Northumberland's* masts were named fore, main, mizen, jigger and after jigger.

Other ways of naming five masts were fore, main, mizen, jigger and spanker; also fore, main, middle, mizen and jigger.

The Giant Jute Clipper "Liverpool."

The largest sailing ship under the Red Ensign at the beginning of the nineties was the four-masted full rigger *Liverpool*, which was specially built by Russell & Co. for the Calcutta jute trade.

This magnificent vessel registered 3330 tons, was 333 ft. in length, and could stow 26,000 bales of jute, a deadweight of nearly 6000 tons. Unfortunately, the days of sail in the jute trade were nearly over; and after her launch on December 7, 1888, R. W. Leyland & Co. sent her to London to load a cargo for Melbourne. Captain Thomas Calder was given the command of the new clipper. He sailed from London on March 9, with one cabin and 10 steerage passengers. The *Liverpool* passed through the Downs on the 11th and took her departure from the Start on March 13, arriving at Melbourne on June 9, 88 days out.

This seems to have been an average passage for the new ship.

On her second voyage Captain Calder was obliged to take his vessel to Frederickstadt for an outward cargo.

The following details of this voyage were taken from the *Liverpool's* log:—

Sept. 2, 1890. Sailed from Frederickstadt in tow of four tugs. 2 p.m., cast off tugs.

„   5, 6 p.m., off Christiansand.

„   6, Westerly gale.

„   13, Fair Isle bore South.

„   21, Lat. 49° 14′ N., Long. 20° 8′ W.   Course S. 17° W.   Distance 297 miles. Wind N.W., fresh gale.

Oct.   4, First of the Trades.

„   7, St. Antonio, Cape Verde, N.N.E. 40 miles.

„   19, Crossed the Equator in 23° 35′ W.

Nov.   8, Crossed the Greenwich Meridian in 40° 50′ S.

„   16, Lat. 42° 37′ S., Long. 31° 33′ E.   A four-mast ship in company.

„   27, Lat. 43° 10′ S., Long. 86° 22′ E.   Course N. 89° E.   Distance 300 miles Wind north to west, strong to gale force. Passed four-mast ship *Muncaster Castle* in p.m.

„   28, *Muncaster Castle* dropping astern fast.

„   29, Lat. 43° 30′ S., Long. 99° 38′ E.   Winds north, N.N.E. fresh gale. Distance 323 miles.

Dec.   12, Anchored in Hobson's Bay, 101 days out.

In February and March loading wheat, wool and horns. Loaded 5045 bales wool; 29,353 bags of wheat, 3112 bags of flour, besides horns, bark, leather and tallow.

Mar.   24, 1891. Towed to sea. 7.30 a.m., tug left the ship.

April 25, 53° S., 88° W.   Blowing a hurricane from N.W., under lower topsails, Distance 210 miles.

„   26, 50° S., 83° W.   Blowing a hurricane from N.W., under lower topsails. Distance 200 miles.

„   29, Off the Horn, 36 days out.

May   21, Crossed the Line.

June 27, 10 p.m. off St. Catherines. At noon took tug *Hibernia*, agreement £70.

„   28, Sunday—moored at Gravesend.

„   29, Left Gravesend 1.30 in tow of *Iona* ahead and *Victor* alongside. 5.30, entered S.W. India Dock and moored in the basin, 96 days from Melbourne.

This voyage is a good example of the *Liverpool's* work. She was undoubtedly very powerful in strong winds.   Her best passage to Calcutta was, I believe, made in 1894, being 83 days from Liverpool. In 1899 she made another good run up the Indian Ocean, arriving in the Hooghly on August 27, 92 days out.

When outward bound from Antwerp to San Francisco in 1902 under Captain Lewis, this magnificent ship went ashore in a fog on the rocky coast of Alderney on February 25. She was under all plain sail at the time, and the crash on the rocks broke her back: at the Inquiry it was found that sufficient allowance had not been made for the indraught at the height of spring tides.

Her crew of thirty-five were saved, but the ship became a total loss.

The Four Skysail-Yarder "Peter Rickmers."

Another beautiful four-mast ship, built by Russell in 1889, was the *Peter Rickmers*, for the famous Bremerhaven firm of Rickmers.

This vessel was the very last thing in sailing ship design and construction, and was more up to date than the *Liverpool* though some 400 tons smaller.

She was constructed of steel throughout with a midship bridge deck, but owing chiefly to her lofty sail plan—she crossed four skysail yards above double topgallants—the *Peter Rickmers* never looked clumsy and unsightly as was the case with some giant sailing ships. In fact, she was in many ways the most beautiful ship ever launched from a Russell slip.

The following list of passages shows an extremely high average for the Eastern trade:—

1890	Left	Cardiff	4468 tons coal	arrived	Oleleh, Sumatra	100 days
,,	,,	Rangoon	4370 ,, rice	,,	Bremen	116 ,,
1891	,,	,,	4368 ,, coal	,,	,,	93 ,,
1894	,,	Cardiff	4347 ,, coal	,,	Singapore	84 ,,
,,	,,	Bassein	4400 ,, rice	,,	Bremen	122 ,,
1895	,,	Cardiff	4298 ,, coal	,,	Singapore	94 ,,
,,	,,	Rangoon	2390 ,, rice	,,	Bremen	118 ,,
1896	,,	Cardiff	4322 ,, coal	,,	Singapore	89 ,,
1898	,,	New York	118,916 cases petroleum	,,	Hiogo	123 ,,
1899	,,	Rangoon	4365 tons rice	,,	Bremen	109 ,,
1900	,,	New York	117,716 cases petroleum	,,	Hongkong	106 ,,

1900	Left	Rangoon	about 4350 tons rice	arrived	Dover	110 **Days**
1901	,,	Portland, O.	4443 tons wheat	,,	Antwerp	131 ,,
1902	,,	Astoria	4429 ,,　,,	,,	Birkenhead	115 ,,
1903	,,	Astoria	about 4440 tons wheat	,,	Plymouth	113 ,,
1904	,,	Rangoon	4384 ,,　coal	,,	Bremen	113 ,,
1905	,,	New York	117,734 cases petrol	,,	Singapore	104 ,,
1907	,,	Penarth	4303 tons coal	,,	,,	95 ,,

In the following year the *Peter Rickmers* went ashore at Long Island, U.S.A., after just on 20 years' successful voyaging in the Asiatic trade, and became a total loss.

Handy Three-Mast Barques.

Although most owners in the nineties fought steam competition with big carriers of from 2000-3000 tons, a few noteworthy firms clung to the handy and economical three-mast barque of moderate tonnage.

In the days of the racing clipper ships there were also a number of clipper barques, and though they did not come so much into the limelight as the ships they were very popular with seamen.

Later again, many a full-rigged flyer, including most of the "Loch" three-masters, was cut down by having the yards stripped off her mizen. It was easy to tell those cut-down ships, for the true barque has only cross-trees on her mizen. In some cases the reduction of a full-rigged ship to a barque actually caused an improvement in her passages, because it allowed indifferent helmsmen to steer her straight. Many ships were very hard-mouthed, but it was rare to find a barque that steered badly, and this was one of the reasons which made them popular with seamen.

"Parsee" and "Assaye."

In the year 1868, whilst *Thermopylae* was building at Aberdeen, Robert Steele on the Clyde was at work on two beautiful little main skysail sister ships: these were the 1200 tonners, *Assaye* and *Parsee*, built for J. & W. Stewart for their Eastern and Colonial trade.

During the eighties these ships had the yards stripped off their mizen masts, and as the illustration of *Parsee* shows, they made very handsome barques.

Wreck of the "Mallsgate."

As an example of an iron clipper-built barque I cannot do better than recall the *Mallsgate*, which was built at Harrington by Williamson in 1877 to the order and, I believe, the design, of Captain James Sprott. Every shipmaster who is worth his salt longs to be able to build his ideal ship; and in innumerable cases these ships have been built and proved themselves very successful.

It is probable that no more beautiful barque was ever built than Sprott's *Mallsgate*. Indeed it is reported that she was built without regard for cost, and the bill very nearly ruined the old skipper. As she was meant to sail, she was therefore as sharp as a knife with a long run, and consequently loaded a very small cargo.

Captain Sprott, when he found that she ran away with more money than he could afford, was glad to let his brother (of the firm of Fisher & Sprott) take her over.

The *Mallsgate*, besides being very much admired for her good looks, made a number of outstanding passages, such as Hull to Sydney, 78 days in 1884; and Barrow to San Francisco, 113 days in 1886. An Australian newspaper correspondent who had access to her logbooks stated in print that she actually maintained an average of 300 miles a day for nine days on one of her passages out to the Colonies, her best run being 357 miles.

At the end of 1888 Captain Sprott, who had commanded her himself for some years, handed her over to his chief officer, Mr. M'Adams. Under M'Adams she went out to Brisbane in 1889, making the very fair passage of 89 days. After discharging at Brisbane she went to Newcastle, N.S.W., and loaded coal for San Francisco. She left Newcastle on July 17, and immediately fell in with hard gales from south-east to east, the weather being very thick with mountainous seas.

At 6 p.m. on Sunday, July 21, a rumbling noise was heard, and before anything could be done the barque struck on Middleton Reef, and was immediately swept from stem to stern by the heavy breakers. In a moment all was confusion. Amidst the thunder of the surf and the crash of falling spars there came a wild cry of "She's filling!"

Captain M'Adams gave the order to cut away the masts in order to prevent the vessel heeling over, and to give time to provision and lower the boats. By the time that the pinnace and life-boat were in the water, the coal composing the ship's cargo was washing about the cabin floor, and the decks had been burst asunder.

Although it was pitch dark and the boats under the lee of the wreck were almost swamped by every bursting sea, provisions, water, boat compasses and navigation instruments were brought up from below and, in the confusion of the moment, placed in the life-boat, so that when the boats were compelled to leave the ship it was found that the pinnace contained only 2 gallons of water, one tin of fresh herrings, and 1 lb. of bread.

About two hours after the *Mallsgate* had struck she began to break up, besides lurching violently as each heavy sea swept her fore and aft. Captain M'Adams now ordered the boats away. The pinnace, which was a boat 21 ft. long, contained Captain M'Adams, J. J. Fisher (the second mate and son of the owner), E. H. Bate (third mate), two apprentices, the carpenter and three A.B.'s The life-boat contained the mate, bosun, steward, cook, and the remaining A.B.'s.

In fetching clear the pinnace had her rudder broken, and a jury rudder had to be fixed. At this the life-boat tried to take the pinnace in tow, but owing to the darkness of the night and the heavy seas this was found to be impossible; and in less than 10 minutes the boats had separated never to meet again.

We will follow the adventures of the pinnace, as she had by far the worst time of it.

All night the gale blew furiously; and the boat's crew, who were thinly clad in shirt and trousers, having had no time to dress, were kept busy bailing. At dawn a jib was rigged as a storm try-sail, and under this the pinnace lay hove to for the next 24 hours. Towards evening on Tuesday the weather cleared, and the captain set a double-reefed mainsail. The wind continued to go down, and by Wednesday night it was almost calm. On Thursday the wind again freshened and it was necessary to heave to under the storm jib.

That night was a bad one for the castaways. The wind blew hard from the nor'west. All hands, through lack of food and water, had lost strength. Indeed two already lay unconscious at the bottom of the boat, whilst the man who was bailing required help to lift the bailer over the boat's side. But for the never-failing cheeriness of Captain M'Adams it is probable that the crew of the pinnace would have entirely lost hope.

Before the dawn one of the men had died, and his body was dropped over the stern. By noon on Friday the gale was again so heavy that the boat could only carry a reefed jib. That night the wind dropped with a shift which caused a cross sea. In this the boat very nearly came to her end, two seas falling upon her at once from opposite directions and nearly filling her.

"Bail out, boys," cried the undaunted skipper, and those who were strong enough set to with hats and anything that came handy. The pinnace was no sooner freed than she was again overwhelmed, and so it went on all night, their exertions in bailing telling badly against the weakened men.

All this time the daily allowance of water had been a wine-glass per man at sunset. In vain they begged for more, but Captain M'Adams was firm. One man had secretly been drinking salt water, and on Friday he became a raving lunatic. Before night his spirit departed, and he was envied by his shipmates because his sufferings were over.

On Saturday the wind was still high, but the boat made good progress; another miserable night, however, was spent fighting the high wind and sea with only four of the boat's crew able to do anything—the others lay in the bottom of the boat calmly waiting their end.

On Sunday morning the wind moderated, and Captain M'Adams set the mainsail and jib. At 10 o'clock land was sighted. At 2 p.m. the land was made out to be Moreton Island, and an effort was made to get into the bay by the south passage, but the breakers were too heavy and Captain M'Adams was compelled to head off shore.

About this time a local steamer, believed to be the *Laura*, was sighted crossing ahead. The captain, carpenter, second officer and one of the apprentices took to the oars, but they were obliged to desist as, owing to their weak condition, the flesh of their hands stuck to the oars and came off in lumps. They then held up an oar with a large handkerchief tied to it. The steamer stopped her engines for a short time, but then steamed away round Cape Moreton. This seemed the last straw. Water had long since been finished, and everyone felt the end approaching. The boat was now opening her seams and leaking terribly; there was a long unbroken line of surf beating on the east shore of Moreton Island, through which it was impossible to beach her, so another night had to be spent at sea.

Happily the current set towards the Cape and the boat was soon in smooth water; thus at 8.30 on Tuesday morning the survivors were able to make a landing near Yellow Patch, a mile from Cape Moreton. Their first action on gaining shore was to crawl to a water hole and drink. Their troubles, however, were nearly over. The "Comboyuro" lighthouse signalled to the local steamer *Advance,* which took the shipwrecked men on board and hurried with them to Brisbane.

When taken aboard the *Advance* only Captain M'Adams, the carpenter and the third mate could stand on their feet. Of the others several appeared to be dying, and it was only by real hard work on the part of the chief engineer of the *Advance* and those assisting him that animation was restored to the sufferers.

These survivors from the pinnace were loud in praise of their captain, and declared that they would never have weathered it out but for his firm discipline, cheery courage and clever handling of the boat.

The life-boat with the mate in charge made the land some 200 miles further north after an almost equally trying time, and all hands were re-united in Brisbane Hospital.

The Speedy "Selkirkshire."

A worthy rival of the *Mallsgate* was Law's pretty little *Selkirkshire* built the following year. In Vol. I., I mentioned her record passage from Yokohama to Portland (O.) and other good performances.

One of her old apprentices, writing to the P.S.N. Co. Magazine, *Sea Breezes*, credits her with a passage of 26 days from Buenos

"DARTFORD"

Lent by Captain Shultze

"MINERAWA"

Photo Captain Shultze

[*See Page* 34

"KILLARNEY"

[See Page 36

"TACORA"

[See Page 39

Ayres to Delagoa Bay, July 7 to August 2, 1903; and vouches for a speed through the water of over 16 knots.

Let me quote his words with regard to the latter statement:—

In March, 1903, we were bound for Cadiz from Leghorn (as our articles had run out the crew had been paid off in Leghorn, and we had signed on a crew of Italians, mostly fishermen). We sighted Gibraltar about sundown with a strong wind from the east. As the wind increased we clewed up our royals, and we boys made them fast. When we entered the Straits it was blowing a gale, so we clewed up the fore topgallant sail, but when the men were ordered up to make it fast they refused because there were no life lines on the yards, so it ended in the boys again going aloft. On coming to deck again we went aft and hove the log. The line was marked up to 16 knots; that all ran out and dragged the man holding the reel to the rail, where it broke from the reel and went overboard just as the glass ran out.

He follows this with a tribute to his ship—

The *Selkirkshire* was a smart little vessel, both in speed and looks; she had more brass and teakwood aboard than you could shake a stick at; she was built for the emigrant trade to the Colonies, and used to run to Rockhampton. Her 'tween decks were pierced for ports fore and aft. We also carried a condenser and a donkey in the deckhouse.

I can bear him out in his remarks about the *Selkirkshire's* lines and looks, for I have Birrell, Stenhouse's half model of this vessel.

Birrell, Stenhouse & Co., of Dumbarton.

This firm only built about 50 sailing ships, but they gave place to no other builder, not even Steele for beauty of line and ênish.

At the end of 1924 a little 750-ton barque, named the *Ingrid* and flying the Danish flag, arrived at Leith in order to be broken up. The local experts at once pronounced her to be a thoroughbred; she turned out to be the *Countess of Derby*, another of Birrell's designs of the seventies. This barque bore testimony to the careful finish of the Dumbarton firm; besides a very fine figure-head and much artistic carving and gingerbread work at bow and stern, her pooprail and the handrail round her midshiphouse were beautifully carved in the form of a rope.

The Handy "Forfarshire" Sails between the Reefs.

As an example of a fast iron barque of the eighties I cannot do better than mention Law's *Forfarshire*, another of Birrell's

D

productions; she was 100 tons larger and slightly fuller than the *Selkirkshire*, and equally handy, if not quite such a flyer.

As an instance of her handiness: on May 2, 1894, she sailed from Cardiff bound for Kossiene, New Caledonia, *via* St. Helena; after discharging at St. Helena she continued her passage in ballast on August 18. On Sunday, November 4, she arrived off the reef-bound coast of New Caledonia. There was no tug available, and the passage into the Kossiene anchorage through a gap in the coral reef was very narrow, the width of the entrance being less than the barque's length.

Whilst his mate conned the ship from the fore upper topsail yard, Captain Evans himself took the wheel and steered his vessel through the barrier. It was a perilous business even with a handy ship, but the *Forfarshire* reached the anchorage without coming to grief.

Here she found the *Nairnshire* of the same company loaded and ready for sea. The *Nairnshire* sailed on November 13 and the *Forfarshire* followed her a month later on December 15, both ships being bound for Antwerp. Though the *Nairnshire* was by no means a slow ship the *Forfarshire* arrived in the Scheldt on April 16, five days ahead of her.

The Tiny "Minerewa" and the Training Ship "Dartford."

There are just two other barques which I should like to mention before turning to the more modern specimens of that rig. Both of these, the *Minerewa* and the *Dartford*, were very well known in Australian and New Zealand waters.

The *Minerewa*, of 371 tons, which was built by Murdoch & Murray in 1884, and was first of all called the *Vale Royal*, was considered a very smart vessel in the inter-Colonial trade. She was eventually lost with all hands in the Tasman Sea.

The 1300-ton *Dartford*, which was one of Mounsey & Foster's build, came out in 1877, and in her old age she was fitted out as a training ship by the Union S.S. Co. of New Zealand. She was hulked in 1913, refitted for service in 1918, and reverted to a hulk in 1921.

Sweet "Cupica" and Her Sisters.

After this glance at one or two of the best known of the iron barques, we now come to the more modern steel barques dating from 1888, the year in which Bigger of Londonderry built the *Cupica*—*Sweet Cupica*, as Masefield calls her—for Macvicar Marshall & Co.; Workman & Clark built *Lorton* for Peter Iredale & Porter; and Duncan built *Harold* for Thomas Stephens & Sons, the owners of the famous Colonial passenger clipper *Thomas Stephens*.

Charles J. Bigger of the Foyle Shipyard, Londonderry, like Birrell of Dumbarton, did not build many sailing ships—his last, the *William Mitchell*, being only numbered 32 in his yard list—but those he did build were outstanding vessels. I do not know whether he set the fashion for 1200-1500 ton barques when he launched the *Cupica*, but certainly every sailing ship builder of any note seems to have followed his example in trying to produce an economical, good-carrying yet fast sailing, steel three-mast barque of this size.

The keen eyes of retired sailormen in the ports of the Antipodes were quick to note the arrival of a stranger, and especially a maiden voyager; and their criticisms were always very much to the point and inclined to be on the severe side, yet they pronounced the *Cupica* to be the handsomest steel barque they had ever seen. That she was a success is proved by the fact that she was followed by three sister ships, the *Camphill*, launched in 1889, and the *Craiglands*, launched in 1891, both for Squarey & Kendall of Liverpool, and the *Silverstream*, launched in 1891 for W. P. Herdman of Carrickfergus.

These little barques looked from a distance to be flush-decked, for their 25 feet of fo'c'sle head and 40 feet of raised quarterdeck did not show above the mainrail, and this added to their good looks.

The sail plan of the *Camphill* gives one a great idea of compactness and handiness: though the spar measurements are ample with fore and main lower yards of 77 feet, the short spike bowsprit and short mastheads gave these Londonderry barques a look of power, whilst the lower and topmast in one and the single topgallant yards add an appearance of neatness aloft which is somehow absent from the bald-headed rig which in 1888 had just been introduced.

The first of these four sisters to go under was the *Camphill*, which, after being sold to J. & J. Rae & Co. in 1905, went out to Talcahuano from Liverpool and on her way north to load guano was stranded, October 6, 1906, on a sunken rock in rounding the Tumbes Peninsula.

The *Cupica* was sold about 1907 to the Germans and registered at Hamburg as the *Gretchen Hartrodt*. A curious accident happened to this ship in 1895. She left Hull on November 18, with 1800 tons of coal for Algoa Bay. Whilst beating down the North Sea in charge of a pilot she stranded on a wreck about five miles north of the Winterton Light. After hanging for about half an hour she was backed off, but was then found to be leaking, and had to put back to Hull for repairs to her bottom. On this occasion the pilot was severely reprimanded and the captain censured for the untrustworthy condition of the ship's compasses.

Craiglands was sold by Squarey & Kendall about the same time as the *Camphill*; she went to Larvig and was renamed the *Margit*.

Silverstream remained under the same ownership till 1909 when she was sold to the Italians. I believe that Captain Dagwell commanded her during the whole of her life under the British flag; she was sunk by the Germans in 1916.

I do not propose to give a detailed account of all the steel three-mast barques which came off the stocks during the last years of the nineteenth and the first years of the twentieth century, for they would need a whole book to themselves if given their due.

The biggest fleet of small steel barques was that of George Milne's Inver Line which, with the exception of one or two bought ships, came from the yards of McMillan and Russell.

The Dundee "Glens" were even smaller than the Aberdeen "Invers." The largest of the fleet, with the exception of the big four-posters *Glencona* and *Glenclova*, was the *Glenesk* of 1369 tons, which was built by Russell in 1889.

The steel barque *Harold* will be best remembered under the flag of Walmsley & Co. The *Killarney*, built by Evans, also belonged to Walmsley.

The ancient yard of the Hills of Bristol, in which the *Saucy*

Arethusa of glorious memory was built, produced as its last square-rigged sailing ships the three sisters, *Penrhyn Castle, Powys Castle,* and *Favell.*

The Ritsons of Maryport.

There was no more enterprising firm of shipbuilders than the Cumbrian family of Ritson, whose yard was situated on the bank of the narrow Ellen. In all they built close on a hundred ships, their last sailing ship, the fine steel full-rigger, *Acamas,* being numbered 67.

The part of the river on which their shipyard faced was only 60 ft. from bank to bank at high water, and yet in this narrow space they managed to launch the *Auchencairn* which was over 2000 tons register, $287\frac{1}{2}$ ft. in length, 40 ft. 2 ins. in breadth, and drew 25 ft. There was only one way to launch a ship of this size into a river only 60 ft. wide, and that was broadside on; indeed the Ritsons became so noted for their wonderful broadside launches that whenever a launching date came round there was always a large crowd gathered on Moat Hill, which rose straight up from the river bank just opposite to the firm's building slips.

After three trusty shipwrights had knocked away the chocks and let go the tackles, the ship to be launched would slowly start to glide down the ways; and her speed would gradually increase until in the end she fell with a resounding crash off the dock wall into the river, raising a wave which often wet more than the feet of the spectators crowded on Moat Hill. The ship itself usually gave one or two heavy rolls from rail to rail and then quickly steadied up as the mooring lines were tautened.

Four steel three-mast barques were built by Ritsons at the beginning of the nineties: the *Criffel,* launched in1891 for McDiarmid & Co.; the *Wythop* in 1892 for R. Ferguson of Dundee; the *Ladas* in 1894; and the *Midas* in 1895, both for themselves. These were all very fine specimens of the 1300-1400 tons barque.

The Weatherly "Ladas."

The best known of the four was undoubtedly the *Ladas,* which was called after Lord Rosebery's horse which had won the Derby just three months before her launch. This barque, besides being very handy, was unusually fast for her type when the yards were on the backstays.   Her first commander was Captain T. Messenger, one of those fearless sailormen who were never happier than when they were hanging on to the topgallant sails in a really hard blow; in the *Ladas* he had a ship which bore driving, though he treated her without mercy.   Luckily, the Ritsons had some fine riggers, they also made their own sails and so there was no fear of anything carrying away through indifferent gear.

Captain Hodgson, who served his time in the ship, in writing to the P.S.N. Co. Magazine, relates two nasty experiences of the *Ladas* on her first voyage.

The first of these was when she was running down the Easting bound for Newcastle, N.S.W., from the W.C.S.A. Captain Messenger was threading his way through the great mass of field-ice and bergs which blocked the South Atlantic in 1895-6. It was, as a matter of fact, in March, 1895, in about 53° S. and 29° W.   Whilst passing between two large bergs the *Ladas* collided with a broken off piece which was about 100 feet long and barely rose above the water. This bit crashed along her port side shearing off the heads of a number of rivets. It says much for the good construction of the *Ladas* that her plates were not broken in; indeed, it was not until some months later that the ship began to leak badly. By this time she had crossed the Pacific and was at Victoria, B.C. Here she was put on Bullen's slip at Esquimalt, and repaired.

It was on her passage home from Victoria with a rather crank cargo of canned salmon that the *Ladas* had her second unpleasant experience. Whilst carrying on with a strong easterly wind in the South Atlantic she was caught by a hard squall in the middle watch. Though the topgallant halliards were let go, the *Ladas* heeled too much for the yards to run down and lay flat with her hatches in the water. For about twenty minutes her crew, clinging like flies to the weather rail, expected their ship to turn right over; then she suddenly paid off, brought her spars upright, thus allowing the yards to come down with a crash, and straightway lay over on her starboard side, being caught by the lee. This time, as the topgallant yards had come down, she did not lie over quite so far, and her badly scared crew presently managed to square the mainyard and get her once more under control.

At the end of this voyage Captain Messenger went to the *Midas*, and Captain R. Dixon left Ismay's *Copley* to take over the *Ladas*. Captain Dixon was also a sail carrier. According to Captain Hodgson he made the outward passage from West Waterloo Dock to Honolulu in the splendid time of 119 days, then covered himself with glory by beating Spreckels' *W. G. Irwin* in the run from Honolulu to 'Frisco.

Amongst the ships which Captain Hodgson remembers passing in the *Ladas* were the smart little *Brier Holme*, the big *Fingal*, Shankland's *Miltonburn*, Carmichael's *Talus*, Goffey's *Eurasia*, and Milne's *Invercoe*.

These are some very creditable scalps for a little barque of under 1400 tons.

The *Ladas* eventually went to the Norwegians, and was broken up in 1921.

The Beautiful Barquentine "Tacora."

Nicholson & McGill of Liverpool, who owned a number of small iron and steel barques, such as the *Bolivia, Valdivia, Orellana, Villalta, Dochra* and *Lochinvar*, were the first British firm to try a four-mast schooner in general trading.

John Reid was their favourite builder, and in 1888 they commissioned him to build a four-mast fore and aft schooner of 900 tons. This was the *Tacora*, a beautiful little thing with fine lines and a large sail area.

It was expected that she would prove herself to be very fast, but on her maiden voyage it was soon realised that fore and aft sails are not satisfactory except with beam winds; also, in light airs and anything of a sea with their heavy booms and gaffs they not only thrash themselves to pieces but are very hard on the gear.

Captain Thornton, her master, proposed square sails on the foremast at any rate, and before her second voyage five yards were sent aloft; this turned an indifferent fore and aft schooner into a lovely little four-mast barquentine which was easily capable of a 24-hour run of over 300 miles in the Roaring Forties.

On her second voyage Captain Thornton took her out to Adelaide and on her third to Sydney. I have a note of this passage. She left Antwerp with general cargo on April 11, 1891, took her departure from the Lizard on the 14th, crossed the Equator 25 days out, and experienced very bad weather running her Easting down, going as far south as 47° 50′, where she sighted ice. Her best run was 305 miles.

The Leeuwin Meridian was crossed on June 27; very rough weather was met with on the coast especially in Bass Straits; King's Island was abeam on July 7, 84 days out, and *Tacora* reached Sydney on July 15, where she was much admired.

In 1892 she arrived Plymouth June 29, 77 days from Talcahuano.

Here is a smart round voyage which she made in 1897 under Captain Ullathorne.   Sailed from Cardiff April 28, arrived Mauritius July 16, left Mauritius and arrived Newcastle, N.S.W., September 20; left Newcastle, N.S.W., October 3, arrived Tocopilla November 24, left Tocopilla December 15, passed the Lizard April 5, 1898. Voyage 11 months 11 days.

In 1899 *Tacora* ran from Prawle Point to Mauritius in 73 days, and then crossed from Newcastle, N.S.W., to Valparaiso in 36 days. In 1903 she made the passage from Dover to Hobart in 92 days. These records are very good work indeed for a vessel of her rig which was very economical in man power but had few other advantages.

The *Tacora* was eventually sold to the Norwegians, and she came to her end in 1911, when, laden with a valuable cargo of ebony, she went to the bottom at Gorontalo in the Celebes; and now lies amongst the fishes in 900 feet of water.

Owing to the little *Tacora*'s speed and good looks a few more four-mast barquentines were built. In 1892 John Reid built the *Rimac* of 946 tons for Nicholson & McGill. Lloyd's registered her as a four-mast schooner; she certainly had not anything like the speed of the *Tacora*, 141 days from the Tyne to Calcutta in 1893 being an average example of her work.   After a few years under the British flag she also went to the Norwegians.

"CARL VINNEN"

[*See Page* 44

"LANCING"

[*See Page* 46

"LANCING"

DECK SCENE "LANCING"

[See Page 46

Russell's Barquentines.

Early in 1893 Mr. James Fairlie, who had been thinking deeply on the problem of how to make sailing ships pay, went to see W. T. Lithgow of Russell & Co., and suggested building a four-mast barquentine with a water tank amidships which would come right up to the 'tween decks and be available for either water ballast or cargo. Lithgow, who had already launched the *Donna Francisca* with a water ballast tank, and had proved its use, at once fell in with Fairlie's idea, and the result was five sister four-mast barquentines, the *Oberon* and *Titania,* for Mr. James Fairlie, the *Renfield* for J. Archie Russell, *Sound of Jura* for Charles Walker, and the *Westfield* for Nicoll & Co., of Dundee.

The first of the fleet, the *Oberon*, was launched in October, 1893. With a gross tonnage of 1119 tons, and net of 1054, she carried 1740 tons of deadweight. Her ballast tank amidships had a capacity of 500 tons, and proved a great economy; for instance, on her first voyage she took coals from Glasgow to Rio, and arrived in the Brazil port right in the middle of a revolution. The British shipping in the port was under the control of the British Admiral, who gave each arrival instructions as to where she was to anchor. This was a good deal further from the town than the usual anchorage, owing to the fighting being as much on the water as ashore, the Brazilian navy being on the side of the revolutionists. All day long tugs and small gunboats were making dashes along the water front and firing into the town; then, when the return fire became too hot to be pleasant their favourite dodge was to take refuge behind the shipping lying in the bay.

Most of the foreign merchant ships were lying idle, owing to the fact that they could not obtain any ballast in the shape of stiffening, the quarries from which it came being constantly under fire. When the consignee of *Oberon's* cargo found that she could discharge her cargo to the last ton without requiring any stiffening, he said he would take delivery as fast as they could discharge if only the captain would move his ship to a certain berth which was a bit nearer the town. The captain went to the Admiral for permission, but was told that if he dared to shift his ship he would do it at his own risk, and if anyone on board got killed he, the captain, would be hauled up for manslaughter.

Captain Selley of the *Oberon* lay still for a few days, but then he could stand it no longer, and weighed and went into the berth his consignee wanted him to take up. As he had a donkey winch he soon had his cargo out and was ready for sea again, and luckily got clear of the flying bullets without any casualties.

The second of Fairlie's barquentines, the *Titania*, was launched in October, 1895, and Captain Selley left the *Oberon* to take her.

I think I should now say something about the rig of these barquentines, for sailors credited them with some very queer sails. For instance, *Titania's* jack yard topsails seem to have been miscalled "Jimmy Greens," and her three-cornered lower sail on the jigger was called by her mates a "spinnaker." Mr. James Fairlie, in describing to me the sail plan of *Oberon* and *Titania*, writes as follows:—

In planning her (*Oberon*) out I decided to make a few alterations aloft, so as, if possible, to lighten the work and make her easier to handle. In the ordinary barquentines there is what is called a "triatic stay" from the mizen masthead to the main masthead as you could not have the ordinary fore and aft stays as on a square-rigged vessel. This means that when you go about you have to take in your gaff topsails, and shift both tack and sheet over the triatic stay, which entails a lot of work and wasted time.

I therefore had a boom fixed with a gooseneck on the main and mizen mastheads, with guys and a tripping line for the tacks, which were double, so that when the ship was put about the gaff of the lower sail went underneath, and the boom of the topsail went over the top of the triatic stay, so that all you had to do was to trip up the weather tack after she was round, and haul down on the lee one. In the first instance I had the gaff topsails made of a size to haul out to the gaff in the ordinary way with the usual check block on the gaff end, and everything ready to set in the usual way. But the booms proved themselves quite successful, and very easily handled. When the *Oberon* came off her first voyage the captain was highly pleased with her, his only complaint being the weight of the booms and gaffs on main and mizen.

I thought I would obviate this on the *Titania*, which by this time I had already contracted for, by having short lower gaffs on these masts, the gaff topsails with their independent booms remaining the original size. To make up for the curtailed canvas I had jack yards put on the mizen and jigger lower masts with a three-cornered topsail and lower sail. The inner leach of the lower sail worked up and down a stay set up on the forward side of the lower mast by hanks and the head was hauled out to either yardarm by outhauls. A single hank on the head of the leach working on a wire stay which stretched from yardarm to yardarm guided the sail across. The topsails were worked pretty much the same as a studding sail. The sail area was considerably in excess of an ordinary barque of the same tonnage. Every sail was effective, and arranged in such a way as to preclude any flogging of other sails; the whole arrangement, in fact, worked easily and satisfactorily.

According to Mr. Fairlie, these queerly rigged barquentines were able to hold their own with the square-rigged deep-watermen of their day. They could all make 300 miles in the 24 hours under favourable circumstances. On one occasion the *Oberon*, when bound to Fiume with a cargo of nitrate, and rather foul, being nearly a year out of dry dock, ran neck and neck with one of the Cunard Line Mediterranean steamers for the best part of a day, and it was only when the wind lightened towards sundown that the liner went ahead.

The last of them in active service was the *Sound of Jura*, which had a small steam engine fitted in 1916 and just sufficient power to drive her ahead at 2 to 3 knots in a calm. Her last owners were the Kerguelen Whaling and Sealing Co., and she was commanded by Captain Cruickshank, a son, by the way, of one of the owners of the Liverpool Crown Line. He tells me that she was not a flier but a wonderful vessel at rolling. She used to leave Cape Town in September with coal for the Kerguelen sealers, and remained down South as a store for the whale oil until the steam freighter came down in February, when she returned to the Cape. In June, 1927, she was dismantled in Simon's Bay.

Of the others the *Oberon* was a coal hulk at Saldanha and the *Renfield* at Leith.

"Alta" and "Mozart."

In 1900 Duncan built the 1300-ton four-mast barquentine *Alta* for San Francisco owners. This vessel was intended for the lumber trade, with a carrying capacity of 1,700,000 feet. Her yards on the foremast were tremendously square; her steel foreyard being just under 100 ft. long, but like the others she was no flier. Her last days were spent under the single star of Chile.

In 1904 the Grangemouth Dockyard Co. built the *Mozart* of close on 2000 tons for A. C. De Freitas & Co. of Hamburg. This ship was also tremendously square forward with stump top-gallants. She was allotted to the French Government at the end of the war, who sold her to the Finns.   She was scrapped in 1935.

Queer Rigs.

When the war was over and shipping resumed its normal trading various laudworthy attempts were made to preserve the sailing ship to the world.

In 1919 the Gray's Harbor Motor Ship Co., of Aberdeen, Washington, built three wooden 1600-ton five-mast barquentines for the lumber trade: these were *Forest Pride, Forest Friend,* and *Forest Dream.*   They were classed 12 A1 and registered at Seattle. Besides six yards on the foremast they also crossed a very square yard on the middle mast which must have been a great help in fair winds.

The *Forest Dream* in January, 1928, arrived at Antwerp, having been sold to the Swedes, for whom she brought a cargo of guano from Peru *via* the Panama Canal.   She made a long passage and gave underwriters some anxiety though they certainly did not expect a fast run from a vessel of that rig.

The palm must be awarded to the German "Vinnens" for their enterprise in devising an entirely new rig, as seen in their "Vinnen" auxiliaries.

The rig of the old Yankee four-master *Olympic* used to be described as a "schooner chasing a brig"; and in the case of the "Vinnens" one might call them "three-mast topsail schooners chasing two-mast topsail schooners."   These "Vinnens" were large carriers rather than passage makers; for instance, *Carl Vinnen* left Rosario on October 24 with 2380 tons of maize, called at Falmouth, November 27 and arrived at Southampton, her port of discharge, on December 1.

Vinnens converted two of their auxiliary schooners to full power before the last war.   They sold their auxiliary four-masted barque *Magdalen Vinnen* to the North German Lloyd in 1936. She was converted into the training ship *Kommodore Johnsen.*

CHAPTER II.

THE LIMEJUICERS OF 1888-9.

Dub-a-dub, dub-a-dub, thus strike their drums;
Tan-ta-ra, ta-ra-ra, the Englishman comes!

The Wealth of Language.

I HOPE my quotation from the old Elizabethan song on the winning of Cadiz by the English will not bring down a wealth of language upon my head from those to whom the mention of the word "English" is anathema. It will be noticed that the verse headings of the chapters of this Volume are chosen from Elizabethan poets. I have selected these in an effort to show that once upon a time this little island of Great Britain possessed men with the gift of language; though in these days one has to admit that all the wealth of imagery, the richness of expression and the variety of expletive in the language of the Old Country is only to be found overseas.

It is curious how the language of a nation and the vocabulary of an individual are affected by the air they breathe. It is a well-known fact that the stronger the air the stronger the language and the more varied and vivid the adjectives and similes.

When mountaineers swear their language far transcends that of the lowly plain dweller: and even at sea most sailing ship men will agree that the worst language is used up aloft when taking in sail, and specially is this the case when struggling in the grip of a westerly gale when the lungs are filled with ozone.

The Cockney, breathing the very often badly used-up air of the Metropolis, though he is as sharp as a knife in intellect, has a very poor vocabulary, with the expletive "By Our Lady" shortened into the adjective "Bloody" doing duty for every occasion.

In North America the air is as invigorating as champagne.

45

It is therefore not surprising to find that the English language has been enlarged and decorated—one might almost say re-written and re-spoken—by the great American and Canadian peoples.

This brings me to my point. I have often been asked by landsmen as to the meaning and origin of the words "Limejuicer" and "Windjammer."

According to the Act.

The words "Limejuicer" and "Windjammer," the first denoting a British sailing ship and the second any kind of sailing ship, though generally used to describe a square-rigger, were undoubtedly invented by the American sailor, and of the two "Limejuicer" was the first to be broadcast round the world. This word dates from the passing into law of the B.O.T. regulation for the prevention of scurvy, and was invented, I believe, by some contemptuous Yankee after a period of service in a ship where a pannikin of limejuice was served out every day at noon. Thus the word came to denote a ship of British nationality alone, for no other nation instituted this limejuice regulation for its sailors.

The word "Windjammer" does not appear in any of the old nautical dictionaries, and I doubt if it is fifty years old; indeed, I am not certain that the American sea writer, T. Jenkins Hains, did not invent it when he put it on the title page of his first book.

At one time it was used a great deal by the officers of steamers, who considered themselves a cut above those who still clung to sail, and was a sneer of contempt in their mouths. Remembering these sneers with evidently some considerable bitterness, several old sailing ship men have expostulated with me for putting it on to the title page of this book: but the poor old "Windjammer," after being looked upon as a leper of the seas, has in her death-throes come to be regarded by the whole world with admiration and affection, and the term is now no longer one of contempt but of endearment.

The Wonderful "Lancing."

In the autumn of 1888 the well-known French trans-Atlantic mail steamer *Pereire* appeared on the seas as the four-mast ship,

Lancing, flying the British flag. She was the last and by far the most successful of the many conversions from steam to sail.

The well-known Blue-nose skipper, Captain George Alfred Hatfield, of Yarmouth, Nova Scotia, was primarily responsible for her conversion, and it is said that Mrs. George Hatfield planned the new cabin accommodation. The work was very well done at Blyth, though I believe that the man who did it was ruined through undertaking the contract.

This famous vessel (which was undoubtedly one of the most remarkable as well as one of the fastest ships under sail that have ever come out of a British yard), was designed by the late Sir William Pearce, and most perfectly built by Robert Napier & Sons at Glasgow. She was launched as far back as November 4, 1865, as an iron screw barque heavily rigged with a large sail plan to aid her 1000 horse-power engines.

The following account of her launch was given in the *Glasgow Herald*:—

On Saturday Messrs. Robert Napier & Sons launched from their building yard at Govan one of the largest and finest screw steamers which has been built on the Clyde. Mrs. John Napier, at the special request of the company, named the vessel the *Pereire* in honour of the family of the president of the company. The vessel has been designed and constructed for the Compagnie Generale Transatlantique, of Paris, who carry the mails between France and Mexico and the United States. It is expected that she will surpass in speed any mail steamer afloat, although it will be no easy task to beat the famous Cunard screw steamer *China*, also built by Messrs. Napier, which has just made one of the fastest, if not the very fastest, passages from New York on record.

For the next 22 years the *Pereire* carried mails and passengers between Havre and New York. She soon proved herself more than a match for the "flying *China*," and may be considered to have been on a par with the beautiful *Russia*, which was launched from Thomson's yard on the Clyde in 1867. Both vessels were barque-rigged with single topsails, topgallant sails and royals, but the *Russia* had double the horse-power. However the *Pereire* was always hard to beat and held her place as one of the "greyhounds" of the Atlantic. Her career as a steamer seems to have been devoid of much incident, except that it was in her cabin that the Emperor Napoleon III. approved the plans for the improvements to the port of Havre.   Her last commander under the French was Captain Daure.

As a mail steamer her registered tonnage and dimensions were:—1755 tons net; 3150 tons gross; 345 ft. length; 43·5 ft. breadth; 29 ft. depth of hold.   When converted to a sailing ship she came out at 2546 tons net; 2785 tons gross; 356 ft. length; 43·8 ft. breadth; 27·3 ft. depth.   Her overall length was 405 feet.

When re-rigged her main and mizen masts were 200 feet from keel to truck and 175 feet from the maindeck.   Her main and cross-jack yards were $92\frac{1}{2}$ feet long.   The shortest spar aboard her was a very stumpy spike bowsprit, which only carried three headsails, and her appearance certainly would have been improved if this spar had been a few feet longer.

When the engines and boilers were removed her water ballast tank, holding 1200 tons, was left in her, and this was the case also with the stokehold and engine-room bulkheads.

Her maindeck was of iron and was unpopular with the men, for it gave a nasty slippery foothold in bad weather.   She had the usual maindeck capstans for braces, etc., and powerful crabs for the halliards.

Her old-fashioned first class saloon was aft with alleyways on either side, and its roof made a magnificent poop deck.   Right aft was the wheelhouse, rising from the level of the maindeck to the height of the poop skylight, with a lifting roof, so that the helmsman by craning his neck could see the mizen royal.

Over her wide but shapely counter was the usual steamer's half-round of her date.

There used to be a model of her steering gear and a picture of the old ship as a mail steamer in the South Kensington Museum.

When viewed in dry dock her sharp lines both of bow and stern were very noticeable.

Her shaft tunnel was plugged and the space once occupied by a screw was filled in with an iron plate, which addition to her run was considered a great help to her speed.

After her conversion the *Lancing* drew 24 feet when fully loaded and $17\frac{1}{2}$ feet with 1200 tons of water ballast.   With her great length and heavy yards she was not an easy ship to handle, and the

ON THE FOREYARD "LANCING"

[See Page 46

"SINDIA"

[See Page 58

"BUCKINGHAM"

[See Page 59

"MARION INGLIS"

[See Page 62

Norwegians certainly seemed to have got the hang of her better than her British officers as I can find no specially good passages under the Red Ensign.

Captain S. J. Hatfield, who took turns with his uncle Captain G. A. Hatfield in commanding her in her early days, declared that she was very fast under certain conditions. With a head wind in narrow waters she was doubtless more than a handful, and I should much like to know if either of her British masters was in the habit of putting her about when tacking, as her Norwegian masters always wore her round on to the other tack.

Mr. Wallace, the well-known author of *In the Wake of the Wind Ships,* quotes the following anecdote from a letter of the younger Hatfield, written after a passage from Dundee to New York in 1890.

> On the voyage in question we were boarded by a New York pilot off George's Banks. When he put his foot on the rail—it was dark at the time—he asked if this was the *Frederick Billings.* When I told him it was the *Lancing,* he informed me that he had seen us coming, and that he was looking for steamers yet he told his mate that he would not let this four-mast ship go past. He had given his discharges to the skipper of the pilot boat, he said, as the steamer would be at Sandy Hook at least four hours ahead of the ship. This was at 4 a.m. At 8 a.m. when he came on deck he was surprised to see his pilot boat so far astern that you could just see the top of her masthead. He asked "How fast is your vessel going?" I told him that I had no patent log as a shark had taken it. "Well," he said, "our boat is doing her best 14 knots." So one can imagine how fast the *Lancing* was going.

During the whole of her career she was only twice put on the overdue list.

Her last commander, Captain P. T. Pedersen, assured me that she would have broken all records if she had not been either loaded too heavy or ballasted too light. He declared that she never had a real chance to show what she could do for this reason, added to the fact that her complement of 28 men all told was insufficient to allow of hard sail carrying; in fact, it was often a hard job for all hands to get her mainsail on to the yard and the gaskets passed.

Nevertheless her sailing records under Captains S. B. Johnson, N. B. Melsom and P. T. Pedersen were nothing short of amazing. The most astonishing entry recorded in her logbook was an average of 18 knots for 72 running hours, whilst on a passage from New York to Melbourne. This is scarcely believable and has never been

E

approached by any other ship. Another wonderful bit of sailing in her logbooks was 76 miles in 4 hours. She was at her best, of course, in strong quartering winds, but she was so long—as long and straight as a barracouta, the Australians called her—that once she had got up speed she carried her way in the most astonishing manner.

The following extracts from a passenger's log, as an illustration of her speed and seaworthiness, when over 55 years of age, make interesting reading:—

GLASGOW TOWARDS MONTE VIDEO, IN 1920.

February 17.—Lat. 56° 16′ N., Long. 11° 28′ W. Course N. 27 W. Distance 154 miles. About 2 a.m. it fell a dead calm, most mysteriously, with very heavy rain and we continued rolling about helplessly in the heavy sea till 7 a.m., when gradually the long prayed-for breeze from the N.E. set in gently and increased gradually with heavy rain all the time, till at noon we were bowling along with most of the sail set, at least 12 knots straight on our course south. . . . I was pretty feeble still, but crawled up on deck for a few minutes towards evening to see the sight which was grand beyond words. It was a high and wild sea. From the water's edge to the poop where I was is 20 feet, and the waves as they came along behind must have been 20 feet higher than I was, *i.e.* 40 ft. waves, but the ship just rode over them as easily as a gull, every sail including royals set, rolling from side to side so as to take an occasional wave over in the waist, but rushing along with a far easier motion than a steamer, so much so that in one's cabin one can hardly hear anything except the swish of the water rushing past and the creaking of the woodwork.

February 18.—Lat. 52° 7′ N., Long. 17° 23′ W. Course S. 40 W. Distance 325 miles. We have had 24 hours of magnificent sailing, averaging 13½ knots. At one time we were doing 14½ knots for 4 hours.

February 22.—Lat. 36° 11′ N., Long. 19° 14′ W. Course S. 15 W. Distance 227 miles. It is extraordinary how the *Lancing* slips along in a comparatively light breeze. Sitting in the cabin when she is going 10 knots you would imagine, but for the rolling, that you were at anchor in harbour.

February 26.—Lat. 24° 59′ N., Long. 21° 13′ W. Course S. 16 W. Distance 273 miles. For two hours during the night we were going 14 miles an hour and the whole day's average is faster than most tramp steamers and some passenger ones.

March 6.—Lat. 0° 32′ S., Long. 25° 58′ W. Course S. 6. W. Distance 135 miles. From Lamlash to the Equator 21 days a very rapid passage: only 16 days from the latitude of the Lizard.

March 10.—Lat. 5° 53′ S., Long. 28° 10′ W.   Course S. 11 W.   Distance 68 miles.   Still no wind to speak of, only a light breath coming away from S.E.   It is wonderful how the *Lancing* gets along in it, as she does from 2 to 3 knots all the time.

March 16.—Lat. 20° 38′ S., Long. 35° 9′ W.   Course S. 32 W.   Distance 125 miles.   We overtook and passed two full-rigged ships going the same way.   First saw the very tops of their masts above the horizon in the early morning and gradually raised all the masts and sails and then by evening had left them behind again.   The ships were too far off to the West for us ever to see their hulls, but it was interesting following them by their sails only.

March 19.—Lat. 28° 9′ S., Long. 42° 3′ W.   Course S. 43 W.   Distance 262 miles.   Average about 11 knots, and we are going for short spells as much as 14.   There was a high short sea on the starboard quarter, but the *Lancing* is a wonderfully dry ship and only took occasional dollops aboard.   It is fascinating watching her tearing through the seas, the sails all as stiff as boards and doing their work perfectly silently, so different from a steamer with its everlasting rattle, noise and vibration.   In my cabin this morning there was no more noise of any kind than when we were at anchor at Greenock.

March 20.—Lat. 29° 38′ S., Long. 43° 23′ W.   Course S. 38 W.   Distance 113 miles.   At 6 this morning, wind having gone round to South, Captain wore ship and we are now going along on the port tack close hauled, all sail set except royals, pitching into a heavy head sea, which the pampero has brought up from the South, but getting along fine, nearly 8 knots.   It is grand to see her lashing through the heavy sea, putting her nose into it at times, but taking very little aboard.

Ardrossan to Cape Chatte, in 1921.

July 24.—About 10 a.m. after wearing ship to starboard tack a fierce storm from N.W. descended upon us and blew for nearly 20 hours with regular fury.   I have never been in such a furious gale.   The wind blew the foam from the crests of the waves like smoke.   Sail was taken in till we had only foresail and lower topsail on foremast, upper and lower topsails on main and mizzen and lower topsail on jigger.   With these she rushed along at 10 knots, close-hauled, jumping about much but taking little water aboard, she is so high out of the water.

Cape Chatte to Ardrossan, in 1921.

August 31.—Fine breeze from N.N.W. about 2 a.m.   We are bowling along a good 12 knots.   Simply walked past a steamer going the same direction.   Our men crowded on foc's'le-head and cheered as we passed, offering steamer the end of a tow rope.

September 4.—Wind has freshened and we are sometimes going 15 knots, average 10 knots, through dense fog most of the time; a fairly high sea with seas coming over the rail occasionally, but ship going wonderfully steady. This cargo of spool wood has been very carefully loaded and she is in fine trim.

September 6.—Grand sailing all day, at nearly 10 knots. *Lancing* has a very heavy cargo (draws 24½ feet) and a very dirty bottom, not having been in dock for a year, so not much more than 10 or 11 knots can be got out of her.

GLASGOW TO SANTOS, 1921.

January 4.—Last night was a bad one, pitching and rolling badly, ship washed by seas, wind full gale. Wore ship at 1 a.m. This morning it is almost calm, but heavy swell makes us roll much. The ship is very stiff this voyage, loaded with briquettes, more weight than usual being low down.

January 10.—A big four-mast barque has been keeping us in company these days (8th to 10th) but too far off to signal. She goes ahead sometimes in lighter puffs as she is in ballast, but we have caught her up again to-day.

January 12.—Sighted Madeira . . . . passed Funchal Point about 5 miles off, which took away what little wind we had.

January 13.—The barque came near enough for lamp signalling last night. She is the Norwegian ship *Bellhouse* of Tonsberg, 46 days out from Sundsvall, Baltic, with planking for Melbourne. All day she has been sailing alongside, not a mile off. Sometimes we haul ahead when breeze strengthens, then she comes up again when wind is lighter. Her cargo of wood makes her much cranker and she does not roll anything like us. There is a very long high swell from N.W. quite a quarter of a mile between each top.

January 15.—*Bellhouse* was quite near us during the night and asked captain to report her on arrival at Santos. Since then she has steered more southerly and is out of sight.

February 1.—Wore ship with all hands in half an hour, not bad time for a four-master of *Lancing's* size.

February 5.—Passed a big four-mast barque going same way this morning. Sighted her at dawn about 7 miles ahead and by noon she was out of sight astern.

When the above notes were made the *Lancing's* complement consisted of:—Captain Pedersen; Mate A. Larsen; Second Mate Henrikson, Third Mate Hansen, bosun, carpenter, two sailmakers, donkeyman (for four steam winches), 10 A.B.'s, 2 O.S.'s, 7 boys, 1 cook, 1 steward, and passenger, signed on as storekeeper, 31 in all.

Captain Pedersen took command of the *Lancing* in 1919. His previous ship was captured and sunk off Ireland during the war, but no lives were lost.

The second mate's ship was also captured and sunk in the Bay of Biscay, all being drowned except himself and one man.

The third mate's ship was sunk off Hartlepool, only Hansen and another man being saved.

Johansen, the sailmaker, was serving in the *West Lothian* when she was captured by a U-boat in the North Sea, April 18, 1917, and then sunk. In this case all were saved.

The old *Lancing* was always a happy ship, which was not surprising as she was liberally run under Norwegian colours with the following splendid dietary scale, which apparently is that laid down by the Norwegian Government:—

	Breakfast 8 a.m.	Dinner Noon	Supper 6 p.m.
Sunday	Porridge eggs and bacon coffee	Vegetable soup tinned stewed beef fruit grut	Tea, mince and potatoes
Monday	Porridge bacon coffee	Pea soup salt beef or pork potatoes, tinned pineapple	Tea, hash and potatoes
Tuesday	Porridge curried rabbit coffee	Vegetable soup tinned bully beef fruit grut	Tea dry hash
Wednesday	Porridge baked beans and bacon, coffee	Rice and milk, salt cod, potatoes omelette	Tea stewed meat.
Thursday	Porridge eggs and bacon coffee	Vegetable soup, bully beef fruit grut	Tea liver and bacon
Friday	Porridge bacon coffee	Pea soup salt beef or pork potatoes, tinned pears	Tea dry hash
Saturday	Porridge eggs and bacon	Fruit soup salt fish and meat balls ground rice	Tea and stew

Besides a cup of coffee at 6.30 a.m. and coffee and biscuits at 3 p.m., jam was allowed *ad lib.* at breakfast and supper. In the cabin the officers got exactly the same food as the men, taken from the same pot in the galley, with a few extras such as an extra allowance of Ideal milk.

The fruit soup on Saturdays was made of all kinds of dried

fruits, apples, barley, currants, prunes and raspberry vinegar; and was most excellent.

The rice and milk on Wednesdays was thin like soup and very good. The men were served with one tin of Ideal milk each per week. The salt beef and pork were excellent and the coffee was always delicious.

I very much fear that the *Lancing* had no such provender when she was under the British flag.

The accommodation aboard the ex-mailboat was naturally very extensive and far superior to that of an ordinary cargo carrier, both forward, aft and amidships. Forward her complement of 20 men had room to lose themselves in her fo'c'sle. Aft each mate had his own cabin, and there was also a mates' messroom, besides the cosy saloon where the captain and his passengers had their meals.

If her sailing was wonderful, her food scale luxurious and her accommodation without compare, the old *Lancing* should be even more admired for her strength and the perfection of her construction. Her strength was almost beyond belief. On one occasion towards the end of her life the *Lancing*, travelling at the rate of 11 feet per second, ran full tilt into an iceberg on the Newfoundland Banks; she then swung broadside on to the weather side of the berg, where she remained, grinding and bumping, for about half an hour. Yet the only damage done was seven loose rivets in her stern and two of the lower yard trussbands broken.

Amongst Lloyd's surveyors she was called one of the wonders of the world. The Lloyd's surveyor at Glasgow who passed her through her last special survey could not find a dent in any of her shell plates, nor was there any record in Lloyd's Register of her hull having to be repaired. She passed a No. 2 survey when 57 years old and retained her class of 100 A1 to the end of her existence.

During her long life of sixty years from 1865 to 1925 the *Lancing* visited every part of the world. Her first few years as a sailing ship were evidently difficult ones: she was managed by A. E. Kinnear & Co., of London, who, I am afraid, did not succeed in making her pay.

Just before she was sold to J. Bryde of Sandejford, Norway, in 1893, she was sued by the Liverpool Towage Co. for a debt of £84, and narrowly escaped the disgrace of having a bailiff on board.

On her first passage as a sailing ship the *Lancing* left London with 18,000 casks of cement. According to *Lloyd's List* she took her departure from Plymouth on February 24, 1889, and we next hear of her at Melbourne on June 21. I believe Captain Persson was in charge this voyage.

In 1890 Captain George Hatfield took her out himself and came home to Dundee with a jute cargo.

Her next outward passage was from New York to Melbourne in 1890-1, and Captain Pedersen says that it was running her Easting down on this passage that she averaged 18 knots for 72 hours.

Most of her homeward passages during the early nineties seem to have been with jute to Dundee. Her first spell under the Norwegian flag was not a long one, for about 1896 she was bought by Mr. Frank Ross of Quebec and we find Captain Hatfield, who had evidently retained his interest in the old ship, once more in command. Cargoes, however, were not easily come by and she spent some months laid up in Sausalito Bay in hopes of a grain cargo.

Whilst in San Francisco waters, I think towards the end of 1896, she was chartered by an American syndicate to take a party down to Peru in search of Aztec treasure. I suppose the treasure was not forthcoming, for at the beginning of 1897 we find Captain Hatfield taking her across to Sydney, where she arrived on February 26. She was back again in San Francisco that summer.

In July, 1899, I saw her myself in San Francisco loading for Australia. She was then commanded by Captain F. W. Chapman. It was not until 1901 when she was sold to J. Johnson & Co. of Christiania for £6500 that she really began to gain a great name for herself as a passage maker. On June 13, 1901, she arrived at San Francisco from Newcastle, N.S.W., under Captain S. B. Johnson, having made the run across the Pacific in 59 days. Her next passage of note was from St. John's, New Brunswick, to Melbourne in 69 days. This was, I think, in 1902.

In 1903 we find her on the overdue list at 10 guineas per cent.

As I have already mentioned, she was only twice on the overdue list, and the first time was on a jute passage to New York when 5 guineas was paid.

Captain S. B. Johnson had the old ship until 1906 when he handed over to Captain N. B. Melsom. Under Johnson she seems to have been mostly in the Melbourne trade, and in 1904 we find her coming home to Queenstown with 29,562 bags of Melbourne wheat. But except for the run from St. John's to Melbourne, none of Captain Johnson's passages seem to have aroused attention.

Captain Melsom commanded the *Lancing* until 1918, and throughout that time hardly made a passage that was not considerably above the average. Captain P. T. Pedersen who followed him was also a great passage maker; I am therefore going to give a complete list of her passages from 1908 to the end. These are taken from the ship's logbooks.

1908

Left Langesund March 1, arrived Melbourne, May 15—75 days out. (A record passage
   at that time, cargo timber.)
Melbourne to New Caledonia—40 days. (Very bad weather throughout.)
Left Nehoue, N.C., August 12, arrived Hampton Roads for New York—100 days out.

1909

Left New York, March, for Tusket Wedge. (Made the run in 4 days.) Laid up at Tusket
   Wedge till August.
Tusket Wedge to Buenos Ayres—50 days. (Cargo 2,100,000 superficial ft. of timber
   under deck; 172,000 ft. on deck; total 2,272,000.)
Laid up at Buenos Ayres for three months.

1910

Buenos Ayres to Plum, New Caledonia—59 days.
Plum, N.C., to Rotterdam—97 days.
Rotterdam to the St. Lawrence, St. Lawrence to Ardrossan (cargo of sawn timber)—
   13 days. (Total number of days from Rotterdam—81.)

1911

Left Monte Video, January 21, arrived Pouembout, New Caledonia, March 8—46 days.
Left Pouembout, N.C., April 5.
Passed Prawle Point (for Rotterdam), July 18—104 days.

"GOLDEN GATE" EX "LORD SHAFTESBURY"

Photo Captain Schutze

"GOLDEN GATE" EX "LORD SHAFTESBURY

Photo Captain Schutze

[*See Page* 60

"PASS OF BALMAHA"

[See Page 62

"GLAUCUS"

[See Page 70

1912
Left Clyde December 27, 1911.   Arrived Monte Video February 11, 1912.—46 days.
Left Monte Video, April 19.   Arrived Poro, N.C., June 19—61 days.
Left Kouaoua, N.C., July 5.   Arrived Glasgow October 27—114 days.

1913
Left Clyde November 29, 1912.   Arrived Monte Video January 28—1913—60 days.
Left Buenos Ayres March 18.   Arrived New Caledonia May 17—59 days.
Left Poro, N.C., June 16.   Arrived Glasgow September 22—98 days.

1914
Left Glasgow December 5, 1913.   Arrived Rio January 17, 1914—43 days.
Left Rio March 6.   Arrived New Caledonia May 12—68 days.
Left New Caledonia June 2.   Arrived Channel September 25—115 days.

1915
Left Leith February 17.   Arrived Valparaiso May 17—89 days.
Left Antofagasta September 9.   Arrived New York November 25—77 days.

1916
Left New York February 2.   Arrived Aarhus February 25—23 days.   (*Lancing* passed
through Pentland Firth—15 days out. She beat the Danish mailboat
Frederick VIII from New York to Aarhus by one day.)
Left Aarhus March 24.   Arrived Halifax April 15—21 days.
Left Halifax May 10.   Arrived Glasgow May 24—14 days.   (2407 miles; average per
day 172 miles.)
Left Glasgow June 10.   Arrived Cape Chatte July 3.—22 days.
Left Capucines July 26.   Arrived Ardrossan August 15—19 days.
Left Greenock September 11.   Arrived Quebec October 10—29 days.
Left Quebec November 10.   Arrived Glasgow 24 November—14 days.   (2730 miles;
average per day 194 miles.)

1917
Left Lamlash December 26, 1916.   Arrived Baltimore January 31—35 days
Left Baltimore March 28.   Arrived Aarhus April 25—27 days.
Left Christiania May 24.   Arrived Matune June 19—24 days.
Left Cape Chatte July 15.   Arrived Ardrossan August 9—24 days.
Left Ardrossan September 16.   Arrived Quebec October 13—26 days.
Left St. Ann November 18.   Arrived Queenstown November 30—12 days.   (2336 miles;
average per day 194 miles.)

1918
Left Glasgow March 9.   Arrived Santos May 7—58 days.
Left Santos May 30.   Arrived Melbourne July 15—45 days.
Left Melbourne July 30.   Arrived Barbados November 6—99 days.
Left Barbados November 11.   Arrived New Orleans November 28—17 days.

1919

Left New Orleans December 15, 1918.   Arrived Queenstown January 12, 1919—27 days.
Left Havre March 3.   Arrived Hampton Roads April 11—38 days.
Left New York May 27.   Arrived Aarhus June 21—24 days.
Left Aarhus July 10.   Arrived Cape Chatte August 27—37 days
Left Cape Chatte September 14.   Arrived Ardrossan September 30—16 days.

1920

Left Lamlash February 14.   Arrived Monte Video March 27—41 days.
Left Buenos Ayres May 29.   Arrived Queenstown July 18—50 days.
Left Belfast August 13.   Arrived Cape Chatte September 9—27 days.
Left Cape Chatte September 26.   Arrived Ardrossan October 29—33 days.

1921

Left Glasgow December 17, 1920.   Arrived Santos February 12, 1921—57 days.
Left Santos March 5.   Arrived Bermuda April 6—32 days.
Left Bermuda May 1.   Arrived Mechin May 14—13 days.
Left Mechin June 8.   Arrived Ardrossan June 24—16 days.
Left Ardrossan July 12.   Arrived Cape Chatte August 11—30 days.
Left Cape Chatte August 27.   Arrived Ardrossan September 12—16 days.

The *Lancing* was laid up from September, 1921, to June, 1922, when after being dry-docked at Greenock she went round to Hull and loaded for Cape Chatte.   Her trans-Atlantic voyage in 1922 was a bad one, the weather being very unfavourable.

On the return passage from the St. Lawrence to Ardrossan, with the usual spool wood cargo, the *Lancing* was a month fighting against hard easterly gales.   Once more she was laid up in the Gareloch.   In the spring of 1924 she was given a much needed overhaul and fitted out for one more run to Canada.   This time she left the Tail of the Bank on May 14 and arrived at Cape Chatte on June 15, 32 days out.   The passage home was also nothing remarkable.

The end of her active service had now arrived.   On Christmas Eve, 1924, the famous old ship was towed away from Ardrossan *en route* for Genoa where the Italian ship-breakers awaited her.

"Sindia" and "Holkar"—The Last of Brocklebank's Sailers.

In the years 1887 and 1888 Messrs. Harland & Wolff launched the last sailing ships to be built for the famous firm of Brocklebank.

These were the two magnificent four-mast barques *Sindia*

and *Holkar*, said to be the largest sailing ships in the world when they came out.

Of course they were large carriers rather than clippers, but, like all Harland & Wolff's productions, they were faster than their carrying capacity would make one suspect, and they were as handsome as the earlier Belfast ships with the characteristic rake of mast and powerful sheer. After a few years in the Calcutta trade they were ousted by steam and forced into the ranks of the grain carriers.

Then, when the Brocklebanks sold their sailing ships, *Sindia* was bought by the Anglo-American Oil Co., and was kept busy carrying kerosene oil to the East and returning to America with chrome ore.

She came to her end in December, 1901, on her homeward passage from Kobe, Japan, to New York. Whilst searching for Delaware Bay during a winter blizzard, she stranded at Ocean City, New Jersey, and became a total loss though her crew was saved; the greater part of her cargo was salved. The wreck is still to be seen half buried in the sand.

The *Holkar* survived until 1925, when she was broken up in Holland.

The first captain of this ship was the veteran Captain William Ellery, whose sea time began as far back as 1856, when he sailed as an apprentice in Brocklebank's barque the *Hindoo* of only 256 tons.

The *Holkar* was his twelfth as well as his last sailing ship, for he left her at the end of her maiden voyage in order to take over the steamer *Ameer*. Captain Peterkin was the next commander of the *Holkar*. In 1901 she was sold to D. H. Watjen & Co., of Bremen, and disguised under the name of *Adelaide*. The Germans sold her to Norway in 1913, when renamed *Odessa*, later changed to *Souverain* and then *Hippalos*. She was broken up in 1924.

"Muscoota" ex "Buckingham" and her famous Figure-head.

The next ship to the *Holkar* in point of size to be launched in 1888 was the *Buckingham*, built by Thomas Royden for Macvicar

& Marshall's Palace Line.   This four-mast barque is wrongly said to have been the only vessel of the British Mercantile Marine that was launched by Queen Victoria; and she had a very beautiful figure-head of the Queen holding a rose.

In spite of such a propitious start, the *Buckingham* seems to have had a somewhat chequered life.   Macvicar & Marshall sold her to the Germans in 1901, who changed the name to *Bertha*. She was later sold under German flag and renamed *Ottawa*.   During the war she was taken over by the American Shipping Board, who spent over £50,000 in reconditioning her, after which she was re-christened *Muscoota*, by Mrs. Wilson, the wife of the President, and sent to sea.   But the American Shipping Board soon disposed of her to a syndicate of Americans and Australians for the sum of £7400. In the autumn of 1922 the *Muscoota*, under Captain A. C. Wilvers, loaded two and a half million feet of timber at Port Ludlow, Puget Sound, and crossed the Pacific to Melbourne in 69 days.   When off Wilson's Promontory on Christmas Day, 1922, she was in collision with the steamer *Yarra*, and the famous figure-head of Queen Victoria was left in the steamer's galley.

The *Muscoota* succeeded in making port, but in the lawsuit which followed Captain Wilvers claimed £150 for the lost figure-head, which was still more damaged by souvenir hunters.   In the end damages to the extent of £5267 were awarded the owners of the sailing ship.

In the spring of 1924 the old ship was bought by the Wallarah Coal Co. and became a hulk in Sydney Harbour.

"Galgate" and "Lord Shaftesbury."

The next largest sailing ships of 1888 were the steel four-mast sister ships, *Galgate* and *Lord Shaftesbury*, built at White-haven, the former for Joyce and the latter for Herron's Liverpool Lord Line.

They, also, were big carriers, yet with a surprising turn of speed on occasions.   In May, 1900, the *Galgate* went from Shanghai to the Columbia River in 27 days, during which she covered 2600 miles in 10 days, her best run being 295 miles.

In 1895 she made one of the quickest passages from Calcutta

to New York, arriving April 26, 102 days out.   And in 1902 she arrived at Queenstown on January 6, 112 days from Astoria.

The *Galgate* fell a victim to a German submarine in 1916.

The *Lord Shaftesbury* will perhaps be better remembered as the American *Golden Gate*.   One of her best passages under the Red Ensign was 88 days from New Caledonia to the Delaware Capes in 1904.   In 1912 she had a very nasty experience off the Horn, being swept from stem to stern by what the reporters called a tidal wave, which took boats, deckhouses, and one man overboard; very shortly after this, the ship became surrounded with ice, and had one or two nasty crashes before she got free.

After the war she had a trying passage from 'Frisco to Runcorn *via* the Panama Canal.   The *Golden Gate,* as she was now called, sprang a leak soon after leaving San Francisco and it became necessary to man the pumps every watch; indeed, Captain Hackell did not expect to get his ship home.   She was 48 days to Panama and 98 to Ellesmere Port, where she was run aground but refloated afterwards with help from the shore.

Not long before her arrival the pumps broke down and had to be repaired, and the ship was then considered to be in such danger of sinking that a Cunard liner stood by whilst the pumps were out of action.

The *Golden Gate* was laid up in Oakland Creek along with many another well-known windjammer.   She was scrapped in 1934.

"Marion Lightbody" and her Stowaways.

One of the smartest four-masters, launched in 1888, was the steel ship *Marion Lightbody,* built by Henderson to the order of Rogers & Co.   This vessel was commanded by Captain William Cordiner from her launch until Rogers parted with her to Trinder, Anderson & Co. in 1911.

The *Marion Lightbody* was a fair sailer for her type.   In 1893 she sailed from Liverpool for Melbourne with general cargo at the beginning of October, and the very first day out made a run of 300 miles.   Yet, such is the luck of the winds, that in spite of this good start she took 36 days to the Line owing to the lack of N.E. Trades.

This passage was enlivened by three little Liverpool shoe-blacks who had stowed away. These boys, on being discovered, turned to with such a will that Captain Cordiner refused to give them in charge on his arrival.

In 1903 *Marion Lightbody* again had stowaways aboard on a passage from Liverpool to Melbourne. This time there were two boys, one said he was an orphan but the other admitted that he had run away from his widowed mother in the most heartless way, and Captain Cordiner was by no means so well-disposed towards him as to the shoe-blacks.

Marion Lightbody was the fourth of the "Marions." The ships before her were steel three-masters, the *Marion Crosbie*, *Marion Inglis* and *Marion Ballantyne* (first named *Olymp*).

To show the way in which sailing ships were still paying in the nineties, it is worth recording that the 1600-ton full-rigger *Marion Inglis* paid a dividend of 30 per cent. in 1898 on a twelve months' voyage besides carrying a good amount to reserve.

The *Marion Chilcott*, which made the 34-day record from Newcastle, N.S.W., to Honolulu under Captain Weedon, did not belong to Rogers' fleet. Though she made this run under American colours, she was the old Russell-built ship *Kilbrannan*.

After paying only £4300 for the *Marion Lightbody*, Trinder, Anderson & Co. sold her to the Finns the following year for £7600. The ship was on her way from Geelong to Queenstown at the time. She reached Queenstown safely, but on being ordered to Limerick for discharge was very nearly lost in a furious gale off Galway, where she was reported in distress with a heavy list to starboard.

"Pass of Balmaha" as a German Raider.

The 1500-ton steel full-rigger, *Pass of Balmaha* was built by Duncan for Gibson & Clark of Glasgow: she was Duncan's 237th, and though like every other builder at this date he had to consider carrying capacity before sailing qualities, he managed to give the *Pass of Balmaha* a good turn of speed for a full-built ship. But she will be remembered rather as the German raider *See-Adler* (Sea Eagle) during the war, when she was so ably commanded by the daring Graf Felix von Luckner, who sank millions of pounds' worth of French and British shipping, including, alas, some fine square-riggers.

Some of her sailing performances in her early days are worthy of record. In 1899, under Captain Scougall, she went from Newcastle, N.S.W., to Sourabaya in 42 days. Then in 1900 Captain Scougall sailed from Buenos Ayres to Newcastle, N.S.W., in 42 days. The *Pass of Balmaha* had strong westerly winds as far as Bass Straits, where a head wind induced her master to bear away south to round the Island when he got a fair wind again. The *Pass of Balmaha's* average was 236 miles per day, her best run being 336 miles.

In 1901 the ship arrived off the Isle of Wight, 103 days out from Caledonia.

In 1908 the *Pass of Balmaha* broke the record between the River Plate and Boston, making this run in 34 days. She had just been sold by Gibson & Clark to the River Plate Shipping Company, and was commanded at the time by Captain Dick Lee, a very fine example of a Blue-nose shipmaster.

When war broke out she was commanded by a New England skipper named Scott, and was on a passage from New York to Archangel under the American flag when a suspicious British cruiser held her up and sent her to Scapa Flow under a prize officer and six men. Then whilst she was on her way a German submarine popped up and took the old ship, prize crew and all, into Cuxhaven.

After the battle of Jutland the German naval authorities realised that there was little hope of their cruisers being able to avoid the enemy on the high seas, and decided that camouflaged merchantmen were their only chance as commerce destroyers outside the radius of their submarines. The *Pass of Balmaha* was a very clever choice for their desperate object, as none of the allied cruisers were likely to suspect a windjammer of being a German warship. Luckily for the success of the enterprise, there happened to be a German naval officer who was perfectly suited for the command of such a vessel. This was Commander Graf Felix von Luckner, who had commanded cruisers at the battles of Heligoland and Jutland; at Jutland his vessel had been sunk and he was picked out of the sea severely wounded. The Count, however, was a tough customer; not only was he a champion swimmer but he held the German record for saving life from drowning, so that it is not surprising that he managed to keep afloat until he was rescued, in spite of being badly wounded. His chief hobby was yachting, and he was a devotee of the out-of-date square-rigged sailing ship, having not only served in the past for a year as A.B. in a Norwegian windjammer, but also in the fo'c'sle of the British four-mast barque. *Pinmore,* as mentioned in Volume I.

The Germans were as thorough as even they could be in the preparation of the *See-Adler,* as the *Pass of Balmaha* was re-named; everything was thought out down to the tiniest detail.

First of all, the ship was fitted with an auxiliary engine of 1500 horse-power; besides two four-point-twos, machine guns, carbines, bombs and a powerful wireless plant were concealed behind secret doors; hidden accommodation being even prepared for future prisoners.

Next came the selection and training of the crew. To the number of 64, they were all picked men from the Naval Reserve, most of whom had served in the merchant ships of many nationalities besides their own. Although von Luckner, his navigating officer and most of his crew could speak Norwegian, this in itself was not considered sufficient to disguise the raider into an innocent Norwegian trader.

For several weeks before sailing the crew were trained in Norwegian ways and methods of carrying on at sea. All orders were given in that language, and the Count himself was so thorough in playing his part that he grew a beard and learnt to chew tobacco and spit brown. All naval discipline and habits were strictly tabooed, for fear of the keen eyes of the British naval officer.

As soon as von Luckner was satisfied that his deck hands would pass as Norwegians and that his gun crews were efficient, the *See-Adler,* as we will now call her, took on board a deck cargo of very heavy timber, which effectually blocked all entry to the hold, except by secret doors. Next sufficient provisions were taken in for a three years' cruise. Perhaps the most important and skilfully contrived deception of the lot were the ship's papers. These showed that the *See-Adler* was the Norwegian ship *Irma,* bound out to

"CARRADALE'

[See Page 70

"ANDRINA"

[See Page 78

"GRACE HARWAR' AND "FRIEDA"
After hurricane at Mobile

Lent by H. E. Earp   [See Page 97

"CARRADALE"

Lent by Gregory Robinson   [See Page 70

Melbourne, to which the rubber stamp of the British Consulate bore witness.

The *See-Adler, ex Pass of Balmaha,* left German waters for the high seas on December 21, 1916, and such bad weather was experienced in rounding the Scottish coast that no enemy ship was sighted. However, at 9.30 a.m. on Christmas Day, when about 180 miles south of Iceland, the new raider sighted the British auxiliary cruiser, *Avenger.* First a blank and then a shotted charge was fired at the innocent looking full-rig ship, which had all sail set to a light breeze. Captain von Luckner, having gained sufficient time to make his preparations now hove to, whilst the cruiser circled round with every gun trained in his direction. Having had a good look at the strange sailing ship, the *Avenger* now hauled off a few lengths and sent a boat to examine the *See-Adler.*

Von Luckner's plans for just such an emergency were complete. Only five men, all of whom could speak Norwegian, showed themselves on the deck of the raider, besides her captain, who, as the boat came alongside, could be heard bellowing orders in Norwegian whilst his men lowered a rope ladder over the side.

Two officers and an armed party of 12 bluejackets came over the rail to be properly hoodwinked by the daring Count, who almost overplayed his part in his zeal as an actor.

After greeting the boarding officer with "A Happy Christmas to you," he took him aft to his cabin in order to show the ship's papers. I will give what followed in his own words:—

In the saloon, lying on a divan, I had a seventeen-year old boy, dressed as a woman and possessing a very clear complexion and feminine appearance. He was carefully dressed for the part he had to play, and a shawl was wrapped round his head as if he were suffering from toothache.

I introduced this specimen of human camouflage to the officer as my wife, who was "very sick." Whereupon he said:—" I hope you will excuse me, lady, I am only doing my duty, and will only be here for a short time in which to look at the ship's papers." There was only one danger regarding the boy's make-up, and that was his voice, which might have betrayed him by reason of its roughness. Fortunately the supposititious "toothache" excused him from talking. Part of my cabin fittings were Norwegian cushion covers, and on the walls were displayed photos of Norway's King and Queen, also a photo of King Edward VII.

While the officer was proceeding with the examination of my papers a gramophone in the mess-room was playing "It's a Long Way to Tipperary," whilst several of the

F

examining officers' men were taken to the pantry, where the steward supplied them with a glass of good whisky, which made everyone cheerful and created a good impression.

During this time I was chewing tobacco and expectorating on the floor, after the manner of a Norwegian captain.

(I fancy that Norwegian captains will accuse him of overplaying his part here.)

When the examination was finished, the officer shook hands with me and said "Captain, your papers are all right, but you must wait until you get the order by signal to continue your voyage." I thereupon assumed an anxious look and asked if I would be safe from submarines, and could he give me any advice. He replied: "I don't think you will find any so far North as we now are."

The officer and his crew then left my ship and went aboard the cruiser, and in about half an hour the signal, "Continue your voyage," was hoisted. Oh, what a relief was felt by everyone on board when that signal was given. After this the cruiser passed us once more. We gave her three cheers and dipped our Norwegian flag. She then showed another signal "Happy Voyage," to which I replied "Thank you very much." "That is just what I want," said I to my chief officer, and felt indeed a happy man.

The disguised boy in the saloon formed part of a carefully thought out scheme for the recapture of the ship, in the event of the Count's acting failing to convince a suspicious boarding officer. As all credit for this very ingenious stratagem must be awarded to von Luckner, I will again use his own description:—

When my ship was being fitted at Bremerhaven I had the whole of the floor of the after saloon cut out and reconstructed, so that it would become the platform of a hydraulic lift, which could be suddenly lowered about 14 feet. Knowing (in the event of capture) that I would not be allowed to go to my original quarter, but would have to remain on deck, and that only my supposed wife would be allowed in the saloon quarters, I had all my arrangements ready. I knew that one officer of the prize crew would remain on deck while the other would be with the prize crew off duty, below deck.

Doors had been cut in the steel masts of my ship, and in these were concealed uniforms, caps and arms for my crew aloft.

I could conceal 20 armed men under the saloon floor. On the navigating deck was an electric button, which sounded alarm bells in every part of the ship.

At a favourable opportunity, when part of the prize crew were having a meal in the saloon, I would put on my uniform, coat and cap, and with my pistol would make prisoner the officer on duty. Then I would press the electric button, drop the saloon floor and sound the alarm, whereupon my deck crew would seize their rifles and cover the prize crew on deck. The part of the prize crew who would fall with the saloon floor would become an easy prey to my 20 armed men.

My plans were rehearsed many times. At these rehearsals men went down with the floor, so that it could be noted how the furniture would fall. My supposed wife would, when the signal was given, close all doors, and with pistol capture any sentry who might have been posted inside or out. An order would have been previously given to my deck crew to go aloft where they could have got their arms, etc., from the masts. Their position would have given them a great advantage over the prize crew on deck.

He adds:—

Our plans seemed so efficient that we often wished that an opportunity would be afforded of demonstrating them.

As a Britisher, who knows how vigorously his countrymen usually act when taken by surprise, I see a few flaws in the Count's carefully prepared scheme, by which he hoped to recapture his ship without bloodshed, and I think that his long rehearsed words:— "Put up your hands; this is a naval ship. I am the Commander; you are my prisoner," would have led to a nice little scrimmage.

The following is a complete list of the prizes captured by the old *Pass of Balmaha* in her guise as a German raider:—

Name of Prize	Nationality and Rig	Passage	Cargo
Gladys Royal	British steamer	Cardiff to Buenos Ayres	Coal
Lundy Island	,, ,,	Mauritius to Nantes	Sugar
Charles Gounod	French barque	Durban to Havre	Maize
Percy	British aux. schooner	Halifax to Channel	Fish and Lumber
Antonin ..	French 4-mast barque	Iquique to France	Saltpetre
Pinmore ..	British 4 mast barque	Buenos Ayres to Channel	,,
Buenos Ayres ..	Italian ship	Iquique to Gibraltar	,,
British Yeoman	British barque	River Plate to Liverpool	Grain
La Rochefoucauld	French ship	Iquique to France	Saltpetre
Dupleix	French barque	,, ,,	,,
Horngarth ..	British steamer	Buenos Ayres to Liverpool	Maize
Cambronne ..	French barque	Iquique to Mediterranean	Saltpetre
A. B. Johnson	American 4-mast schn'r	San Francisco to Australia	Lumber
R. C. Slade ..	,, ,,	Sydney to San Francisco	Copra
Manila ..	,, ,,	Sydney to Honolulu	Coal

It says a good deal for the skilful management of Graf Felix von Luckner that the capture of these fifteen ships only cost one life. The steamer *Horngarth* would not give in until her engines had been damaged by shellfire. One of her crew received a splinter in the head and died soon after being operated upon by the *See-Adler's* surgeon, his case being hopeless from the start. Von Luckner gave him an impressive funeral, and read the service himself over a coffin draped with the Union Jack, all hands and prisoners being paraded on deck, whilst the ship's band played the "Dead March."

Most of the prizes were caught entirely by surprise, and rounded to at once, but the *Gladys Royal* ran from the raider until five shells had penetrated her stern. But there was a reason for this, the captain having lost his previous ship to the *Moewe*.

Bombs were generally used to sink the captured ships, but these failed in the case of the *Percy* and von Luckner had to resort to shellfire. After a few shots sparks and smoke began to issue from the *Percy*, her oil fuel had caught, and she was soon a mass of flames, lighting up the sky for miles around.

The Frenchman *La Rochefoucauld* was sunk by gunfire in order to satisfy her crew that the *See-Adler's* armament was not a dummy one.

The barque *Cambronne* alone escaped destruction, as von Luckner used her in order to get rid of the 287 prisoners, which at this date—March, 1917—were overcrowding his hold and consuming all his stores. He placed the *Cambronne* under the senior Captain, Captain Mullings, who was given instructions to carry her into Rio. But the Count took no chances. He first of all sawed off her topgallant masts above the topmast caps, dumped all cargo and spare sails overboard, and only gave the prisoners provisions for a month. However, Rio was not far off and they had no difficulty in making port.

Having got rid of his prisoners, von Luckner now steered a course for the Pacific in order to find some suitable place for cleaning the ship's bottom and give his crew a run ashore, after which he hoped to descend like a hawk upon the trans-Pacific trade.

The *Pass of Balmaha* was no stranger to the Horn, but she caught it hot whilst rounding Cape Stiff at the end of March, 1917, being forced a long way to the southward.

After capturing the four-masted schooners in the neighbourhood of the Equator, Count von Luckner anchored off the little known Mopelia Island, Society Group, in August, in order to careen his ship.

Here the coral reef dipped sheer down to unfathomable depths,

so that the ship could be laid close alongside, and hove down.
Unfortunately, whilst half the crew were ashore and the other half
were scraping the raider's plates, an unexpected breaker which
von Luckner called a "tidal wave" lifted the ship up and set her
down right on top of the reef.   This was the end of the *See-Adler* ex
Pass of Balmaha, for there was no way of heaving her off the reef;
with no bottom one could not lay out anchors, and it was soon
recognised that the ship was a total loss.

The sporting Count eventually set off in his launch and experienced many an exciting adventure and queer prison before he saw
the Fatherland again.

NOTE.—This account was written before the publication of *The Sea Devil.*   It is taken
from von Luckner's own description of his cruise, written whilst he was a prisoner in New
Zealand, and published in pamphlet form in August, 1919.   The *Pinmore's* adventure
described in Vol. I. was also taken from the same source.

Carmichael's "Glaucus."

The *Glaucus*, which was launched in March, 1889, was the
only four-master in Carmichael's fleet.   Her best known commander,
Captain Cook, declared that she sailed quite as well as her younger
sisters but did not steer as straight.

Like all Barclay Curle's productions she was a very handsome
ship.   On her first voyage she loaded salt at Liverpool at 27s. 6d.
for Calcutta and made the passage in 86 days; from Calcutta she
took 3214 tons of Indian produce to New York whence she was
loaded back again to Calcutta with 86,947 cases of oil.

Amongst her best passages were the following:—

    1892   'Frisco to Queenstown—105 days.
    1898   Frederickstadt to Melbourne—93 days.
    1898   'Frisco to Falmouth—108 days.
    1899   Melbourne to Lizard—85 days.

Her last passage under the British flag was in 1905, when she
left Astoria on January 6, and arrived at Queenstown at 7 a.m. on
April 26, 109 days out.   She was then sold to the French firm of
Ant Dom Bordes et Fils who re-named her *Almendral.*   Henceforward she became a nitrate clipper.

Mr. Thomas Carmichael relates an amusing story about the
Glaucus.   Whilst bound north along the Brazil coast the ss. *Ionic*

passed **very close** to the *Glaucus*, storming south in the **strong** Trade. A passenger in the steamship took a snapshot of the sailer, which soon found its way to one of the Carmichaels. This photograph showed that the *Glaucus* had every sail set except the mizen royal, whose yard was on deck. On his arrival at San Francisco Captain Cook found a letter awaiting him from his owners asking what had happened to his mizen royal yard. Cook replied that if the *Ionic* had passed the *Glaucus* two hours sooner her passengers would have seen his mizen royal yard coming down in two pieces, which was caused by the fool of a second mate omitting to ease the halliards before taking a pull on the braces.

Years later the same Carmichael was telling this story to the skipper of the Clyde Shipping Company's steamer off the West Coast of Ireland. The master of the steamer said nothing until he got Carmichael alone, then he told him that he was that fool of a second mate, and that though he got the blame it was really the fault of the old fool of a mate, who said he would ease the mizen royal halliards and had forgotten to do it.

If Carmichael, after this, had met the mate, perhaps we should have found the blame put on to Captain Cook himself.

Roxburgh's "Carradale."

Amongst the later ships of the Glasgow Dale Line were the 2015-ton sister ships *Armadale* and *Bracadale*, both built by Stephen in 1887. They were iron four-mast barques, and were followed by the steel four-mast barques *Carradale* launched from Stephen's yard in 1889, and *Fascadale* launched from the same yard in 1890. These were about 70 tons larger.

The last of their four-masters was the *Torrisdale* of 2184 tons, built by Henderson in 1892.

Though these ships were built specially for the Australian trade we find them compelled to seek cargoes all over the world, like most sailing ships in the twentieth century.

It was always easy to recognise these Dale liners, for they were all painted light lead colour with the white ports upside down with the exception of the *Armadale*, which had black and white ports when Captain Duncan was in command

Of the five four-mast barques the *Carradale* was probably the best known.   Whilst she was commanded by Captain Alexander Smith she put up some astonishing records for a full-built ship. Captain J. W. Harris, marine superintendent of the Booth Line, who served his time in the ship, tells me that her best performance while he was aboard was 304 miles two days in succession whilst running the Easting down in November, 1895.   He also remembers her making 290 miles between December 5 and 6, 1898, when loaded down to her marks with coal; on this occasion it was blowing hard from the sou'west, the ship was carrying all plain sail, and (Captain Harris adds) from the fuss she **was** making one would have supposed she was logging 16 knots.

Her best passage was undoubtedly from Barry Dock to Nagasaki in 1897, when she went out *via* Anjer and Banka Straits in 114 days. This was during the sou'west monsoon, and the *Carradale* sailed from Banka to Nagasaki in 19 days.

In 1896-7 the *Carradale* took part in a very interesting race from 'Frisco to Queenstown.   The following seven ships engaged in the contest:—

Springburn	left 'Frisco for Hull September 12, 1896.				
Ditton ..	,,	,,	Queenstown September 13, 1896.		
Loch Linnhe	,,	,,	Cork September 23.		
Formosa ..	,,	,,	Falmouth September 24.		
John Cooke ..	,,	,,	Queenstown September 25.		
Carradale ..	,,	,,	,,	,,	,,
Falls of Afton	,,	,,	,,	October 2.	

The *Carradale*, I may say, had been 15 months out of dry dock, but it is probable that most of the others were in the same condition.

It is interesting to note from the *Carradale's* log the way in which these seven ships were constantly in company with each other

October 14.—*John Cooke* and *Carradale* were in company.

October 21.—*Carradale* crossed the Line 26 days out having had very light Trades.

November 25.—*Carradale* spoke *Loch Linnhe*.

November 26-30.—*Carradale, Loch Linnhe* and *Ditton* in company.

November 28.—The three ships rounded the Horn within sight of each other.

November 30.—In 52° 45′ S., 56° 26′ W., *Carradale* spoke the *Springburn*.

December 1.—In 50° 46′ S., 52° 23′ W., *John Cooke* was again in company with *Carradale*,

December 14.—In 30° 30′ S., 27° 03′ W. *Springburn* again showed up over *Carradale's* horizon.

December 17.—In 27° 30′ S., 26° 50′ W. *Formosa* spoke *Carradale.*

December 20.—In 18° 53′ S., 25° 39′ W., *Falls of Afton* spoke *Carradale.*

December 23.—In 11° 08′ S., 26° 05′ W., *Formosa* and *Carradale* were in company and remained within speaking distance of each other until the night of December 29.

December 28.—*Carradale* and *Formosa* crossed the Line.

January 20, 1897.—In 43° 51′ N., 24° 38′ W., *Springburn* and *Carradale* were again in company.

January 24.—In 48° 32′ N., 21° 35′ W., *Springburn, Ditton* and *Carradale* were all together.

January 26.—In 49° N., 20° W. (dead reckoning), *Ditton* and *Carradale* were together.

January 28.—In 50° 49′ N., 15° W., *Loch Linnhe* spoke *Carradale.*

Finally, at daylight on January 30, *Carradale, Ditton, Falls of Afton, Loch Linnhe,* and two other ships, *Port Douglas* (which had left 'Frisco after the seven) and the *Almora* (which had left 'Frisco before them), were within sight of each other off Queenstown. It was blowing a nor'west gale and the ships were under three lower topsails; they were towed into Queenstown about noon in the order named.

Captain Alexander Smith was probably prouder of his passage from Portland (O) to Queenstown in 1897-8 than of any other, although the *Carradale* took 145 days, for on this occasion he brought his ship home round the Horn without a certificated officer on duty. The second mate cleared out the night before *Carradale* towed down to Astoria, and Captain Smith had no time to procure another second mate.

Carradale left Portland in tow on November 27 and anchored off Astoria at 3 p.m. the next day. That night it came on to blow, and the four-mast barque *Elginshire* dragged her anchor and came down on top of the *Carradale,* her port quarter striking the *Carradale's* starboard cat-head. She then came grinding along the latter's starboard side until the two vessels were almost poop to poop, when the *Carradale's* cross-jack yard brought down her jigger topmast—no damage, however, except the loss of braces and a sprung main royal yard was suffered by the *Carradale.*

On December 2, at 3 p.m., the *Carradale* towed to sea in

"CONISHEAD"

[See Page 77

WRECK OF "PINDOS"

[See Page 78

"EUDORA"

Lent by Captain L. R. W. Beavis

"BRABLOCH"

Lent by Captain D. Kiddie

[*See Page* 86

company with the *Elginshire* and *Cromartyshire*.   Light southerly winds were experienced until December 4, when a fresh gale from the S.E. set in.   The three grain ships were soon forced to shorten sail down to three lower topsails and foresail, and night found the *Carradale* head-reaching slowly off the land on the port tack. On December 5, Captain Smith was compelled to furl his foresail and fore lower topsail, the wind having hauled to sou'west with a high sea and terrific squalls.

December 6 dawned with the ship labouring heavily, hove to on the starboard tack.   At 4 a.m. the weather side of the mizen topsail split and with some difficulty it was goose-winged.   At 7 a.m. during a very heavy squall the ship was forced down on her beam ends.   All hands were called to take in the mizen topsail, but directly the sheets were started the sail blew away.   As the ship did not right herself all hands were sent below *via* the lazarette in order to trim the bags of wheat over to windward. It was found that the cargo had settled down bodily to leeward, leaving a huge space between the bags and the ship's side. Until 10 p.m. that night all hands worked below carrying the bags up from the lee side and dropping them down the space to windward.

December 7 found the *Carradale* still hard pressed by a whole gale from S.W. with her decks swept by tremendous seas.   All hands again worked in the hold till 10 p.m.   During the forenoon, however, a big spare spar on deck broke adrift, and it was only with the greatest difficulty it was secured.   During the operation the mate was knocked down by a sea, and had his right ankle so badly broken that he could not leave his bunk or perform any duty for the remainder of the passage.   After this catastrophe Captain Smith promoted the bosun to mate and the third mate to second mate.   Neither of these officers, however, held a certificate.

At 3 p.m. that afternoon the main lower topsail blew to rags until not a vestige remained except the bolt-ropes.   After this, with incredible labour, a new mizen topsail was bent though it was not set.   At 8 p.m. Captain Smith wore his ship round on to the port tack, in spite of which the ship still listed to port.   Throughout that night the ship lay under a weather cloth in the jigger rigging, labouring heavily in a whole gale and high sea.

On December 8 the gale slightly moderated and Captain Smith set his fore and mizen topsails and a reefed mainsail in lieu of a main topsail. Later on a new main topsail was bent and set and the mainsail furled. That night the wind backed to the S.E. and increased to a whole gale with the sea still running mountains high. At 4 a.m. on December 9, whilst the hands were aloft making fast the fore lower topsail, the wind flew round to the S.W. and caught the *Carradale* flat aback. Luckily no damage was done and Captain Smith hove to on the starboard tack. The weather continued to pipe up until December 13 with the ship either hove to or head-reaching.

At 10 p.m. on the 13th we find the following entry in the log:— "Wind shifted to nor'west, blowing harder."

At daylight on the 14th the *Carradale* was at last squared away on her course, but it was not until the 18th that the weather moderated sufficiently to permit of the anchors being taken aboard. During the whole of this strenuous time Captain Smith hardly left the deck, though he showed that he had plenty of confidence in his two "acting" officers.

The *Carradale* crossed the Line in long. 118° 46' W. on January 6, 35 days out.

At daybreak on February 9, in 54° 54' S., 83° 54' W., *Carradale* spoke the ship *Pleiades* which was only 20 days out from Timaru for London. The wind was northerly and fresh; both ships were under all plain sail heading for the Horn, but although the *Pleiades* was a smart ship she was hull down astern of the *Carradale* by 6 p.m.

Three days later the latter rounded the Horn in light easterly winds and fog. She crossed the Line on March 20 and had a very long spell of the Doldrums. *Carradale* arrived off Queenstown on April 26 where she received orders for St. Nazaire, where she docked on April 29, 148 days out.

Both the other ships made longish passages, the *Cromartyshire* arriving Dunkirk May 3, 152 days out.

The following is an epitome of the *Carradale's* crack passage from Barry Dock to Nagasaki in 1897:—

April 27.—Left Barry for sea.
May 25.—Crossed the Line—28 days out.
June 26.—On longitude of the Cape—60 days out.
July 23.—Sighted Java Heads.
July 25.—Anchored off Anjer Point.
July 26.—Left Anjer, drifted and worked the tides through the Straits, anchoring
          frequently.
July 31.—Sailed through Banka Straits at night and were clear away the morning
          of August 1.
August 19.—Arrived Nagasaki, sailing right up to the anchorage.

In 1898-9 the *Carradale* made her second passage to the East from Barry Dock. This time she was bound to Shanghai. The season was not so propitious and she took the long route round Australia, the following being her dates at chief points on the passage:—

September 21.—Left Barry Dock for sea.
September 30.—Off Madeira.
October 29.—Crossed the Line. Had a long spell of calms.
November 27.—In 40° 32′ S., 18° 57′ E., spoke the ship *Sierra Blanca*, which left Liverpool
          on the day *Carradale* left Barry, both ships being 67 days out.
January 1.—Hove to off Tasmania.
March 19.—Anchored off Woosung.

From Shanghai she sailed in ballast on April 21 for the W.C.S.A. The passage was a slow one of 90 days, her best run being made on May 15—288 miles—with the wind two points abaft the beam.

Arriving Taltal July 21 she received orders to load nitrate at Iquique. *Carradale* left Iquique September 6, was off the Horn in a blizzard October 4; crossed the Line 62 days out November 7; had Flores abeam December 2, and made the Lizard December 12, 97 days out. Here she found a hard north-easter to contend with making it a dead beat up Channel, and she did not arrive at Cuxhaven, her port of discharge, until 10 p.m. on Christmas Day.

The *Carradale* was commanded by Captain Robert Peebles until 1894, when he was succeeded by Captain Alexander Smith. Under Captain Peebles the ship made some steady passages in the Australian trade, loading outwards to Melbourne with timber from Norway, and coming home with wheat and wool.

Captain Alexander Smith had the *Carradale* until a couple of years before the war when Captain Baxter took command.

Carradale survived the war, and her last active service was under the Finns, who sold her to Germany for £3100 in 1924; and the old ship was broken up in 1925. Her sister ship, the *Fascadale*, had a very short life, being wrecked on the coast of Natal on February 7, 1895, with the loss of four lives.

Armadale, *Bracadale* and *Torrisdale* all lived to a good old age. Both *Armadale* and *Bracadale* went to the Norwegians, the former being renamed *Audun* and the latter *Svolder*. *Torrisdale* was sold to Roberts, Owen & Co. about 1910; *Svolder* was wrecked in 1911, *Torrisdale* wrecked in 1912, *Audun*, ex-*Armadale*, scrapped 1924.

Roxburgh's last two ships were the 1650-ton steel three-mast barques *Clydesdale* and *Nithsdale*, built respectively in 1895 and 1896 by Russell & Co. The *Clydesdale* was burnt at Tocopilla on December 10, 1903, and the *Nithsdale* was sold to German owners in the same year and renamed *Cap Horn*. After a few years under the German flag she went to the Norwegians, and must not be confused with Bordes' four-master of the same name. She was posted missing, when homeward bound from Valparaiso, in January, 1915.

Porter's "Ulidia."

In 1889 Richardson, Duck & Co. built the magnificent 2405-ton full-rigged ship *Ulidia* for John Porter, of William Porter & Sons. The *Ulidia* cost £23,000 to build, and loaded 3650 tons of railway iron (11,993 rails) with 50 tons of dunnage and packing.

As regards her sail plan, her mainyard was 91 ft. long and she carried reefs in her single topgallant sails.

The *Ulidia* was commanded by Captain F. Patey throughout her existence and carried a complement of 16 A.B.'s in the fo'c'sle with a donkeyman and an assistant steward amongst her petty officers.

The following passage to Sydney from Maryport is a good example of her sailing powers:—

May 7, 1891.—Towed out of dock and down Channel.

May 8.—3 p.m., abreast of Tuskar. 3.30 p.m., dropped the tug. Fair wind, averaging 11 knots with all square canvas set.

June 1.—Crossed the Line about midnight.

June 12.—In 29° 39′ S., 32° 40′ W., passed a barque to windward heading same way. In 5½ hours she was on *Ulidia's* quarter. So far the *Ulidia* had outsailed every ship she had met.

June 16.—39° 25′ S., 10° E., the old tea clipper *Miako* in company, 50 days out from New York to Natal.

June 28.—Crossed Cape Meridian—52 days out.

July 6.—Abreast of Crozets: hard sou'west gale. Running under reduced sail.

July 19.—Abreast of Leeuwin 21 days from the Cape. Best 24 hours' run—280 miles.

July 27.—10 a.m., S.W. Cape Tasmania in sight—81 days out.

August 4.—8 a.m., took line of tug *Port Jackson* aboard. At noon dropped anchor in Pinchgut Bay—88½ days out.

The *Ulidia* was one of those splendid ships which only had a short life, and has therefore been forgotten. Whilst leaving Fremantle May 18, 1893, bound in ballast for Sydney, she got ashore on Straggler's Reef and became a total loss.

"Andelana" and her famous Workington Sisters.

R. Williamson & Co. commenced ship building at Harrington where they built about 70 sailing ships. It was not until they moved to Workington that they really came to the fore as builders of high-class square-riggers, but the six 2500-ton steel four-masters which they built between 1889 and 1892 made their name, being known far and wide as the famous Workington sisters. Those were the *Andelana*, built for E. F. & W. Roberts; the *Eusemere* for Fisher & Sprott; *Pendragon Castle* for Chambers; *Vortigern* for Brown & Jenkinson; *Caradoc* for the Caradoc Ship Co., London; and *Conishead* for Bourke & Huntrods.

All six vessels were unusually fast for modern four-masters; the last three, *Vortigern*, *Caradoc* and *Conishead*, were of slightly fuller model than the first three so that they could carry an extra 300 tons of cargo. For this reason they were perhaps not quite so speedy as *Andelana*, *Eusemere* and *Pendragon Castle*.

The *Andelana* was a four-mast ship, the other sisters being all barques. Though the former's life was a short one her passages were invariably above the average, and the following are her best:—

1891 Left Hongkong. Arrived San Francisco—31 days.

1892 Left New York May 10. Arrived Shanghai August 30—112 days.

1893 Left 'Frisco February 20. Off Brow Head—88 days out; and put into Holyhead—90 days out, in order to wait for sufficient tide to enter Fleetwood.

1896 Left Yokohama October 1. Arrived 'Frisco October 24—23 days.

The Roberts brothers were Canadians, and in 1896 they asked the well-known Captain George W. Stailing of Nova Scotia to take command of their big Southampton built four-master *Andrina*. On her passage home from India the *Andrina* was rammed by a tramp steamer, but her forward bulkhead kept her afloat and she was towed into Queenstown. As repairs would take some months Captain Stailing was asked to take over the *Andelana*. The voyage that followed seems to have been unfortunate from the start, and ended in tragedy.

Sailing from New York early in 1898 for Shanghai, the big ship was dismasted in a typhoon. After being refitted at Shanghai Captain Stailing crossed to Tacoma in order to load grain for home. In Vol. I. I mention the capsizing and sinking of the *Andelana*, owing to the chain of her ballast boom carrying away. Mr. Wallace, in his book *In the Wake of the Wind Ships*, gives a very full account of this accident, which happened during the night. Apparently no one ashore realised the catastrophe until the ship's gig was found on the beach with the part of her stem which held the ring of the painter torn out of her. The ship had disappeared without leaving any other trace, and it was only after the anchorage had been swept by two tugs that the lost vessel was located.

Mr. Wallace goes on to relate the story of the gallant diver who went down in 180 feet of water in order to place cables in position for lifting the ship. On his second descent the pressure blew out the packing round his air pipes, which he had vainly tried to get renewed, and when the man was hauled up he was found crushed to death by the pressure at that depth of water. After this all ideas of salvaging the *Andelana* were given up, and she still lies at the bottom of Tacoma harbour, forming a tomb for her captain and crew, composing nineteen souls.

"Pindos" ex "Eusemere."

The second of the Workington sister ships was the *Eusemere* launched in June, 1890, for Fisher & Sprott. The following are her passages under the Red Ensign:—

Scilly to Colombo	81 days
Calcutta to New York	105 „
New York to Calcutta	104 „
Calcutta to Dover	119 „
Dungeness to Philadelphia	34 „
Philadelphia to Calcutta	112 „
Calcutta to Isle of Wight . ..	160 „
(Captain washed overboard off Cape of Good Hope)	
Middlesbrough to Calcutta ..	112 days
Calcutta to Beachy Head	118 „

In 1896 *Eusemere* was sold to B. Wencke of Hamburg, and re-named *Pindos*. Though her passages under the British Ensign were steady enough they were not remarkable, but the Germans seemed to have brought out *Eusemere's* powers of sailing better than her British captains. The following are her passages from 1896 to 1901:—

Lizard to Rangoon	105 days
Rangoon to Falmouth	107 „
Dungeness to Rangoon	97 „
Rangoon to Scilly	98 „
Isle of Wight to Rangoon ..	98 „
Rangoon to Lizard	107 „
Dover to Iquique	85 „
Iquique to Isle of Wight	92 „
Antwerp to Iquique	94 „
Tocopilla to Dunkirk	61 „
Iquique to Deal	78 „

and so her voyages go on. Her best passage with a nitrate cargo is given as 57 days to the Channel and 60 to Bremen.

I think the most remarkable passage in her whole career was her outward passage in 1904 from Hamburg to San Pedro, California, in 106 days, when she rounded the Horn in midwinter heavily loaded with a full cargo of cement.

Towards the end of 1911 *Pindos* sailed from Mejillones loaded with nitrate to Falmouth for orders. On a Saturday night of February in the usual thick sou'west weather she came ashore at Coverack. Both the local life-boat and the rocket apparatus were speedily on the spot. The rocket apparatus had five unsuccessful throws; the first throw fell splendidly but the line fouled, the second and third throws fell short, the fourth was too high and the fifth short. However, the life-boat, though her line parted more than once and she manoeuvred in great danger from the broken water round the wreck, was successful in saving the *Pindos's* crew of 27, after being out the greater part of the night.

"Pendragon Castle," afterwards the German "Lisbeth."

The third of the Workington sisters was the *Pendragon Castle* launched in February, 1891, for J. Chambers & Co. of Liverpool. Her first captain was J. D. Wood of *Glengarry* fame; on her maiden voyage she had three very hard case officers who allowed no afternoon watch below and played the bucko with endless hazing and consequent bloodshed, so that the maiden passage of 92 days from Liverpool to Calcutta with salt was by no means a pleasant one to her crew, who were glad to be paid off in Calcutta. The treatment of all hands was no better on the homeward passage. The ship left Calcutta for Hull with a cargo of linseed on June 19, 1891, and came driving up the Humber in a blizzard, 113 days out. This was during the night of October 9; the ship, which was almost out of control, touched on Halle Sands, lost both anchors and chains, and eventually was taken charge of by the Humber tugs, who safely docked her the next day.

After discharging she was ordered round to Cardiff. Whilst towing round the *Pendragon Castle* broke adrift from her tug and was obliged to run for the Downs, where she collided with the American four-mast schooner *Maria O. Teel,* and this accident considerably delayed the commencement of her second voyage. She left Cardiff on February 10, 1892, for Colombo with a cargo of coal under the same master but with new officers. Her passage was one of the best in her career. For 19 days she averaged 229 miles a day and her best 24 hours' run was 343 miles. She arrived at Colombo on April 23, only 42 days from the Equator and 72 days from the Bristol Channel. At Colombo she discharged her coal, took in ballast and sailed for Rangoon, where she arrived only 99 days out from Cardiff. Her homeward passage was spoilt by cholera. Some of her crew died in Rangoon of this scourge, and after leaving for Liverpool on June 22, 1892, Captain Wood was

"NEOTSFIELD"

[*See Page* 92

"SIR ROBERT FERNIE"

Lent by M. M. Brodie

[*See Page* 100

"ELGINSHIRE"

[*See Page* 102

compelled to put into St. Helena for medical assistance. After a passage of continued head winds and calms the ship arrived at Liverpool on November 2, 133 days out. Captain Wood died soon after the ship's arrival home, and Captain Richardson took charge of her on her third voyage when she again left Liverpool for Calcutta loaded with salt. Her third outward passage was remarkable for light winds, no sail having to be furled throughout the 156 days that she took between Liverpool and Calcutta. On her homeward passage with linseed she arrived at Amsterdam on September 28, 111 days out.

On her fourth voyage the *Pendragon Castle* arrived at Calcutta on March 3, 1894, 107 days out from Hamburg which she left on November 16. This is a very good time for a full built ship. On her homeward passage in 1894 she left Calcutta with the usual cargo of linseed on June 1, and arrived at Hamburg on September 28, 119 days out, having beaten quite a fleet of Calcutta wallahs, including her sister ship the *Eusemere*. She made one more Hamburg and Calcutta voyage, and then the competition of steam drove her to Newcastle, N.S.W., and the W.C.S.A.

She was then sold to H. H. Schmidt of Hamburg, who re-named her the *Lisbeth*, under which name she continued to make fine passages until the autumn of 1927 when she was broken up on the Clyde.

Whilst under the German flag she was mostly in the nitrate trade. The commanders of the German nitrate ships were all picked men, for they were expected to race out and home, and many of them were superb seamen. The following example of seamanship by the captain of the *Lisbeth* I have taken the liberty of quoting from Rex Clements' *Stately Southerner*:—

Sometimes a clipper swooped in from the sea and down on her moorings like a plundering Viking on a Saxon hamlet. Such a spectacular piece of seamanship I once witnessed on the part of a four-masted barque in Tocopilla.

Tocopilla Bay forms the segment of a circle, with a bluff headland at its northern extremity and an ugly reef of rocks stretching out to seaward from its southern end. The ships in port lay in a single tier, reaching from close under the lee of the reef to within a quarter of a mile of the headland, and at no great distance from the shore.

One afternoon we saw a barque not far out in the offing standing boldly into the anchorage with every stitch of canvas set. She was heading straight in for the line of

G

shipping before the town and coming along grandly, leaning steeply over, with a flashing bow-wave curling away on either side of her.   To an onlooker from the port, it appeared as though she were determined to pile herself up.

On she came, with never a tack or sheet started.   The men on the nearest ship ran out, thinking there would be a collision.   Still the barque came on, with no sign of shortening sail.   Only, as she approached, she was observed to alter course slightly in order to head between the endmost vessel and the headland.   It was magnificent, or monstrous foolhardiness, just precisely which was not apparent.

The stranger stood unwaveringly in till she was within a few hundred yards of the nearest ship and not more than a cable's length from the headland.   Then we heard a whistle aboard her.   Down went her helm hard-a-port, topsail and t'gallant halliards whined in the sheaves, staysail hanks tinkled swiftly down the stays, and the barque swept boldly down under the stern of the anchored shipping.   With lessening momentum she stood straight down the narrow fairway between them and the shore, clewing up sail in masterly fashion.   A minute or two more, and she ported again.   Then, passing between the end ship and the southern reef, with her bows pointing fair out to sea, and her men furling sail like heroes, she let go her anchor and brought up, in the best berth in the harbour.

It was a superb piece of seamanship—as daring as it was well-timed.   The barque turned out to be a German vessel, the *Lisbeth.*

At the end of the war the *Lisbeth* was handed over to the French Government, but was very soon bought back by the Germans. In 1924 she aroused great interest in Liverpool where she arrived from Pensacola on August 7. The old ship came up the Mersey channel with a fair wind on the quarter under all sail, and was almost up to the Rock light before she took her tug; she was watched by the shipping community with much admiration. On her next voyage she went out to Adelaide in ballast in 86 days, and came home with grain, arriving Falmouth—113 days out—in June, 1925.

Her last voyage contained the following fine passages:—

Santos to Adelaide	..	..	47 days.
Astoria to Callao ..	..	..	64 ,,
Callao to Sydney ..	..	..	59 ,,

her last passage of all being from Sydney to Queenstown, March 8, to July 6, 1927—120 days.

She discharged her grain cargo at Limerick and was afterwards taken to the Clyde to be broken up.

"Conishead," "Vortigern" and "Caradoc."

Of the other three Workington sisters I think *Conishead* had the best record. Her run from Barrow to the Equator under Captain Bromley, of 14 days 8 hours in 1894, has never been beaten. On the same passage she was only 34 days to the latitude of Rio and 42 to the Cape.

Wencke & Son of Hamburg evidently had a keen eye for a smart ship, for besides the *Eusemere* they also bought the *Conishead* and the *Vortigern* at the end of the nineteenth century, *Conishead* being re-named *Athene*; and *Vortigern, Hebe. Conishead* again distinguished herself under the Germans, her best passage being from the Lizard to Melbourne in 73 days, the distance from Cape Meridian to Melbourne being covered in 22 days. This was in 1911. The whole passage from Cuxhaven occupied 87 days, the ship being held up in the Channel for 14 days. Whilst running her Easting down she made three 24-hours' runs of over 300 miles.

Of the other two I have no outstanding records. The *Caradoc* went missing in October 1898, whilst *Vortigern* survived the war, being taken over by the Peruvian Government.

"Garthwray's" Adventures.

Seven months before Messrs. Williamson sent the *Andelana* down the ways they launched a steel full-rigged ship of 1891 tons for J. Chambers & Co. of Liverpool. This was the *Wray Castle* which, as the *Garthwray*, made her name notorious for the longest passage between two ports, of which there is any record. This statement sounds as if the *Wray Castle* was the slowest ship ever built, but this was far from being the case. At the time of her launch she was considered a very fine specimen of a steel sailing ship, and her performances under the flags of Chambers and afterwards J. B. Walmsley & Co. showed that she possessed quite a good pair of heels for a full-built vessel.

At Workington they say that she was the first ship built with lapped butts though she was only lapp-butted to the turn of the bilge, above which she had the old-fashioned inside butt straps. She was also the first ship at Workington to have lower masts and topmasts in one.

Before the war she made several good passages in the West Coast trade, and in 1907 she distinguished herself by beating the French barque *Duquesne* by four days in the run from 'Frisco to Runcorn.   Captain Hay, who was in command when she was bought by the Marine Navigation Company of Canada and her name was changed to *Garthwray*, told me that she was a very fair sailer for a big deadweight carrier, being capable when down to her Plimsoll mark of an easy 10 knots under topgallant sails.

Like many another ship, after voyaging all over the world with hardly a serious accident, her luck suddenly seemed to desert her.   Fate called and, after a desperate struggle to survive, she went to her end.

On June 12, 1922, she cleared from Grangemouth, Firth of Forth, with a cargo of briquettes for Iquique under the command of Captain Mann.   Light winds and calms gave her rather a slow passage down the Atlantic, but her crew considered themselves fortunate to arrive off the Horn in summer time.

The *Garthwray* was lucky in having her half-deck filled up with nine strapping apprentices, three of whom were soon out of their time, and the senior of whom was acting as third mate.   Her fo'c'sle, also, contained an average crowd of seamen for those days, so that one cannot put down her misfortunes to insufficient man power.   It is probable that much of her gear wanted renewing, as this is the only possible reason one can find for the way in which her masts went by the board.

The first time that she was dismasted the hands were aloft furling sail off the pitch of the Horn, when a fierce squall burst over the ship.   For two hours this squall was at its height, and whilst it raged the *Garthwray* lost her topgallant masts, had her rudder damaged and her steering gear thrown out of action.   Captain Mann, who had been congratulating himself with the thought that he would soon be round the corner, had, perforce, to put back to some port where he could re-fit, and avoiding the Falklands he made for Monte Video.   On arriving off the River Plate the lame duck signalled an inbound steamer asking that a tug might be sent out to her, and she finally anchored off Monte Video on September 9, 1922.   Here a delay of four months held her up while she waited for her new spars to come out from home. Captain Mann, also, was relieved by Captain Henry, the marine superintendent of the *Garthwray's* owners.

The voyage was resumed on April 12, 1923. This time the ship took 32 days to reach the spot where she had been dismasted. Captain Henry was no luckier than Captain Mann. He managed to reach 58° 22′ S. and about 70° W., when his ship was once more overwhelmed. For 48 hours she struggled against hurricane squalls from the west-sou'west with driving hail and snow. At the end of this time Cape Stiff had again conquered and Captain Henry put up his helm and ran for Cape Town with fore and main topmasts sprung, and other damage.

The battered *Garthwray* made a quick run to the Cape, but on making Green Point light her luck again deserted her, and she was blown back, taking another five days to get in touch with Signal Hill. At last, on July 20, the tug *Ludwig Weiner* picked up the unfortunate ship, which by this time had added a heavy list to her other troubles, and towed her in to Table Bay. She was dry-docked at Cape Town and had 3 feet of grass and tons of barnacles scraped off her bottom.

Here Captain Henry gave up the task, the mate also went home, and even Miggs, the ship's cat, which had been seven times round the Horn, deserted the luckless *Garthwray*. There remained, however, the nine stalwart apprentices, amongst whom was a boy named T. V. Ward, who had previously been in the *Garthforce* when she rammed an iceberg to the southward of the Cape.

After leaving the Cape the *Garthwray* made one more call before reaching her destination—this was at Hobart in order to replenish her provisions. The rest of her passage seems to have passed without incident, and Iquique was reached on December 23, 1923, 559 days out.

The only members of the crew who sailed from Grangemouth and reached Iquique were the carpenter, steward, and nine apprentices.

The *Garthwray* sailed in ballast from Iquique on the March 15, 1924, for Talcahuano. When 38 days out she stranded on the island of Santa Maria during a dense fog and became a total loss.

This time her crew had to desert her, for the ship at low tide was almost high and dry, with the rocks poking through her bottom. After photographing the wreck with her sails still set, the *Garthwray* argonauts gave the poor old ship a deep-sea blessing and pulled away for Coronel.

Devitt & Moore's "Tamar."

During the nineties there were three full-rigged, full-built sailing ships which gained an excellent reputation for speed amongst the cracks of the Colonial wool and grain fleet. These were the *Tamar*, *Brabloch*, and *Neotsfield*. The largest of the three was the *Tamar*; she was launched in May, 20, 1889, by Napier, Shanks & Bell of Glasgow for Devitt & Moore, and was a steel ship of 2112 tons gross.

Her commanders under Devitt & Moore's house-flag were J. R. Brown, and the well-known H. N. Forbes. Both of these captains were old and trusted commanders of Devitt & Moore's; Brown, who commanded the *Tamar* from her launch until 1896, had the following passages to his credit:—

1895	Sydney to Channel	..	84 days
	Barry to Adelaide ..	..	77 ,,

The best passages made by Captain Forbes, who took over in 1896, were: in 1897 Sydney to London with 7428 bales of wool—87 days; in 1898, Newcastle, N.S.W., to San Francisco—51 days. Both of these passages were the best of the year for the respective runs.

In 1900 the *Tamar* was sold to T. A. Shute of Liverpool and henceforward was mostly in the West Coast trade.

In 1903-4 the outward record from the Channel round the Horn to both Chile and Peru was broken by Thomas Shute's vessels. The *Tamar* sailing from the Tyne under Captain J. C. Amberman passed Dover on November 24, 1904, and arrived Callao—68 days out, whilst the *Eudora* taking her departure from the Lizard at 10 p.m. November 30 arrived at Coquimbo at 9 a.m. on January 27 —57 days 16 hours out.

On her next voyage the *Tamar*, when bound from Hamburg to Seattle under a new captain, aroused alarm at Lloyd's by suddenly

turning up in Plymouth Sound. It appears that her new captain
was a hard drinker, and whilst the ship was bound down Channel
he suddenly took out his revolver and fired at the man at the
wheel. This headstrong method of inducing good steering brought
the mate on deck on the jump. It was about two in the afternoon,
and all hands perceived that their commander was so drunk that he
could hardly stand up.

Worse was to happen, for the skipper next proceeded to alter
the course of the ship, and soon after dark the mate was astonished
to recognise the Vierge light, near Ushant. In order to make
certain he asked the captain for the light book. This put the drunk-
en man into a furious rage, and he proceeded to tear up the light book
and other navigation books which were in the charthouse. The
mate, having satisfied himself that the light was that of the Vierge
and that the ship was heading straight for the rocks, next made an
attempt to put the helm up, upon which the captain swore that he
would shoot anyone who attempted to change the course.

At last in desperation, when the ship was less than two miles
from the rocks, the mate again besought the captain to allow him
to alter the course before the *Tamar* went ashore. He got the
usual drunken response, "I'll shoot you if you interfere with the
management of the ship. Let the ship go to the bottom, I am
responsible." He backed this up by firing a shot at the mate which
whistled past the latter's right ear. This was too much. The mate
went forward, fetched the second mate and all hands, and after
seizing the captain and placing him in irons, headed the ship back
for Plymouth.

Tamar was the last survivor of Shute's fleet. She survived the
war and was laid up at Bordeaux until May 1923, when she was
towed to Rotterdam for breaking up.

"Brabloch" and Captain David Kiddie.

The *Brabloch*, which was launched in the Clyde from Barclay,
Curle's yard a month later than the *Tamar*, was built for Robert
Kerr Holms-Kerr of the Glasgow Stock Exchange, but she was
managed by Aitken, Lilburn & Co. She cost about £8 10s. a ton,
and like all Barclay, Curle's ships was greatly admired for her good
looks. Indeed, it is said that it was owing to Mr. Rose, of Donald-

son, Rose & Co., seeing the *Brabloch* on the stocks that Barclay, Curle received the order for *Cromdale* and *Mount Stewart*.

The story goes that Mr. Rose handed over the *Cromdale* to one of his sons, and the *Mount Stewart* to the other, and told them to run the ships and in that way work for their living.

The *Brabloch* was a powerful full-built ship, which stood up to her canvas, and was capable of logging 14 to 15 knots in strong fair winds.   One of her best sailing performances was on her passage to Melbourne in 1894 under Captain David Kiddie.   Leaving London on October 5 she took her departure from the Lizard on the 9th.   From October 22 when she was in 28° 49′ N., 21° W., to October 29, when she was in 22° 39′ N., 23° 53′ W., the *Brabloch* was in company with the *Hesperus* in calms and light airs. (*Hesperus* had left London the tide before the *Brabloch* and she arrived at Melbourne the tide before *Brabloch*.)

On November 10 *Brabloch* crossed the Equator in 31° 23′ W. On the 15th she passed Fernando Noronha.   On November 30 the Meridian of Greenwich was crossed.

In running her Easting down the *Brabloch* covered a distance of 6724 miles in 27 days, giving an average of 249 miles a day. This was from 31° 5′ S., 21° 39′ W., her position on November 25, to 41° 16′ S., 134° 29′ E., her position on December 23; her best 24 hours' runs during this time were 312, 339, 302, 300 and 295.

From December 2 until 8 the ship had to be cautiously navigated through ice.   On December 28 the Otway was signalled and at 3.40 a.m. on the 29th the pilot came aboard off the Heads; the anchor being dropped in Hobson's Bay at 8.20 p.m., 85 days from London and 81 from the Lizard.

In the year 1896 a number of the vessels which loaded coal at Newcastle, N.S.W., had to fight against fire.   Amongst these was the *Brabloch*.   She loaded 3154 tons of coal and arrived at San Francisco with the flames bursting through her hatches and ventilators.   She was quickly towed on to the Sausalito Flats where she was filled with water and the fire extinguished.   Afterwards she was pumped out and taken to an anchorage off the berth where she was due to discharge.

The *Alexandra,* which was bound from Newcastle to Los

"BUTESHIRE" SINKING

"ELGINSHIRE"

[*See Page* 102

"CALIFORNIA": Last Sailer of the White Star Line

Lent by Messrs. Ismay, Imrie & Co.

[*See Page* 108

Angeles, also put in to San Francisco with her coal alight and was scuttled.   The *Republic* was not so fortunate: she had to be aband- oned with her coal on fire when 300 miles from 'Frisco.   Her crew was taken off by the *Hollinwood*, which had also had trouble.   She had put into Lyttelton with her coal on fire, and had discharged and re-stowed it.

The fifth ship, the well-known *Knight of St. Michael*, put back to Newcastle with her coal heated and discharged.

Captain David Kiddie, who served in the *Brabloch* as mate and master from 1891 to 1898, was an excellent example of a sail- trained seaman.   His father was a London master-rigger who worked for a number of firms including that of Herron, Dunn & Co.   Fathers in those days were stern disciplinarians.   Young Kiddie left school on a Friday in July, 1876, and his father sent him to sea the following week with Captain Bailey, the senior master of Herron, Dunn & Co., who was notorious as the worst sea bully under the Red Ensign.

According to Captain Kiddie, Bailey made a practice of whack- ing all hands and after beating up his crew from mate to cook reserved any spare energy he possessed for the ship's boy.   This was aboard the Sunderland-built ship *Highmoor*.   The voyage was from London to Cape Town, Calcutta, Madras, Vizagapatam, Bimlipatam, Coronada, and back to London.   The homeward passage took 180 days and Captain Bailey was forced to put in to St. Helena for provisions.

Captain Kiddie's second voyage was under Captain Roberts in the *Mornington*.   On the outward passage the rudder head broke off, and the vessel was steered into Rio de Janeiro by means of a boom out on each quarter with tackles from the iron of the rudder.   Whilst in Rio half the crew, including Kiddie, went down with yellow jack.

In this ship the mate was a bucko; he and the bosun had a terrific fight with capstan bars on the fo'c'sle-head whilst the ship was lying in Rio harbour, which resulted in the bosun being paid off.

The *Mornington* went on to Huaniloss to load guano and whilst she lay there a Blue-nose ship arrived, in which the late bosun of the *Mornington* was second mate.

On the homeward passage the *Mornington* called for orders at

Queenstown where the bucko mate asked to be paid off, as he was afraid that he would receive a bad hammering from all hands if he went on to the port of discharge.

After this second voyage Captain Kiddie started with his father as a rigger, and one of his first jobs was the fitting of double top-gallant yards to the *Old Kensington*, and when that ship was ready for sea in April, 1880, Kiddie shipped under old Captain Underwood. The *Old Kensington* went out to Melbourne in 70 days, and often when running heavy before the westerlies Captain Underwood used to haul Kiddie out of his berth to take the wheel. The latter received an additional five shillings a month to his pay on this voyage for fitting wire footropes to each yard. The job took him most of the voyage, the wire necessary for the work having been put aboard by his father. There was sufficient for all the footropes except that of the starboard fore lower topsail yard. When the ship arrived in the London River, Kiddie was roundly cursed by his father for being careless and cutting off too much for the splices, but he was thanked by Captain Underwood for his good work.

After two voyages in the *Old Kensington* he passed for second mate in the old St. Katherine's Dockhouse. Soon after he passed he met old Bailey whose ship, the New Brunswick built *Star of India*, was in Cubitt Town dry dock. Bailey gruffly asked him what he wanted; Kiddie replied that he was looking for a second mate's job. "Well, you aren't coming here," retorted Bailey; at which Kiddie returned hotly, "Thank you, but if I went with you I'd give you a little of what you gave me when I was a boy of fourteen."

The Nipper and the Skipper.

Captain Kiddie's experience as a first voyager was no unusual one in the days of sail. I fear there are some terrible stories of ill-treatment of ships' boys and apprentices right up to the end of the nineteenth century, but even in the seventies good officers strove to find punishments for unruly boys which were not cruel or brutalising. In the Navy when mast-heading was abolished a favourite punishment for a middy was to order him, just before the gunroom dinner hour, to look out for the Swiss fleet and report when sighted. This meant that the hungry mid had to keep a close watch on the horizon whilst his mess-mates were eating every scrap of the gunroom dinner.

Though the commanders and number ones in the R.N. were invariably hard-hearted martinets, when they became captains their hearts softened, and I could give the names of a number of these soft-hearted captains in the last days of the wooden walls. Only lately a naval correspondent to the papers recalled how his "old man" aboard the *Raleigh* used to send his steward with a tray of sandwiches, perhaps a slice or two of duff and a small bottle of wine to a middy who, he had noticed, was on the look-out for the Swiss fleet. This welcome meal was offered "With the captain's compliments, and don't let the commander catch you."

In the Mercantile Marine one of the most common punishments for apprentices besides the usual dirty jobs of cleaning out the pighouse, etc., was riding the boom. This was a bitterly cold and sore business when the ship was plunging or rolling in the rough weather of high latitudes. A correspondent of mine tells the following amusing experience when he was a first voyage apprentice. I will put it in his own words:—

It was the second dog-watch. I was supposed to be keeping the time and I fell asleep under the break of the poop. The captain, who was sitting in a deck-chair on the weather side of the poop enjoying a cigar, noticed that I failed to strike the bell, and on discovering that I was asleep sent forward for a couple of buckets of water. However, one of the other apprentices aroused me just in time to avoid being doused; whereupon the skipper ordered me to carry the two buckets of water up and down the deck as a punishment.

After a time the weight of the buckets began to try my strength very severely and in desperation I began to empty a little water out of each every time my beat took me to where a life-boat hid me from the captain's view. I repeated this ruse until I was carrying empty buckets.

At last the captain, seeing that I was bearing up much better than he expected, ordered me to bring my buckets on to the poop for his inspection. On finding that they were empty he sternly ordered me to fill them again and to march up and down the poop under his eye. Here there was more motion than on the maindeck and I had great difficulty in staggering up and down with the heavy buckets. The man at the wheel also amused himself by trying to increase the ship's motion with the helm. At last, just when I was passing the spot where the captain was sitting, the ship gave an extra heavy lurch and I was thrown with the buckets of water right on top of the captain.

His deck-chair capsized and the pair of us, well soaked by the spilt water, slid in a mixed heap to the lee rail. I just remember the captain in his rage ordering the second mate to his room for laughing, whilst I cleared off to the end of the bowsprit where I stayed until I thought it was safe to return to the deck.

This little incident became the laugh of the ship, and put me in the captain's bad books for the rest of the voyage.

Captain David Kiddie was succeeded in the command of the *Brabloch* by Captain W. S. Hawkins, who made a long homeward passage in 1899, namely Melbourne to Beachy Head—132 days. He was succeeded by Captain A. S. Baxter, who made the following fine passages:—

1900	Dover to Adelaide.. ..	74 days
1900-1	South Stack to Hongkong	111 „
1901	Astoria to Roches Point ..	114 „
1902	Liverpool to Sydney ..	84 „

Captain Baxter remained in the ship until 1908 when Captain A. McKay took over.

In 1912 the *Brabloch* was sold to the Norwegians for £4250. Four years later she was resold to another Norwegian firm for £56,000.

At the end of the war she was still classed 100 A1 and known as the *Vinga*. In 1922 she went out from Frederickstadt to Melbourne in 112 days. This was her last voyage, and at its close she was sold to Spanish ship breakers.

"Neotsfield."

The *Neotsfield* will be better remembered in Australian waters than even the *Tamar* or the *Brabloch*, for she was owned for the first dozen years of her existence by F. H. Dangar of Sydney, N.S.W.

She was one of the last of the iron ships built by McMillan, and though a good carrier had quite a good turn of speed. She made her name by a great piece of work in June, 1906, when she sailed from Cape Town to Port Hunter in 30 days, beating the steamer *Howick Hall* (which left East London for the same port three days later), by one day.

Her passages from Sydney to the Channel in the nineties were seldom over 100 days. Captain J. B. Rugg commanded under Dangar's ownership, but he gave up the command in 1902 when the *Neotsfield* became the property of R. Thomas & Co.

After a life which was singularly free from accident, the *Neotsfield* was sunk by a German submarine in 1917.

"Grace Harwar."

The *Grace Harwar* was the first steel ship built for W. Montgomery of London. Though a large carrier she has several good passages to her credit, and as late as 1922 sailed from Melbourne to Tocopilla in 37 days.

The first of her commanders was Captain B. Hunt, then J. G. Briscoe had her from 1897 until 1906, when Captain C. Frazer took over. In 1909, on the sale of the Montgomery's *Fitzjames*, her commander, T. C. Fearon, was given the *Grace Harwar*.

Captain Fearon's last voyage in the *Grace Harwar* before retiring was an adventurous one. He sailed from London with a cargo of Portland cement in barrels on July 30, 1910, for Talcahuano, Chile. After summer weather in the North Atlantic the Equator was crossed on September 2—34 days out. Light fine weather was again experienced down to 50° S., but the *Grace Harwar* had the usual nasty time off the Horn, and she was nineteen days from 50° S. Atlantic to 50° S. in the Pacific.

Talcahuano was reached on October 25—87 days from London. After discharging his cargo in Talcahuano, Valparaiso and Huasco, Captain Fearon sailed in ballast on December 7, 1910, from Huasco to Newcastle, N.S.W. The Pacific was crossed in 56 days, and loading coal at Newcastle the *Grace Harwar* made the return passage to Coquimbo in 39 days, arriving on April 15, 1911. After discharging her coal the *Grace Harwar* loaded nitrate for Europe.

Whilst she was lying in the tiers a most unusual six-hour hurricane swept over the port. It started at 11 p.m. on June 11, blowing right off-shore from the N.E. There was soon trouble amongst the shipping through the anchors which the ships had out astern dragging. Captain Fearon was compelled to slip his stern lines in order to allow the ship to swing head to wind; but this brought the *Grace Harwar* under the stern of the French steamer

Magellan which was also riding head to wind, and although the sailing ship's chain was slacked away until the whole 120 fathoms was outside the hawse-pipe the *Grace Harwar* could not drop clear of the French steamer. The result of the collision between the two ships was the loss of *Grace Harwar's* figure-head, head gear and bowsprit which was knocked right up on end. At last her cable parted and the ship swung clear. Captain Fearon then dropped his spare bower anchor with a steel wire bent on to it.

At 2 a.m. the calm period of the hurricane arrived and lasted for five minutes; then the wind started again out of the sou'west, the opposite quarter from which it had been blowing. It was pitch dark, the air was full of sand and dust blown off from the shore, and the screaming of the wind and the roar of the surf drowned the noise of the crashing ships. With the shift of the wind the *Grace Harwar* had to contend with a four-masted German. The two ships ground together for a few hectic moments and then dragged apart.

The gale continued to blow until daylight. There were 27 ships in port at the time, and every one of them was more or less damaged. A large Frenchman dragged into the surf and became a total loss; an Italian ship sank at her moorings; half the lighters in port were either sunk or put out of action, and Captain Fearon relates that it took a week to get the tiers squared up and the ship remoored. Then on the night of June 21 another of these sudden hurricanes came along, and once more all the ships broke adrift and came crashing into each other. *Grace Harwar's* opponent this time was a large German steamer which dropped down under her bows and still further smashed up things forward. In fact, the steel bowsprit was so mangled that it was necessary to cut it off 10 feet from the knightheads.

Before leaving Iquique, Captain Fearon employed a diver to fish up his lost anchor and chain. The diver shackled a wire to the end of the cable, and this was taken to the windlass. Whilst heaving in, owing to the tremendous strain, the wire slipped off the drum, and, catching the officer in charge of the work, cut off one of his feet. After this Captain Fearon allowed his anchor and chain to remain at the bottom of the harbour.

Being unable to obtain a new bowsprit at Iquique Captain Fearon, having gained a certificate of seaworthiness, decided to sail his ship home without one. All went well until Falmouth was reached on November 17, 114 days out from Iquique; but whilst the ship was sailing in to the Carrick Roads in charge of a pilot, she took charge in a squall and ran into the port side of the Italian steamer *Oriana*, both vessels being damaged. In this collision the *Grace Harwar's* port anchor was carried away and lost overboard, so that this, added to the one lost at Iquique, left the ship with only one anchor, and before proceeding in tow for Hamburg Captain Fearon had to re-fit his ship with anchors and chains.

After discharging at Hamburg the *Grace Harwar* was towed to Cardiff where she loaded coal in February, 1912.

Captain Fearon now decided to retire. He had been 41 years at sea, and except for sixteen months in 1885-6 these had all been spent in sailing ships. He was undoubtedly one of the most experienced windjammer men in the last days of sail, having commanded in turn the *Dawpool, General Roberts, Fitzjames,* and *Grace Harwar*. As an example of his seamanship and resource I will give the following story of the *Dawpool* off Cape Horn.

A Close Call off the Horn.

On May 16, 1891, the *Dawpool* left San Francisco with a cargo of grain for Liverpool. There was a good deal of excitement on the water front as the local newspaper correspondent reported that there were heavy bets on the race to Liverpool between her and the American ships *Henry B. Hyde* and *R. D. Rice*, which sailed about the same time.

The *Dawpool* rounded the Horn in some of the worst weather ever served up by Cape Stiff. Captain Fearon kept his ship running before a tremendous sea until he was in 53° 44′ S. and 52° W. That afternoon the *Dawpool* logged 14½ knots; the log line was marked to 14 knots. At 9.30 p.m. when it was hove, the line all ran off the reel and snapped before the glass had run out. Hardly had the sandglass been turned when the main topgallant sheet carried away, the thrashing chain of which soon split the upper topsail.

Captain Fearon immediately had all hands called to shorten sail. After a tremendous struggle both topgallant saii and upper topsail were made fast.

The Cape Horn greybeards were now threatening every moment to poop the ship, so Captain Fearon determined to heave to, and gave the order for the foresail to be hauled up; whilst all hands manned the fore buntlines the mate sent one of the apprentices aft for some spare gaskets. The boy noticed whilst he ran the gauntlet of the flooded maindeck that the main hatch had been stove in; he immediately went on to the poop and reported the damage to Captain Fearon. The captain, on examining the hatch himself, found that the fore and aft beam had been broken by a sea, and allowed the whole hatch to fall in. He at once ordered the mate to leave the foresail and get the hatch secured. The first attempt nearly ended in disaster, a big sea raged aboard and washed the men and the sail they were striving to put over the hatch the length of the maindeck.

The second attempt was no better. When the mate and the ship's company had picked themselves up from another cruise along the maindeck they retreated forward and took refuge under the fo'c'sle-head. In such a crisis it would have been all over with the *Dawpool* if her captain had been either a weak man or a poor seaman. It was pitch dark, the huge seas rolling up astern poured over on to the maindeck on each side and flooded the hold through the broken hatch; the ship was running like a scared stag and the smallest mistake of the helmsman would have meant a broach to. In this desperate situation Captain Fearon went forward and harangued the thirty cowed men and boys under the fo'c'sle-head. He told them to "come out and fight for their lives like men and not to die like rats in a trap." His scornful words brought forth the second and third mates, the bosun, sailmaker and carpenter, the five apprentices who were all *Conway* boys, and two of the A.B.'s. The rest, headed by the mate who had quite lost his nerve and was crying like a child, remained still panic-stricken under the fo'c'sle-head.

Captain Fearon superintended the third attempt at securing the hatch himself, and after a terrific struggle he and his gallant band succeeded in stopping the water from getting below. He next

"SIMLA"

"LORD TEMPLEMORE'

[*See Page* 109

"SWANHILDA"

Lent by Captain Lee

[*See Page* 110

"HINEMOA"

Lent by Captain L. R. W. Beavis

[*See Page* 113

turned his attention to bringing his ship to the wind, and this by consummate seamanship he succeeded in doing without shipping any heavy water.

Captain Guy de Mattos, who was one of the *Dawpool's* apprentices on this occasion, wrote in his log "a truly terrible night; one not to be easily forgotten. Captain Fearon behaved with remarkable coolness." The captain himself in a letter to me wrote that the night was one of the worst he ever put in at sea.

Owing to the captain's splendid handling the *Dawpool* came out of her trouble with only the loss of 500 tons of wheat—some of the cargo which was in the hatch. This, from being wet, had swollen, and for this reason had to be thrown overboard.

The *Dawpool* did not succeed in winning her race, but the report of her close call had preceded her to Liverpool, where she arrived on September 19. The next day, a Sunday, the crews of the *Henry B. Hyde* and the *R. D. Rice* (the first of which had beaten her by 12 days and the second by 16) came aboard and chantied her through the three docks. Quite a big crowd of Liverpool shipping people came down to see her dock owing to the report of her narrow escape getting into the papers. It was a calm, quiet Sunday. With the three crews chantying on the capstans, as the lines were hove in, the singing was most impressive. Indeed, people said that they had heard the capstan chanties on St. James's Mount, where Liverpool Cathedral now stands.

After this digression we must return to the *Grace Harwar*. She was sold to the Russians in February, 1913. On July 5, 1916, she was again battered by a hurricane. This happened at Mobile, when the wind reached the velocity of 107 miles an hour, and practically every building in the city received more or less damage. The *Grace Harwar* with another Russian ship, the *Frieda*, better known as the old *County of Edinburgh*, was washed right up on to the docks of the Texas Oil Company. As shown in the illustration the *Grace Harwar* suffered severe damage aloft. She was not the only vessel to come to grief, for a number of craft were blown ashore, and others were driven as much as two miles up the Mobile River, whilst the U.S. snagboat *William J. Twining* was blown right on top of the wharf of the Mobile and Ohio Railway Company.

H

Altogether the damage done by this hurricane amounted to millions of dollars without mentioning the loss of life.

The *Grace Harwar* was broken up in 1935.

"Port Patrick's" Adventures.

The *Port Patrick* was the first steel ship built for Crawford & Rowat's Port Line. She was one of Russell's standard size 1700-ton full-riggers, amongst which were the *Dumbarton Rock, Ardnamurchan, King Edward, Dechmont*, and *Kensington*.

The *Port Patrick* will be remembered more for her unusual adventures than for her speed, yet she was by no means a slow ship, and in 1894 made the best passage of the year from Oregon to Queenstown where she arrived on January 10—98 days out.

The first of her adventures happened in 1901, when she was bound from Port Elizabeth to Newcastle, N.S.W., in ballast. Whilst the ship was on her way up the coast making about $2\frac{1}{2}$ knots under full sail with a light northerly wind, she was struck by a sudden and very fierce west-sou'west squall which, although her canvas was handled as speedily as possible, almost overwhelmed her. The ship broached to against her port helm and nothing the captain could do would make her pay off. In this predicament the ship rapidly drifted inshore, and Captain Galloway was compelled to let go his anchors about a mile west by south of Cleft Island in order to prevent the ship going ashore; but at first the anchors did not hold, and the vessel dragged until her stern was almost in the breakers, which were beating on the rocky coast of Cleft Island.

As it was now blowing hard with the sea making fast, Captain Galloway decided to abandon his ship, and succeeded in leaving her safely with all hands; he was later picked up by the steamer *Abergeldie*, which was bound from Port Pirie to Sydney. As soon as it became known that there was an abandoned ship anchored under Cleft Island, near Wilson's Promontory, there was a race between the tugs *Eagle* and *Champion* in order to salvage her, in which *Champion* was successful. She found the *Port Patrick* still hanging to her anchors with most of her sails in tatters, but still just clear of the rocks. Without much difficulty a line was got aboard her and she was towed back to Melbourne.

Just on five years later—to be exact, on January 2, 1907— the *Port Patrick*, when leaving Astoria homeward bound with grain, came into violent collision with the lightship, which was severely damaged; and as if this was not an unlucky enough start to her passage, the very next day she struck on an uncharted shoal and for some time was in very great danger. Heavy seas broke over her stern, damaging the rudder, flooding the cabin, bursting in doors, and wrecking fittings on the maindeck. The carpenter also, while attempting to repair damage, was swept overboard and drowned. The ship, however, was soon floated though leaking badly, and Captain Sainty put back to Victoria for repairs.

The *Port Patrick* was sold to the Russians in 1913 on her arrival at Dunkirk, 130 days out from Caleta Coloso.

She survived the war, and in 1922 was still sailing the seas along with the four-masters, *Port Caledonia* and *Port Stanley*, under the Finnish flag. The *Port Caledonia* was lost on the coast of France in the winter of 1924-5, the *Port Stanley* and the *Port Patrick* going to the ship breakers.

The Speedy "Puritan."

This ship, which was built for Sir R. W. Cameron by John Reid in 1889, was a steel four-mast barque with some good sailing records to her credit. Perhaps her best performance was a run of 15 days from New York to the Butt of Lewis in the winter of 1899, being bound for Leith with a cargo of grain. In 1911 she left Newcastle, N.S.W., coal laden for San Francisco. On June 17, when 800 miles from Tahiti, the *Puritan* sprang a bad leak during a heavy gale. For 10 days whilst the crew fought the leak the bad weather continued, and on June 27, although it was still blowing hard, the captain decided that the ship must be abandoned; three boats were launched at midnight and got safely away from the ship. For two days they managed to keep together, then the weather grew still worse and they soon lost sight of each other. The captain's boat, containing twelve men, eventually reached Tahiti, 800 miles away, with her crew more dead than alive after seventeen terrible days. The mate's boat containing himself and nine men was never heard of again, whilst the third boat, which only contained three men, was picked up by the Auckland steamer *Talune,* when her occupants were at their last gasp.

The Sister Ships "Glencaird," "Cairniehill," and "Sir Robert Fernie."

In 1889 Russell & Co. built these fine steel four-mast barques, the first two for W. T. Dixon & Sons, and the *Sir Robert Fernie* for W. J. Fernie.

The *Glencaird* was lost on Staten Island when making for the entrance to the Le Maire Straits in October, 1901.

The *Cairniehill* was burnt and sunk in New York harbour in 1895. The wreck was bought by Flint & Co., raised, and renamed the *Charles R. Flint,* only to be again lost by fire in April, 1896.

The *Sir Robert Fernie* survived her two sister ships by many years. Her life, though, seems to have been rather humdrum. Her best sailing performance was in 1893, when she made the quickest grain passage of the year, namely 105 days from San Francisco to Queenstown. In 1907 she was sold to the Germans and re-named *Elisabeth*: two years later she was bought by the Compania Peruana de Vapores y Digue, dismantled, and used as a store ship at Callao until 1917, when she was taken to San Francisco to play her part in the Great War, being re-rigged as a four-mast barque.

The *Syren and Shipping,* in their *More Survivors of a Glorious Era,* give the following list of her passages under the Peruvians:—

Puget Sound to Callao	103 days
Peruvian ports to Talcahuano	18 ,,
Talcahuano to Callao	18 ,,
Peruvian ports to Buenos Ayres ..	58 ,,
Buenos Ayres to Copenhagen	73 ,,
Copenhagen to Norfolk, Virginia (in ballast)	62 ,,
Norfolk, Va., to Buenos Ayres	58 ,,
Buenos Ayres to Rotterdam (calling at Queenstown for orders)	68 ,,
Cardiff to Newcastle, N.S.W. (in ballast)	97 ,,
Newcastle, N.S.W., to Callao	76 ,,
Callao to Columbia River (in ballast) ..	45 ,,
Columbia River to Sydney, N.S.W. ..	91 ,,
Newcastle, N.S.W., to Callao	73 ,,

This is good steady work on the part of the old ship. In August, 1924, she was chartered to load guano for London, but was wrecked at Lobos Island.

"Falkland" and "Hollinwood."

In 1889 Potter built the big *Falkland* and Royden the *Hollinwood* for Macvicar, Marshall & Co.'s Palace Line. Neither of these huge four-mast barques lasted very long. The *Hollinwood* when homeward bound from Sydney for London with a mixed cargo, which included 2306 bales of wool, was abandoned with her wool on fire before the end of the nineteenth century; whilst the *Falkland* capsized and disappeared off the Bishop Rock in June, 1901, having left Tacoma under Captain Gracie on January 30 for Falmouth.

"Alice A. Leigh."

The biggest sailing ship ever built by the Whitehaven Shipbuilding Co. was the steel four-mast barque *Alice A. Leigh*, which registered over 3000 tons gross.

She was constructed to the order of J. Joyce & Co. of Liverpool and came out as a four-mast ship, but was reduced in 1901 to a barque. This mighty ship was a large carrier without any pretensions to speed, and there was a good photograph published in October, 1927, showing Law's *Elginshire* in the act of sailing round her. This insulting business of sailing round a ship means that you first of all sail through her lee, then luff up across her bows, until you are giving her what racing yachtsmen call a "weather bower".

In her later days the *Alice A. Leigh* was owned in New Zealand, being called the *Rewa*, but since 1923 she has been laid up at Auckland and will never go to sea again.

"Lord Rosebery."

A faster ship than the *Alice A. Leigh* was the *Lord Rosebery*, another big steel four-master from Whitehaven. She was at first called *Windermere*, but was renamed almost at once.

In 1895 she raced *Benares* out to Adelaide, both ships arriving on December 30, the *Lord Rosebery* being 74 days from Dover, and the *Benares* 75 from Hamburg. Others of her passages were not up to this standard; for instance, in 1899 she took 160 days between Panama and Taltal. Another long passage was 159 days from Calcutta to the Isle of Wight.

In 1910 *Lord Rosebery* was sold to Hamburg and renamed the *Reinbek*. At the commencement of the war she was caught at Valparaiso and eventually allocated to the French.

"Semantha".

This steel four-mast barque was built by Hamilton & Co. for J. R. Haws & Co. of Liverpool. Like their later ships, *Alcedo* and *Alcides*, the *Semantha* was unusually fast for a modern steel four-master. Her best passage was made in 1899 when she sailed from Astoria to Brow Head in 101 days.

In 1911 the *Semantha* was sold to the Norwegians. She was captured in the Atlantic by *Kronprinz Wilhelm*, February, 1915, and sunk.

"Buteshire" and "Elginshire".

In 1888 Messrs. Law & Co. commissioned Birrell to build two steel four-mast barques for the Shire Line. The first of these was the *Buteshire*, launched in July, 1888, and the second the *Elginshire*, launched in May, 1889.

The best-known commanders of the *Buteshire* were W. W. Swinton, who had the ship from 1892 to 1900, and Captain R. Purdie, who was in command from 1901 until her loss.

The following are a sample of the *Buteshire's* passages:—

1896	San Francisco to Hull	129	days
	Middlesbro' to Fremantle	85	,,
1897	Iquique to Hamburg	110	,,
1898	Hamburg to Sydney	96	,,
	Sydney to Honolulu	52	,,
	Honolulu to Portland (O.)	19	,,
1899	Astoria to Queenstown	135	,,
1900	Swansea to San Francisco	148	,,
	San Francisco to Falmouth	130	,,
1901	Barry to Hongkong	142	,,
	Hongkong to Portland (O.)	62	,,
	Portland (O.) to Falmouth	144	,,

In 1909 during her last voyage the *Buteshire* failed to make the passage from Panama to Caleta Coloso. The following letter from her senior apprentice is very interesting as showing the sailing ship's difficulty in working south on the West Coast of South America. He writes:—

We left Panama for Caleta Coloso on April 14, and for five days we ran with a light fair wind, after that the fun began. The wind set in from southward, shifting at times to S.W. with calms until we struggled to 2° 12′ N. We were then standing along on the starboard tack when the land was sighted on the port bow, and as it was approaching dark the captain decided to wear ship and stand out to sea for the night. The helm was put up, the main and crossjack yards squared and the ship got away before the wind so that we could brace the yards up and stand out, but there she stuck, standing straight in for the land while all ways and means of getting the ship to come to the wind were tried.

The order was therefore given to clear away the anchors. By this time we were about a mile from the shore, when the unexpected happened. The ship came rushing into the wind, the yards were braced up and we stood out. Even then we were driven back to 6° N. Again we beat our way down to 2° 37′ N., when the same thing happened. This time, however, the ship would not come round, the starboard anchor was let go. When day broke we found we were about a mile from the shore, with a reef on both sides; and there we lay for five days with the wind on a lee shore.

On May 5 the wind came off the land and gave us a chance to get away, which the captain took advantage of. While lying at anchor one morning a canoe was seen about ½ mile off with a native in it approaching slowly. When he came within hailing distance, one of the sailors, a Chilian, asked him in Spanish why he did not come alongside. So he came up and had a talk with him. The Chilian told me the native had never seen a ship before and when he saw the white men he was frightened as he had never seen any before. Next morning he brought the village to have a look at us.

After having been out 80 days we found we had been driven back to 6° N. again. The captain then decided to put back to Panama to have the bottom cleaned. The ship could not do more than 4 knots when she should have been going 8, as the bottom was so foul. After 91 days at sea we struggled back. Since then we have received fresh orders to go to Portland (O.). Better than on the West Coast which is almost slavery, working 800 tons ballast and putting in 3200 tons of saltpetre, all with hand winch whilst lying at anchor, seldom getting ashore. At Portland we shall be alongside a wharf, get ashore every night and never touch ballast or cargo.

The *Buteshire* eventually crossed to Newcastle, N.S.W., where she loaded coal back to Valparaiso, arriving 61 days out. From Valparaiso she went to load nitrate at Pisagua. Pisagua was left on November 18, and owing to a leak Captain Purdie was obliged to abandon his ship about 6 a.m. on March 27, when 100 miles west of Brest.

It was on March 19 after a hard battle against easterly gales that 13 inches of water was found in the hold, and though all hands, including the captain's wife, were continuously at the pumps from that date, the water gradually gained upon them, so that when the steamer *Ardeola* came along on March 27 Captain Purdie seized the opportunity to save his crew. Captain Purdie thought his ship was likely to sink at any moment, but as a matter of fact she remained afloat until March 29, during which time several vessels reported her; for instance, the captain of the ss. *Milton* reported as follows:—

March 27, 6 p.m. in 48° 47′ N., 7° 19′ W., 73 miles sou'west of Bishop Rock Lighthouse—four-masted vessel *Buteshire* standing to S.E. water-logged and abandoned. Apparently all above rail intact, two boats on fore house and one life-boat on skids, other missing. Vessel rolling very heavily in N.E. sea, and when she plunged did not think she would recover. Stopped close under her stern; stern light burning, also one in cabin and galley. Weather at time moderate gale E.N.E., heavy sea.

Other ships continued to report her until March 29 when the captain of the ss. *Duva* wrote to his owners as follows:—

I saw the four-masted barque *Buteshire* of Glasgow take her departure from the lists of ships on March 29, at about 3 p.m., abandoned, on fire, and a lot of water in her. We stopped and boarded her to see if there was any chance of saving her, but had to get out of her pretty quickly. About ten minutes afterwards she foundered. I got a snapshot photo of her just before she left, position about 28 miles sou'west of Longships.

I reproduce his photograph facing this page.

The *Elginshire* was the last of all Law's sailing ships to remain in commission.

The first skipper of the *Elginshire* was Robert Greig, who, I am afraid, was not one of Law's most popular captains. He left the *Elginshire* (so the unkind said) because she was a bit too big for him, and he took the *Duns Law* from the stocks. He was succeeded by J. G. Hannah, who handed over to David Stott in 1900. Wright followed Stott, and he was followed by Dixon. Finally, in 1919, Captain Roberts had her until 1922. For a while the old ship was laid up in Milford Haven. Captain Roberts lived aboard in charge for three months, but then could stand it no longer, and accepted the command of the *Garthgarry*, whereupon Law & Co. sold the *Elginshire* to the ship breakers.

"STRATHGRYFFE"

"MAYHILL"

[*See Page* 116

"LYNGO" EX "DUMBARTON ROCK"

Lent by F. G. T. Dawson

[*See Page* 119

"GLENESK"

[*See Page* 120

Elginshire was a faster ship than the *Buteshire*, and held the record from New Caledonia to the Clyde, her run being 86 days. Some of her best passages were made under Captain Dixon, such as 42 days from Santos to Cossack, West Australia, when she averaged 224 miles for 36 days and accomplished a 24-hour run of 318 miles.

CHAPTER III.

THE CARRIERS OF THE NINETIES—1890-1891.

So to the sea we came; the sea? that is
A world of waters heaped up on hie,
Rolling like mountains in wild wildernesse,
Horrible, hideous, roaring with hoarse crie,
And is the sea (quoth Coridon) so fearfull?
Fearful much more (quoth he) then hart can fear:
Thousand wyld beasts with deep mouthes gaping direfull
Therein stil waite poore passengers to teare.
Who life doth loath, and longs death to behold,
Before he die, alreadie dead with feare,
And yet would live with heart halfe stonie cold,
Let him to sea, and he shall see it there.
And yet as ghastly dreadful as it seemes,
Bold men presuming life for gaine to sell,
Dare tempt that gulf, and in those wand'ring stremes
Seek waies unknowne, waies leading down to hell.

ED. SPENSER'S
" *Colin Clouts come home againe.*"

The Sea's Lost Prestige.

ON January 14, 1928, an article appeared in the *Times* with the above heading. The writer of the article begins as follows:—

The going down to the sea in ships has been deprived of almost all its terrors and most of its romance. It is no longer a venturing forth upon a great and indefinite adventure. . . . The fear that the sea once inspired, except in rare cases, has vanished; . . . the mysteries of the deep have lost their attraction.

He then proceeds to contrast the lot of the present-day passenger at sea with that of the sailing ship emigrant sixty years ago.

No longer does the courageous maiden, discreetly dressed and wrapped in borrowed oilskins, sou'wester on her head, venture forth, under the protection of the captain, upon the wet and slippery deck to watch the seas breaking over the bows of the ship, and to

106

feel the spray beating on her face. . . . No longer teak barrels bound in brass contain the salt pork and beef of the crew's rations. No longer the ship's cow, which supplied the children and invalids with milk, chews the cud in her roughly built loose-box; nor is dawn to-day rendered poignant by the crowing and cackling of fowls. . . .

His words are true enough in some ways. The sea has lost its prestige as regards frightfulness, such as is so vividly described by Spenser: the sea has become safe to the traveller—safer in many ways than the land; but it has by no means lost its hold over those who have salt water in their veins.

Some people have an inborn antipathy for the Great Deep, and one can never make them understand the charm that it has for so many of us.

There is something majestic, inspiring, almost supernatural about a great storm at sea. At the same time its other moods fill one with a kind of inner spiritual satisfaction—moods of wind and weather, of smiling calm, of sparkling sunshine, of purple wavelets silver-tipped in the glittering moonlight—one could go on recalling these intriguing changes of the sea *ad infinitum.*

The seaman aboard the giant steamship is almost wholly indifferent to these changes, which he calls shortly "weather." He has no chance of observing the wonders of the deep, and even the phosphorescent wave has gone astern before he can focus his night-glass upon it.

As for the passenger, our *Times* correspondent declares that he or she is more interested in the saxophone notes from the band than the musical gurgle of the white water swishing by under the rows of lighted portholes.

It is only when the landsman finds himself aboard a ship, whose only motive power is the breeze of Heaven, that he is brought in close contact with Nature as exemplified by wind and wave, fish and fowl, sea and sky. At first he is only interested as in some "unknown thing," then, as his mind is opened, he realises for the first time the inner truth of Longfellow's words:—

> "Wouldst thou," so the helmsman answered,
>   Learn the secrets of the sea?
> Only those who brave its dangers
>   Comprehend its mystery!"

The Mighty "California."

This ship was built on the lines of the *Sindia* and *Holkar* for Ismay's famous White Star Line. I reproduce her lines, and her model is to be seen at the Sailors' Home in Liverpool. Amongst sailormen she was considered one of the finest four-mast barques ever built; indeed, when lying at anchor in the Mersey she always queened it over the other shipping. John Masefield describes her as "the *California* huge, as slow as Time,"—but this is rather a severe criticism of her sailing capabilities, for under the British flag at any rate she made some very fair passages, as for instance:—

1890	Liverpool to San Francisco	..	130 days.
1891	San Francisco to Liverpool	..	121 „
1892	Newcastle, N.S.W. to 'Frisco	..	53 „

Ismay sold the *California* in 1896 to Messrs. Ritson & Livesey of Liverpool. Their manager, Harold A. Sanderson, sold her a year later to Sloman of Hamburg, who renamed her *Alster*. In 1898 she was again sold to another Hamburg firm, who ran her until 1912 when she was bought by the well-known Schramm of Bremen.

In 1914 the outbreak of war found her in Valparaiso where she was interned. Later on her crew damaged her in every possible way they could in order to prevent her being used by the Allies. Thus, at the end of the war she was incapable of going to sea until she had had a complete overhaul and re-fit. She was allocated to the Italians, who used her for some time as a hulk at Valparaiso.

At last, in 1926, she was fitted out and loaded 5000 tons of nitrate at Caleta Coloso for Norfolk, Virginia.

She was commanded by Captain T. H. Kirkwood, and was so long in making the passage to Panama that 10 guineas per cent. was paid on her; however, she arrived at the entrance to the Canal on March 28, 1927. It may be interesting to note her costs in the Canal. Tonnage tolls, tug hire, etc., amounted to 4302 dollars.

Sailing from Colon on April 11, she again caused anxiety amongst the underwriters, who could gain no news of her until a belated report declared that she was ashore on the island of Old Providence, and likely to be a total loss. This report was only too true. She stranded on the island on April 15, and there she remained.

"Lord Templemore."

Another sister ship of the two last Brocklebank sailers was the *Lord Templemore* belonging to the Irish Shipowners of Belfast. This ship had a very aristocratic reputation! One man assured me that she was commanded by a peer of the realm. Another declared that her captain was the younger son of the Marquis of Downshire. As a matter of fact she was commanded in her early years by Captain Walker, son of the Right Honourable Sir Samuel Walker, Lord High Chancellor of Ireland. Captain Walker was afterwards Superintendent of the Mercantile Marine Office and B.O.T. Examiner at Dublin.

Lord Templemore was bought at the end of the nineteenth century by the Act. Ges. Alster of Hamburg, the same people who had bought the *California* and was renamed *Alsternixe*.

On November 26, 1906, she left Callao for Melbourne in ballast, and was posted as "missing".

"Simla."

This ship was the fastest of the five big Russell built four-mast barques launched for Gilbert M. Steeves between 1889 and 1893. These were the *Stanley*, *Simla*, *Sofala*, *Somali*, and *Saratoga*.

The *Simla*, which was launched in March, 1890, distinguished herself by making the best passage of the year from Liverpool to Calcutta. Leaving the Mersey on April 11, 1890, she let go her tug and made sail on the 14th; crossed the Line on May 4, 23 days out; made her best run on May 28—293 miles with the wind abaft the beam under three topgallant sails, and made the Sandheads July 9, 88 days from Liverpool.

Amongst her apprentices in 1907 was Warneford, the man who brought down the first Zeppelin. On this voyage she went from London to Port Adelaide in 100 days, then loaded wheat at Port Pirie for Queenstown. The outward passage was a very comfortable one, but the run home a perfect nightmare. The *Simla* was 70 days to the Horn, during which time neither her maindeck nor her crew were ever dry. She finally arrived at Cardiff 186 days out, and no less than 14 days from Queenstown.

On her next voyage in September, 1908, she caught fire at

Acapulco, where she had arrived with a coal cargo. After this she was converted to a hulk and ended her days as a four-mast barque belonging to the Union Oil Company of California.

"Swanhilda's" Adventures.

One of the fastest four-mast barques built was the *Swanhilda* which was launched from McMillan's yard in July, 1890, for the Nova Scotian firm of J. W. Carmichael & Co. Though nearly all her passages were much under the average, she will always be remembered for her record run of 66 days from Wallaroo, South Australia, to Queenstown, where she arrived on April 18, 1894

Other smart performances were:—

1892	Hakodate to San Francisco	..	23 days.
1895	Liverpool to Sydney	..	82 „

All these were made under the command of Captain Colin Fraser, a Blue-nose skipper.

At one period of her career the *Swanhilda* was bombarded by American newspaper reporters. This was on arrival at San Francisco from Melbourne. It appears that one of her crew was the murderer Frank Britton, who had shipped before the mast under the name of Wheeler. This man had made a habit of taking his victims up into the hills on the plea of showing them a goldmine, and often murdering them. The curious part about the case was that Captain Fraser and his mate, Thomas Meikle, had recognised the man from the description published in the Australian papers soon after the *Swanhilda* had left Port Phillip, but they had kept the matter secret.

When the *Swanhilda* arrived in the Bay two local detectives came aboard with the quarantine officials. The mate pointed Wheeler out, and he was at once handcuffed, taken back to Australia and hanged.

In 1905 the *Swanhilda*, when under the command of Captain Macdonald, made an extraordinarily long and unfortunate passage to Chile. She sailed from Hamburg with a cargo of coke on January 14 for Coquimbo. Going north about she almost immediately ran into bad weather, losing sails, boats, steering gear and compasses, and she was driven in an almost helpless condition as far as the coast of Greenland, her highest latitude being 80 miles north of Cape

Farewell. By this time Captain Macdonald had managed to rig up temporary steering gear. He then succeeded in sailing her safely back to the Clyde without compasses, and with three men at his jury wheel. In order to save any demand for salvage, he even worked his lame duck up the Channel to Innellan before he took steam.

Whilst the *Swanhilda* was being repaired Captain Macdonald lost his wife, and so a new man took the ship to sea on her second attempt to reach Coquimbo.

This second attempt seems to have been no luckier than the first one as regards weather, and the *Swanhilda* was on the point of being posted as "missing" when a telegram announced that she had arrived at Rio de Janeiro, 135 days out, with "rudder jammed, houses stove in, galley rendered useless, considerable deck damage, some spars broken and sails lost, cabin flooded, etc." Her owners now begged Captain Macdonald to proceed to Rio and resume his old command, and under him the ship eventually reached her destination.

There are many unlucky things that you can do aboard a ship, and many persons or animals which it is considered unlucky to have aboard a ship. The best known subjects, of course, are hares and parsons; but there is a superstition of the sea which seems to be borne out by hard fact. Not only is the captain's wife unlucky, but over and over again in the case of shipwreck she is the only person lost. On one occasion two ships collided off the pitch of the Horn. They were swept beam to beam in the hollow between two immense Cape Horn greybeards. The captain of one of them, thinking that his ship was going to be sunk by the collision, attempted, just before their contact, to throw his wife aboard the other vessel. She fell between the two ships and was crushed to death, being the only person in either ship to receive any injury.

This train of thought has been aroused by the fact that the *Swanhilda* was lost in 1910 on a passage from Cardiff to the West Coast, when her young captain, Pine, had his wife aboard, and was in fact making a honeymoon trip of it.

Sailing from Cardiff on March 15, all went well until 5 p.m. on May 6 when, in misty rainy weather with a heavy sea running, land was unexpectedly sighted right ahead, and within half a mile. The ship was immediately wore on to the starboard tack and braced sharp up with her head to the nor'west so as to get clear. After a little while the heavy mist lifted sufficiently to show Cape St. Anthony close on the port bow. Both the heavy sea and a strong current were setting the ship on to the Cape. It was immediately recognised that the *Swanhilda* would not go clear, and the captain gave orders for the lifeboats to be swung out. Before this could be done the vessel struck heavily broadside on.

The starboard life-boat was swung out first, and in the confusion of the moment fourteen of the crew and the master and his wife scrambled into it. It was then lowered with such haste and so unevenly that it was up-ended and shot its occupants into the water, eleven of them, including the captain and his wife, being drowned. The other five, including a man who lost his reason, succeeded in making a landing through the surf.

Meanwhile the port life-boat was safely lowered, and with the thirteen remaining members of the crew on board was pulled out to sea until daylight. This boat succeeded in reaching New Year's Island after thirty strenuous hours, during which one of its occupants died of exposure.

The lighthouse-keepers on New Year's Island sent a wireless message to the mainland which brought an Argentine Government transport to the rescue.

At the subsequent inquiry the mate of the *Swanhilda* was asked why he had not gone to the help of the drowning people of the starboard boat. His reply was that the boat and the drowning men had been washed into the breakers, and he did not consider it advisable to endanger the lives of those in his boat in attempting what he considered to be an impossible rescue. The mate explained the curious fact of the captain leaving the ship in the first boat by saying that the captain's wife was young and very frightened and refused to get into the boat unless he came with her.

The senior apprentice, who was acting as third mate and only the previous year had suffered shipwreck off the Horn when serving in the *Deccan*, said that he and two others had been lowered to the water in the port life-boat. After the falls were unhooked the

"SPEKE"

Lent by Captain L. R. W. Beavis [*See Page* 121

"VIMEIRA"

Lent by Captain L. R. W. Beavis [*See Page* 126

"DITTON"

"DITTON" IN COLLISION
With *Port Crawford* and *Peeblesshire*

[*See Page* 123

life-boat was swept away from the ship, and they had a job in getting alongside again. Whilst they were adrift and having great difficulty in keeping off the rocks themselves, he saw the starboard boat driven into the surf.

The bosun in his evidence declared that he stopped one man from getting into the starboard life-boat before the captain's wife, but that the captain said to him, "Let them get in. She will not go till I go."

Some time afterwards an Argentine gunboat made a search of Staten Island, and discovered the bodies of four men. These, who were of the starboard boat's crew, had evidently got ashore safely through the surf, but afterwards died of starvation. The insane man was found alive in a cave, and eventually recovered his senses. He declared that he had lost his reason when he had found the bodies of Captain Pine and his bride, washing to and fro in the surf, but still locked in each other's arms. He said that he and the other four had lived for some time on tins of grease, and when the grease was exhausted resorted to shellfish.

The wreck of the *Swanhilda* seems under the circumstances to have been unavoidable, but the loss of life was certainly needless, for the ship showed no signs of breaking up, and if only her company had remained aboard until the weather moderated they would all have been saved.

"Hinemoa's" Fatal Ballast.

The beautiful *Hinemoa*, which was built by Russell in 1890 to the order of John Leslie, was fitted with freezing machinery for the frozen mutton trade from New Zealand.

Though she was a handy, well-behaved ship with a very good turn of speed, she suffered from ill-luck from the very start. Many declared that a curse had been put upon her, which chiefly affected her masters and her freights.

On her first voyage when she was commanded by Captain R. de Steiger, who, it is said, was a German baron, four of her apprentices died at Lyttelton from typhoid, the germs of which were believed to have been in her ballast. This ballast was rubble from an old London burial ground, and it was most unlucky stuff,

I

for on the outward passage whilst she was running her Easting down it had broken down the shifting boards, piled down to leeward and laid the ship on her beam ends.

Soon after the ship's arrival in New Zealand a local coasting schooner came alongside to take some of this ballast. The *Hinemoa's* crew gravely warned the schooner of its evil properties. However, the latter sailed away with sufficient of it to bring her very near to destruction, for it shifted in her hold as it had done in the *Hinemoa's* and she also was laid on her beam ends.

The *Hinemoa's* ballast was also made responsible for the continual breaking down of her freezing machinery, but its most fatal effect was upon the ship's many captains—I will not mention names.

One of her captains went mad, another was dismissed for a criminal offence, a third was a drunkard, and after the ship had sailed for the West Coast he became so outrageous that the crew took charge and put the ship back. Her fourth captain, or it may have been her fifth, was found dead with a revolver beside him, and they brought it in as suicide. The man who succeeded him did not die a violent death aboard the *Hinemoa*, but whilst he was mine-sweeping during the war he shot himself outside Lowestoft one morning. Her captain in 1908 was severely censured for letting his ship drift ashore in the vicinity of Lorne Jetty.

In spite of her fatal ballast the *Hinemoa* managed to make some very fair records, as follows:—

1894	The Downs to Melbourne	..	.. 77 days
1895	The Lizard to Melbourne ..	..	.. 83 ,,
1901	Newcastle, N.S.W., to 'Frisco	..	.. 60 ,,
1902	'Frisco to Old Head of Kinsale	..	.. 101 ,,
1902	Frederickstadt to Melbourne	..	.. 94 ,,

(On this passage she had two hands washed overboard.)

By this time the freezing machinery had been taken out of her and she had become a general trader.

Law's "Dumfriesshire."

In December, 1889, Russell launched the steel four-mast barque *Dumfriesshire* for the Glasgow Shire Line. She was the biggest ship in the fleet, registering 2565 tons.

In their four-masters Thomas Law & Co. seem to have tried out the various sail plans, and *Dumfriesshire* was given three skysail yards.   She had a midship bridge with a large house on top of it, and was a very up-to-date ship in every way.   Being a very large carrier a great deal was not expected with regard to sailing power, nevertheless she made some very respectable passages, both under that splendid shipmaster Captain McGibbon, who commanded her until the end of the nineteenth century, and Captains Swinton and Furneaux who followed him.

On her maiden voyage the *Dumfriesshire* left Antwerp on March 15, 1890, and arrived San Francisco August 21, 158 days out; and sailing from San Francisco on October 28, she reached Hull on April 7, 1891, 159 days out.

As an example of her best work the following passages are worth noting:—

1893	'Frisco to Queenstown	112 days.
1894	Newcastle, N.S.W. to Antofagasta	42 ,,
1898	Newcastle, N.S.W., to Valparaiso	39 ,,
1898	Newcastle, N.S.W., to Valparaiso	39 ,,
1901	Portland (O.) to Falmouth	114 ,,
1910	Tacoma to Falmouth	127 ,,

Amongst her worst passages were:—

1897	Iquique to Hamburg	196 days.
	(Put in to Rio leaking 2/7/97 and left Rio 20/8/97.)	
1899	Dunkirk to New York	45 days.
1900-1	Philadelphia to Hiogo	163 ,,
1909-10	Mejillones to Hamburg	114 ,,
1910	Hamburg to Honolulu	140 ,,

In comparison with other ships of her date she showed up very fairly; for instance, here are a few passages from Newcastle, N.S.W., to the Pacific Coast in the early nineties:—

Torrisdale	72 days.
Earl of Dunmore	67 ,,
Gowanburn	65 ,,
Dumfriesshire	64 ,,
Beacon Rock	58 ,,
Falkirk	57 ,,

Her worst passage on this route was 84 days in 1893.

One has to be careful not to mix up this ship with Goffey's *Dumfriesshire*. The latter had a curious experience in 1904. She stranded under full sail on one of the New Caledonia coral reefs, and her captain thought it wise to abandon her. The following morning when the castaways looked for their ship on the rocks nothing was in sight, so they concluded that she had foundered during the night. They themselves were then picked up by a steamer and taken to Noumea. The Goffey's *Dumfriesshire*, however, had floated on the rising tide, sailed along the coast for about thirty miles, then drifted into a bay where she was secured by a settler, whose claim for salvage was a heavy one.

Law's *Dumfriesshire* outlived her small rival by many years and figures on the sailing ship Roll of Honour, for she was torpedoed off the Smalls in 1915, and went down in five minutes.

"Mayhill."

One of the fastest four-mast barques built in 1890 was the *Mayhill*, belonging to W. II. Myers and managed by Ismay, Imrie & Co.

Unfortunately her life was a very short one, for she was wrecked on August 10, 1895; but she hardly made a bad passage, her best being:—

1891-2 Downs to Melbourne	..	..	..	74 days.
1892　Newcastle, N.S.W. (with 300 tons of coal)				
to San Francisco ..	..	..	..	57 „
1893　Newcastle to 'Frisco	..	..	..	50 „

"Strathgryfe."

Another fast four-mast barque was the Russell built *Strathgryfe*, but she did not do much under the British flag.

In 1910 she was sold to the Germans for £3850 and renamed *Margretha*. On her very first passage under the Germans she sailed from Rotterdam to Melbourne in 82 days, throughout which, it must be confessed, the winds were very favourable; her best run was 297 miles.

She seems to have had a life which, for a ship, was somewhat humdrum, her most thrilling moments being in June, 1905, when she was crossing the Pacific from Newcastle, N.S.W., to Pisagua.

On the twelfth day out she broached to and carried away her topgallant masts. For some time her condition was critical. However, she finally righted herself and proceeded to her destination without further incident.

Five years before this when bound out to Melbourne, the *Strathgryfe* picked up a shipwrecked crew belonging to a foreign barque in mid-ocean and brought them safely to port.

She was seized by Portugal in the war and remained the *Graciosa* and in 1918 was sunk by U-boat.

"Cambrian King" and "Cambrian Hills."

The last two ships built for Williams's Cambrian Line were the *Cambrian King* and *Cambrian Hills*, the first built by Russell in 1890, and the latter by A. Rodger & Co. in 1892.

These Welshmen were fine 1700-ton steel full-riggers with a good turn of speed. For instance, in 1894 the *Cambrian Hills* went from Rotterdam to Port Pirie in 77 days, and came home from Wallaroo to Queenstown in 88 days; in August, 1898, she sailed from Shanghai to Astoria in 31 days; and in 1902 arrived Queenstown, March 1, 104 days out from San Francisco.

The sail and spar plan of the *Cambrian Hills* will be found in the Appendix.

Neither vessel had a long life, the *Cambrian King* being posted "missing" in 1901. The *Cambrian Hills* left Iquique for Havre on November 27, 1904. All went well until she was off the Scillies when the ship seems to have been overwhelmed by a terrific squall. According to the account she sprang a leak, slowly settled down on her side, and presently capsized. Before this her crew had taken to the boats; they were picked up by a passenger steamer and landed at Queenstown.

The Last of the "Passes" and "Capes."

There were three "Capes" and three "Passes" launched in the nineties, all of them steel four-mast barques with the exception of the last, the *Pass of Killiecrankie*, launched in 1893, which was a three-mast barque. Three out of these six ships were built off the same lines by Duncan. These were the *Pass of Brander* launched in 1890, and the *Capes Wrath* and *Clear* launched two years later.

With the exception of the *Pass of Killiecrankie*, which was a large carrier with a small sail plan, and therefore very slow, these last "Passes" and "Capes" were good sailers.   Here are a few of their best passages:—

Cape York	..	Barry to Adelaide	..	..	..	..	72 days in	1893
		Newcastle, N.S.W., to Mollendo	..		..	38	,,	1899
Cape Wrath	..	Newcastle, N.S.W., to San Francisco		..	53	,,	1894
Cape Clear	..	Calcutta to Beachy Head	..	..	..	102	,,	1894
Pass of Brander		Cardiff to Callao	..	..	..	..	58	,,	1909

The Lyles, who for so long had been connected with the East Indian sugar trade, gave up sailing ships about the end of the nineteenth century.   The last three ships disappeared from the Register about the same time, the last to survive being *Cape Wrath*, which was posted "missing" in 1901 when on a passage from Callao to Astoria.   It was thought probable that she had capsized in heavy weather owing to the shifting of her shingle ballast.

As regards the "Passes" the *Pass of Melfort* foundered with all hands at the entrance to Barclay Sound, Vancouver Island, in December, 1905.

The beautiful *Pass of Brander* fell a victim during the war. She was sold to J. & J. Rae & Co., of Liverpool, some half-dozen years before the war and renamed *Bengairn*.

The *Pass of Killiecrankie* went to the Norwegians, being renamed *Stifinder*.

"Ainsdale" and "Hawksdale."

These two fine steel sister ships were built by Bigger of Londonderry for Peter Iredale & Porter in 1890.   The *Hawksdale* was wrecked on January 26, 1899, but the *Ainsdale* survived until recent years.   On February 15, 1916, when 200 miles sou'west of Cape Clear she was left in a sinking condition by a German submarine, her crew having been made to abandon her.   She did not sink, however, and was towed into port a week later as a derelict by the s.s. *Basuto*.   She was then re-fitted and an engine put into her.   In April, 1918, she had another encounter with a U-boat whilst under convoy from Norway to the United Kingdom.

"Dumbarton Rock."

This ship was one of Russell's standard 1700-ton full-riggers. She was built for the Rock Line and sold to A. Yule & Co., of Calcutta, in 1893.   Messrs. Yule & Co. only had her for a very short time, and then sold her to H. Burmester & Co., of Hamburg, who renamed her the *Lika*.   She later came into the hands of the Norwegians, and was renamed the *Lyngo*, being owned by the Norwegian Whaling Co., whose base was at Walfisch Bay (now Walvis Bay), South Africa.   She was in Cardiff as late as February, 1925, still full-rigged and looking as handsome as ever.

"Andromeda."

Another ship which survived until recent years was the Duncan-built main skysail yard four-mast barque *Andromeda*. She was built for G. F. Smith, the owner of the *Galatea, Constance Timandra* and one or two small wooden barques.

Though registered in Glasgow *Andromeda* was really a Blue-nose, as G. F. Smith belonged to St. John.   On the death of Mr. Smith she was owned for a short time by his widow, and managed by A. W. Adams of St. John, but in 1901 she was sold to Black, Moore & Co., of London.   Though she was a fine handsome ship like all Duncan's products, I cannot find that she made any passages worthy of record, though Blue-nose skippers as a rule had a way of getting a ship through the water however poor a sailer she might be.

"Drumalis'" "Andrada" and "Andorinha."

These big four-mast barques were built by William Pickersgill & Sons of Sunderland, the first for Peter Iredale & Porter, and the other two for the Roberts brothers.

All three were tall ships with a reputation for speed.   The *Andorinha* was specially lofty with her three skysail yards.   She had an evil reputation as a wet ship owing to hard driving, and amongst seamen she was spoken of as a man killer, who washed a man or two overboard every passage.

There used to be a dispute between the crews of the *Drumalis* and *Andorinha* as to which of the two held the record from Cape Town to Newcastle, N.S.W.   In 1898 the *Drumalis*, on arrival at

Newcastle, N.S.W., announced her passage from Cape Town to be 24 days.   In 1900 the *Andorinha* made the same run in 24 days and some odd hours.   The Andorinhians claimed that the *Drumalis's* passage should have been 24½ days, but the matter was never really settled one way or the other.

Andrada's best performance was from Antwerp to San Francisco, 117 days in 1897.   This ship has been missing since December 11, 1900.

Drumalis came to grief on Cape Sable in August, 1902.   The lofty *Andorinha* was eventually bought by Ant. Dom. Bordes & Fils, and renamed *Helene*, being the biggest ship in the French nitrate fleet for a number of years.

The "Glens" of Dundee.

Messrs. W. O. Taylor & Co., the owners of the Dundee "Glens," seem to have been very partial to the barque rig.   Their ships until 1890 were all small handy iron or steel barques, mostly built by A. Stephen & Sons.   The last of these were the *Glenmark* and *Glenesk,* sister barques of 1257 tons net.   They were built by Russell and were very good examples of his small barques, being handy, economical and with a very fair turn of speed.   Both had long lives and remained under the Glen house-flag until just before the war.   They were followed by two big steel four-mast barques, the *Glencona,* of 2631 tons, launched by Russell in 1890, and the *Glenclova,* of 2369 tons, launched by Connell in 1893.   Both these were considered fast ships of their type; the *Glencona* in 1902 sailed from San Francisco to Liverpool in 117 days, considered a fair passage at that date.   The *Glenclova* will be remembered for her passage of 81 days from Table Bay to Puget Sound, which is still a record for that run.

Glencona came to grief on July 16, 1903.   The *Glenclova* was sold to H. H. Schmidt of Hamburg about six years before the war and renamed *Mimi.*

The Wreck of the "Speke."

When T. R. Oswald removed from Southampton to Milford Haven in 1890 his career as a prolific builder of sailing ships was

"DITTON" IN COLLISION
With *Port Crawford* and *Peeblesshire*

"DITTON" IN COLLISION
With *Port Crawford* and *Peeblesshire*

[*See Page* 123

"TALUS"

[*See Page* 126

"ROSS-SHIRE"

[*See Page* 132

almost ended.   He only built four square-riggers at Milford Haven, but these four were notable ships, namely *Speke,* numbered 260 in his yard list, and *Ditton,* both launched in 1891; *Lyderhorn* and *Windermere,* both launched in 1892.

The first two were the biggest full-rigged ships ever built by Oswald, and were specially designed to gain good deductions in tonnage, for instance they registered:—

Speke	..	2875 gross	2712 nett.
Ditton	..	2901 ,,	2699 ,,

They were indeed tremendous ships for only three masts, and although their mainyards were 106 feet long, with a ship's length of over 310 feet, it will be seen that, even when the yards were braced sharp up, there must have been a big unfilled space between the masts.   It was for this reason chiefly that these two huge full-riggers had no claims to speed, although they were very lofty, crossing a main skysail over a single topgallant sail.   Like all ships of over 2500 tons, the *Speke* and *Ditton* had their accommodation amidships, with separate fo'c'les for each watch of ten A.B.'s.

Messrs. R. W. Leyland & Co. were firm believers in the three-master, but seamen had one strong objection to them.   They declared that the lower yards of these big ships were so great in circumference that, when they were on the foot-ropes, they could not reach over far enough to pick up the sail in furling or reefing.

The *Speke* was launched in March, 1891, and her first commander rejoiced in the name of Gyllencreutz.   He was succeeded in 1899 by F. Stott.   Finally Captain Tilston, who had been mate for three years before taking up the mastership of the *Wavertree,* took over the *Speke* at Los Angeles in 1904.   From Los Angeles the *Speke* crossed the Pacific to Newcastle, N.S.W., and loaded coal back to Peru.   Captain Tilston then again returned to Australia in ballast and, calling off Sydney Heads, received orders for Melbourne.

During the night of Wednesday, February 21, whilst beating down the coast, Captain Tilston mistook the Cape Shanck light for that on Split Point, and so set a dangerous course.   At daybreak on Thursday morning the *Speke,* on the port tack, found herself close in-shore and heading for the rocks on the southern side of Phillip Island. It was blowing hard and there was a big sea running. Captain Tilston immediately tried to wear round, but the *Speke* refused to bear up, and as a last chance to save the ship both her anchors were let go, but one of the chains parted almost at once, and the other anchor dragged. From midday, as one of the crew said, "We knew it was all up with us; the only question being whether we would go ashore at a bad spot or not, as in that wind and sea nothing could save the ship."

The *Speke* then drifted into Kitty Miller's Bay, and did not touch the ground until she was within a few fathoms of dry land. The surf, however, was terrific, and, directly the ship struck, began to sweep her from stem to stern. The captain gave orders for the port and starboard life-boats to be launched without delay, but this was easier said than done. The starboard life-boat, which was put over the port side with four men in her, was immediately capsized, and one of the men, Frank Henderson, was drowned, being swept away from his mates by a huge breaker. Meanwhile the port life-boat was swinging in the davits with the cook, a very stout elderly man, aboard her waiting to be lowered. However, as soon as they saw the fate of the starboard boat, the cook was hurriedly assisted back to the ship's deck. For a few moments after this there was a good deal of confusion and excitement, but the shore was close aboard and a boat soon succeeded in carrying a line through the surf, by means of which all hands safely reached the beach. In handling the lifeline and getting the men ashore Cook (the second mate) and an able seaman named Herman, particularly distinguished themselves. Herman conducted the fat cook along the lifeline: unfortunately for the pair of them the men slacking away from the ship were confused by the shouting on shore, and let go too quickly with the result that Herman and the "doctor" were half drowned in the surf.

In spite of the stress and danger there were one or two comical incidents in this shipwreck. For instance, the mate, Williams, came on deck with two panama hats, which he had bought in South America, in his hands. These were soon torn from his grasp to the amusement of the crew, but he had the satisfaction of finding one of them on the beach the next morning. The men's parrot was the first of the ship's company to get ashore; he flew off to the cliff, but immediately returned to the ship and perched on the taffrail where he was speedily overwhelmed by a sea and drowned.

The *Speke* had two apprentices. The first of these packed his mother's portrait in the middle of his kit-bag and chucked it aboard the ill-fated starboard life-boat. The second apprentice put his pocket book with all his worldly possessions into the breast pocket of his jacket, and threw that into the boat. The portrait and the pocket book were found next day washed up on the shore, but the kit-bag and jacket were never seen again.

In the inquiry the captain had his certificate suspended for twelve months because he should have known that he was within the radius of Cape Shanck light and therefore had set a dangerous course.

The "Ditton" and her Collisions.

The *Ditton* was just about an inch larger all round than the *Speke*. Her deadweight capacity on a draught of 24 feet was 4500 tons. In spite of her huge spars she seems to have been a popular ship with seamen, and in 1904 when the desertion of ships' crews on the Pacific coast was exercising the authorities, the *Ditton* distinguished herself at San Francisco by losing only one man from desertion. This record beat that of any other British ship sailing through the Golden Gate that year.

The *Ditton's* first master was Captain H. Stap, who for a number of years commanded the *Great Britain*, the only successful auxiliary ever built. The *Ditton's* first voyage was to Sydney, N.S.W., where she was the cause of a great deal of interest on the part of the shipping community. On her second voyage she went out to San Francisco and again she queened it over all her rivals. On her third voyage she sailed for Melbourne *via* Rio.

She will always be remembered in Newcastle, N.S.W., for the way she ran amuck in that port in 1902. The Newcastle pilots found the *Ditton* was more of a handful than they could do with. Captain William Davis had only lately taken over the ship from Captain Stap. Arriving off Newcastle in ballast in squally southerly weather he made the mistake of only engaging one tug. The

Ditton was drawing only 13 feet forward and 13 ft. 6 in. aft, and thus showing a tremendous high side.   The *Port Crawford* and the *Peeblesshire* were lying at the Farewell buoys, loaded and waiting to go to sea, when the *Ditton* came in under tow.   Just as she was abreast of the Farewell buoys a fierce squall gave her a sheer.   She broke her towrope, took charge, and ran slap into the *Port Crawford*, her steel bowsprit knocking the foremast out of the latter and breaking it off just above the deck like a carrot.   Just at the last moment the mate of the *Ditton* let her starboard anchor go with a run. The terrified crew of the *Port Crawford* thought at one moment that the huge lump of metal was going to land aboard their ship, but it just missed the rail and acted as a fender between the two vessels.   The *Peeblesshire*, lying on the other side of the *Port Crawford*, lost some of her port backstays and sundry blocks, which came tumbling down on top of the half-deck, which in that ship was in the fore part of the midshiphouse.   The *Ditton* of course lost her spike bowsprit which was broken short off a few feet outside her figure-head.

Although steel spars, iron blocks and heavy wires rained down on the decks of all three ships only one man was killed. He happened to be out on the *Ditton's* bowsprit making fast the outer jib, and when the bowsprit went he was crushed and killed between it and the *Port Crawford's* backstays.

This accident happened in April.   The damages to the three vessels were made good, the *Port Crawford* and *Peeblesshire* sailed for their different destinations, and the *Ditton* went under the hydraulic cranes to load her coal cargo.   About the middle of July the big ship was down to her marks, and a pilot was engaged to shift her out into the stream, but once more the *Ditton* was too much for the pilot, and this time she charged into the barque, *Sardhana*, belonging to Weir & Co., and the German ship, *Anemone*.

At the official inquiry into the first collision it was found that the anchors of the *Ditton* were not let go as soon as the order had been given by the pilot, there being some considerable delay on the fo'c'sle-head.   At the same time the Court considered that it was an error of judgment to bring such a big ship into that crowded port with only one tug ahead.

The inquiry into the second collision condemned the pilot for adopting an improper course in moving the *Ditton*.

Two years later Britain's biggest full-rigger was nearly lost by stranding. She was on a passage from Newcastle, N.S.W., to San Francisco. Captain Davis ran into foggy weather on September 8, 1904, and the ship went ashore on the night of the 13th. However, the *Ditton* was re-floated without much difficulty, and continued her successful career.

During the last two or three years before the war the few remaining Leyland ships ,of which the *Ditton* was one, were managed by J. H. Welsford & Co. The old ship was sold to C. Bech & Co. of Tvedestrand, Norway, in 1911 and renamed *Nordfarer*. Soon after the end of the war her name was again changed to *Bragdo*. In 1921 she came home from Wallaroo to Queenstown in 85 days, and discharged at Liverpool, but on her way back to her home port she was wrecked at Boobjerg on November 2.

Carmichaels' "Talus."

In 1891, although they were not dissatisfied with the *Glaucus*, the Carmichaels returned to their first love, the full-rigged ship, and the *Talus* was launched to their order from a Barclay, Curle slip in March of that year. She was a magnificent ship of 2090 tons gross and 1954 tons net, and she could load 3359 tons of wheat or 3381 tons of coal. Like all first-class modern ships she had fore and aft bridges for getting about in bad weather when the maindeck was dangerous; her midshiphouse, also, was extended to the full width of the vessel, and its railed-in top made a handy place of refuge when the maindeck was under water.

With a topgallant fo'c'sle of 40 feet, a midshiphouse or bridge deck, as Lloyd's called it, of 36 feet, and a poop of 36 feet, the *Talus* in her superstructure rather resembled the French bounty ships. With their large carriers Messrs. Carmichael deserted the tapering main skysail yard, though in all other respects their ships were as pleasing to the eye as ever. I have been twice in port with *Talus*, and on each occasion I was much impressed by her good looks.

Captain E. C. Bennett, of *Thessalus* fame, took the *Talus* from the stocks. His first voyage was a very fine performance to get out of a full-built ship of the nineties. *Talus* went from Liverpool to Melbourne in 81 days; Melbourne to Newcastle, N.S.W., in 6 days; Newcastle, N.S.W., to San Francisco in 48 days; and from San Francisco to Queenstown in 113 days. Her passage across the Pacific was the best of 107 ships.

Captain Bennett made another very fine passage in 1893, when he anchored his ship off Monte Video only 41 days out from Cardiff. *Talus's* later passages, although they were nearly all good, were not remarkable, and she was rather overshadowed by the splendid *Peleus*, the last—and many sailors will declare, the finest—ship of Carmichael's fleet. Captain Bennett handed over to Captain Stenhouse in 1896, as the Carmichaels wanted him to take over the *Glaucus*. After commanding the *Glaucus* for half a dozen years the old skipper retired from the sea.

He was one of the most trusted of the Carmichael captains. After serving his apprenticeship with the Hills of Bristol, about 1858 we find him in Carmichaels' employ as mate and then master of their old wooden *Jason* in the sixties. His next command was the little *Medea*; then he had the *Thessalus*, one of the fastest iron ships ever built, from her launch until the Carmichaels asked him to take over the *Talus*.

The dispersion of the Golden Fleece fleet began soon after the turn of the twentieth century, and *Talus* went to W. Lewis & Co., of Greenock. During her last days she was chiefly in the W.C.S.A. trade, taking Welsh coal out to the West Coast ports and bringing nitrate home. On June 14, 1914, she left the Clyde in ballast for New York, and was posted as "missing."

"Vimeira" and "Pyrenees."

Captain Hardie of the Clutha Shipping Company was one of the last owners to remain true to sail; indeed Hardie's *Archibald Russell* was the last big square-rigger launched from a British yard for general cargo trade.

The following appreciation of John Hardie was given lately in the magazine *Sea Breezes* by one of his old captains:—

Captain John Hardie was the founder of the firm of Messrs. J. Hardie & Co. He must have been a seaman of the first order. I understand that all his sea-going career was spent in George Smith & Sons' City Line. He was their Commodore-captain, and took command of the first steamer. He started shipowning in the early seventies. His ships were all strongly built, well found, fast sailers, and good carriers of cargo, and this is the reason why the firm retained their ships up to within a couple of years ago, when other sailing ship firms had to dispose of their vessels long before, owing to their not being able to make ends meet. Messrs. J. Hardie & Co. treated their masters like one of themselves, and consequently managed to get all that was best out of a man. During the time that I was with them they had good loyal men in command of their ships, who studied their interest at all times.

The best known of Hardie's earlier ships was the beautiful *Talavera* which I have described in Vol. I. She was followed in 1885 by a 1500-ton steel ship, the *Albuera*, then with the nineties came no less than seven magnificent steel four-mast barques launched from various Clyde shipyards. The first two of these were the well-known sister ships *Vimeira* and *Pyrenees*. In 1891 Connell built four 2200-ton ships from the same lines. These were Hardie's *Vimeira* and *Pyrenees* and Clink's *Thistle* and *Valkyrie*, the first three being four-masters and the last a full-rigged ship. For full-built ships the *Vimeira* and *Pyrenees* gave a very good account of themselves, but they were lucky enough to be taken from the stocks by two very fine shipmasters—Captain D. Steven commanding the *Vimeira*, and Captain R. Bryce the *Pyrenees*.

Here is a description of Captain Steven, and Mr. Gordon, the *Vimeira's* mate, written by one of the ship's apprentices about 1907:

Two more accomplished seamen never sailed under square sails. Both were Scotsmen, and the captain was a lean, keen, pretty-mannered man, more like a clever sort of doctor to look at than a sailor. He had nerves too, so it was said; but he made little enough of them on many an occasion when there was excuse and to spare. He would come on deck in his oilskins, his long coat close-buttoned about his meagre body, and take a 24-hour turn of driving his ship through a spell of ugly weather without turning a hair.

Gordon, the mate, was a grey old bulldog of a man, roughened by 30 years of salt and sea, with a delicate-handed adroitness in his work that was wonderful to see in a man of so coarse a mould. In the half-deck we hated him, and the mate who is hated by apprentices is commonly a most efficient and exacting officer.

He then goes on to describe the foremast hands aboard the *Vimeira*:

One could not imagine a crowd better than that which the *Vimeira* carried at the time I made my first voyage with her. They were shipped at Barry Dock, and the story was that the "old man" had hunted them up one by one from the boarding-houses. They numbered 18, all good upstanding able seamen, in the best sense, and—what was infinitely more wonderful—all British. Twelve were Irishmen, splendid strapping fellows, and the best sailors imaginable, since they added to the mastery of their trade that good humour which one could not rely on in English sailors. It would make an ordinary mate's mouth water to see these fellows at work—say tightening up the gear in the first dog-watch after decks had been swept down; nine of them on a brace, and the line would go as straight as a bar as soon as the weather brace was let go.

They not only did their work, but they put a polish on it, and all with the most cheerful way about them. We of the half-deck gained as much as anybody by having them for shipmates, for those Irish taught us twice as much as the mates and the captain all put together, and the lessons were a good deal more pleasant too.

This was at sea. In Colombo they were given shore leave, and every single man had to be taken out again by the police, mastered by violence, and brought off to the ship under guard. Most of them were hoisted on board hugging trophies, the spoils of riot and destruction.

This description of a windjammer's crew half a dozen years before the war may astonish some of my readers, for real seamen were supposed to be almost extinct at that date.

On her maiden voyage the *Vimeira* sailed from Birkenhead to the Sand Heads in 92 days, and leaving Calcutta on January 18, 1892, arrived at Dundee 109 days out from Saugor on May 9. Her second voyage consisted of the following round: Cardiff, Rio de Janeiro, Newcastle (N.S.W.), San Francisco, Falmouth, Havre. None of the passages was anything out of the way. On her third voyage she crossed from Havre to New York, and made the passage from New York to Calcutta in 104 days to Saugor, and arrived back in New York on March 4, 1895, 99 days out from Saugor and 102 from Calcutta.

Her fourth voyage was from Barry to Colombo and the East India sugar ports of Sourabaya and Benjowanjie, then back to Philadelphia where she loaded kerosene for Hiogo, making a long passage of 190 days, and arriving Hiogo January 18, 1897.

Captain Jones was succeeded by Captain Mason in 1905, then Captain Stewart had the *Vimeira* from 1906 to 1909. On her last homeward passage from Caleta Buena to Dunkirk the *Vimeira* put into Queenstown on February 21, 1909, when 117 days out, having been in collision on February 19. The next voyage Captain Thompson took her out to Caldera from the Tyne.

"ROSS-SHIRE"

Photo Adamson

[See Page 132

"OWEENEE"

[*See Page* 136

"AUCHENCAIRN"

[*See Page* 140

The *Vimeira* continued to go her steady way until May, 1924, when she was sold by Hardie & Co. to be broken up.

Here are a few of her best passages up to the date of the war:—

1897	San Francisco to Antwerp		111 days
1899	Tacoma to Antwerp		115 „
1901	Astoria to Plymouth		115 „
1901	Antwerp to San Francisco		137 „

(127 days from Dungeness. This was her ninth voyage, and Captain Jones had taken over from Captain Steven. The *Vimeira* was only 20 days to the Equator and 52 to the Horn.)

1902	Newcastle, N.S.W., to Taltal		44 „
1902	Pisagua to Hamburg		93 „

(87 days to Prawle Point.)

1904	Iquique to Dunkirk		98 „

Captain R. Bryce, who commanded the *Pyrenees* throughout her life under the Red Ensign, had previously been mate and master of the little *Salamanca*. He has been described to me as one of the finest sailormen in the world.

On her maiden passage the *Pyrenees* sailed from the Tail o' the Bank to Sydney in 85 days, crossed from Newcastle, N.S.W., to Valparaiso in 39 days, went back again to Newcastle from Callao in 42 days, then sailed to Diamond Island from Newcastle in 58 days, and loading at Bassein called at Queenstown on September 7, 1893, 143 days out, and finally discharged at Bremerhaven.

On her second voyage she loaded Baltic pine at Frederickstadt and made the run out to Melbourne in 84 days from Tory Island. From Melbourne she loaded home to London, making the passage to St. Catherine's in 92 days.

Other good passages under the British flag were:—

1895	New York to Anjer		97 days
	Cheribon to Delaware Breakwater		93 „
	(91 days from Anjer)		
1896	Philadelphia to Nagasaki		136 „
	Tacoma to Queenstown		108 „
	(Discharged at Hamburg)		
1897	Hamburg to Sydney		97 „
	(90 days from Dungeness)		
	Newcastle (N.S.W.) to San Francisco		52 „

K

1898	San Francisco to Falmouth				120 days
	(14 days to Equator, 40 to the Horn, and 67 to the Equator Atlantic.)				
	Liverpool to Sydney				86 ,,
1899	San Francisco to Queenstown				136 ,,
1900	New York to Shanghai				121 ,,
	(Passed Anjer May 25, 88 days out.)				
	Shanghai to Port Townsend				45 ,,
	(22 days from Yokohama.)				

The *Pyrenees* loaded at Tacoma and sailed for Leith on October 14. She took fire on November 16, as described in Volume I., page 32, was beached on Manga Reva Lagoon on December 2, salved by two American master mariners, and brought into the American Registry under the name of *Manga Reva* in 1902. Under the Americans she made a number of good passages, the best being 102 days from San Francisco to Philadelphia in 1909.

In 1913 her name became of interest to newspaper reporters owing to the mutiny of her crew 200 miles from the Delaware Capes, when bound from San Francisco to New York under Captain Townsend.

"Thistle" and "Valkyrie."

All J. D. Clink's ships were built by Charles Connell with the exception of the *Pinmore*, and all were called after celebrated racing yachts with the exception of *Pinmore* and the *Fiery Cross*. Besides the two famous tea clippers of that name there was a very fast country ship named *Fiery Cross*. Clink's *Fiery Cross*, by the way, was a sister ship of his *Fiona,* both registering 1399 tons and being launched in 1878.

The *Thistle* and *Valkyrie* being full-built carriers could not maintain the sailing records of their predecessors, though they easily kept off the overdue list. *Thistle,* under the command of Captain J. McNeill, was lost on the Palmerston Reef in the South Pacific on November 8, 1905. Apparently at midnight on the 7th Captain McNeill altered his course so as to pass closer to the reef, and went below at 1.30 a.m. Soon after the change of the watch at 4 a.m. the look-out reported land on the starboard beam. Captain McNeill immediately hurried on deck, but before anything could be done the ship struck and became a total loss.

The *Valkyrie* was taken from the stocks by Captain Maitland, later well known as the commander of Devitt & Moore's training ships *Harbinger*, *Illawarra*, and *Port Jackson*.   On her maiden voyage Captain Maitland took the *Valkyrie* out to Calcutta *via* Rio, and loaded home to Boulogne.   Her second outward passage was a more testing one, being out round the Horn to San Diego. Coal was loaded at Cardiff, and on April 25, 1893, the *Valkyrie* was towed to sea by the tug *Black Cock*, in company with the ship *Terpsichore* behind the *Storm Cock* and the *Susannah* behind the *Knight of St. John*.   The *Valkyrie*, by the way, was a bald-header, with a 96-ft. mainyard, and a mainsail which her sailmaker boastingly declared to be the largest ever made on the Clyde.   She was also equipped with every kind of labour-saving appliance, such as halliard winches.   Like many of the big full-riggers built in the nineties she was very difficult to steer.   On her passage to San Diego the *Valkyrie* made a good run south.   When off the Plate she safely weathered out a pampero, which luckily gave warning of its approach by a vast bank of cloud on the western horizon; this put the sun to bed half an hour before his time.

A light easterly breeze held until four bells in the middle watch, when it fell calm and the stars were blotted out by the black pall of cloud, which was now over the ship.   The topgallant sails were now handed, after which for a few minutes there was a sort of deadly silence only broken by the swish of the water round her bends, as the ship rolled in the dying swell.   Then a dull moaning to the westward gave the officer of the watch notice that the pampero was upon him.   The order for the upper topsail halliards to be let go, and for the courses to be hauled up, was at once given, but before the men were above the sheerpoles the first breath of the pampero caught the *Valkyrie* aback, and there was a rush to the braces.   Luckily the wind came in short bursts for a while and it was not blowing at its full fury until all hands were laid out along the topsail yards.   It was a two-hour fight with the slatting sails and roaring wind, not to speak of the pelting rain, before the gaskets could be passed, but the ship had her heavy weather suit bent and nothing carried away.

When the *Valkyrie* got down to 50° S. Captain Maitland ordered that every sail should be reefed before being furled.   This was a very unpopular order with his crew, and they called it "the 'old man's' tuck." This is not to be wondered at, because it usually meant that the hands were twice as long aloft as they would have been if no reefing was required.

The *Valkyrie's* first passage round the Horn was made in midwinter, Staten Island being sighted on July 6. On the following day the *Valkyrie*, in company with the American ships *Sterling* and *A. G. Ropes*, actually ran past the Horn before a fair south-easterly breeze, passing more than a dozen eastward bound ships head-reaching under small sail. The splendid *A. G. Ropes* soon ran ahead of the *Valkyrie*, but the *Sterling* dropped astern. The three ships were to the westward of the Diego Ramirez rocks before the usual westerly Cape Horn snorter stopped their progress, and the *Valkyrie*, at any rate, had a very unpleasant time fighting her way to the westward. On July 31 Captain Maitland was able to test his ship against the *Tillie E. Starbuck*, one of the few iron ships sailing under the Stars and Stripes. The two ships were very evenly matched, for they were constantly in company all the way up the Pacific. *Valkyrie* eventually reached Point Loma early on September 20, and at noon the tug *Sante Fe* towed her to the San Diego anchorage.

After discharging her coal the *Valkyrie* sailed to Portland, Oregon, in ballast, and loaded grain home to Cardiff. Here Captain Maitland left her owing to illness, his next command in Clink's fleet being the steel barque *Calluna*, ex *John Carswell*, which had been built for J. Carswell by Connell in 1891, being afterwards bought by J. D. Clink.

The *Valkyrie* only just survived the nineteenth century, being lost in collision in 1901.

Law's "Ross-shire."

This ship was the only one built by Scott of Greenock for the Shire Line. She was a very handsome and a very powerful vessel with quite a respectable turn of speed; but she was something of a handful for a watch of ten hands, there being no aids to man-power in the shape of donkey engines, halliard winches and the like beyond four maindeck capstans. Neither had she any bridges to help her crew to get about when the maindeck was flooded, which was generally the case in heavy weather, for Captain Andrew Baxter was a driver and the ship owed her good passages more to his nerve and seamanship than to her qualities as a clipper. With her long lean bow and heavy stern, the *Ross-shire* bore driving to the limit that her canvas would stand. But she knew how to scoop up the sea over either rail. The most dangerous place in the whole ship when Captain Baxter was driving her was the half-deck, under the break of the poop, for the *Ross-shire* had a way of filling up under the break of the poop, and the half-deck was often two blocks with water so that the apprentices of the watch below were very nearly drowned.

On one occasion whilst the ship was running before a howling westerly gale in the North Atlantic, there nearly was a tragedy in the half-deck. Luckily all hands were on deck except for a sick apprentice. This boy, as it happened, was a very fine swimmer, and when the house filled up, by laying back his head and bumping his nose against the deck beams, he just managed to catch a short breath each time the ship rolled. In this way he saved himself from drowning, for the water took some time to run off, each sea filling the half-deck up afresh through the broken door panels.

Aloft, the *Ross-shire* was as strong as any sailing ship could be, all her masts and yards were of steel, and her rigging, except for purchases and spilling lines, of steel wire.

Captain Andrew Baxter took the *Ross-shire* from the stocks. He was one of Law's most trusted masters. When he was second mate under old John Peattie, the latter declared that he was a born sailor. As soon as he passed for mate he was made chief officer of the *Stirlingshire*, and two years later, when he received his master's ticket, he was given the command of the *Dumbartonshire*. This was in 1882. Five years later he left the *Dumbartonshire* and took the *Kirkcudbrightshire*, and he left her in 1891 for the poop of the *Ross-shire*. Here are a few of the *Ross-shire's* best passages:—

1891	Greenock to San Francisco	..	..	..	..	108 days
1892	San Francisco to Queenstown		..	..	..	114 ,,
1893	Calcutta to Lizard	..	..	..	..	..	103 ,,
1893/4	Portland, Oregon, to Lizard	..	..	..	..	106 ,,
1894/5	Portland, Oregon, to Queenstown	..	..	..	98 ,,

1895	Newcastle (N.S.W.) to San Francisco			..	..	58 days
1896	Sydney to San Francisco	..	..	..	..	64 ,,
	San Francisco to London	..	..	..	..	116 ,,
1897	London to Philadelphia	..	..	..	..	28 ,,
	Philadelphia to Hiogo ..	..	..	..	..	140 ,,
1898	Hiogo to Port Townsend	..	..	..	..	29 ,,
	Portland, O., to Queenstown ..	..	..	..	116 ,,
	Hamburg to Philadelphia	..	..	..	..	47 ,,
1899	Philadelphia to Kobe ..	..	..	..	..	149 ,,
	Moji to San Francisco ..	..	..	..	..	40 ,,
	San Francisco to Birkenhead ..	..	..	..	123 ,,

At the end of this passage Captain Baxter retired from the sea in order to take charge of Weir's Bank Line agency in New York.

Under Captain Baxter the *Ross-shire* never made a bad passage, and she also weathered out several fierce cyclones without losing more than a few sails. The first of these was on her passage home from Calcutta in 1893. She had left Diamond Harbour on January 23, and took her departure from the Eastern lightship at 4 a.m. on the 24th. After experiencing a very light north-east monsoon the *Ross-shire* crossed the Equator on February 2. The wind remained light and variable until the 12th, when the ship was in 11° 25' S., 86° 55' E. The barometer now began to fall, and by midnight it was blowing hard from the nor'west, and the ship was throwing a heavy confused sea all over her.

Captain Baxter was compelled to furl his royals, topgallant sails, mainsail and crossjack. At dawn the weather gave all the hurricane warnings; the dark sky was covered with torn, ragged clouds hurrying before the wind, the sea was very high and confused. Captain Baxter immediately snugged down to lower topsails, calculating that the cyclone was travelling W.S.W. A few hours later the wind shifted to the east-south-east and blew very hard, with fierce squalls and sheets of rain, whilst the sea filled the main deck to the rail; but the glass now began to rise, and as the E.S.E. wind flattened out the westerly sea Captain Baxter gradually made sail, and in the first twenty-four hours after the glass had started to rise the *Ross-shire* made 288 miles.

She ran out of the influence of the cyclone into that of the south-east Trades.   On February 27, Captain Baxter had another and much worse experience of a cyclonic storm.   At midnight on that date it was blowing fresh from the sou'west, and the ship was under whole topsails and foresail, reefed mainsail and crossjack with the yards hard on the backstays.   The barometer at 6 a.m. was 29° 28′ and falling fast, and a heavy black bank to the southward gave warning of what was to come.   At noon Captain Baxter furled his courses.   At 4 p.m. the upper topsails had to come in.   Four hours later the ship was brought to the wind on the port tack under lower mizen topsail and fore topmast staysail.   It was now blowing a hurricane from south-south-west with a high, dangerous, easterly sea and torrents of rain.   The ship lay down with her lee rail under water, and the wind was so terrific that no canvas would stand. The fore topsail soon went to pieces.   Captain Baxter eased away the sheets of the mizen topsail in an effort to spill the wind, but the lining along the foot of the sail had already begun to go, when at midnight on February 28 in lat. 26° 48′ S., long. 48° 30′ E., the *Ross-shire* suddenly found herself in the calm centre of the cyclone. At 1 a.m. the wind came away again from the opposite quarter, the N.E.   With expert officers, a good crew, and seven hefty apprentices Captain Baxter was able to get his ship braced up on the starboard tack before the wind reached hurricane force.   At 6 a.m. Captain Baxter's log recorded:

> Still blowing a hurricane with torrents of rain and a mountainous confused sea, ship with lee bulwarks under water, otherwise behaving splendidly.

The strength of the gale did not take off until four bells in the first watch, but then Captain Baxter bent a new topmast staysail, set a reefed foresail and fore and main lower topsails, and kept the vessel away on her course.   The *Ross-shire* was not entirely clear of this hurricane until noon the next day.   Captain Baxter reckoned that he had hit the cyclone on the recurve as it turned south between Mauritius and Madagascar.

The *Ross-shire* came through this second blow unscathed, but a few days later she came up with Brocklebank's *Majestic* which had sailed from Calcutta 20 days ahead.   *Majestic* was jury-rigged forward, had lost her main topmast head, and topgallant mast, crossjack yard, and lower mizen topsail yard.   When asked if she wanted assistance she held up a blackboard, showing:—"Crippled entirely and wishing to be reported all well."

Majestic had evidently experienced the same cyclone as the *Ross-shire*, but had not come through it so easily.

Captain William Couper succeeded Captain Baxter. Couper was a real old Scottish shellback, and as hard a driver as Baxter. After commanding the *Kinross-shire* for six years he had retired from the sea in 1898, but found that he was unable to stand shore life, and was soon haunting Law's office and begging for another ship. In the spring of 1900 he took the *Ross-shire* out to Sydney in 84 days, crossed from Newcastle, N.S.W., to Valparaiso in 41 days, and then went to Pisagua, by way of Caldera, to load nitrate. On Christmas Eve, 1900, *Ross-shire* caught fire, or, as some say, was set on fire; she was completely burnt out and finally sank at her moorings.

The Blue-nose Flyers "Oweenee" and "Muskoka."

Two of the fastest ships in the last days of sail were the Stockton-built four-mast barques *Oweenee* and *Muskoka*, which were managed by F. C. Mahon of Windsor, Nova Scotia. The *Oweenee*, which was launched in August, 1891, before the *Muskoka*, in October, 1891, was the larger of the two ships by 75 tons, and on a draught of 22½ feet loaded the following cargoes:—

3709 tons of nitrate	3721 tons of wheat
3713 tons of coal	94,578 cases of oil
17,062 bales of hemp	2,111,000 feet of lumber

Both ships crossed three skysails over single topgallant sails, which gave them a very handsome appearance aloft; with Blue-nose officers it goes without saying that they were beautifully kept.

The *Oweenee* was built for Captain Burchell, and the *Muskoka* for Captain Crowe, who were both Blue-nose sailors and great rivals in the matter of passage making. When the ships were planned Captain Burchell thought that he would make certain of having the faster of the two by giving the *Oweenee* an extra 8 feet in length, but he did not do this by lengthening out the bow lines, but by cutting the plan in half and lengthening out the midship

"MUSKOKA"

"MUSKOKA"

[*See Page* 136

"CAROLINE" EX "MUSKOKA"

"CAROLINE" EX "MUSKOKA"

Lent by Captain L. R. W. Beavis

[See Page 140

section. This, according to Captain Crowe, was a fatal error, and made the *Oweenee* slightly slower than her rival.

Captain C. M. Burchell commanded the *Oweenee* from her launch until she was sold to Lewis, Heron & Co. of the Thames and Mersey Shipping Company, when he retired in favour of Captain J. Jones. He was afterwards lost at sea when in command of a Canadian coasting steamer.

The following are some of *Oweenee's* best passages:—

1891-2	Middlesbro' to Port Pirie	71 days
	(66 days from Prawle Point. Arrived January 7.)	
1893	Yokohama to Tacoma	26 ,,
	(Cargo tea. Arrived September 27.)	
1899	New York to Sydney	85 ,,
1900-6	Downs to Sydney	78 ,,
	Newcastle, N.S.W., to 'Frisco	57 ,,
	Barry to Cape Town	48 ,,
	Dungeness to Los Angeles	125 ,,
	Dungeness to Portland, Oregon	126 ,,
	Beachy Head to Newcastle, N.S.W.	92 ,,
	Dublin to New York	26 ,,
	Astoria to Valparaiso	58 ,,
	Astoria to Queenstown	104 ,,
	Saigon to Falmouth	102 ,,
	New York to Shanghai	124 ,,

In 1912, under Captain Jones, she made the following passages:

Taltal to Astoria	63 days
Astoria to Dublin	103 ,,

In 1913 Captain Collins succeeded Captain Jones, and made the splendid run in ballast of 73 days from Dublin to Newcastle, N.S.W. A correspondent of the American magazine, *Sea Stories*, wrote as follows:—

In 1915 I made a passage from Liverpool to Sydney in the British four-mast barque *Oweenee*. . . . My experience in this fine big ship was one that I shall never forget, although it seems ages since I joined her in the fog and murk of the great Mersey-side seaport. We were what is known as a "happy ship." The officers were all very able men, and the crew was, I believe, above the average for a sailing ship at that time. Except for a rather dusty passage down St. George's Channel, and the usual weather that is encountered in the Southern Ocean, we had an uneventful passage.

The *Oweenee* carried on through the war until 1917. I received the following report of her conversion:—

I saw Mahon's *Oweenee* in Glasgow in 1917. She lay for month's alongside the ill-fated submarine, K. 13, in No. 3 Dry Dock, Govan, being converted into an oil-tanker for the Anglo-Saxon Petroleum Co., and is now renamed the *Ortinashell*. Her "gossamer," I expect, was sold as scrap. She has been stripped of every spar and even her bowsprit is gone.

Muskoka's passages as long as she was commanded by Captain Albert Crowe were never approached by any of her contemporaries. Captain Crowe came of a well-known Nova Scotia shipping family; his father was a shipbuilder, and four of his uncles commanded clipper ships. He himself was undoubtedly one of the best passage makers ever known. Whilst he commanded the *Muskoka* she was considered the fastest sailing vessel afloat. After he left her she seems to have dropped suddenly into oblivion.

This splendid shipmaster gave up the command of his magnificent vessel in order to settle at Portland, Oregon. In 1913, when surveyor in the Columbia River district for the San Francisco Board of Marine Underwriters, Captain Crowe was drowned in attempting to salve the barque *Miami*, which was stranded on Nehelan Sands. The *Miami* broached to and capsized in the heavy surf, and Crowe with 15 men was drowned.

During the first half dozen years of her life *Muskoka* was engaged in the Eastern trade either conveying kerosene from New York, or coals from Wales to China and Japan. Her best passages from New York were the following:—

New York to Shanghai	..	..	..	..	113 days
,, ,,	..	..	..	..	104 ,,
,, Nagasaki	..	..	..	..	114 ,,

Her best homeward passage in the early nineties was from Portland, Oregon, to the Channel in 99 days. On January 25, 1898, she arrived at Queenstown from San Francisco in 98 days. On her next outward passage she loaded steam coal at Cardiff for the American fleet in the East, and made the run out to Hongkong in the extraordinary time of 85 days. The American war with Spain was on, and the fleet badly needed coal, thus a race took place between a number of ships from the Welsh ports to Hongkong. This race was of course won by the *Muskoka*, but the *Metropolis*, which had sailed five days ahead of her, arrived at Hongkong on the same day, June 19, 90 days out. The third best passage was that of the *Renee Rickmers*, 93 days from Barry: then came the *Celtic Bard*, 107 days from Barry.

From Hongkong *Muskoka* loaded to New York, and made the run in 109 days. After this Captain Crowe kept his ship chiefly in the San Francisco grain trade, in which the *Muskoka's* passages were without rival. On January 7, 1900, Captain Crowe signalled the Lizard 111 days out from Astoria. In 1901 the *Muskoka* left Astoria within a day or two of the German training ship *Herzogin Sophie Charlotte*, the *Ardencraig* and the *Marion Lightbody*. Each captain considered that he had a flyer under him, and bets were freely laid on the result, but the other three ships had no chance with the *Muskoka*. She was off the River Plate only 50 days out from Astoria, but was then becalmed for nearly a fortnight. Her best run of the passage was 332 miles. She anchored off Queenstown on April 9, 101 days 20 hours from Astoria. The ships at anchor round her were astonished to hear a round of cheers aboard the new arrival. It was the *Muskoka's* crew cheering their captain on learning that none of the other ships had arrived, and that they had therefore won their wagers.

This was indeed a fine passage, for it was a season of unfavourable winds, and many of the fastest ships in the trade took three to four weeks longer than the *Muskoka*, and her race rivals were all over the 115 days.

In 1902, Captain Crowe's last grain passage, the *Muskoka* made a still better run to Falmouth, being 96 days to the Bishops, and the victor of the following race:—

					Arrived			
Henriette	..	left 'Frisco Dec.	16			Falmouth	March 31—105 days
Kilmeny ..	..	„	„	„	17	„	„	April 5—109 „
Largiemore	..	„	„	„	18	„	„	March 31—103 „
Clan Buchanan ..		„	„	„	18	„	Kinsale	„ 31—103 „
Anglesey ..	..	„	„	„	22	„	Queenstown	April 2—101 „
Clackmannanshire		„	„	„	24	„	„	„ 13—110 „
Hinemoa ..	..	„	„	„	25	„	Kinsale	„ 5—101 ..
Muskoka ..	..	„	„	„	27	„	Bishops	„ 2— 96 „

After this victory Captain Crowe handed over the command to Captain R. McDonald, who remained in the ship until she was sold to A. D. Bordes in 1908. At Dunkirk she was registered as the *Caroline.* Under the French the following are examples of her passages:—

1912	(Captain Gautier)	Iquique to La Pallice	..	91 days
1912-3	(Captain Le Mentec)	Port Talbot to Iquique	..	87 ,,
1913		Iquique to Dunkirk	..	104 ,,

My latest news of the *Muskoka* takes her to July, 1920, when she was reported in *Lloyd's List* as " on fire and beached" at Antofagasta, being still under Borde's house-flag. This was the end of *Caroline* (*ex Muskoka*).

Ritson's "Auchencairn."

The *Auchencairn* was the largest of all the ships which were launched on their sides at Maryport; she was also one of the fastest. The Ritsons ran her themselves until the end of the nineteenth century when she was sold to the Germans and renamed *Nomia.* Whilst under the command of Captain Nelson she made the following smart passages:—

1893	United Kingdom to San Francisco	..	..	110 days
1894	United Kingdom to Portland, Oregon	..	..	108 ,,
1894-5	Astoria to Queenstown	..	..	..	..	110 ,,
1895	Fleetwood to Portland, Oregon	..	..	..	116 ,,

On her return passage this year she left Portland in November, and arrived at Antwerp on March 7 after calling at Falmouth, and the whole voyage from Fleetwood out to the Pacific coast and back to Antwerp only totalled eight and a half months.

Whilst owned in Bremen she continued to maintain her sailing reputation. On July 10, 1912, she left Newcastle, N.S.W., for Antofagasta and was posted "missing" on December 18, 1912.

Haws' "Alcedo."

This steel four-mast barque, which was built by Royden, also made a great reputation in the San Francisco grain trade. Under Captain R. Coutts, who took her from the stocks, she did the following good work:—On her maiden passage she left Liverpool on November 10, 1891. Captain Coutts was obliged to put into Holyhead for shelter. He sailed again on November 14, cast off from tug *Black Cock* when abreast of the Tuskar on the night of

November 15, and arrived at San Francisco on February 27, 1892, 104 days out from the Tuskar.

In 1895 Captain Coutts made another splendid outward passage round the Horn, namely, Liverpool to San Francisco, 102 days, and leaving 'Frisco on November 28 with 3900 tons of wheat, he was back in the Mersey in 104 days.

The far-sighted Germans snapped up the *Alcedo* as soon as she was for sale. Curiously enough, her last passage before being sold was from Bremen to New York, and the ship had barely cast off her tug before it was discovered that the crew, which had been shipped at Bremen, were really landsmen—German emigrants who had paid a crimp for their passage. It was lucky for the *Alcedo* that she had a fine passage across, for none of these sham sailors could be induced to go aloft.

After being bought by the Act. Ges. Alster of Hamburg the *Alcedo* was renamed *Alsterschwan*. At the end of the war we find her in the hands of the British Shipping Controller under the name of *Barthold Vinnen*.

"Afon Alaw."

The last two ships to be built for the Windmill Line, belonging to Hughes & Co., of Menai Bridge, were the sister ships *Afon Alaw* and *Afon Cefni*, which were launched from the slips of A. Stephen & Sons in 1891 and 1892 respectively. The latter was lost almost at once, having been "missing" since January 5, 1894.

The *Afon Alaw* was one of the best known of the Welsh wind-jammers during the last period of square sail. It is not easy to estimate her qualities as a sailer as she made some very long passages, such as 172 days from San Francisco to Kinsale in 1901, and she also made some very quick passages. She certainly showed herself a fast ship under Captain Evan Jones. Under him she went out to Mejillones from Barry in 77 days in 1907-8, and, loading nitrate at Mejillones, arrived back at Falmouth on July 7, also 77 days out. One of her apprentices who served under Captain Jones wrote to me as follows:—

She could sail like a witch, but as her gear was pretty rotten, I doubt whether she was at her best. Coming up from Jervis Bay to Sydney we logged 16, watch after watch.

He credits her with the following passages:—

Cardiff to Port Nolloth, South Africa	..	..	34 days
Port Nolloth to Newcastle, N.S.W.	..	..	37 ,,
Newcastle, N.S.W., to Coquimbo ..	..	..	28 ,,
Coquimbo to Newcastle	..	..	54 ,,

In 1910 she made the poor passage of 121 days from Frederickstadt to Melbourne, but was only 28 days from the Cape.

Hughes & Co. sold her to W. Thomas, Sons & Co. in 1904 and she was still under the Cambrian house-flag when war broke out.

The "Dunsyre."

This big steel full-rigger was built for Potter Brothers by W. Hamilton in 1891.   Like most full-riggers of over 2000 tons, the *Dunsyre* was no flyer; however, in June, 1919, she arrived at Wellington from San Francisco only 38 days out, having made the run from land to land in 31 days.   On this occasion she was commanded by Captain Theodore W. Peters, a Sydney bred sailorman of only 23 years of age.   At the time she belonged to the Robert Dollar Co., of San Francisco.   They sold her to J. M. Botta, and the following is a description of her as she lay among a fleet of old windjammers in Oakland Creek, by a correspondent of *Blue Peter*:—

I spent much time aboard her, and saw the old light at Dungeness in my imagination, and the old Beachy light, and Owers light; and smelt a hard north-easter coming down-Channel with a hard ,bright sky, over a sharp, cold green sea.   But *Dunsyre* doesn't look as she looked when she knew those seas.   The paint hangs in great rolled-up flakes on her masts; an old ship-keeper was painting her rails with red lead, so that she didn't look altogether forgotten, but on the poop deck is nailed canvas.   All over her poop they've nailed strips of canvas—they've done a first-rate near job and they've painted it red.   They did it to save her poop deck, which was in very bad condition.   I was in her master's cabin, and in the mate's rooms, the steward's pantry, and everywhere else.   A sorry sight for a sailor; she has been all fitted up with electricity, and all manner of crazy newfangled gadgets—such as pipes for fresh water.   However, she still shows her breed.

After being laid up at Oakland she ended her days as a towing barge.

The Last of the "Drums."

I have said a few words about the end of the *Drumrock* in Vol. I., but she deserves a further mention, as she was undoubtedly one of the finest steel sailing ships ever built.   She was fitted by Ramage & Ferguson with a complete hospital under the poop and also baths for all hands, an unheard of luxury aboard a windjammer. She also put up some good sailing performances in her early days.

In 1894 she sailed from San Francisco to Tacoma, anchorage to anchorage, in 5 days 6 hours 15 minutes.   This was in November, at which date she was the largest vessel ever seen in Puget Sound, and she loaded the record grain cargo from Tacoma, namely, 5000 tons of wheat.   Three years later she raced the *Thistlebank* out to Calcutta. *Drumrock* arrived from Liverpool on August 10, 85 days out.   The *Thistlebank* arrived on August 7, 88 days out from the Lizard.

Drumrock's first commander was Captain T. S. Bailey, and he commanded her from her launch until 1899, when she was sold to F. Laeisz, and, under the name of *Persimmon*, became one of the best known of his nitrate clippers, some of her best passages in this trade being the following:—

1899	Ushant to Taltal	..	..	..	..	73 days
1899	Iquique to Prawle Point	..	..	..	79	,,
1900	Dungeness to Taltal	..	..	..	76	,,
1901	Dover to Valparaiso	..	..	..	71	,,
1901	Iquique to Dungeness	..	..	..	87	,,
1903	Dungeness to Valparaiso	..	..	..	75	,,
1903	Iquique to Scilly Islands	..	..	..	80	,,

In her old age, after forming one of Vinnen's fleet for a number of years, she came under the Canadian flag, and was converted to a barge at Vancouver in 1925.   Her job now was to carry logs from Queen Charlotte Island to the mainland mills.   Early in 1927, whilst being towed by the *Pacific Monarch* from Masset to the Powell River, she got on the rocks in Takuish Harbour, Smith's Inlet, Queen Charlotte Sound, broke her back, and became a total loss.

"Robert Duncan."

This steel four-mast barque originally belonged to Leitch & Muir of Greenock.   I have two notes with regard to her passages. On January 24, 1899, she passed the Isle of Wight only 78 days out from Melbourne—this was the shortest passage from Melbourne made that year.   In 1903 she took 101 days between Wei-hai-wei and Puget Sound, 90 guineas being paid in re-insurance.

About five years before the war she was sold to A. P. Rolph, and renamed *William T. Lewis*.   During the war she was shelled by the Germans and left to sink; but her wood cargo kept her afloat and she was safely towed into Bantry Bay.   In October, 1925, I received the following information from a Seattle correspondent:—

The old barque *William T. Lewis* is anchored in Lake Union about five minutes' walk from my home: she had been idle over a year and will ,I suppose, end her days where she is tied up.

The *William T. Lewis* was converted into a towing barge, owned at Victoria, B.C.

The Wreck of the "Dundonald."

The Belfast barque *Dundonald* will be chiefly remembered for her tragic end.   She was built for T. Dixon & Sons, but at the time of her loss was owned by Kerr, Newton & Co.

On February 17, 1907, she sailed from Sydney, N.S.W., for the United Kingdom under Captain J. T. Thorburn.   The passage went wrong from the start; contrary winds were followed by fierce gales: then came a calm when three sharks were caught, and her crew hoped to bring up a fair wind by nailing a shark's tail on to the end of the jibboom.   However, the charm failed to work, for besides a continuance of calms and head winds the compass began to behave erratically, so that it was impossible to be sure of the course set being steered.

At one bell (12.30 a.m.) on the 17th day out, whilst the ship was plying her way through a squall of rain, hail and sleet under small sail, there came a wild cry from the look-out forward, "Land on the starboard bow!" and then a second later, "Breakers ahead!"   The mate, Peters, and third mate, Knudsen, who were on watch, saw the land at the same instant, and immediately had the ship brought as close to the wind as she would lie.   Captain Thorburn and the watch below were then called.   By this time it was clear to everybody that the ship was embayed, and that she would not clear the land on that tack.   Captain Thorburn thereupon decided to wear her *short round*.   Though the hands on the braces moved quicker and pulled harder than they had ever done, it was no use.   Suddenly there came a tremendous shock and everyone realised that the ship had bumped over a rock.   Then whilst all hands were still hauling

"JUTEOPOLIS" LATER "GARTHPOOL"

[*See Page* 149

"ARDNAMURCHAN"

Lent by Jas. Randall

[*See Page* 152

MASTS AND YARDS IN A LONDON DOCK

By Courtesy Port of London Authority

[See Page 155

on the weather braces the ship struck again and again with such force that her crew were flung off their feet.

In the midst of the turmoil, with the sails flogging, their chain sheets knocking sparks out of the steel yards, the sea boiling and hissing alongside, and the ship crashing and thumping on the rocks, the mate's voice rose above the awful din, crying "Let go the topsail halliards." Down came the yards with an almighty crash, and the topgallant sheets carried away. The captain now gave orders for lifebelts to be served out, and the boats to be cleared away, and whilst the second mate, Daniel McLaughlin, and the sailmaker were serving out the lifebelts, the ship became wedged on the rocks, stern on to an overhanging cliff which was 200 feet high. Here she grounded and pounded whilst the tremendous surf lifted her up and thumped her down again. It was no use attempting to lower the boats, for in the pitch darkness all that could be seen from the ship was a mass of broken water showing grey against the dark loom of the cliffs. By this time all hands had assembled on the poop. Anderson, the man at the wheel, asked if he might leave it; the captain said "Yes," but he had scarcely let go the spokes before the rudder was struck by a rock, and the wheel spun round until it went to pieces. The ship had drifted in opposite to a hole in the cliff, through which the sea roared with the noise of thunder. Amidst the surging soapsuds around the ship huge pieces of kelp 20 feet in length were tossed hither and thither. It was hoped that the ship would remain together until daylight, but to everyone's horror it soon became evident that either she was settling down, or else the tide was rising.

The mate now advised that all hands should take refuge on the fo'c'sle-head, but this also was soon being washed by green seas, until presently a big one came along and swept everyone away. Only the most active members of the crew survived this wave. One man, a Russian Finn, managed to get ashore from the jiggermast. Two others got on to a ledge half-way up the cliff, by means of the mizen upper topsail yard. The only other survivors of that sea crawled up into the foretop. One of the apprentices, Charles Eyre, and John Judge, an Irish seaman, reached the fore upper topgallant yard, and succeeded in throwing one of the topsail spilling lines to the

L

Finn, who made it fast to a rock, and by this means the survivors, by working their way hand over hand were able to gain the cliff. That morning as soon as it was light, the roll was called, when it was discovered that out of twenty-eight hands twelve were missing, including Captain Thorburn and his little son.

The castaways were on Disappointment Island, which lies 5 miles from the north-west end of Auckland Island, the latter being some 180 miles south of New Zealand. The first day after getting ashore the survivors ate raw mollyhawks, and they were unable to get their matches dry for three days. A fire was then lit and never allowed to go out for the next seven months.

The *Dundonald's* foremast remained standing for 12 days, during which time the castaways salved as much canvas as they could, and with this they made a sort of tent, but with the advent of May and winter time in the Southern Ocean it was necessary to build a strong shelter from the constant storms of snow and hail and the bitter cold. They thereupon dug holes in the ground with their hands; over these they built a framework of sticks, upon which they placed sods of earth, and in these makeshift huts they managed to survive through the winter, their only food being seals and sea-birds.

From the start both the mate and the second mate were ill from exposure. The second mate recovered, but the mate died.

It was known that there was a food depot on Auckland Island, and the survivors of the *Dundonald* succeeded in making a canvas boat, pieces of clothes and blankets being sewn together by means of a needle made from a bird's bone with a hole bored in it. These were stretched over a framework of sticks and the resulting boat was successfully navigated by three men across the 6 miles to Auckland Island. They left on July 31, but failed to find the provision depot, and returned to Disappointment Island on August 9. A second boat was built in September, but this was broken up in the surf at its very first trial. A third boat was launched in October, and with Knudsen, Eyre, Walters and Gratton, crossed the 6-mile strait, but was smashed on a rock in making a landing. The four men managed to get ashore, but the piece of lighted turf which they had carried in the boat in order to make a fire was put out. They only had two matches, and it took three days to dry these before they could get a light from them.   On the fourth morning, after struggling through 15 miles of bush and scrub to the other side of the island, they discovered the depot, and also a boat. The boat, however, had no sails, so the undefeated castaways cut up their clothes and made them into a sail.   This action in such a climate sounds a desperate one, but I should explain that they found warm clothes in the depot.   Besides these they found ship's biscuits and tinned meat, but nothing else beyond an old pattern gun.   The depot had apparently been rifled some time or other of its tea, butter, sugar and coffee.

The day after reaching the depot an attempt was made to return to Disappointment Island, but the weather was so bad that they were nearly lost, and had a great struggle to get back to the depot.   On the following day, however, they succeeded in returning to their old camp.   Here they were hardly recognised, for they had cut their hair and beards, and clad in their depot clothing looked like Antarctic explorers.   The rest of the survivors were transferred to the depot hut on Auckland Island in two trips.   There was a piece of paper in the depot stating that the *Tutaneki* had called there on February 1, and that another Government boat would call in six months.   This put heart into everybody.   A flagstaff of sticks and branches was lashed together, upon which a home-made flag with the word "Welcome" upon it was hoisted.

On October 16 the steamer *Hinemoa* arrived and took off the *Dundonald's* castaways.   During their long sojourn on Disappointment Island the shipwrecked crew lived almost entirely on mollyhawks, sooty albatrosses, mutton-birds, whale-birds, and an occasional sea-lion.   Their only vegetable was the root of a plant called stilbo-carpa polaris.   They were very clever in making whatever they needed, such as ropes of grass fibre, shoes of sealskin, wooden spoons, wooden hooks, bone needles, and oars of the crooked veronica elliptica, the only wood on the island, with blades of canvas sewn round forked sticks.   A sou'wester served as a cup.

Previous to the *Dundonald* the following vessels are known to have been wrecked on the Auckland Islands:—*Minerva* on May 10, 1864, was the first of which there is any record, four survivors only being rescued in March, 1865.   Then came the *Invercauld, General Grant, Derry Castle, Compadre, Spirit of the Dawn, Daphne, Kakanui,* and the French barque *Anjou,* which was wrecked on January 22, 1905.   I think it was after the tragedy of the *General Grant* that the depot was placed on the Island.

The Loss of the "General Grant."

The *General Grant,* a passenger ship of 1200 tons, left Melbourne on May 4, 1866, with £10,000 worth of gold dust, 12 saloon and 33 first and second cabin passengers.

On the night of May 13 she drifted up against the perpendicular cliffs of Auckland Island in a calm.   The first crash carried away the jibboom.   She was then carried stern first by the current for about half a mile to another projecting rock.   This time she lost her spanker boom and rudder, and the wheel in spinning round broke in the ribs of the helmsman.   This collision canted the ship's head into a huge cave which was about 250 yards long.   As the *General Grant* was swept into this cave on the top of the swell the foremast struck the roof and carried away close to the deck.   The main topgallant mast followed it.   Large rocks also fell from the roof and stove in the fo'c'sle-head.

For the rest of the night the ship lay bumping and crashing against the roof and walls of this awful cavern, until at last her mainmast was driven through her bottom and she began to sink. The boats were hurriedly lowered, but were nearly all capsized in the surf, only 10 survivors, including the stewardess, getting safely ashore.   Captain Loughlin, when last seen, was waving his hand to the boats from the mizen top.   The *General Grant* sank 10 minutes later and took her commander down with her.

After being on the island for eighteen months the *General Grant* castaways were eventually rescued by the *Amherst* (Captain Gilroy) from Bluff Harbour.   Since that date many attempts have been made to salvage the treasure from the *General Grant,* but although a few pieces of wreckage were found no diver has ever located any of the gold.

One could hardly imagine two more terrifying wrecks than those of the *General Grant* and the *Dundonald*.   *General Grant* was hurled by the never-ceasing swell of the Southern Ocean into a gigantic fissure in the face of the Auckland cliffs. Although it was calm she was almost in a worse position than the *Dundonald*, which was slewed stern first hard up against the cliff, and became locked, as it were, into a dock of rocks. At first glance one is inclined to think that the loss of life in both cases could have been avoided, but in such shipwrecks the factors of darkness, noise, fatigue and cold weight the scales heavily against those who are fighting for their lives, and at such times a leader's judgment and sea-sense often prove to be at fault—one false step, an order hurriedly given, a boat hurriedly lowered, or a rope hurriedly let go, meaning all the difference between life and death.

"Garthpool" ex "Juteopolis," the Last Square-rigger under the British Flag.

This ship was built for the Calcutta and Dundee jute trade. Under Barrie's house-flag she was commanded by Captain W. Linklater. At the beginning of the twentieth century, by which time sailing ships had been driven out of the jute trade, the *Juteopolis* was sold to the Anglo-American Oil Company, and her adventures under the management of J. Macdonald will be described in another volume. However, I cannot resist mentioning here the extraordinary sugar passage of the *Juteopolis* in 1903-4. After leaving Iloilo on April 30 she was becalmed for two whole months off the Caroline Islands. For twelve days she beat about one little island in the Pacific making one mile ahead and two to leeward. During this time her crew anxiously watched the canoes of the natives, whom they suspected of a desire to capture the ship. At last, on September 10, the *Juteopolis* had to put into Honolulu for provisions and water. After this she continued to experience very light weather, and as her bottom had a fine growth of weed and barnacles her voyage lengthened out until her crew began to despair of ever reaching New York. At length an end was made to the dreary passage on February 11, 1904, by which time the ship was 287 days out. When the Anglo-American Oil Co. sold their sailing ships just before the war the *Juteopolis* was bought by George Windram & Son of Liverpool for £6500. At the end of the war she appeared under the name of *Garthpool* and the ownership of Sir William Garthwaite.

She later proved herself the luckiest, if not the fastest, of all the Marine Navigation Company's fleet, her greatest mishap being a rudder damaged off the Horn in 1926, when she was compelled to put into Rio for repairs.   She arrived at Falmouth on September 5, after the long passage of 70 days from Rio.   She was ordered to discharge at Liverpool, and aroused a great deal of admiration amongst the old salts on Mersey-side by dispensing with a tug and sailing up to an anchorage off New Brighton.   She passed the Bar lightship at 1 p.m., and although there was an anxious moment off Crosby when the wind backed and fell light, she carried her way over the ebb under a main topgallant sail, and finally dropped her hook in full view of an enthusiastic crowd.   She left Liverpool again on November 23, 1926, in ballast for Adelaide.   She loaded 4100 tons of grain at 41s., and, sailing from Adelaide on April 11, proceeded *via* the Cape of Good Hope and arrived at Queenstown on August 10, 121 days out.   Her port of discharge was Dublin.

It is interesting to compare this passage with that of the speedy *Lawhill*, which, coming by way of the Horn, reached Queenstown 121 days out from Geelong.   *Garthpool* sailed from Dublin on October 13, 1927, for Australia again, and reached Adelaide on January 13, 1928, after a good passage of 92 days.   After loading grain at Wallaroo, the *Garthpool* sailed for the United Kingdom on March 22. An attempt was made to proceed by the Cape of Good Hope route, but, after experiencing continual head winds, the *Garthpool* was at length squared away for the Horn.   She reached Queenstown on August 14, 1928, 145 days out, and was ordered to discharge at Belfast.

The *Garthpool* was commanded by a very experienced seaman who has already been mentioned in these pages; this was Captain David Thomson, amongst whose previous commands were C. S. Caird's last ship, the beautiful *Euphrosyne*, the fatal *Hinemoa* and the *Garthneill*.   He got 14 knots out of the old ship, and several days runs of 300 miles. He had the honour of commanding the sole representative of the British flag amongst deep-watermen.

Garthpool was wrecked at Boavista in 1929, and Captain Thomson died in 1948.

"Ancaios" and "Ancenis."

These two sister ships were large carriers, and thus had no speed. They carried 2900 tons deadweight on a draught of 20 ft. 8 in., and could load 155,000 cubic feet of timber. As regards ballasting they required 50 to 60 tons of ballast for shifting in dock, and 800-900 tons when under sail.

The *Ancaios* was managed by G. T. Soley & Co., but her chief owner was Captain R. K. Kelley. She was sold to John Porter who renamed her *Ravenhill*. He sold her to an Australian lumber company the year before war was declared. She was sunk by the Germans, and her crew had a very rough experience in the boats, which Captain Roberts, her commander, never got over. He soon afterwards went blind and died.

The *Ancenis* was built for J. Y. Robbins of Yarmouth, Nova Scotia, and her first name was the *Lillian L. Robbins*. For five years she traded to the East from American ports, then in 1897 Captain R. K. Kelley bought her, changed her name to *Ancenis*, and reduced her to a barque. She was sold to the Norwegians about 1909. On December 24, 1924, she arrived at Ardrossan with scrap iron, 100 days out from Port Natal, and was then broken up.

"Celtic Queen," "Celtic Race " and "Carnedd Llewelyn."

These were the last three ships built for the Celtic Line, and were typical steel full-rigged ships of the nineties. Though good carriers they were faster than most three-masters of over 2000 tons, but they were not fast enough to figure in the annual lists of record passages.

There was a still later ship, which I had almost forgotten, named the *Celtic Bard*, built in 1895. She, however, had a very short life, having been "missing" since September 19, 1898.

The *Celtic Monarch* as the *James Rolph* was laid up in Oakland Creek, December, 1924, and after a spell of service as towing barge, was scrapped in 1934.

The *Carnedd Llewelyn* went "missing" off the Horn in 1908 on a passage from the W.C.S.A. to the United Kingdom. She was commanded at the time by Captain Thomas Evans, but had only an acting second mate; also there was a great deal of ice and bad weather at about the time she would have been off the Horn. Another ship was posted "missing" about the same time, and that was Weir's *Falklandbank*.

From Punta Arenas came the information that a party of Tierra del Fuego Indians had found a derelict ship's boat containing two bodies of European seamen and some nautical instruments. Evidence showed that the occupants of the boat had starved to death. At the same time the British steamer *Devon*, which rounded the Horn on June 21, 1908, observed large fires burning on one of the islands in the neighbourhood of the Horn. These were taken to be of volcanic origin by those on the steamer. But afterwards it was suggested that they may have been lit by castaways either from the *Carnedd Llewelyn* or the *Falklandbank*.

Mr. Robert Hughes-Jones, the managing owner, believed that a collision with icebergs accounted for the loss of his ship.

Celtic Queen was sold to the Norwegians in 1911. Both she and the *Celtic Race* were afloat when war started.

"Banklands," "Bankleigh" and "Bankburn."

These were the last ships of William Just's Bank Line, the first and last being handy little three-mast barques, and the *Bankleigh* a steel and iron barque of under 1500 tons, which had first been known as the *Annie Speer*.

In 1896 the *Banklands* arrived at Valparaiso on March 15, 71 days out from Ardrossan, having managed to beat the *Bankburn*, which arrived at the same port from Barry in February, by one day.

I have no notes of any further passages of these little barques. The *Bankburn* was broken up in 1925. The *Banklands*, as the *Skien*, went "missing" in 1913 when carrying coal from Swansea to Luderitz Bay. The *Bankleigh* was sold to Norway, 1907, and became *Ceres*, later renamed *Iona*, which was scrapped in 1924.

"Ardnamurchan."

There is just one more ship that I should like to mention in this chapter, and that is the steel full-rigger *Ardnamurchan*, a

ANTWERP

Photo by Jas. Randall.

NEWCASTLE, N.S.W.

[*See Page* 157

LUMBERMEN: Puget Sound

very fine specimen of Russell's handiwork.   She was built for Hugh Hogarth.   Her deadweight capacity on a gross tonnage of 1718 tons was 2800.   She was a steady-going ship without being brilliant. Hogarth ran her until 1909, when she was sold to Genoese owners, and re-named *Speranza*.   In 1912 she was bought by the Norwegians, and her name changed to *Gunda*.   The Norwegians drove the old ship from Melbourne to Buenos Ayres in 42 days, and this was probably the best passage of her career.

Her last passage was from Rosario to Antwerp in the spring of 1924.   After this she was laid up for two years, then in 1926 she was sold to Dutch ship breakers.

CHAPTER IV.

THE CARRIERS OF THE NINETIES, 1891-2.—*Continued.*

Salarino—Your mind is tossing on the ocean;
There, where your argosies with portly sail—
Like signiors and rich burghers of the flood.
Or, as it were, the pageants of the sea--
Do overpeer the petty traffickers,
That curt'sy to them, do them reverence,
As they fly by them with their woven wings.

Salamio—Believe me, sir, had I such venture for**th,**
The better part of my affections would
Be with my hopes abroad.   I should be still
Plucking the grass, to know where sits the wind;
Peering in maps, for ports, and piers, and roads;
And every object that might make me fear
Misfortune to my ventures, out of doubt,
Would make me sad.

Salarino—My wind, cooling my broth,
Would blow me to an ague, when I thought
What harm a wind too great might do at sea.
I should not see the sandy hour-glass run,
But I should think of shallows and of flats;
And see my wealthy Andrew dock'd in sand,
Vailing her high-top lower than her ribs,
To kiss her burial.

(Merchant of Venice.)

The Sailing Ports of the World.

VENICE, the Queen of the Adriatic, was the greatest port in Europe throughout the Middle Ages.   Her hundred-oared, double-banked galleys ruled the Mediterranean in spite of the might of Genoa.   Her lateen-rigged buzo-nefs with their painted sails lorded it in the Black Sea and the Bosphorus in spite of the Turks' displeasure, whilst her lumbering galleons and heavy carracks knew the narrow seas and stormy waterways of

Northern Europe. Her merchant princes, wise in the ways of the sea and of greedy men, were the first to institute a Plimsoll mark on the side of their ships. This was a gaily painted cross usually of metal but often curiously carved.

Venice rose when Tyre, the last stronghold of the Phoenician merchant-seamen, fell in 1123 A.D. Her fleets became so numerous that, when the Fourth Crusade was organised, they contracted to transport 4500 horses, 9000 knights, 20,000 foot and one year's provisions to the scene of operations. Her merchants, like Shylock, required their pound of flesh. Besides their contract price of 85,000 silver marks for the hire of the ships, they claimed, when the Crusaders captured and sacked Constantinople in 1204, as their share of the spoil "a half and a quarter of the Roman Empire"—and they received it.

Although her neighbours, the stubborn Genoese and the hard-fighting Turk, trimmed her wings on several occasions, Venice maintained her position as the first port of the known world until Diaz rounded the Cape, and the enterprise of Henry the Navigator and his captains turned all eyes to the sunny port of Lisbon.

The Pool of London.

It was not until some 400 years after the death of Henry the Navigator that his mother's country became the leading maritime nation, and the London River the great shipping highway of the world. In the time of Charles II. the Pool of London was no more crowded than it is at the present day, and the wharves, which were mostly called quays, such as Galley Quay, Bear Quay and Crown Quay, and extended along the north side of the river for about 1100 feet between the Tower and London Bridge, were ample for the trade of London. Here in 1660 one saw perhaps half a dozen full-rigged ships flying the Red and Blue Ensigns, the East Indian gridiron, and a few dead and gone flags from the other side of the North Sea. The smaller vessels, coasters and the like, were mostly ketch-rigged, with square yards forward. Besides them, the gurgling tide of the Thames was covered with spritsail barges which were much like those of the present day; watermen's skiffs with wide sternsheets; and Thames passenger boats, called tilt-boats, because the whole of their after ends were hidden under a canvas tilt, much like that on a Cape waggon. These tilt-boats had two short masts with spritsails, the foremast being pitched right in the eyes of the boat, which possessed no bowsprit or headsail. There were also a few square-rigged cutters plying to and fro in the lower reaches of the river.

Two hundred years later, say about 1860, the Pool of London presented a very different sight. The yellow flood could now hardly be seen for the hulls of ships which lay head and stern in tiers, five, six and seven abreast. The city clerk, leaning over the stone balustrade of London Bridge during his luncheon hour, then looked upon a forest of masts and yards, from which, on a fine sunny day, a thousand sails would be hanging out to dry.

This forest of masts has since been replaced by funnels and derricks, and though the scene is still a busy one, and full of interest, its beauty has gone for the lover of the sailing ship. The old Thames-side docks, also, St.Katherine's, London, Millwall, East and West India on the North side, and the Surrey Commercial, and Greenland on the South, which in the sixties were crowded from end to end with the finest sailing ships in the world, now present a very forlorn appearance.

Crossing the Mersey Bar.

Though Liverpool shipowners hung on to their sailing ships for years after the great London firms had entirely capitulated to steam, the Mersey-sider is now roused to unusual excitement by the mere sight of a lone windjammer sailing into his port.

I wonder how he would have felt if he could have watched the scene on the Mersey River during the evening of Tuesday, January 23, 1866, when Pilot-boat No. 8 led the African Royal Mail steamer *Athenian* and eleven sailing ships across the bar into safety. A fierce sou'west gale had been raging for several days, and the sea was far too rough for pilots to be trans-shipped. Many of the vessels were damaged, and it was imperative that they should gain the refuge of the port. Thus it was that the pilot-boat, a sturdy little schooner, surging along under a spitfire jib, reefed fore staysail, and double reefed foresail, led the way over the bar with the distressed shipping in her wake. She was closely followed by the barque

Richard Cobden from Bombay, which had lost her fore topmast, then came the ship *Lord Dufferin* from Savannah, with sails blowing from her yards in tatters, and the African mail steamer *Athenian*, rolling rail under. After these came a procession of smaller vessels headed by the schooner *Persia*, each one under the merest rag of a sail.

The Mersey can produce no such stirring scene as the above in these days, and when the old *Juteopolis* sailed up to her anchorage in 1926 men gazed in wonder at such an amazing sight.

Antwerp and Hamburg.

The last sailing ship ports in Europe are those of Antwerp and Hamburg, which, since the beginning of the twentieth century, have been doing their best to filch the trade from the ports of Great Britain, and as far as square-rigged deep-watermen are concerned not without a fair measure of success. The photograph of Antwerp, which was taken a few years before the war, lends point to this statement.

The German has been wise enough to refuse a second mate's ticket to anyone who has not served four years in sail. In this way he has not only preserved his sailing ships, but has provided his seamen with the grounding which, whatever steam-bred officers may say to the contrary, is necessary before a man has any right to call himself a sailor.

Hamburg, then, is likely to be the last home of the windjammer, unless the enterprising Danes and Finns can supplant the great Elbe port with Copenhagen or Mariehamn.

Newcastle, New South Wales.

In the latter days of sail there was no more popular port amongst sailing ship crews and apprentices than Newcastle, N.S.W. Not even the picnics of Sydney or the music-halls of Melbourne gave more amusement ashore. The harbour for the 25 years previous to the war was always a "sight of fair ships"; these, as shown in the illustration, lay alongside the dyke, four abreast in about a dozen tiers, and with their bowsprits poking over each other's sterns, so closely were they packed together. Every sail-trained apprentice will dilate upon the delights of pretty Stockton, where the ships discharged their ballast; nor could he forget the glorious view out to sea from the Reserve.

In 1896, during the coal strike, there were more than 120 deep-watermen in the harbour waiting to load. During the seven months of the second Newcastle coal strike in 1905 there were even more ships in port, and ashore during the height of the strike there were often as many as 400 sailors in gaol. The ships in port at this time represented all nations and all rigs. Besides the big four-masted ships and barques from the Mersey and the Clyde, there were Down-Easters, three and four-masted schooners from the Pacific slope, a lone South Seaman, and the strangely rigged *Olympic*, which has been described as "a fore and aft schooner chasing a brig." Every one of these ships was waiting to load across the Pacific either to 'Frisco and Puget Sound or to the nitrate ports, and there was a great deal of betting as to which ship would make the best passage across the Atlantic. The race was won by the big Anglo-American oil sailer *Daylight*. Right up to the commencement of the war about twelve to fifteen ships a month loaded coal at Newcastle for the South American ports.

Table Bay in the Boer War.

In the old days it was no uncommon sight to see a fleet of 500 sail lying wind-bound in such a roadstead as the Downs. Captain Boultbee Whall, in May, 1870, counted 300 sail within sight of the Lizard. Probably the largest fleet of sailing ships that has ever been gathered together at an anchorage in modern days was one I saw in Table Bay during the Boer War. Besides vessels which were discharging in the docks, I counted over 150 ships awaiting their turn at anchor in the Bay, but even at that time I noticed that the greater number of these were foreigners, many of them being Frenchmen. I took a boatman round the fleet and snapshotted each ship, but unfortunately the films were too hastily developed and are not fit for reproduction.

The Puget Sound Lumber Port.

One of the very last refuges of the big sailing ship was the Puget Sound lumber port. The photograph illustrated in this book I found at the back of a Seattle hotel menu.

No doubt there are many seamen who can remember the early days in Puget Sound, when of a night time the crews of the ships used to gather round huge fires of disqualified timber, sing songs, tell yarns, and, where the apprentices were gathered, eat apple pies as fast as the Chinese cook of the woods could bake them.   Clams, crabs, and fish were also eaten in great quantities at these midnight barbecues.

This was in the early eighties, when Tacoma was the centre of the largest pine forest in the world, and Puget Sound, that ideally beautiful inlet, was hardly known to the outside world. In those days the Sound was mostly frequented by wooden ships with the Stars and Stripes at the spanker gaff.   These would tie up alongside a lone sawmill in the forest, and load the lumber by means of their own man-power.   Later, when the iron deep-watermen began to appear in the Sound, the great difficulty was the want of man-power, and you had to be careful not to straggle back to your ship in ones and twos, or you were liable to be sand-bagged in some quiet corner near a pile of lumber by a crimp's runner.

Seattle began as a sawmill village grouped round Yester's Mill, and, as the old Puget Sound chanty relates, was the "place to have a spree."   Seattle in the nineties was in truth a tough little spot, where you could lose your money in double quick time at faro, roulette, or stud-poker; where you could be shot for refusing a drink of fire-water; but where you could outfit and take steamer for the Golden North.   This was the lure that emptied the fo'c'sles of the sailing ships in the late nineties, and caused the crimps of Seattle and Tacoma to outdo their celebrated rivals at San Francisco and Portland in the matter of shanghai-ing.

"Earl of Dunmore" on Fire.

Amongst the West Coast ships one of the best known was the *Earl of Dunmore*, which I have mentioned in Vol. I as being somewhat notorious for the wild crowd of boys which she carried in her half deck.   This four-mast barque was managed by J. D. Thomson of Glasgow.   She was not a fast ship, being rather lightly rigged, and I can find no outstanding passages in her record.   She was a lucky ship, for she survived two serious fires.   The illustration shows her on fire in Sydney harbour.   On this occasion the fire was smothered by the simple method of letting the water in, but she had a much narrower escape when homeward bound from Melbourne to London in 1901.

On this occasion the fire was discovered when the ship was 900 miles from land.   She was in 37° 30′ S., 32° 50′ W., on March 21, when smoke was seen coming out of the main ventilator.   As soon as the after hatches were lifted, smoke came up in volumes.   After a difficult examination Captain Hay decided that the seat of the fire was between No. 3 and No. 4 hatches, and he gave orders for water to be poured down these two openings.   The fire seemed to have got a firm hold, for, in spite of the water, in a very few hours the smoke had found its way into the cabins and lazarette.   The usual method of boring holes through the deck was thereupon attempted, but when the carpenter removed the planking from the steel deck it was found that the latter was red hot, and the water vanished into steam as soon as it was poured on it.   Not only the smoke but flames prevented the crew from getting near the fire, and as the water seemed to be doing no good Captain Hay ordered the ship to be battened down fore and aft and all air passages to be closed up. This gradually took effect, and after two days the fire seemed to be smothered.   Captain Hay then had the hatches opened, and nothing but dead damp smoke could be seen below.

On March 27 some of the cargo was dug out of the hold, but no further signs of the fire were seen.   The *Earl of Dunmore* reached London on June 4.   On the cargo being discharged, a large quantity of it was found to be either scorched or burnt.   Many of the steel deck plates were buckled, some of the beams twisted, and any wood below, such as dunnage wood, completely burnt.   The ship evidently had a very narrow escape.   This fire is interesting as an example of a successful smothering of fire by preventing the admission of air.

The *Earl of Dunmore* eventually fell a victim to the war, being sunk in March, 1917.

The Famous "Howard D. Troop."

It will be noticed that nearly every ship which stood out in the twentieth century as a fast sailer and maker of quick passages

"EARL OF DUNSMORE" ON FIRE

[*See Page* 159

"HOWARD D. TROOP"

[*See Page* 160

"DALGONAR"

"PELEUS"

Lent by Thomas Carmichael, Esq.

[See Page 169

was commanded by a Blue-nose skipper. The *Howard D. Troop* was not only the last, but the largest and fastest of the fleet which from 1840 was owned and run by the Troop family of St. John, N.B. She was called after the son of the founder of the firm, who was one of the leading Canadian shipowners of his time. The ship was built by Robert Duncan under the superintendence of Captain Raymond Parker, who took command of her from the stocks. His maiden passage was one of the most remarkable ever made across the Atlantic. The Troops had accepted a time limit charter to load case oil at New York for Shanghai. Owing to the usual last minute delays whilst the ship was in the builders' hands, Captain Parker was left with very little time to reach New York. He sailed from Greenock on February 12, 1892, and after dropping the tug at Tory Island was held up for two days by head winds. Then when he was almost in despair of saving his charter, he was lucky enough to get a slant which he carried almost the whole way across the Atlantic. The *Howard D. Troop* anchored in New York on February 26, only 13 days 2 hours out from Tory Island, her best run being 330 miles.

Captain Parker then handed over his new record maker to Captain J. McLaughlin, who loaded 92,000 cases of oil for Shanghai. The *Howard D. Troop* seems to have been fond of running the time limit down to the last second. In January, 1899, she left Hongkong in ballast for Astoria. From Hongkong to Japan she took 35 days, and Captain D. W. Corning, who was now in command, began to despair of saving his charter. However, the westerlies piped up when the ship was off Yokohama, and she made the rest of the passage in 22 days, arriving at Astoria just before dark on the very day that her charter expired. On this occasion she saved her owners 5000 dollars by arriving in time.

Perhaps her best known and most successful master was Captain Ervine A. Durkee. In 1905-6 Captain Durkee made the run from Chefoo to Sydney in 49 days, then, loading 3500 tons of wheat at Sydney, reached Falmouth on May 11, 1906, only 82 days out. Another passage worthy of record was from Singapore to Manila in 9 days 16 hours. This was in 1904. The *Howard D. Troop* made the run also from Melbourne to Newcastle, N.S.W..

M

in 2½ days.   Her best passage was undoubtedly that made in September, 1909, when she sailed in ballast from Yokohama to Astoria in 21 days.   Previous to this passage the "Troop" had very nearly come to her end by fire, which could only be smothered by scuttling the ship.   Captain Durkee suspected incendiaries amongst his crew, and hauled the suspected men before the British Consul at Yokohama for examination.   However, there was not sufficient evidence to prosecute, whereupon the crew refused to work and demanded their discharges.   Captain Durkee was evidently glad to get rid of them, and he shipped Japanese for his record-breaking run.

Sailing from Yokohama at 6 a.m. on September 6, he made the Columbia River lightship at 8 a.m. on September 26, and anchored off Astoria at 2 p.m.   The best 24 hours' run was made on the 21st, being 351 miles with the wind strong at S.S.W.   Other runs worthy of note were 312 on the 22nd, 312 on the 16th before a strong southerly gale, and 297 on the 13th.   This passage was a day better than that of the little *Selkirkshire* made in October-November, 1897.

In 1912 after the death of Howard D. Troop, the ship was sold to James Rolph of San Francisco for £7250.   In spite of the fact that the ship's figure-head was a fine likeness of the late Mr. Troop, her name was changed to *Annie M. Reid*.

On November 25, 1912, the "Troop," under her new name of *Annie M. Reid*, arrived at Adelaide Semaphore only 37 days out from Monte Video.   I think her last passage was from Honolulu to San Francisco in 1921.   On this occasion she took 34 days, and afterwards formed one of the fleet of square-riggers which were laid up in Oakland Creek.   She was finally scrapped in 1934.

Gracie, Beazley's "Dalgonar."

When the well-known sailing ship designer and builder, T. R. Oswald, left the Itchen for Milford Haven, the Southampton building slips were taken over by a company called the Southampton Naval Works Ltd.   Besides some half-dozen small steamers this company built four large sailing ships.   The first of these was the *Agnes*, a steel full-rigged ship of 2199 gross tons, launched in January, 1891, for D. H. Watjen & Co. of Bremen.   Then came the four-mast barque *Crocodile* of 2555 tons, launched June, 1891; followed by the mighty *Dalgonar*, a steel full-rigger of 2665 tons, launched in December, 1891; and the steel ship *Annie Maud* of 2036 tons, launched May, 1892.

The *Dalgonar* cost £23,361. On February 11, 1892, she left Southampton in tow of the *Flying Serpent* for Barry Dock. Here she loaded 2677 tons of coke, and sailed for Port Pirie under Captain John Gray on March 21. The passage was made in 107 days. She then crossed the Pacific from Newcastle, N.S.W., to San Diego in 80 days with the usual coal cargo; left San Diego in ballast on February, 1893, and sailed up to Tacoma in ballast in 18 days, where she loaded 3936 tons of wheat; and sailing from Puget Sound on March 17, was off the Old Head of Kinsale 131 days out, and docked in the Herculaneum Dock, Liverpool, on July 27, 133 days out. This was considered quite a satisfactory maiden voyage for a full built full-rigger of her size.

On her second voyage she loaded 3903 tons of salt on a mean draught of 22 ft. 6 ins., and after being dropped by the tug *Gladiator* at 11 a.m. on September 10 off the Bishops, she arrived at Calcutta on Christmas Day, 1893, 107 days out. At Calcutta she loaded just under 4000 tons of linseed on a mean draught of 23 ft. 1 in., left the Hooghly on April 17, 1894, passed Agulhas on July 21, and sighted St. Catherine's on September 23, 159 days out. She discharged her cargo in the Alexandra Dock, Hull, where Captain Gray handed over to the well-known Captain James Kitchen.

Captain Kitchen was ordered to New York to load case oil for the East. He left Hull on November 3, 1894, with 2630 tons of linseed in bags and 90 tons of stiffening, was badly held up in the North Sea and Channel by light head winds, and, taking his departure off St. Catherine's on November 16, arrived at New York just in time for Christmas, being 50 days out from Hull. The *Dalgonar* sailed from New York on February 5, 1895, with 106,300 cases of oil, which, with 90 tons of ballast stowed in the after run, put her down to a mean draught of 22 ft. 7 ins. On February 21 in 13° 28′ N. 28° 35′ W., a fire broke out in the paint locker which was situated in the fore peak. It was, however, got under after an hour's strenuous work.

The *Dalgonar* crossed the Equator 23 days out, and arrived at Anjer on May 14, 98 days out. Finally she reached Yokohama on June 16 after a very good passage of 131 days. She left Yokohama again on August 29, with 4974 tons of cargo consisting chiefly of tea and curios, and arrived at Tacoma on October 7, 39 days out. Here she loaded 66,710 bags of wheat (3992 tons), and, sailing on December 10, made Kinsale Head on the morning of April 17, 1896, 129 days out. Here she received orders to discharge at Liverpool, where she arrived two days later.

On her fourth voyage she was very nearly destroyed by fire. She left Liverpool on June 27, 1896, for Sydney with a general cargo and 20 tons of gunpowder in the after hatch. She made a good run South and was about 15 days out when a man who was working at the main cross-trees putting on chafing gear happened to notice that smoke was coming out of the top of the steel mainmast (*Dalgonar* had her lower and topmasts in one and the topmast head was open). He immediately slid down the nearest backstay and gave the alarm. As soon as the hatches were taken off thick smoke came up. The first thought in everybody's mind turned to the gunpowder stowed on the after hatch; in spite of the suffocating smoke all hands threw themselves upon the boxes of powder, and the 20 tons were overboard in less than thirty minutes. The fire then had to be fought. Captain Kitchen was a commander of the good old sort, a man and a gentleman, who was very popular with those he sailed under. He was an old man of great experience, and all hands had every confidence in his being able to cope with the situation. By the time that the gunpowder was overboard one boat fully provisioned was already towing astern, whilst two others were swung out ready for lowering. The *Dalgonar* had a 2½-inch pipe running under her topgallant rail with a branch to which a hose pipe could be screwed at about every 20 feet of her length. The hatches were soon battened down, hoses connected up, and the pump set going. Meanwhile the carpenter started to cut a hole in the deck near the after hatch, but the half-inch steel deck underneath the wooden one was too much for him. The ship was within a few hours' sail of St. Vincent, and Captain Kitchen immediately altered his course for the island. That night, whilst all hands were fighting the fire, a tramp steamer stood by, but continued her voyage after receiving the *Dalgonar's* thanks as soon as it was light.

Amongst the cargo of the burning ship were paint, sheep dip, oakum and sundry chemicals. The smoke and fumes from these turned out to be very poisonous. On the morning after the steamer had left the *Dalgonar*, Captain Kitchen ordered the cables to be got out of the chain locker. The first man who went down lost consciousness just as he had hitched a line to the end of the cable. Another hand then went down with a bowline round him; he just had time to sling his unconscious mate when he too dropped. The pair of them were pulled out unconscious and it took some time to bring them round.

The weather was very light, and the *Dalgonar* took three days to reach St. Vincent; then whilst a donkey boiler was forcing steam into the hold, the crew braved the smoke and poisonous fumes below and discharged the cargo into lighters. This was a nasty job, and the natives of St. Vincent absolutely refused to face it. Each man of the crew stayed below for about an hour. It was all he could stand; and immediately on coming up into the fresh air he was bowled over at once and lay gasping like a man in a fit.

The *Dalgonar* had arrived at St. Vincent on July 18, 1896. Three weeks later the tugboat *Blazer*, which had been sent from Liverpool to her assistance, arrived at St. Vincent with two pumps on board, but by this time the fire had been conquered, whereupon the cargo was re-stowed, and on August 11 the *Dalgonar*, with her royal and topgallant yards on deck, set off for home in tow of the *Blazer*. The latter had a long hard tow, for it was not considered safe to set anything more than a lower staysail on the *Dalgonar*, added to which there was a head wind most of the way to the Channel. On August 24 the *Blazer* with her tow anchored at Funchal, Madeira, and, leaving the next day, was spoken in 42° N., 13° W., on September 1. Holyhead was made at 6 p.m. on September 7, and the *Dalgonar* docked at Liverpool on the following day. On November 28, after a full re-fit, the big ship once more sailed for Sydney, and again she caused her owners a good deal of anxiety, for, on December 6 she was spoken in the Bay of Biscay with her fore topgallant mast gone, and again on January 5, 1897, Captain Kitchen, in 1° N.,

27° W., asked the ss. *Zero* to report him with loss of sails and fore topgallant mast.   However, the *Dalgonar* arrived safely in Port Jackson on March 24, 1897, 116 days out.   She then crossed from Newcastle to San Francisco in 82 days, and finally docked in the Albert Dock, Hull, 164 days out from San Francisco.

The passages of Captain Kitchen's last voyage in the *Dalgonar* were as follows:—

1898	April	23	Left Hull at 7 p.m.
	,,	26	Passed Prawle Point 8.15 a.m.
	May	28	Arrived Philadelphia 5 p.m.—35 days out.
	July	2	Left Philadelphia (cargo 105,500 cases of oil).
	Dec.	15	Arrived Kobe, Japan, 166 days out.
1899	Feb.	8	Left Kobe (with 1500 tons of ballast).
	Mar.	25	Arrived Port Angeles, 45 days out.
	June	3	Arrived Tacoma.
	July	4	Left Tacoma.
	Dec.	13	Arrived Queenstown—162 days out.
	,,	29	Docked in Alexandra Dock, Hull.
1900	Feb.	27	Left Hull in tow for London.
	Mar.	1	Docked in South West India Dock, London.

Captain Kitchen now handed over his command to Captain Isbister, and retired from the sea to his home at Hoylake.   He died about twenty-five years later.

Captain Isbister commanded the *Dalgonar* for the rest of her life, and I have described his death, along with the capsizing of his ship, on page 18 of Vol. I.

As I have given the dates of the *Dalgonar's* first five voyages I may as well give those of the rest, especially as they give a good idea of the work of a large carrier in the dozen years just previous to the war.

1900			*Dalgonar* sailed from London for Sydney.
	,,	16	Off Beachy Head at 3 p.m.
	June	20	Arrived Sydney—97 days out.
	Sept.	7	Left Newcastle, N.S.W.
	Nov.	7	Arrived Tocopilla—57 days out.
1901	Jan.	12	Left Tocopilla.
	April	29	Arrived Falmouth—107 days out.
	May	4	Left Falmouth in tow for Hamburg.
	,,	10	Arrived Hamburg. (Grounded going up the river. Discharged 3956 tons of nitrate.)

1901	July	21	Left Hamburg for Sydney.
	,,	26	Passed St. Catherine's.
	Nov.	6	Arrived Sydney—108 days out.
1902	Jan.	25	Left Sydney.
	June	2	Arrived Falmouth—128 days out.
	,,	5	Left Falmouth.
	,,	13	Docked at Liverpool.
	Aug.	31	Left Liverpool.
	Dec.	17	Arrived Sydney with fore topmast sprung—108 days out.
1903	April	6	Left Newcastle, N.S.W.
	June	12	Arrived San Francisco—67 days out.
	Aug.	24	Left San Francisco.
1904	Jan.	19	Arrived Liverpool—148 days out. (Passed No. 3 Survey.)
	May	12	Left Liverpool.
	Aug.	19	Arrived Sydney—99 days out.
	Sept.	29	Left Newcastle, N.S.W.
	Nov.	9	Arrived Coquimbo—41 days out.
1905	Jan.	12	Left Coquimbo.
	,,	17	Arrived Antofagasta.
	Feb.	15	Left Antofagasta.
	June	21	Arrived Plymouth—126 days out. (Left Plymouth in tow for Antwerp Dock. Towage £80).
	June	26	Arrived Antwerp 8 p.m.
	Aug.	19	Left Antwerp 1 p.m. (2660 tons of coke, 650 tons ballast, mean draught 20 ft. 10½ in.).
	,,	21	Left Flushing 5 p.m.
	,,	25	23 miles South of Prawle Point.
	Dec.	1	Arrived Valparaiso—102 days out.
1906	Mar.	11	Left Valparaiso.
	,,	21	Arrived Iquique.
	April	28	Left Iquique. (1000 tons of nitrate and 200 tons of ballast.)
	May	18	Arrived Antofagasta.
	June	27	Left Antofagasta.
	Oct.	9	Passed Lizard 7.55 a.m.
	,,	13	Arrived Rotterdam—108 days out.
	Nov.	19	Left Rotterdam 10 a.m. in tow for Antwerp. (720 tons of ballast.)
	,,	21	Arrived Hamburg. (Extract from captain's letter: "She was as stiff as a church; would not, of course, have had enough hold in the water to do any sailing.")
1907	Jan.	7	Left Hamburg.
	,,	21	Parted with tug off Isle of Wight 11 a.m.
	June	27	Arrived Astoria—159 days out.

1907	Oct.	9	Left Astoria.
1908	Feb.	26	Arrived Kingstown (for Dublin)—140 days out.
	April	6	Arrived Liverpool from Dublin. (700 tons of sand ballast.)
	May	30	Left Liverpool.
	Sept.	10	Arrived Sydney—103 days out.
	Nov.	28	Left Newcastle, N.S.W.
1909	Jan.	18	Arrived Coquimbo—51 days out.
	Mar.	17	Left Coquimbo.
	,,	31	Arrived Talcahuano.
	June	18	Left Talcahuano. (Full cargo of wheat.)
	Sept.	12	Arrived Queenstown—86 days out.
	,,	26	Arrived Hull (in tow of tug *Blazer*).
	Dec.	2	Left Hull in tow. (700 tons of pig-iron ballast.)
	,,	4	Arrived Tyne 2.10 p.m.
1910	Jan.	6	Left South Shields. (Cargo of coke.)
	,,	8	Anchored Southwold in sou'west gale.
	,,	20	Passed St. Catherine's with light nor'west wind.
	,,	27	Arrived Seattle (172 days from the Tyne, 158 from St. Catherine's).
	Oct.	5	Left Seattle.
1911	Feb.	26	Arrived Queenstown—143 days out.
	Mar.	4	Left Queenstown.
	,,	15	Arrived Rochefort.
	April	25	Left Rochefort in tow.
	May	3	Arrived in Mersey.
	June	17	Left Liverpool.
	Sept.	24	Arrived Sydney—99 days out.
	Dec.	16	Left Newcastle, N.S.W.
1912	Feb.	10	Arrived Coquimbo—56 days out.
	May	13	Left Taltal.
	Sept.	5	Arrived Dunkirk 6 p.m.—115 days out.
	Oct.	4	Left Dunkirk in tow.
	,,	7	Entered West India Dry Dock. Passed Survey.
	Nov.	20	Left London. (Cargo 4025 tons cement, paper and scrap iron.)
	,,	23	Passed Portland Bill 2.5 p.m.
1913	Mar.	5	Arrived Melbourne—105 days out.
	June	2	Left Newcastle, N.S.W.
	July	25	Arrived Callao—53 days out.
	Sept.	24	Left Callao for Taltal.
	Oct.	9	Ballast shifted, vessel thrown on beam ends; in trying to launch lifeboat captain and three men drowned.
	,,	10	French four-mast barque *Loire* hove in sight.
	,,	13	*Loire* took survivors off *Dalgonar*.

"THE HIGHFIELDS"

[See Page 170

"WISCOMBE PARK"

[See Page 174

"PROCYON"

Lent by Jas. Randall

[*See Page* 176

"SPRINGBURN"

Lent by Forbes Eadie

[*See Page* 176

The old ship refused to sink, and after drifting for some 5000 miles stuck fast on a coral reef off the Island of Mopihaa, belonging to the Society Group.

The Splendid "Peleus."

The last of Carmichael's fleet was as grand a looking ship as any of her predecessors, and for a full-rigger of over 2000 tons her sailing records were extraordinarily good. She was launched in March, 1892, and was an up-to-date ship in every way. Like the *Talus*, she had a midship bridge, but this was just aft of the main-mast, whereas that of *Talus* was just abaft the foremast. *Peleus* had lifting bridges running the whole way from the break of her poop to her topgallant fo'c'sle, the forward one being over 100 feet long in sections. With a 'tween deck capacity of 1297 tons, and a hold capacity of 2948 tons, the *Peleus* was able to load 3396 tons of coal, 3405 tons or 33,040 bags of Californian wheat, and 962 standards of Frederickstadt flooring boards, with 600 tons of pigiron stiffening. I give her spar measurements in the Appendix. With a 90 ft. mainyard and 45½ ft. royal yard, she was square without being overhatted.

Captain George Shapland, who had previously commanded the beautiful *Siren*, took *Peleus* from the stocks, and was in command during the whole of her life under the Golden Fleece house-flag. When the *Peleus* was in Antwerp in 1903, four masters of large steamers, who had been apprentices with Captain Shapland in the *Siren*, came aboard to call upon him. Though they greatly admired the *Peleus* they refused to admit that she was in any way superior to the old *Siren*. The following are a few passages made by *Peleus* under the Red Ensign:—

1st Voyage—

Liverpool to Sydney	87 days
Sydney to San Francisco	55 ,,
San Francisco to Hull	112 ,,

2nd Voyage—

Swansea to San Francisco	124 ,,
San Francisco to Liverpool	110 ,,

3rd Voyage—

	Cardiff to Cape Town	.. ..	..	57 days
	Cape Town to Newcastle, N.S.W. ..		..	39 „
	Newcastle, N.S.W. to 'Frisco	..	..	72 „
	(At the worst season of the year.)			
	San Francisco to Falmouth ..	..	..	148 „
	(This was the worst passage of her career.)			
1897-8	Barry to Cape Town	.. ..	..	53 „
	Cape Town to Astoria	.. ..	..	94 „
	Astoria to Falmouth ..	.. ..	..	113 „
	Falmouth to Dunkirk	.. ..	..	2 „
1898-9	San Francisco to Falmouth ..	..	..	110 „
1899	Barry to San Francisco	.. ..	..	111 days
1900	Liverpool to Sydney	.. ..	..	86 „
1901	Frederickstadt to Melbourne	..	..	86 „
1902	Liverpool to Melbourne	.. ..	..	86 „
1903	Newcastle, N.S.W., to Valparaiso ..	..	..	42 „
	Caleta Buena to Antwerp	.. ..	..	88 „
1904-5	San Francisco to Liverpool ..	..	..	123 „

This was the ship's last passage under the Red Ensign, for in 1905 the Carmichaels sold her to A. D. Bordes. She was renamed *Adolphe,* and was broken up in Holland in 1923.

"The Highfields."

This fine Stockton-built four-mast barque was the last sailing ship owned by the famous Liverpool shipping auctioneers and valuers, C. W. Kellock & Co., who, in 1920, celebrated the centenary of their existence. Though Messrs. Kellock never owned more than half a dozen ships at a time, you may be sure that with their expert knowledge no ship sailing under their flag was anything but first-class in every way. Since the eighties they have owned the following ships:—*Childwall, Evelyn, Lord Canning, Gateacre, Combermere, Sudbourn, Adderley* and *The Highfields.* The latter distinguished herself on her maiden passage by making the best run out to Calcutta of the year. Under Captain T. Stevenson she arrived in the Hooghly on July 25, 83 days out from Liverpool. Messrs. Kellock only owned *The Highfields* for a few years, and before the end of the nineteenth century she came under the flag of Macvicar, Marshall & Co.

Her end was a tragic one.   On a passage from Cardiff to Table Bay with coals the Cape was made in August, 1902, in the worst of weather.   After many sails had been blown away Captain E. R. Dunham hove his ship to, but the weather continued so bad that he decided to run for his port.   It so happened that the German steamer *Kaiser* was lying just outside the breakwater blocking the road of the sailing ship.   In attempting to pass her, *The Highfields* fouled the steamer's cables and a collision was the result.   *The Highfields* sank almost at once, taking down with her the master, second mate, and 21 of the crew.

" Nal" ex " Lord Ripon."

Lord Ripon was the last ship built for John Herron's Lord Line.   She was launched from the Grangemouth Dockyard in January, 1892, and without a doubt was one of the finest ships built that year.   I remember seeing her lying in Antwerp soon after she had been sold to the Germans, and was much impressed with her looks.   She was a tall ship, crossing three skysails over double topgallant yards, and was fitted with the fashionable midship bridge connected to poop and fo'c'sle by bridge gangways, and, what was somewhat unusual in a British ship, she had a large wheel-house aft.

She was taken from the stocks by Captain W. Butler, a very tough nut of the old tyrannical type of shipmaster, some of whose exploits I related in Vol. I.   Here are a few of her passages under the British flag:—

1893	Calcutta to New York	..	..	..	98 days
1894	Barry to Rio ..	..	..	..	33 „
	Calcutta to Lizard	..	..	..	104 „
1896	Sydney to London	..	..	..	107 „
	(2507 bales of wool.)				
1897	London to Sydney ..	..	..	..	83 „

In 1898 the *Lord Ripon* was sold to the Rhederei Visurgis of Bremen and renamed *Nal*.   One of her best passages under the Germans was in 1904—New Caledonia to Delaware Breakwater, 88 days.

She survived the war, and after the Armistice was handed over to the French Government, who sold her to British buyers for £2750.   Her last owners belonged to Danzig.

She was lost off the Horn under rather mysterious circumstances on January 16, 1922.   Apparently during a gale off the pitch of the Horn she sprang a bad leak and became unmanageable.   With 15 to 16 feet of water in her hold she drifted past False Cape Horn, and grounded somewhere in the neighbourhood of Lort Bay, Hardy Peninsula.   Her crew then abandoned her, and eventually turned up at Buenos Aires early in February.   Meanwhile the ship had floated before the boat's crew were out of sight, and was taken by the current towards the Washington Channel.   The news of the derelict was not long in reaching Punta Arenas, whereupon the officer in command of the naval station ordered the mine-layer *Orompello* to go in search of the missing ship, which had not only been reported as "adrift inside the Hermite Islands," but "sunk off Wollaston Islands."   After hunting round False Cape Horn without success the *Orompello* went across to Romanche where she found an Argentine cutter, whose people gave the following account of the *Nal*.

They stated that they first of all saw her in Lort Bay apparently under sail.   This was on January 16.   On January 17 the *Nal* was seen to be heading for Bertrand Island, running before a north-west wind, and at about 5 p.m. it was noticed that she was aground off Hall Point.   On the following day the cutter's people boarded the derelict.   They found her lying on the ground with a slight list. As far as they could see nothing seemed to be wrong with the barque. They, however, were unable to stay aboard her for long, owing to the threatening weather.   Whilst they were running for shelter they declared that they saw the *Nal* float clear of Hall Point, with her head towards New Island.   Their last information about her was on January 20, when they noticed her disappearing behind Barnfet Island.   The *Orompello* then searched along the East Coast of Wollaston Island, but apparently failed to find any trace of the *Nal*.

After the failure of the *Orompello* to find her, other vessels took up the search, and the last news came from Lloyd's, who reported her as "lying sunk off Wollaston Island."

"Hawaiian Isles."

This Scottish rigged four-mast barque was built by Connell for A. Nelson of Honolulu. On her maiden passage she sailed under Captain O. Kustel for San Francisco from Swansea, and after vainly attempting to round Cape Horn turned tail and took the Eastern route, finally arriving inside the Golden Gate on October 12, 1892, 188 days out.

The *Hawaiian Isles*, however, was not a bad sailer, and made many better records. For instance, in 1909 she sailed from Delaware Breakwater to Honolulu in 128 days, and from Kahaualea to Philadelphia in 108 days. In the following year she was sold at Puget Sound for 60,000 dollars. This big price, which was almost 40,000 dollars higher than the market price of a 2000-ton steel four-mast barque at that date, was paid by the Alaska Packers' Association, who renamed the ship *Star of Greenland*.

"Dominion."

The last of Thomas's fleet was the Doxford-built steel four-mast barque *Dominion*. This ship registered 2539 tons gross, but was heavily sparred, and was expected to be as fast, if not faster, than the 1800-ton iron four-masters, such as *Principality*, *Metropolis*, and their sisters. Captain W. Meredith, who took the *Dominion* from the stocks, was a great carrier of sail.

The *Dominion* had a short and full life. On her maiden voyage Captain Meredith had trouble with his crew, who refused duty on the grounds that the ship was over-sparred and under-manned. It is probable that she was a heavy working ship and, as regards being under-manned, every sailing ship launched in the nineties was under-manned when compared to her predecessors of the seventies and eighties.

Here is a quotation from Stevenson's *By Way of Cape Horn*, which speaks for itself:—

I sailed in the British ship *Dominion* once from Barry to San Francisco, and I never did see such sail carrying. As for the main deck, you could not put your foot on it in bad weather without fear of going overboard. One night in the Pacific, about 45° S., in a southerly gale, there came a crack, and away went all three topgallant masts overboard, all through carryin' on.

The best passages in the *Dominion's* short record are the following:—

| 1894 | Start Point to Rio | .. | .. | .. | 33 days |
| 1897 | Swansea to San Francisco | .. | .. | .. | 118 „ |

In January, 1899, Captain Meredith sailed from Honolulu for Vancouver, and never arrived.   As an explanation for the *Dominion's* disappearance in the Pacific it was suggested that she had been insufficiently ballasted and had probably capsized in a squall.

"Trade Winds."

This big steel four-masted barque was built by Ramage & Ferguson for G. N. Gardiner & Co., of Liverpool, the owners of the well-known Newcastle-built full-rigger *Four Winds.*

In February, 1891, the date of her launch, the *Trade Winds* was considered to be the finest, as well as the biggest, ship ever built at Leith.   With a gross tonnage of 2859, she had a deadweight capacity of 4400 tons.   She was intended for the Calcutta jute trade, and was by no means as full-built as the usual deep-watermen of her day; it was therefore expected that her passages would be well above the average.   In this, however, I think her owners were somewhat disappointed.

Her first commander was Captain Ritchie, and the best passage made under the Red Ensign, so far as I know, was in 1892— Hamburg to Calcutta, 107 days, with 3100 tons of salt.

In 1897 the *Trade Winds* came under the house-flag of J. Joyce & Co., but two years later they sold her to D. H. Watjen of Bremen, who changed her name to *Magdalene.*   A little while before the war the ship again changed hands, and her name, going to Hamburg owners as the *Ophelia.*   During the war she was interned at Caleta Colosa.   After the Armistice she sailed to Bruges, being allocated to the French Government under the Treaty.   However, in 1922 she was sold back to the Germans, and was later broken up at Wilhelmshaven in the Imperial Navy Yard.

"Wiscombe Park."

This 2000-ton full-rigger was launched in November, 1891, for G. Windram & Co., of Liverpool, the owners of the "Scottish" fleet. She was a large carrier without any pretensions to speed, and I can find no sailing records in her history.

In 1909, after a passage of 150 days from San Francisco to Brow Head, she was sold to Chadwick, Wainwright & Co. She survived the war, and soon after the Armistice came under the flag of Bureau Freres of Nantes, being renamed *Edouard Bureau.* After lying at Rotterdam for some time she was bought by the Germans as a training ship for apprentices, and renamed *Greif.* This was in 1924. When outward bound to Adelaide in 1925, after experiencing very bad weather in the Bay, she turned up at Plymouth. At this time, I am told by those who visited her, her gear was in such bad condition that it was positively dangerous to go aloft. She was evidently given a thorough re-fit, and in 1926 we find her racing out to Adelaide against the five-masted Danish training ship *Kobenhavn.* The dates of the two passages were as follows:—

		Grief	*Kobenhavn*
1926	Sept. 19		Left Copenhagen
	,, 29		60 miles south of Land's End
	Oct. 4	Left Valencia, Spain	
	,, 5		Passed Madeira
	,, 6	Passed Tarifa	
	,, 10	Passed Teneriffe	
	,, 12		Passed Dakar
	,, 31	Spoken in 3° S., 33° W.	
	Nov. 10		Passed Cape of Good Hope
	Dec. 6		Arrived Adelaide, 78 days out. 68 days from Land's End
	,, 12	Arrived Adelaide, 69 days from Valencia	

The *Grief* loaded as one of the Australian grain fleet to the United Kingdom, which included most of the square-rigged deep-watermen still afloat. She sailed from Port Pirie on February 1, 1927, and on the passage to the Horn had a four days' gale, during which she was swept from stem to stern by tremendous seas. On the main deck everything movable was washed overboard. Her bulwarks were stove in, twelve stanchions being broken, and two of the life-boats, according to a newspaper report, were hurled 60 yards into the sea. Besides this two of her hands were swept overboard and drowned. The *Greif*, however, weathered out this gale, and arrived at Falmouth on June 7, 126 days out. She was ordered round to Belfast to discharge, but on her way grounded on the Twin Rocks. She was towed off, however, and safely docked at Belfast. Her owners were evidently not prepared for a large repair bill, and as soon as her cargo was out she was handed over to the Irish shipbreakers.

"Orion" and "Procyon."

Three-mast barques of 2000 tons were never common for the reason that the sail-spread was insufficient for a vessel 280 feet long. There were, however, three large three-mast barques which were built by Ramage & Ferguson to the designs of John S. Croudace which were by no means slow; these were the *Castor*, launched in 1886; the *Orion*, launched in 1890; and the *Procyon*, launched in January, 1892. They were practically sister ships, and sailed under the house-flag of W. S. Croudace of Dundee.

The *Procyon* will always be remembered for her smart maiden passage under Captain Dundas, when she arrived at New York on March 2, only 15 days out from Leith. On the death of Captain Croudace about 1895 the *Castor* went to G. Gordon & Co., of Dundee, whilst *Orion* and *Procyon* were bought by J. Wilson, of Dundee.

The *Orion* was wrecked in January, 1906: *Procyon*, which does not seem to have made any other exceptional passages, was sold to the Russians in 1910: and the older *Castor* went to the Germans in 1911 for breaking up.

Shankland's "Springburn."

Springburn was probably the best known of all the big 2500-ton bald-headers which were built between 1889 and 1893 by Barclay, Curle & Co. for R. Shankland's Burn Line. These ships were all intended for the jute trade, but before the end of the nineties steam had captured that trade from the sailing ship, and Shankland's "Burns" were relegated to the San Francisco grain trade, in which the *Springburn* made some astonishing records whilst commanded by Captain William Howard-Rae.

Although bald-headed, *Springburn* was very heavily rigged

"THISTLEBANK"

[*See Page* 179

"CEDARBANK"

   [*See Page* 181

"OLIVEBANK"

[*See Page* 181

"LYDERHORN"

[*See Page* 186

with a mainyard 103 feet long, lower topsail yard of 84 feet, and upper topgallant yard of 72 feet.

Captain Howard-Rae was specially noted for his skill in weathering the Horn when bound to the westward.   He always drove the *Springburn* well to the southward, thrashing her through it with all the canvas she could stagger under, and very often on his first tack to the northward he was able to weather the land, so that it was rare for the *Springburn*, under his guidance, to be more than a week off the Horn.   During a summer passage in 1896 he went down as far as 71° S., and was across to 50° S. in the Pacific in his usual quick time. Yet several vessels that were off the Horn with the *Springburn* were as long as six weeks trying to weather Cape Stiff.

On her first passage after Captain Howard-Rae had given up the command, the *Springburn*, under a master who was frightened of her, was battling off the Horn for 48 days, and took 145 days to San Francisco.

The following are some of her sailing performances under Captain Howard-Rae:—

London to San Francisco	103 days
San Francisco to Queenstown	98 „
Cardiff to Cape Town	37 „
(Cardiff to the Equator, 17 days.)	
Newcastle, N.S.W., to San Francisco ..	42 days
(On this passage she had 14 stowaways on board.)	

In San Francisco, as I have related in Vol. I., her apprentices in 1896 won undying renown by successfully shanghai-ing the notorious Shanghai Brown out of 'Frisco for a winter passage round the Horn.

Springburn was sold in 1906 to A. Dom Bordes & Fils and re-named *Alexandre*.

The sister ships of the *Springburn* were the *Janet Cowan* and *Kelburn* launched in 1889, the *Celticburn* launched in 1892, and the *Miltonburn* and *Otterburn* launched in 1893.

The *Janet Cowan*, which was the second ship of that name, had a very short life, being wrecked on December 31, 1895.   The other four were sold abroad when Messrs. Shankland started the Burn Line of steamers in 1907.   *Celticburn*, which was sold for £7000 in

N

1908, was later the auxiliary *Circe Shell*. *Miltonburn* became the *Goldbek*, and then the *Steinsund*. She went "missing" April, 1920. *Otterburn* went to D. H. Watjen & Co., of Bremen, and became the *Anna*. *Kelburn* was sold to J. J. King & Sons for breaking up in 1910. She was stranded in August, 1910, but re-floated.

" Fort Stuart."

This vessel, besides being one of the largest three-masters, was one of the finest ships ever built in Sunderland, which is saying a good deal. She was designed by Mr. Henry Claughton, the well-known Liverpool naval architect, and she was built by the Sunderland Shipbuilding Co. for Stuart & Douglas, of Liverpool. Captain J. H. Vanstone superintended her construction, and took her from the stocks.

In her midshiphouse she had a steam winch with donkey boiler and fresh water condenser: she had a direct steam windlass, and Hastie's patent halliard winches for hoisting and lowering the upper topsail and topgallant yards. Aft, the officers' quarters were unusually luxurious for a latter day sailing ship. The saloon was panelled throughout in solid oak, with pilasters, caps and mouldings.

The *Fort Stuart* registered 2433 tons, and had a deadweight capacity of 3825 tons. Unfortunately she had a very short life, being abandoned at sea in 1899.

Andrew Weir's Bank Line.

In 1891-2 there were no less than eight vessels added to Andrew Weir's Bank Line. The first Lord Inverforth began ship-owning in a very small way with one or two cheap secondhand barques, but so great was his insight into the business of owning and running ships that he progressed by leaps and bounds. In 1887 there were only three ships registered under his ownership: the *Anne Main*, the first *Thornliebank* and the *Willowbank*.

By 1895 there were no less than 25 ships under Andrew Weir's house-flag, and this number had been raised to 30 without counting 11 steamers by the beginning of the twentieth century. Some of these ships had been bought, but most of the "Banks" had been built specially for the firm. Amongst the bought ships were the celebrated

Abeona from the Allan Line; the Australian clipper *Nebo*, which Weir renamed *Forthbank*; the *Gantock Rock*, which had formerly belonged to Cornfoot's Rock Line; the *Dunbritton*, another of Allan's; the *Trafalgar*, a fast four-mast barque originally owned by A. Brown; *Collessie*, a 1500-ton steel ship built for G. Gray Macfarlane & Co., of Glasgow, in 1891 by Russell; the *Isle of Arran*, a 1900-ton steel ship built by Russell in 1892 for W. Jeffrey & Co.; the *Gifford*, built by Scott in 1892 for Briggs, Harvie & Co.; *Pomona*, another famous Allan liner; the ship *River Falloch*, built for W. D. Denny by Russell in 1884; the iron barque *Sardhana*, bought from W. & J. Crawford; the Dobie-built barque *Trongate*, another of W. D. Denny's; and the little iron barque *Mennock*, originally owned by Bramwell & Gardiner of London.

Of the ships with names ending in Bank, the greater number were built by Russell, but three of the finest ships in the Line, the *Olivebank*, *Cedarbank* and the *Falklandbank*, came from the slips of Mackie & Thomson.

There was a strong family likeness between all Russell's four-mast barques, and there was very little difference between the following seven ships:—

Comliebank	..	.. 2179 net tons	..	built 1890
Thistlebank	..	.. 2332 ,,	...	,, 1891
Gowanbank	..	.. 2205 ,,	..	,, 1891
Beechbank	..	.. 2154 ,,	..	,, 1892
Levernbank	..	.. 2242 ,,	..	,, 1893
Laurelbank	..	.. 2237 ,,	..	,, 1893
Springbank	..	.. 2237 ,,	..	,, 1894

With the exception of the *Gowanbank*, which was abandoned on fire on April 23, 1896, *Laurelbank*, which has been "missing" since January 25, 1899, and the *Levernbank*, which was abandoned dismasted in the Bay of Biscay in 1909, all these Russell-built four-masters were afloat in 1914.

"Levernbank" Abandoned.

The rescue of the ship's company from the dismasted and sinking *Levernbank* by the liner *Russia* in the Bay of Biscay during a gale of wind was one of the most gallant affairs in the annals of the British Mercantile Marine.

The *Levernbank* had rolled her masts out of her during a very severe gale in the Bay; first the foremast fell, and this was followed in turn by the main, mizen and jigger.   How none of her crew were killed it is hard to understand, for the heavy spars crashed through the deckhouses, and even through the deck itself; the crew's house forward was completely wrecked; and the donkey engine was smashed up by the falling spars so that it could not be used to clear the wreckage.   The weight of the gear to leeward gave the ship a heavy list; and the pounding of the heavy spars against the ship's side soon started her plates.   Though the crew worked desperately to cut the wreckage adrift, in the huge sea running and the furious wind the work was not only very dangerous but extremely slow. Then, when it was discovered that the ship was leaking, the pumps could not be manned because they had been wrecked by the falling spars.   Nor was there any hope of escape from the sinking ship by means of the boats, because they had been smashed up during the dismasting.

In this desperate situation the captain ordered rockets to be fired and tar barrels to be lighted as signals of distress.   This brought the *Russia* on the scene, but so wild was the sea that to launch a boat would have been courting death, and the liner could only stand by until the weather moderated.   All that night she kept close to the wreck, and soon after daybreak managed to launch a life-boat which got safely away from her side.   The weather, however, was still very bad, and the boat had all it could do to keep afloat.   It managed, however, to pull in under the lee of the *Levernbank*, but dared not go alongside.   However, a line from the *Levernbank* was caught and made fast, and by this means the barque's crew of 29 in number were hauled through the sea into the life-boat.   Nor dared the boat go alongside the liner on her return with the rescued crew, and once again it was a case of hauling the rescued and the rescuers through the sea by means of life-lines from the *Russia*.

The newspapers called it "an heroic rescue," and they were certainly right.   The Bay of Biscay has seen many fine efforts at life-saving, but none of them was finer than that of the *Levernbank*.

Weir's Small Barques.

Andrew Weir, who in his early days had been associated with Captain Barr of Hatfield, Cameron & Co., seems to have shared Captain Barr's partiality for the economical three-mast barque of 1300 to 1500 tons.   Five of these vessels were built for the Bank Line; the first of these was the iron barque *Thornliebank*, built by Russell in 1886; she was burnt on February 6, 1891.   Then came the steel barque *Hawthornbank*, of 1288 tons, built by Russell in 1889; this barque was sold in 1910 for £2250.   She was followed in 1892 by the steel barques *Fernbank* and *Oakbank* from McMillan's yard.   The *Fernbank* was wrecked on October 21, 1902, and the *Oakbank* on May 30, 1900.   The last of the five was the steel barque *Castlebank*, of 1656 tons gross; this vessel went "missing" in September, 1896, when on a voyage from Newcastle, N.S.W., to Valparaiso.

" Cedarbank" and "Olivebank."

These two big sister ships were the pride of the Bank Line, and though full-built had, I believe, the best sailing records of the fleet.   *Cedarbank* nearly came to her end on her maiden voyage, when, as I have described in Vol. I., she arrived in San Francisco with her Newcastle coal alight.   It seems that in 1892 there was a peculiar grade of coal loaded at Newcastle which was extremely dangerous in a ship's hold, being very gassy and ready to burst into flames if at all heated.   Also when a large amount of smalls and dust was loaded in the hot weather, an outbreak of fire was almost inevitable.   The *Cedarbank*, owing to the heroic efforts of Captain Andrew D. Moody and his crew, not only managed to reach San Francisco, but to so disguise the state of affairs aboard that the Yankee tugboat took her up to the anchorage from the Golden Gate at the very cheap towage rate of 70 dollars because he was unaware that she was on fire.

As soon as the anchorage was reached Captain Moody had his ship towed on to mudflats, and contracted for two tugs with fire-fighting appliances to pour water into the hold, and then pump it out again.   This took a matter of 36 hours, after which the vessel was taken to her discharging berth.   The damage done by the fire was then discovered: many of the 'tween deck beams and stringer plates were buckled and twisted, and a few of the shell plates also buckled. The ceiling was burnt through in about twenty-five different places, and a good deal of the deck planking was charred. The newspapers, both in California and Australia, made great fun of the tug captain who had failed to detect that the *Cedarbank* was a red-hot shell hiding a flaming furnace. The usual reporters had boarded the ship on her way up the Bay but, after taking a glance through one of the ventilating scuttles on the poop, they decided to return to their boat, and they showed remarkable activity in getting over the side. Although the hatches had been blown off the night before making the Farallones, Captain Moody and his gallant men had so battened down the flames and smoke that only a thin wisp of smoke, coming out from under the fo'c'slehead, was noticeable. The tug man had indeed asked the mate what was causing this smoke, but he replied nonchalantly that the crew had been burning out some paint pots.

After this inauspicious start the *Cedarbank*, under Captains Moody, J. A. Robins, B. A. Batchelor, J. Henderson, and J. Boyd, proceeded to make a name for herself as a successful trader. Some of her passages were extremely good for a full-built ship. In 1900 she arrived at Queenstown on December 9, 103 days out from Portland, Oregon. In 1901, under Captain Batchelor, she left New York on April 25 and reached Melbourne 84 days out. Whilst running the Easting down on this passage she did a week's work of 2007 miles, and actually averaged 316 miles a day for five consecutive days. This was followed by a passage from Philadelphia with case oil to Melbourne. After being towed for 116 miles down the Delaware River through the ice, the *Cedarbank* arrived in Hobson's Bay, only 86 days out, although the winds were not favourable in the South Atlantic. Her best work on this passage was 676 miles in 48 hours, which, I believe, was the finest bit of sailing ever done by the ship.

One of her best homeward runs was from Melbourne to Queenstown in 87 days with 38,334 quarters of wheat in 1904.

Captain Batchelor, besides being a great passage maker, was the stern enemy of unscrupulous boarding-house masters and bloodsucking crimps. He knew the inward truth of the lines:—

It's nursin', Johnnie, nursin', your achin', breakin' pate,
  An' cursin', Johnnie, cursin', the crimp that sealed your fate;
It's pulley haul, an' tackle fall, an' bunkboards bare your bed,
  With five days flood behind you, an' twelve months ebb ahead.

On one occasion at Hongkong Captain Batchelor refused to buy sailors from the crimps, and leaving port with only 9 A.B.'s in his fo'c'sle instead of 18, but with 8 hefty apprentices in the half-deck, he made the run across to Portland, Oregon. Here he resumed his battle with the crimps. The *Cedarbank* was hardly at anchor before they were alongside with their bottles of rye-whisky and tales of El Dorado, whilst a note was handed to the skipper stating that the port blood-money per seaman was now at £60. Captain Batchelor's reply was to drop the ship's anvil into the boat, which sank immediately. Her occupants, however, were picked up by the boats of the other crimps, who then kept a safe distance, but managed to entice two of the crew overboard. As soon as the *Cedarbank* had made fast to her wharf, two other members of the crew were arrested on a trumped up charge (neither having ever been in the port before) and taken into custody, whereupon the outraged skipper went for the crimps on the wharf. Two hours later he was arrested for attempted murder and assault. Before leaving the ship he handed over his revolvers to his officers with instructions to allow no man ashore on any pretext.

At the trial it was discovered that the sheriff who had arrested Captain Batchelor, and the crimp who had been assaulted, were brothers. Although the charge of attempted murder was dismissed, Captain Batchelor had to serve a month's imprisonment without the option of a fine, for ill-treating the sheriff's brother. On returning aboard after serving his term in prison he found that although one of his men had been lost, the mate had managed to capture another to fill his place, and had him safely locked up in the lazarette. By this time the ship was loaded and ready for sea. On the following morning, whilst she was towing to sea, the vindictive crimp and his brother the sheriff gave chase in a launch and ordered Captain Batchelor to return to port as his vessel was too short-handed to be seaworthy. They also held up warrants for the arrest of two members of the crew on the charge of stealing greatcoats.

It is almost needless to state that neither of the two men charged had left the ship whilst in port. The skipper put the sheriff off with an offer to inquire into the matter as soon as the ship reached the Bar, but there he paid his enemies in the old-fashioned style with his fore sheet, and, setting sail with a crew of 5 men and 8 boys, made the run to Queenstown in 99 days.

Three years later the *Cedarbank* again arrived on the Pacific Coast. This time her port was Vancouver. The boarding-house masters immediately received a telegram from the American crimps saying "Snout *Cedarbank*!" This was an order to put every difficulty in the way of her captain as regards getting a crew. However, once more Captain Batchelor was too much for the crimps, and he sailed as soon as he was loaded without paying one dollar blood-money, being the first captain for many years to get away without paying heavily for his crew.

In 1909, under Captain Henderson, the *Cedarbank* sailed from Santa Rosalia to Melbourne in 47 days. In 1910 Captain Boyd took the command, and, like most of the biggest of the British deep-watermen, the *Cedarbank*, during the last few years before the war, was in the nitrate trade. In 1912 Captain Boyd made the passage from Port Talbot to Antofagasta in 99 days. Loading nitrate at that port he was 106 days to the Isle of Wight, and arrived at Hamburg on March 13, 1913, 110 days out. On her next passage she took 111 days from Hamburg to Callao. It will thus be seen that, although her work was steady, she was no rival for the nitrate clippers of the "P" Line. The old ship escaped the submarines, as did her sister ship, and in 1919 we find her under the Norwegian flag.

The *Olivebank* also had a narrow escape from fire. Whilst in Port Guaymas in 1911 a fire broke out and she had to be scuttled. She was, however, raised and repaired.

Her first master was Captain J. N. Petrie. He was followed by D. Young, J. Henderson, J. Carse and D. George. I cannot find that the *Olivebank* ever equalled the passages of her sister ship, but I do not think any of her captains pushed her as hard as Batchelor did the *Cedarbank*.

In 1900 she came home from Melbourne to Falmouth in 87 days;

"ORANASIA"

Lent by Captain L. R. W. Beavis
Photo by H. H. Morrison

[See Page 187

"ORANASIA"

Lent by F. G. T. Dawson

[See Page 187

"ELLESMERE"

[*See Page* 186

"AUSTRASIA"

Lent by Captain Lee

[*See Page* 187

in 1909 she made a passage of 60 days between Santa Rosalia and Newcastle, N.S.W.; in 1913, after running from Callao to Newcastle, N.S.W., in 56 days, and back to Antofagasta in 52 days, the *Olivebank* was sold to the Norwegians. After that date she changed hands three times: in 1917, in 1922 when she fetched 85,000 kroner; and in 1924 when she came under the flag of Captain G. Erikson. The Norwegians called her the *Caledonia*, but Captain Erikson, as was his custom with all his ships, put her old name back on her stern.

In 1925 she sailed from Melbourne to Queenstown in 113 days; on April 24, 1926, she left Melbourne for the Seychelle Islands, having been chartered to load guano to New Zealand. Failing to round the Leeuwin, her captain turned round and navigated his ship through the Torres Straits, arriving at Mahe on June 27, 64 days out. The *Olivebank* is said to have been the largest sailing ship that ever went through the Torres Straits. Leaving Port Victoria, Mahe, on August 16, she reached Dunedin on November 13, 89 days out.

The *Olivebank* was employed in the South Australian grain trade until outbreak of last war. She was sunk by a mine in the North Sea in September, 1939.

"Beechbank's" Dismasting.

The *Beechbank*, the other four-master built for Weir in 1892, was sold to the Norwegians just before the war.

On October 18, 1915, she left Mejillones with nitrate for Copenhagen. On January 18, 1916, when the ship was in 60° N., 9° W., she was boarded by a British armed liner. The boarding officer, with an armed guard, gave the captain orders to take his ship to Kirkwall for the usual examination. That afternoon it blew very hard, the wind swinging round from S.S.E. to West from which direction it continued to blow until the 21st. On this date the foremast carried away below the top. On the next day, soon after midnight, the main topmast, with all spars above the topsail yards came crashing down on the deck, breaking holes in it so that the water got to the cargo. An hour or so later the mizen topmast carried away just below the doubling, and did still worse damage

on deck, besides smashing the lifeboats.   At daylight next morning
the Muckle Flugga lighthouse, Shetland, was sighted, whereupon a
distress signal was hoisted.   The weather still continued very bad
until the 24th, when the ship was in 61° 23′ N., 2° 5′ E.   Another
British armed liner then hove in sight and offered to tow the lame
duck into Lerwick harbour.   There was, however, too heavy a sea
running for a line to be passed between the two ships, whereupon
the steamer stood by through the night.   After some clever seamanship a tow rope was made fast about noon on the 25th, and the
Beechbank was successfully anchored in Lerwick harbour during
the morning of January 27.   She caused a great deal of excitement
in Lerwick, whose inhabitants at first thought that she had been
battling with the Hun.   About a month later the dismasted ship
was towed to London.   She was still afloat in 1922 under the
name of *Stoveren*, but was scrapped in 1923.

"Windermere" and "Lyderhorn."

The *Windermere*, which, as I have already stated, was built
at Milford Haven by T. R. Oswald, was the largest ship built for
Fisher & Sprott, the next in size to her being the iron four-mast
barque *Ellesmere*, which was built by Oswald at Southampton in
1886.   The *Ellesmere* registered 2530 tons, but the *Windermere*
was 300 tons larger.   Both these two ships were bought by the
Germans before the end of the nineteenth century.   The *Ellesmere*
became the *Schiffbek* of Hamburg, under the flag of Knohr &
Burchard, whilst the *Windermere* became one of the Rickmers' fleet,
and was renamed *Paul Rickmers*.   She has been "missing" since
July, 1902.

Lyderhorn was the last of the De Wolf's famous fleet.   She will
be remembered for a very long and adventurous passage from
Liverpool to Vancouver.   The first worry for her owners came with a
telegram from Pernambuco, where it appeared she had arrived
with most of her crew in irons.   These men, who had broached the
liquor in her cargo, and had been drunk for days, were exchanged
for dagos.   The new hands mutinied off the Horn, and a fight took
place, in which several men were injured.   One of them was so bad
that when the ship arrived after a very long passage he was expected

to die in hospital, whereupon the officer who had hurt him thought it wise to disappear.

The *Lyderhorn* was sold to the Germans in 1910 for £5500 and renamed *Jersbek*. After the war she was allotted to the French Government and was converted into a hulk.

"Rathdown" and "Howth."

These two big carriers were built in 1891-2 by Workman, Clark & Co. for Sir R. Martin of Dublin, the *Rathdown* being a full-rigged ship, and the *Howth* a four-master. Neither of them figured amongst the clippers of the nineties; for instance, in 1903 *Howth* left San Francisco on October 12, a day behind the *California*, the latter arrived at her port of call on February 12, 125 days out, but the *Howth* did not reach Tor Bay until May 1, being then 201 days out.

Rathdown has been "missing" since October 4, 1900. *Howth* was sold to J. Edgar & Co. in 1904, and sailed under their house-flag until 1913, when she was sold to Windram & Co. During 1914-18 war she was converted into the tanker *Horn Shell*, and was scrapped after that war.

"Austrasia" and "Oranasia."

These two sister ships were very fine examples of Russell's work both in design and build. Colonel Goffey, who was one of those owners who took a personal interest in his ships, and stinted them in nothing, watched their construction and fitting-out with an eagle eye. Though their measurements were the same, the *Austrasia*, which was launched in March, three months ahead of *Oranasia*, registered 12 tons more than her sister ship. Though large carriers they were heavily rigged. The fore, main and crossjack yards were 106 feet long and weighed $7\frac{1}{2}$ tons, the lower topsail yards were 95 feet long, upper topsail yards 90 feet, lower topgallant yards 75 feet, upper topgallant yards 66 feet, and royal yards 50 feet.

Captain Parkes of Seaforth, who had previously commanded the tea clipper *Guinevere*, *Baron Aberdare*, and *Eurasia*, and was one of the most experienced and also most popular skippers afloat, took the *Austrasia* from the stocks. She was fitted out in the James Watt Dock, Greenock, alongside of the unlucky *Thracian*. It will be remembered that this vessel capsized whilst being towed round to Liverpool in ballast by the *Sarah Joliffe*, the runners who formed her crew being drowned. The *Austrasia* was also towed round to Liverpool from the Clyde, and loaded a cargo of salt for Calcutta. The sailing day happened to be a Friday at the end of May, 1892. Colonel Goffey asked Captain Parkes if he minded sailing on that day, but the captain treated such superstition with scorn. Soon after the ship had cast off her tug abreast of the Tuskar tapping was heard by the fore hatch, and on the hatch being opened six stowaways appeared on deck.

All went well with the *Austrasia* until July 25, when she was 56 days out, and running her Easting down in 38° S., 13° W. The barometer was very low, and the ship was running before a moderate nor'west wind under six topsails and foresail. At 8 p.m. the wind shifted in a hurricane squall from the S.E. which caught the ship flat aback. Luckily she paid off before any damage was done; sail was then reduced to three lower topsails and storm staysails, under which the ship was hove to.

All night it blew very hard with a tremendous high sea. At 8 bells in the morning whilst the watch was being changed, it was noticed that the lee clew of the mizen upper topgallant sail was adrift. The second mate ordered some hands aloft to make it fast. Luckily the men were not above the sheerpole when the mizen topmast, without any warning, buckled over and crashed to leeward, dragging the jigger topmast with it. This disaster left the upper yards on the main swinging about uncontrolled by the braces. Hands were at once sent up the main to reeve off preventer braces, but before they had reached their dangerous job the main royal yard broke its parrel and dived over the side. Whilst the men were on the main upper topsail yard, the fore topmast suddenly bent over to leeward. This carried away the fore upper topsail brace, the runner of which swept one of the men off the main upper topsail yardarm. This man had wound a couple of turns of a gasket round his body for safety; for a few seconds he swung from the yardarm, and then, as the gasket gave, he fell into the sea. He fell amongst the wreckage over the side, and just when all hands were wondering what could be done, as the ship's boats had been smashed to pieces by the falling spars, he crawled up on to the poop apparently unhurt, though it was afterwards found that he had severe internal injuries.

Soon after this, although preventer braces had been successfully rigged out from the main topsail and topgallant yards, the main topmast went over in its turn, and by 11 a.m. the ship lay helpless, whilst the south-east gale was blowing harder than ever. The main topmast broke below the doubling; the topgallant and royal masts with their yards did not go overboard, however, but remained inboard entangled in the rigging. The fore topmast broke just above the lower masthead, and in its fall crashed down on to the topgallant fo'c'sle; the topsail yards landed across the fo'c'sle-head, and the topgallant mast went right through the deck. But the most dangerous part of the wreckage was the mizen gear, which was pounding heavily alongside with every roll of the ship; the lower mast cap had broken off with the topmast, and these, being jammed in the collar of the mizen stay, prevented the wreckage from going clear.

Captain Parkes was a fine leader of men, and on such an occasion his great experience wasted no time in doing the wrong thing. He gave orders for the mizen gear to be cut away without delay, but in order to free the mast the stay had to be cut through, a dangerous and difficult task, which Mr. Bygot, the third mate, and an A.B. named Charles Turner, volunteered to do. Going aloft on the shaky mast with axes, they managed somehow to cut through the heavy wire of the mizen stay; this allowed the wreckage to go overboard, and with the upper rigging and other gear already cut adrift the tangle of spars over the side then drifted clear of the ship.

The heavy weather continued until July 28, by which time the decks had been cleared up. Captain Parkes now steered for Rio, under his courses, main lower topsail, and staysails. The *Austrasia* carried a fresh south-east wind right up to the Rio anchorage, where she arrived on August 18. Here Captain Parkes, on finding that he could get no help from the Brazilians, proceeded to jury rig his ship. This took six weeks, and at the beginning of October the *Austrasia* set off for the Mersey under a rig which consisted of three courses, a lower topsail and topgallant sail at the fore, two topsails at the main, and a jib-headed topsail at the mizen with lower topmast and middle staysails between the fore, main, and mizen, three headsails, jigger staysail, and jib-headed spanker; with this small sail plan she reached the Mersey on December 18, 1892, 75 days out. She never met a single ship from the latitude of the Line until midnight on December 17, when she was picked up by a tug off the North Arklow Lightship. The night was pitch dark, and it was raining in torrents, so that the tug-master never noticed that he was picking up a lame duck, and he therefore contracted for the usual towage rates. What he said at daylight when he saw what he had got hold of can well be imagined.

The *Austrasia* was docked on a Sunday morning in the Herculaneum Dock, and Colonel Goffey's first words, roared from the dock-side to the captain on the poop, were:—"This comes of leaving on a Friday. No more Friday sailings for my ships."

Captain Parkes's jury rig was such a work of the seaman's art that Tommy Gray, the rigger, refused to send it down bit by bit, but lifted the masts out with all gear on them by means of a heavy crane so that he could examine it at his leisure on the quay. The ship was then re-rigged and towed to London in ballast where she loaded cement for San Francisco.

Captain Parkes was succeeded in 1897 by Captain W. Ewart, who had the ship till about 1905; then Captain Hughes had her until 1907. I think it was about 1903, under Captain Ewart, that the *Austrasia* was obliged to put back from the Horn to Port Stanley owing to a leak. Luckily her donkey engine was in order, and this connected with the pumps kept the ship afloat whilst she fled under all the sails she could carry before a snow-filled Cape Horn snorter.

Captain Hughes, on his last passage in *Austrasia*, distinguished himself, besides winning a private wager, by beating the *Vimeira* and *Port Jackson* in a race home from Sydney. The *Vimeira* and *Port Jackson* sailed out of Sydney harbour in company on January 10, but the *Austrasia* did not get away until eight days later. Nevertheless she arrived at Falmouth on April 16, 88 days out, and 24 hours ahead of the *Vimeira*, the *Port Jackson*, in spite of her 30 cadets, being third. In this passage the *Austrasia* covered 900 miles in three successive days.

The start of her next passage was a tragic one. The ship

sailed from Barry on June 29 with a new captain and a crew of 30 men, nine of whom were coloured. The newspaper accounts of what happened between Barry and Rio are very confusing, but the main facts seemed to be as follows:—

For some time the captain had been acting strangely and seemed to be in a very excited state. On August 13 he gave orders for a start to be made with shifting sail from the much patched light-weather suit to the heavy-weather one. As the ship was in the tropics the crew refused to start work, declaring that it was too soon. It happened, however, that on the very next day a very heavy squall was experienced, which some of the witnesses described as cyclonic, and this blew the light sails to tatters. That same day the second mate, Charles Bew, went to the captain and told him that several of the men in the fo'c'sle had revolvers. The mate at this time was apparently laid up owing to injuries about which there seems to have been some mystery. According to the evidence of the second mate, the captain turned upon him, and saying, "I am running this show," fired at him and wounded him in the thigh so badly that he could not leave his bunk until September 10. That night the captain locked himself in his cabin, but at 7.30 the following morning the crew broke in the door, secured him, and put him in irons.

The *Austrasia* was worked into Rio with her captain in irons, both mates incapacitated and off duty, and many of her sails hanging from the yards in ribbons. Here the police took charge of the crew, and the British Consul held an inquiry which resulted in the captain, the bosun, and three coloured members of the crew being sent back to Liverpool in order to stand their trials, the captain (who was evidently off his head) for shooting the second mate; the bosun for firing a revolver to the danger of those around him; and the three sailors for refusing to obey orders. In the captain's case he was proved to be insane; the unfortunate bosun was condemned to three months' imprisonment; and the three men were sentenced to 28 days each.

Captain J. Wolf now took charge of the *Austrasia*, and had her until she was sold to the Germans in 1910 for £5200, or at the rate of £2 a ton. Her new owners renamed her the *Gustav*. She was at

Mejillones when war broke out, and remained there until the armistice, when she was awarded to the French Government under the Reparation scheme. They sold her in 1921 to the Vinnen Company. In 1927 the Vinnens sold her to the Altona Company for £4200, after she had arrived at Queenstown, 123 days out from Sydney. This was during the summer of 1927.

The ship sailed for Melbourne again from Vifstavarf on September 30, but put into Queenstown on October 31, having received some damage through heavy weather. She resumed her voyage to Melbourne on December 24.

Her sister ship, the *Oranasia*, was launched on June 1 from Russell's Kingston yard, and was taken from the stocks by Captain Parkes's old crony, Captain A. Greig. The cargo capacity of these two ships, by the way, was 4100 tons. The *Oranasia* seems to have had a more humdrum life under the British flag than the *Austrasia*, but after being sold was constantly having her name changed.

Her best passage under Captain Greig seems to have been 112 days from Prawle Point to San Fransisco in 1893-4. Captain J. Rowe succeeded Captain Greig in 1904, and held the command until the ship was sold in 1909-10 to the Akt. Ges. Alster of Hamburg, who renamed her *Alsterfee*.

She found many old rivals in the Alster fleet, such as the *Alster*, which had once been the White Star liner *California*; the *Alterschwan*, which was the old *Alcedo*; and the *Alsterdamm*, once the *Somali*. After being the *Alsterfee* for a few years only she became the *Lucy Vinnen*. Then her name was changed to *Tamara VI*. That name soon gave place to *Mayotte* when the ship in 1921 was sold to the Greek Government. She was next acquired as a training ship for Danzig, and her last name was the *Hedwig Hemsoth*. Then in May, 1925, she was laid up at Dunkirk, and purchased by British shipbreakers for £2900 at the end of that year.

Potter's Big Ships.

The last six sailing ships on Potter's yard list were the five mighty four-mast barques, *Dunfermline*, *Forteviot*, *Osborne*, *Balmoral* and *Dunstaffnage*, built for Macvicar Marshall's Palace Line, and the *Wanderer*, launched in September, 1890, for themselves.

"DUNFERMLINE"

[*See Page* 193

"FORTEVIOT"

Lent by Captain L. R. W. Beavis
Photo by H. H. Morrison

[*See Page* 195

FIGURE-HEAD OF "FORTEVIOT"

(Queen Margaret of Scotland)

Lent by W. Donovan

[See Page 195

FIGURE-HEAD OF "FALKIRK"

[See Page 270

These ships were all built of steel with the exception of the *Balmoral*, which had iron plates.

Dunfermline, which was launched in September, 1890, was taken from the stocks by Captain B. S. Forbes, who was succeeded by J. Woodward in 1897. During the nineties she made several smart passages, the best being:

| 1897 | Liverpool to Calcutta | .. | .. | 95 days |
| 1899 | Barry to Port Pirie | .. | .. | .. | 77 „ |

The Mutiny of the "Dunfermline."

The most exciting episode in the life of the *Dunfermline* whilst she was under the Red Ensign occurred during her passage home from Tacoma to Belfast in 1905-6.

Sailing with a full hold of grain on November 28, 1905, the *Dunfermline* struck very bad weather to the northward of the Line, and on the tenth day out Captain John Woodward was washed overboard and drowned. The first officer, a young Irishman from Co. Down, of only 25 years of age, then took command, and, calling all hands together, announced that he proposed to proceed with the ship; whereupon Arthur Barnes, who in the subsequent legal proceedings was called the bosun's mate, protested that the ship had been so damaged in the recent bad weather that she was not fit to continue her voyage. The trouble with the crew came to a head on January 20, when the ship was approaching the Horn. Whilst all hands were snugging her down owing to the threatening weather, the third mate fell overboard. The young captain, David Bailie by name, apparently was aloft on the fore upper topsail yard helping the men. The ship was quickly rounded to, lifebuoys were thrown over, and after some unpleasantness, in which Barnes complained about the davit tackles, a boat was lowered, and after an hour's search picked up the mate, who was hanging on to a lifebuoy and defending himself against a large flock of mollymawks and Cape hens.

The next unpleasant incident was a row between the captain and Barnes in the cabin; upon which Barnes rushed forward and tried to induce the crew to take the ship and put the captain in irons. Captain Bailie then handed revolvers to the second mate and

o

the steward, and going up on to the poop called to the crew to come aft. He then ordered them to put Barnes in irons, but they refused. This ended in a confused struggle between Barnes, the steward, and the captain, in which one of the revolvers went off and the bullet whizzed past Captain Bailie's head. He also charged Barnes with striking him with the pistol during this mix-up.

Perhaps I should now give the story in the captain's own words:—

When I was going down the ladder 25 men rushed on top of me—all the crew except the third officer, the apprentice Patterson, and the steward. Two got hold of me and put me down on the poop. They got me by the neck, arms, and back, and dragged the gun out of my hands. I managed to escape into my cabin. The men followed me and some of them tried to get down the skylight. I ordered the steward to screw down the skylight, and he did so, and I locked the cabin door. I loaded my guns—three of them. Some time later matters quieted down, and I ordered the crew aft. They obeyed, but they refused to obey my instructions to put Barnes in irons.

On the ship's arrival at Belfast, her port of discharge, Barnes was brought up at Belfast Petty Sessions and charged that "He did on January 20, 1906, on the high seas, feloniously shoot a gun loaded with gunpowder and leaden bullet at David Bailie with intent to murder; and on the second count, with intent to disable; and on the third count, to do grievous bodily harm; and on the fourth and alternative count, for wounding."

Most of the *Dunfermline's* crew were in Court and watched the proceedings with very great interest. The counsel for the bosun's mate stated that he could produce witnesses to show that Captain Bailie was drunk and incapable on several occasions during the voyage, and that it was Bailie, and not Barnes, who ought to be in the dock.

"It is significant," added Mr. Tughan, "that it was the prisoner who threw the guns overboard, his object being to prevent any harm being done. Was it an offence to take the three weapons from a drunken captain? In the logbook kept by Bailie there is not one word as to disobedience on the part of Barnes."

It is only fair to add that the magistrate, before committing Barnes for trial, remarked: "I saw the captain in the box for six hours yesterday. He was exposed to a scathing cross-examination, and I am bound to say that in my opinion he appeared to be a thoroughly reliable witness." Unfortunately we shall never know the truth of this so-called mutiny, as when the case came for trial before the Recorder of Belfast on May 7, 1906, the Crown was unable to get evidence, and a "nolle proseque" was entered.

Dunfermline was sold to the Germans for £6150 in 1911, and became the *Carl Rudgert Vinnen*.

" Forteviot."

The second of Potter's big ships was the *Forteviot*, launched in June, 1891. On a register of 3145 tons gross she could lift a cargo of 5030 tons. Like nearly all the big carriers of the nineties, her midship-house stretched the full width of the vessel, with what looked like a steamer's bridge over it. It will be noted in the deck plan of the *Dumfriesshire* that all hands, from captain to cabin boy with the exception of the carpenter, sailmaker, cook and his mate, were berthed amidships. In the case of the *Forteviot* the crew and petty officers were berthed amidships, but the captain and officers had their quarters aft.

The *Forteviot* was not, of course, expected to be a crack sailer, but her passages were very steady, and the following is an average sample of her early work:

In 1896 she left New York on June 19, under Captain J. N. Jackson, who had taken her from the stocks. The Line was crossed on July 24, and the Cape Meridian on August 3. The *Forteviot* was in the longitude of the Leeuwin on September 21, and made the Otway on September 28, arriving Melbourne 102 days out.

In 1898 Captain A. F. Gilmore took over the command. He was followed by W. R. Kidd in 1900, and J. Finlay in 1903.

Under Finlay the *Forteviot* had a very similar experience to the *Dawpool* off the Horn, whilst bound from Antwerp to Tacoma in 1904. Her hatches, like those of the *Dawpool*, were either stove in or else the hatch covers were washed away, so that the vessel was in imminent danger of foundering. In this crisis the crew got the funks, and refused to come out on to the main deck, saying that they would either be killed or washed overboard, whereupon Captain Finlay and his officers tackled the job alone, and after a terrible struggle, in the course of which Captain Finlay was severely injured, they succeeded in making the hatches watertight, and thus saved the ship.

On May 17, 1905, Captain Finlay, his mate J. C. Willan, and also the third mate, were presented with cheques by the Underwriters' Association of Liverpool, in recognition of their bravery in bringing the *Forteviot* safely to port.

The *Forteviot* was the cause of a curious tragedy in 1908. Whilst leaving the Elbe, bound from Hamburg to Santa Rosalia, she refused to answer her helm when off Brunshausen, and taking a sheer, capsized her tugs *Fair Play* 3 and *Fair Play* 8 before their crews could cut the tow lines, with the result that five of the tug-men were drowned. The *Forteviot* then grounded, but she was got off at high water without difficulty after sacrificing an anchor and 150 fathoms of chain.

Like the *Dunfermline*, she was sold to Vinnen in 1911, and renamed the *Werner Vinnen*. The *Werner Vinnen* was captured at sea, September, 1914, condemned as prize and renamed *Yawry*. She was taken over by Bell & Co., in 1916 and renamed *Bellands*. I have copies of her captain's abstracts whilst she was commanded by Captain D. Williams between August, 1921, and August, 1922; after which runs she was sold to the Norwegians. Captain Williams, whose previous command had been the training ship *Medway* during the war, had served as second mate of the old ship under Captain Kidd on a voyage from Antwerp to Puget Sound and back to Falmouth and Runcorn in 1900. He took command of her under her new name of *Bellands* at St. Nazaire, and sailed on August 31, 1921, for Port Lincoln.

The following quotations from his abstracts may be of interest as showing the life aboard one of the very last British square-rigged deep-waterman:—

August 31.—3.45 a.m. Hove up and proceeded to sea in tow of two tugs from St. Nazaire roads.

September 10.—Sighted Madeira at daylight.

September 16.—Distance 207 miles, fresh to moderate trade. Passing Cape Verde.

September 17.—4 p.m. Boat muster; swung out both life-boats and lowered to the rail, and put back in chocks.

September 30.—Crossed the Equator. Fresh to strong trade; logging 11 to 12½ knots; all sails set; yards braced sharp up; steering full and by.

October 5.—14° 51′ S., 34° 47′ W.　Distance 178 miles.　Lost S.E. Trade at 8 a.m.

October 10.—27° 10′ S., 26° 55′ W.　Distance 127 miles.　Wind W.N.W.; heavy W.S.W. swell.　Ship rolling heavily; lightening up mizen shrouds and backstays; changed main topgallant sails; had to keep ship two points off her course owing to heavy beam swell.

October 15.—34° 16′ S., 18° 24′ W.　Light easterly airs.　Caught several albatross and Cape pigeons, and let them off again.

October 17.—11.30 p.m.　Logging 11 to 12 knots; royals furled; wind gusty.

October 18.—37° 12′ S., 10° 34′ W.　Distance 246 miles.　Wind N.N.W.　3.30 a.m., main lower topsail sheet carried away; furled the lee side.　4 a.m., loom of Tristan da Cunha abeam approximately 15 miles south of us.　6 a.m., furled mizen upper topgallant sail.　8 a.m., wind freshening.　10 a.m., wind force 7, heavy rain; logging 11 to 12 knots. Noon, moderate gale.　2.30 p.m., took in fore and main upper topgallant sails.　2.45 p.m., terrific squall from N.N.W.　Lowered upper topsails, but the yards only came down about a third of the hoist owing to the force of the wind; fore and crossjack tacks carried away, and the crossjack and foresail were blown to ribbons; midship capstan completely broken off through the crossjack tack block giving way; capstan thrown clean overboard by the crossjack; the bosun swore he saw the capstan going over the topsail yard.　During this heavy squall the second mate was found unconscious in the lee scuppers with a wound on his forehead.　I think he was in the act of letting go the main upper topsail halliards when the crossjack tack gave way, and probably he was knocked down by the tail end of the block.　2.45 p.m., starboard fore lower topsail sheet carried away; the starboard side of sail blown to ribbons, also fore topmast staysail and inner jib sheets carried away and the sails split.　Weather moderating after the squall; bent new foresail and hoisted upper topsails.　7 p.m., set lower topgallant sails.　8.30 p.m., furled mainsail. 11 p.m., furled mizen lower topsail, a hole in the centre.　Midnight, moderate W.N.W. gale and squally.

October 19.—38° 16′ S., 5° 57′ W.　Course S. 74 E.　Distance 229 miles.　Fresh gale; frequent hard squalls.　9 a.m., furled mizen lower topgallant sail.　0.30 p.m., furled mizen upper topsail; inner buntlines carried away and sail split in the seams next to outer buntline cloth; all buntlines being wire from last voyage, have decided to do away with all wire buntlines, using rope instead, being best and cheapest in the long run.　No sails set on the mizen now; ship logging 11 knots; fresh gale, high following sea, rolling heavily at times.

October 27.—41° 10′ S., 26° 24′ E.　Course N. 89 E.　Wind N.W. to W.S.W., freshening.　4.45 p.m., sighted an iceberg 3 points on port bow.　7.12 p.m., iceberg bearing north, distant 12 miles, height about 300 feet in three conical pinnacles, length about ½ mile.

November 8.—39° S., 81° 50′ E.　Course S. 81 E.　Wind fresh, N.W. gale. Distance 270 miles (best run of the passage.)

November 10.—Midnight to 4 a.m., gale increasing with most violent squalls and vivid lightning in S. and S.W.; furled fore and main upper topsails, and a relief to get them in; eased off considerably the fore sheets and mizen lower topsail sheets; blowing a whole gale, very fierce and very high sea from 3 to 4 a.m.

November 11.—7.30 a.m., furled foresail; ugly appearance of weather.   10 a.m., furled mizen lower topsail; ship now under fore and main lower topsail and fore topmast staysail; strong N.W. gale; several large whales passed close to bound west.   2.30 p.m. to 2.45 p.m., squall of hurricane force with very heavy rain; wind shifted from N.W. to W. Barometer jumped up two hundredths, then in a lull, wind and sky cleared; very high N.W. and W.S.W. sea.   After 4 p.m., gale renewing again with violent squalls of wind and rain. Barometer falling all night; ship logging 7 to 8 knots under two lower topsails.

November 14.—Blowing a whole gale, with violent squalls; sea like a boiling cauldron.

November 23.—1 a.m., sighted Cape Borda light.   2.30 a.m., hove to.   3 a.m. stood off on port tack.   5 a.m., signalled Cape Borda; squared away for Port Lincoln. 7.30 p.m., entered Boston Bay through North Channel.   8.25 p.m., anchored in Boston Bay 3 miles N.N.E. of Port Lincoln town; passage 84½ days from St. Nazaire; distance sailed 13,637 miles; daily average 162 miles.

After discharging at Port Lincoln the *Bellands* went up to Sydney to load for the United Kingdom.   She sailed from Sydney at 9 a.m. on Good Friday, April 14, 1922, and had the usual stormy time rounding the Horn.

Here are a few more entries from the captain's log:—

April 22.—3 a.m., terrific snow squall.   Had to keep ship before the wind and furled fore upper topsail and squared the yards.   4 a.m., assumed position 30 miles South of Snares.   7.30 a.m., furled main upper topsail and mizen lower topsail.   4 p.m., all hands furled the foresail; blowing a whole gale all day with terrific snow squalls and very high following sea.

April 25.—47° 29′ S., 174° 22′ W.   Course S. 84 E.   Distance 180 miles.   Moderate westerly gale; squally, rough sea.   5 a.m., set upper topgallant sails; main lower topgallant outer buntline carried away; pointed yard to wind and furled lee side, then clewed up weather side; foot of sail torn along lee side through flapping; heavy squall on at the time. 11 p.m., starboard main lower topsail yardarm carried away; lowered main upper topsail and furled it.

May 19.—56° 20′ S., 80° 12′ W.   Course S. 50 E.   Distance 184 miles.   N.W. gale with violent squalls of hail and snow; very high N.W. sea, running with gale on port quarter under 3 lower topsails, foresail, and fore topmast staysail.   3 p.m., furled mizen lower topsail; 4 p.m., all hands furled foresail; running all night under 2 lower topsails.

May 21.—Logging 10 knots.   Midnight, 30 miles south of Diego Ramirez.

May 27.—47° 51′ S., 47° 37′ W.   Course N. 45 E.   Distance 180 miles; wind N.W. to S.W.   2.10 p.m., sighted very large iceberg on starboard bow.   4.30 p.m., another iceberg on starboard beam; passing patches of kelp.

June 20.—8 a.m., crossed Equator in 28° 12′ W.

July 27.—7.30 a.m., signalled Lizard.   9.30 a.m., pilot motor boat arrived alongside; pilot brought off letters with owners' instructions to proceed to Belfast.   1.30 p.m., engaged tug *Sarah Joliffe* to tow us to Belfast for £260.   Passage to Lizard 104 days 9 hours; distance sailed 14,555 miles; average per day 140 miles.

July 30.—7 a.m., anchored in Folly Roads.   4.30 p.m., berthed in York Dock.

The *Bellands* discharged 4838 tons of cargo leaving 200 tons of ballast on board.   On August 22, 1922, Captain Williams handed over his command to Captain P. G. Araldsen, the *Bellands* having been sold to the Norwegians.   Her name was now changed to *Yavry*.   In 1923, on a passage from Rotterdam to Taltal, she put into Monte Video damaged, when 75 days out.   In 1925 she arrived at Falmouth 121 days from Port Lincoln, and after discharging at Sunderland was handed over to the shipbreakers at Blyth.

The Lovely but Unlucky "Wanderer."

We now come to the subject of John Masefield's famous poem, which begins:—

> All day they loitered by the resting ships,
>   Telling their beauties over, taking stock:
> At night the verdict left my messmates' lips,
>   "The *Wanderer* is the finest ship in dock."
>
> I had not seen her, but a friend, since drowned,
>   Drew her, with painted ports, low, lovely, lean,
> Saying, "The *Wanderer*, clipper, outward bound,
>   The loveliest ship my eyes have ever seen—"

Masefield, it will be remembered, goes on to describe how the *Wanderer* sailed from Liverpool only to put back with all her sails

> Torn into tatters, youngster, in the gale;
> Her best foul-weather suit gone.

But the ship had suffered worse than loss of sails, and as Masefield continues:

> The sea that stove her boats in killed her third;
> She has been gutted and has lost a man.

Once more he describes her towing to sea only to put back again, after a still worse experience.   Let me give Masefield's splendid lines:—

> Towing to dock the *Wanderer* returned,
> A wounded sea-bird with a broken wing.

A spar was gone, her rigging's disarray
    Told of a worse disaster than the last;
Like draggled hair dishevelled hung the stay,
    Drooping and beating on the broken mast.

Half-mast upon her flagstaff hung her flag;
    Word went among us how the broken spar
Had gored her captain like an angry stag,
    And killed her mate a half-day from the bar.

The *Wanderer* was in truth a beautiful ship, as Masefield states, of graceful lines—heavily but handsomely rigged with the dainty skysail yard at the main, and very handsomely painted with black topsides, black ports on white band, and a light blue boot-top over a salmon bottom. Her figure-head was a woman of such loveliness that many an amorous Jack Tar fell hopelessly in love with the cold, white beauty. Yet there was something fatal to man in this ship's psychology. She behaved like a siren luring man after man to his doom. Masefield's poem refers to her maiden voyage. When she was partially dismasted off the Tuskar on her second attempt to gain an offing, the skysail yard in falling killed her master, Captain Currie. Captain J. T. Brander was then offered the command. He had just arrived home from Chile after being wrecked in Rankin Gilmour's *St. Magnus* during a "norther" at the port of Buchapero.

Sailing from Liverpool on November 21, this being the ship's third attempt, Captain Brander arrived out in San Francisco on March 15, having made the splendid passage of 114 days. The *Wanderer*, however, lived up to her reputation. In the South Pacific the cargo caught fire, and though Captain Brander battened everything down and kept the fire in check until he reached port, the ship was so badly damaged that she had to pay a large repair bill at San Francisco. After this she was laid up at Sausalito for a couple of months, during which she narrowly escaped being badly stranded owing to the cable parting. Two of her men also came to grief while she was waiting to load. The first fell overboard from the main topsail yard, but was safely picked up; the second fell from the jigger truck to the deck, and broke both legs.

After loading a grain cargo, the *Wanderer* sailed from San

"WANDERER"

"WANDERER"

[*See Page* 199

"OSBORNE"

Lent by T. H. Wood, Esq.

"DUNSTAFFNAGE"

[*See Page* 203

Francisco on August 21, and arrived at Queenstown in December, 102 days out. The famous American four-master *Shenandoah*, and Roxburgh's *Bracadale* sailed from 'Frisco on the following day, and did not arrive until December 14, 116 days out, *Shenandoah* reaching Liverpool on that date, and the *Bracadale*, Queenstown. After awaiting orders at Queenstown for a couple of months the *Wanderer* was towed to Liverpool to discharge.

On her second voyage she sailed across the Atlantic to Philadelphia and reached that port with only one casualty, a seaman fell from the mizen topgallant yard and broke a leg. After the ballast had been removed at Philadelphia the ship proceeded for Point Breeze in tow of three tugs, two of them going ahead whilst one was lashed alongside. She had no sooner been pulled out into the river than the wind caught her on the port side and blew her back against the wharf, squeezing up the tug, which was lashed alongside, like a concertina. In this predicament the captain and crew of the tug jumped over the side of their vessel like so many crack hurdlers, and they were followed by the tug's funnel. After getting a very powerful tug in place of the crushed one, a second attempt to tow round was made. This time the *Wanderer* again took charge in spite of all three tugs. After running head on into a ferry steamer and sweeping everything from her upper deck, the *Wanderer* then took a stern board which so damaged her rudder that it had to be unshipped and repaired. After this series of mishaps the rest of the voyage seems to have been quite humdrum for such a hoodoo ship as the *Wanderer*. She loaded out to Calcutta, and returned with jute to Dundee.

On her third voyage in 1894 she also escaped trouble, taking salt from Liverpool to Calcutta and running home to Dundee with jute. On her fourth voyage she loaded at Barrow-in-Furness for Calcutta, and again loaded jute home. Her next outward passage was from Liverpool with salt to Chittagong. This time she struck a bad cyclone in the Bay of Bengal. She came out of it with the loss of all her sails, blown in ribbons from the yards out of double gaskets; besides which most of her running rigging was chafed through, frayed, or stranded. The cyclone left the ship with 3 feet of water in her pump well, and she had to be towed to Calcutta for repairs.

She then loaded for Philadelphia, and on her homeward passage **two** of the fo'c'sle hands died.

Captain Brander gave up the command at the end of this voyage, and was succeeded by Captain Tupman. This was in 1896. After her usual voyage out East, the *Wanderer* stranded close to Dunkirk, but was refloated. Captain T. Dunning took over the command about 1900, with Jack Spencer, the son of the captain of *Largiemore*, as his mate, and H. Daniel, second mate.

I have not mentioned the times of any of her passages since her first voyage. In 1895 she arrived on June 2, having made the run from Calcutta to the Lizard in 98 days. In 1901 she sailed from Shanghai to Port Townsend in 30 days. In 1902 she arrived at Queenstown on July 14, 109 days out from San Francisco. On April 14, 1907, whilst she was lying at anchor off Altenbruch, near Cuxhaven, being bound in ballast from Liverpool to Hamburg, she was run into by the Woermann liner *Gertrud Woermann*, between 2 and 3 a.m. The steamer struck her on the port bow. The *Wanderer* fell over to port and sank in 24 fathoms, settling down into quicksands and becoming a total loss.

There are two curious incidents in connection with the wreck of this unlucky ship. The first was this—the following morning after the *Wanderer* had been sunk, the *Isle of Arran*, with Captain Dunning's son as an apprentice on board, on her way up the Hamburg River, passed close by the wreck, which was then lying on her side with her yardarms in the air. We may imagine the anxiety of young Dunning until he discovered that his father and the crew of the *Wanderer* had been taken off by a tug and landed at Cuxhaven.

The second incident comes from the *Wanderer's* old commander. On the night the ship was sunk, Captain Brander woke out of his sleep and roused his whole household, telling them that he had had a vision and seen his old ship run into and sunk by a steamer. The vision was so clear in detail that he even saw the crew leaving the *Wanderer*, and the ship herself slowly turn over as she sank. Captain Brander had no knowledge at the time of where the ship was, but when he read the report in the papers the next day it coincided exactly with his dream, even the time agreeing to the minute.

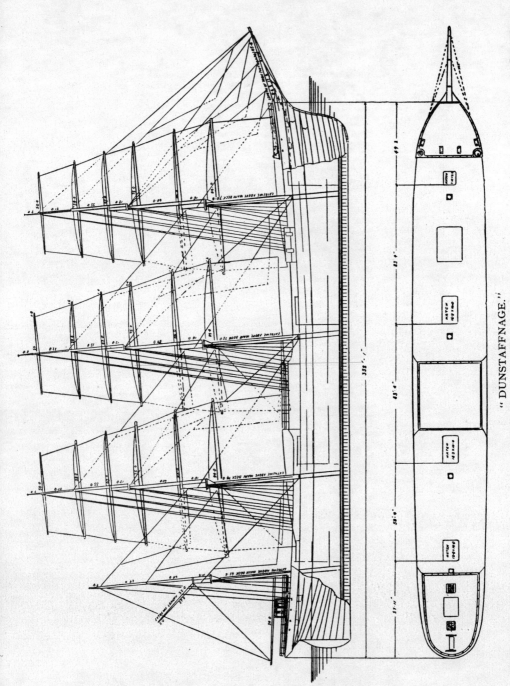

"DUNSTAFFNAGE."

Printed by Brown, Son & Ferguson, Ltd., and inserted in "The Last of the Windjammers."—Vol. II.

[See Page 203.

"Osborne" and "Balmoral."

The next two ships for the Palace Line from Potter's yard were the *Osborne* and *Balmoral*. The *Osborne* was a big steel carrier like the *Forteviot*. The *Balmoral*, besides being 600 tons smaller, had iron plates, only her beams being of steel. The *Osborne* distinguished herself in 1894 by making the splendid passage of 47 days from Newcastle, N.S.W., across the Pacific to San Francisco; this was the best run out of 57 ships. In 1902 she arrived at San Francisco on July 21, 60 days out from Newcastle, having beaten 71 ships. The *Balmoral* was a slower ship than the *Osborne*; for instance, on her maiden voyage she took 156 days from Calcutta to Dundee. This ship was sunk by the Germans in 1916 when the Italians owned her. She had been sold by Macvicar Marshall in 1910 for £5250. The *Osborne* was sold the same year for £6500, realising £2 3s. a ton, one shilling better than the *Balmoral*. *Osborne* became the *J. C. Vinnen* at Valparaiso during 1914-18 war; was taken over by P.S.N. Co. after it, and converted into the hulk *Guardadora*.

"Dunstaffnage."

The last of Potter's sailing ships, and the last ship to be built for Macvicar Marshall's Palace Line, was the huge *Dunstaffnage*. After a few years as a jute clipper she joined the oil sailers, and she had one of the best reputations for speed in the oil fleet. Her best passages with jute were the following:—

1897	Calcutta to Dungeness	..	105 days
1898	„	Boston	..	97 „

In 1899 she failed to get a jute cargo so she sailed from Calcutta to San Francisco, making the passage in 116 days.

Dunstaffnage was also sold to Vinnen in 1910, realising £6350 or £2 a ton. She was renamed *Magdalene Vinnen*. During the war she was lying out on the West Coast.

In 1921 she came home from Antofagasta to Fayal in 116 days, and was handed over to Italy. On December 22, 1923, we find her at Naples, having arrived from Rotterdam *via* Falmouth. She has since been broken up.

"Travancore."

This ship is probably remembered in San Francisco to this day on account of her five-oared racing gig, which not only won the Claude Spreckels' Cup but was never defeated so far as I know.

As regards the *Travancore's* qualities I do not think I can do better than quote the first two verses of a poem composed by her best known captain, J. Jones, who commanded the ship from 1894 to 1902.

> The *Travancore* was a full-rigged ship;
> She carried well, and could do a clip
> Of 13 knots when doing her best,
> Or 10 on a bowline without being pressed,
> And she always behaved like a lady.
>
> Though not a clipper of any renown
> She could make good time running the Easting down
> In "Roaring Forties" weather.
> Being always well found, she would stand a drive,
> And was certainly never the last to arrive
> Of a fleet that left together.

On her maiden voyage the *Travancore* was commanded by Captain F. Horsfall, who made a smart run home from Calcutta, 96 days to the Channel. Under Captain Jones I find the following passages:—

Sharpness to Sydney	..	..	..	96 days
Sydney to Iquique	..	..	..	52 „
Astoria to Falmouth	..	..	..	132 „

These are nothing wonderful, and the *Travancore* was a steady-going carrier rather than a modern clipper. I have no doubt that Captain Jones got the best out of the ship. He was one of those shipmasters who disliked staysails, and never used them except in bad weather, when he allowed a lower staysail to be run up to steady the ship.

On one occasion the *Travancore* sailed from Hamburg in company with the *Cleomene*, whose master, Captain Learmont, was a firm believer in staysails. Captain Learmont had heard Jones's views about the effect of staysails on the lee side of the topsails, but he would not believe it until the fact was demonstrated before his eyes. The two ships were very evenly matched, but the *Cleomene* failed to hold her own, until in desperation Captain Learmont hauled down his staysails, upon which he found that he was able to keep the *Travancore* abaft his beam. After a strenuous race in which they were constantly in company, *Travancore* and *Cleomene* eventually arrived at San Francisco together.

It was whilst the *Travancore* was laid up at Sausalito Bay from June, 1896, to October, 1897, along with a number of other British deep-watermen, that her gig vanquished all comers.

In 1902 Captain Jones decided to take a holiday, and he reluctantly handed over the ship to Captain A. J. Whelan.

In 1904 we find Captain W. C. Chamberlin in charge. He very nearly lost her on Fo Kai Point when bound from Hongkong to Port Angeles on June 1, 1905. Both the captain and mate got into trouble on this occasion, but the *Travancore* was re-floated without suffering much damage. The unfortunate captain, however, had to give place to Captain J. Chrystal, who was in command when the ship was sold in 1908 to Hamburg owners for £4000. She was then renamed the *Claus*. At the outbreak of war she was caught in Valparaiso and remained there until after the Armistice when she was allocated to the French. They sold her to owners on the coast, who renamed her *Laura*.

" Donna Francisca."

This ship was built for J. Hayes & Co. by Russell, and was very well known as a good passage maker, her capacity for cargo on a tonnage of 2277 being 3600 tons. She was very up to date, with a midship water ballast tank which could be filled and emptied in less than twenty-four hours. This was not only a great economy but a great time saver, as the *Donna Francisca* never had to hang about in port discharging ballast or taking in stiffening; also her bottom did not have time to get foul, so that for a full-bodied ship her homeward passages were invariably above the average. For instance, during the nineties she made three consecutive runs from Australia to the Channel in under 100 days, and in 1903 she made the best passage of the year from Astoria to Queenstown, arriving on September 26, 104 days out. She also made three passages in water

ballast from Rio to Melbourne in under 48 days.   Another good run
was from Newcastle, N.S.W., to Valparaiso in 36 days.

Her best-known captain was J. Simon, who commanded her
from 1894 until she was sold to Siemers & Co. of Hamburg in 1910.
The *Donna Francisca* fetched £5200, which is at the rate of £2 8s. a
ton, which was a high price for sailing ships that year, the average
being from £2 to £2 3s. a ton.   She was named *Herbert* by the
Germans and was at Iquique during 1914-18 war; resold Germans
1922 and renamed *Lemkenhafen*.   She was wrecked in 1924.

"Achnashie".

This steel four-mast barque was the last of the fine Duncan
fleet which were built for Thom & Cameron of Glasgow.   She was
commanded in the nineties by Captain E. Pasifull, who was followed
for the rest of her life under the British flag by Captain A. Longmuir.

The *Achnashie* was not a bad sailer for a carrier of the nineties,
but the only record of good sailing which I can find in my notes is a
passsage of 57 days from Newcastle to San Francisco, which was the
best passage of the year for that traverse.   That the *Achnashie*
was an exceptionally fine modern ship is proved by the fact that those
wide-awake Frenchmen of Dunkirk, Ant. Dom Bordes & Co. gave
£10,500 for her in 1907, which was the top price paid for a secondhand
British sailing ship that year, and works out at £4 9s. a ton.   She
entered the nitrate fleet under the name of *Chanaral*.

"Afghanistan", "Arracan" and "Deccan."

These three ships were the last of James Macdonald's British
and Eastern fleet.   The *Afghanistan* and *Arracan* were sister ships
from the Stockton yard, but the first was built of iron in 1888, and
the second of steel in 1892.   The *Deccan*, launched in February,
1897, from Duncan's yard, was a steel full-rigger, the others being
four-mast barques.   Most of Richardson, Duck & Co.'s ships could
sail.   The *Arracan* distinguished herself by sailing from Calcutta to
Falmouth in 97 days in 1894, and from London to Mauritius in 63
days in 1902.   She also made two very long passages in 1901-2—
Newcastle to San Francisco 103 days, and San Francisco to Falmouth
167 days, but it is probable that on these two consecutive passages
the ship was suffering from want of a scrub.

I have described the loss of the *Deccan* off the Horn in Vol. I. The *Afghanistan* was sunk in mid-Channel by collision in June, 1905. The *Arracan* was sold to Lewis, Heron & Co., of the Thames & Mersey Shipping Co., along with Macdonald's other ships in 1908. In that year she sailed from Port Talbot with the usual coal cargo for Iquique. When nearing the Equator the coal caught fire, and 120 tons had to be jettisoned before the fire could be smothered. Worse trouble awaited her off the Horn. After being held up off Staten Island by southerly gales for several days, the *Arracan* managed to reach the longitude of the Horn, but here, during the worst of a Cape Horn snorter, she had her steering gear smashed up, whilst the helmsman had several ribs broken. The castings, arms, and bearings of the wheel gear were all past mending, and the only thing to do was to get lines on to the rudder head, and to lead them to the main deck capstans. This was something of a job, and it was only after nineteen hours of dangerous and heartbreaking work that the ship was once more got under control. Luckily for the *Arracan*, she had a very experienced commander in Captain W. L. B. Kelk, who had been brought up in the British and Eastern fleet, and had been master of the *Arracan* since 1902. Captain Kelk managed to wear his ship round successfully, and then set a course for Port Stanley. However, that night at dusk ice was sighted, and for the next eight days there was little sleep for anybody aboard, all hands being continually at the braces. Captain Kelk now made for the River Plate, and eventually arrived at Monte Video. Here the entire ship's company refused duty, and got six months' rest in the calaboose, leaving the unfortunate boys in the half-deck to do all the work whilst the ship remained in port.

The *Arracan* seems to have been entirely out of luck this voyage, for her coal started burning again at Monte Video. After the fire had been got under it was sold by lots at an auction. The ship was sold to the Germans and renamed first *Carla*, and then *Fehmarn*. She found her way to the shipbreakers in 1924.

"North Star."

The *North Star* was one of the tallest of modern ships, crossing seven yards at fore, main and mizen. Built by the Grangemouth

Dock Co. for A. Bilbrough & Co., the owners of the *Old Kensington*, she was a very handsome and up-to-date vessel. She was only a short time, however, under the Red Ensign, being bought before the end of the nineteenth century by the Alster Company of Hamburg, and known as the *Alsterufer*, until the dispersal of the Alster fleet just before the war.

" Crocodile."

The *Crocodile*, which was one of the four ships built by the Southampton Naval Works, was considered a fast sailer, though I have no notes of any unusually good passages made by her. Her first managers were Peel, McAllester & Son of Liverpool, and her first master was W. Wilson, who commanded her until 1906, by which time she had come under the flag of W. Thomas, Sons & Co., who sold her to the Norwegians in 1915 for £9500.

" Crown of Germany."

This four-mast barque was built by Workman & Clark for William Gibson & Co., of Belfast. She was a fine up-to-date ship with a cargo capacity of 3700 tons on a draught of 22 feet. Besides such labour-saving appliances as a donkey and steam capstans, the *Crown of Germany* was given Shaw & Hastie's patent halliard winches, by means of which one man could lower a topsail in half a minute, and four men could masthead one in five minutes.

During her first years the *Crown of Germany* was well known in the Colonial trade. In 1900 we find her sailing under the flag of the Crown S.S. Co., and managed by J. Reid of Belfast. Later she was bought by Potter Bros., of London. Finally, in 1910 she was sold for £4150 to Hamburg owners and renamed *Fischbek*. On her very first passage under her new flag she was wrecked in Le Maire Straits in August, 1910, when outward bound round the Horn.

" Sofala," " Somali," and " Saratoga."

These big four-mast barques were built by Russell for Gilbert M. Steeves, the owner of the *Simla* and the *Stanley*. They were typical carriers of the nineties without any pretensions to speed. *Sofala* foundered at sea on September 28, 1911, when bound from Monte Video to Sydney, N.S.W., in ballast. When a few days out

"DONNA FRANCISCA"

[See Page 206

"NORTH STAR"

[See Page 207

"CROWN OF GERMANY"

Lent by Captain L. R. W. Beavis
Photo by H· H. Morrison

[*See Page* 208

"MASHONA"

Lent by R. L. Lowden, Esq.

[*See Page* 209

from Monte Video, and about 600 miles from the coast, the ship sprang a bad leak. After finding that the pumps could not keep pace with the water that was coming into the vessel, Captain Evans was forced to abandon his ship. Although a very heavy sea was running, the crew of 30 hands all told got safely away from the ship's side in the two life-boats, and after watching the *Sofala* founder were lucky enough to be picked up by the Norwegian barque *Ingeborg*.

The huge *Somali*, after being laid up in Oakland Creek, San Francisco Bay, under the name of *Mae Dollar*, was converted into a towing barge, latterly named *Island Carrier*. Before this she was the *Adolf Vinnen*. The Vinnens bought her from the Alster Line, under whose flag she was known as the *Alsterdamm*.

The *Saratoga* only had a very short life, as she has been "missing" since August 20, 1896. The *Stanley*, which was launched in 1889, also had a short life, being stranded on March 27, 1896. Gilbert M. Steeves managed one other vessel, a steel three-mast barque of 1361 tons named the *Senegal*. She went "missing" when bound from San Diego to Tacoma in ballast, and has not been heard of since March 15, 1894. There was some talk at the time of her not being sufficiently manned, her ship's company at the time of her loss consisting of master, 2 officers, 3 apprentices, steward and stewardess, carpenter, 6 A.B.'s, and 2 ordinary seamen.

Captain Lowden's "Mashona."

The *Mashona* was the last and largest ship built for Captain William Lowden, who was a splendid example of that dead and gone type of shipowner, the retired ship master.

Captain Lowden was brought up in Brocklebank's from apprentice to commander. After being in command of Brocklebank's ships from 1856 to 1864 he severed his connection with the famous firm in order to take over the teak-wood clipper barque *Huasquina* of 428 tons, which was managed along with several other small ships by his brother, Samuel Lowden.

The *Huasquina* was one of the most notable vessels built by Fell at Workington, and she succeeded the well-known tea clipper *Belted Will* on his slips.

P

Captain Lowden sailed the *Huasquina* with great success until 1872, when his brother died, and he succeeded to his share in the barques *Huasquina* and *Limari*, brigs *Globe* and *Dryad*, and brigantine *Eskett*.   With the management of these vessels now on his hands Captain Lowden retired from the sea, and in 1874 started in partnership with John Edgar, who was a native of Glencaple Quay, near Dumfries, which was also Lowden's old home.

The first vessel built for the new firm was the beautiful little *Greta*, which was always considered the clipper of the fleet.   She was launched in January, 1874.   Then came the *Angerona* and *Candida*, launched respectively in November, 1874, and September, 1875.   These two ships have always been called sister ships of the *Greta*, yet somehow or other their sailing records were never as good. This is easily accounted for, however, as on the same length they drew nearly half a foot more water.

The first master of the little *Angerona* was Captain C. Harwood, who had her for over a dozen years; then Captain Anderson, who had previously been in command of the *Huasquina*, had her for a voyage. He was followed by Captain J. Murdoch; then in 1894 Captain Richard Williams took over the command and sailed her until she was sold to the Norwegians in 1904.

Although she was never quite as lucky nor as fast as the *Greta*, the *Angerona* was a very successful ship, her passages being always up to if not above the average.

When commanded by Captain Williams the *Angerona* twice had to shift ports on the West Coast of America in order to take up charters when time and weather conditions were all against her. However, on both occasions she succeeded in reaching port in time.

In Volume I., I give an illustration of the careening of *Mitredale*. This was an idea of Captain Lowden's and was carried out under his personal supervision.   Some years later the *Angerona's* bottom got very foul through lying in Table Bay for four months during the South African War.   From Cape Town she was sent to Tacoma for a grain cargo home.   Captain Williams determined to careen her so as to clean and coat her bottom.   This he managed with great success, with the result that the little ship made a good passage home.

The *Candida*, which was taken from the stocks by Captain

Mathewson, had a very successful career in the Colonial trade until she was wrecked on February 20, 1898. Captain Mathewson commanded her throughout the seventies and eighties, and eventually handed her over to Captain J. T. Kee at the beginning of the nineties.

Captain Lowden's next ship was the *Ilala*, launched at White-haven in September, 1882. This vessel was fuller built than the previous three and 100 tons larger. She was commanded in turn by Captains Chellew, J. D. Parsell, A. M. Davies, and J. T. Thorburn.

The *Ilala* was never a fast ship, but she made her best passages under Captain Davies, who had come from Newton's *Mitredale*. Captain Thorburn remained in the *Ilala* until she was sold to the Scandinavians in 1903.

The fifth ship to be built at Whitehaven for the firm of Lowden, Edgar & Co. was the big full-rigger *Benicia*. As may be seen from her portrait, the *Benicia* was a very handsome ship. Numbered 60 in their yard list, she was in fact considered one of the finest full-riggers ever turned out by the Whitehaven Shipbuilding Co., and Lowden, Edgar & Co. were very proud of her.

When Lowden & Edgar dissolved partnership in 1890 Lowden retained the *Greta*, *Angerona*, *Candida*, and *Ilala*, but the *Benicia* went to Edgar and remained under the house-flag of John Edgar & Co. until 1912, when she was sold to the Norwegians and renamed *Manicia*. This ship survived the war, and in 1921 arrived in port damaged. She was then sold to the Germans and was broken up by them in 1922.

It was after Captain Lowden separated from John Edgar that he bought the two Newton ships *Eskdale* and *Mitredale*, and Fisher & Sprott's *Rydalmere* and *Thirlmere*. The *Knight Commander* also was bought from Fernie & Sons. Besides these additions to his fleet Captain Lowden managed the small Whitehaven barques *Iron Crag* and *Ladstock* for his overlooker, Captain Thomas Connel.

From this short review of his fleet it is evident that Captain Lowden was a believer in a small handy ship, but in 1891 he allowed himself to be caught in the big ship boom and gave the order for the steel four-mast barque *Mashona* to C. J. Bigger of Londonderry.

Although the *Mashona* registered 2499 tons gross she was very lightly rigged, and was never considered fast. She did, however, make a very good passage across the Western Ocean from Birkenhead to New York half loaded with salt. She was temporarily commanded at that time by Captain Dougal, late of the *Silverhow*, whilst Captain Whettem was taking a lay off. Captain Dougal declared that she worked with a handiness that he had never experienced in the *Silverhow*, and that on a previous occasion she left the smart little *Eskdale* behind in the Channel.

The building of the *Mashona* was superintended by her first master, Captain William Jones, formerly in command of the *Iron Crag*, who was exceedingly proud of her and handled her as if she had been a dainty 1200-tonner like the *Greta*.

Here is a small note I have of her from a San Francisco paper of the nineties:—

The British ship *Mashona* is one of the handsomest and best kept up ships in port. This is her third trip to this port, and Captain Jones brought her in under full sail. Passing Alcatraz the sailors were clewing up the lower topsails, and when the anchor was let go some of her light sails were still drawing.

Under Captain Jones the *Mashona* was a very popular ship, and a number of her foremast hands stayed with her year after year.

Captain Jones was succeeded by Captain S. H. Whettem in 1898. Captain Whettem had been one of the apprentices of the *Huasquina*. He also served as mate under Captain Mathewson in the *Candida*, and was then master in turn of the *Ladstock*, *Candida*, *Knight Commander*, *Mitredale*, and finally *Mashona*, all of which he commanded with great success. He left the *Mashona* in 1904 and took command of Weir's *Ellisland* in 1907, and was lost in this ship together with his wife when she went "missing" about 1910. Captain Lowden, who was one of those owners who made personal friends of their captains, was greatly attached to Captain Whettem, and he was never told of his loss.

Captain J. Henry had the *Mashona* on her last voyage under Lowden's house-flag. She was sold in 1906 to the Norwegians, and in 1911 to Uruguay, and was finally broken up in Italy in 1922.

Captain Lowden took his nephew, Robert Lowden Connel (later Sir Robert Connell) into partnership in 1890. The old man retired about 1904 and died when 85 years of age in 1914.

CHAPTER V.

THE CARRIERS OF THE NINETIES, 1892-9.

Her flagges be new trimmed, set flanting alofte,
  Our ship for swift swimmying, oh! she doth excel;
We fear no enemies, we have escaped them ofte;
  Of all ships that swimmeth she beareth the bell.

Lustely, lustely, lustely let us saile forthe;
  The winde trim doth serve us, it blows from the north.

"THE MARINER'S SONG,"
(From the *Comedy of Common Conditions*,
about 1570.)

The Lost Arts of the Seaman.

ONLY a few of us who chance to be keen sailing yachtsmen care nowadays whether the wind blows from the north or from the south, from the east or from the west. Landsmen can seldom tell you the direction of the wind, unless it happens to be easterly and beasterly, neither is it any longer a matter of vital importance to seamen; indeed the whole art of seamanship seems to be unnecessary to the seafarer of the present day. Some time ago there was a letter in the *Nautical Magazine* from the master of a steamer complaining that his sail-bred watch officer actually dared to leave the bridge for the ship's work. He evidently considered his officer's training in the old seamanship was a hindrance rather than a help to his profession.

As for the present day able seaman, his work is really that of the eighteenth century "swabber," for there is very little that he has to be able to do beyond scrubbing and cleaning, painting and varnishing.

It is sad to think of the lost art of the sea, that art of the fid and marlinspike, of the log-chip and the lead-line, of the Blackwall rigger and the sail trimmer. What able seaman nowadays could turn in a deadeye, cutter stay fashion, or put a Grecian splice into a stranded shroud? What able seaman could clothe a bowsprit or a topsail yard? As regards the latter he would not know the rules for measuring off the necessary amount from the coil for the foot-ropes, stirrups, Flemish horses, bunt slab lines, life-lines, and rope jackstays, such as used to be in every boatswain's head. As for the clothing of the bowsprit, the gammoning has long been a dead and gone lashing, and one could hardly expect a modern seaman to say which of two gammonings, the outer or the inner, should be put on first; nor would one expect him to know how to measure off a "gang of lower rigging."

But there are many seamanship jobs which it would still be useful for the steam-trained seaman to know, in case the engine of a donkey-run crane or derrick broke down; for instance, in lashing sheer legs together, which should be the upper leg if the mast is to be taken in to starboard? This is a small but important point which is often forgotten by yachtsmen when fitting out. In the old days in stepping lower masts it was often necessary to rig small sheers in order to lift the heads of the mast sheers.

Let us now turn to the forgotten lore in the navigator's art. What pilot nowadays knows why his predecessor preferred to heave to under a fore topsail rather than a main topsail? I fancy one could soon stump the present day bridge officer if one gave him a really complicated sailing ship's day's work, with constantly shifting winds, courses, and speeds, leeway and deviation. He no longer has the shifty wind to contend with, nor even a badly steering ship, and his dead reckoning, with the aid of the engine's revolutions and directional wireless, has become a simple matter. Lastly, heaving the log and casting the lead are now entirely mechanical, and the leadsman's song is no longer heard on the narrow seas.

The following incident, which is recorded by Captain Whall in his Blackwall classic, *School and Sea Days*, can never happen aboard the present passenger ship:

> *Jack* (in the chains, seeing a pretty girl passenger leaning over the rail watching him)—"I wish—that girl was—mine."
>
> *Skipper* (wrathful)—"What's that you say, sir?"
>
> *Jack*—"B-y the de-ep—nine!"

Alas, the old sea craft is dead, and the booming double note of the steam whistle, the wail of the siren, and the cough of the choking exhaust, chorus an unhesitating affirmative to Stephen Phillips' question:—

> And must ye utterly vanish and
> Cease from amidst us,
> Sails of the Olden Sea?

> Alas, must ye go as a dream and
> Depart as a vision,
> Sails of the Olden Sea?

The Bonny " Birkdale."

This smart three-masted barque was the last survivor of Peter Iredale & Porter's Dale Line.   Built by Bigger of Londonderry she was undoubtedly a good sailer, though some of her officers complained that she was very wet and a ticklish ship to handle. She was given steel chequered unsheathed decks, and these made her very unpopular with seamen.   Her carrying capacity on a tonnage of 1483 was 2400 tons.   In 1897 she was sold to Chadwick, Wainwright & Co. of Liverpool, and under their house-flag and the command of J. W. S. Davies she put up some remarkable sailing records.   In October, 1910, she made the following run from the Mediterranean:—

> Genoa to Straits of Gibraltar   ..   ..   15 days
> Straits of Gibraltar to Mersey   ..   ..   12 „

She took her pilot off Point Lynas at 7.15 a.m. and, averaging 12 knots, made tide time and got into dock at noon.   This, the steamer *Tordera*, which had taken her pilot at the same place and time, was unable to accomplish.

Other passages of this kind were:—

> Marseilles to Liverpool   ..   ..   ..   20 days
> Gibraltar to Hamburg   ..   ..   ..   17 „

Captain Davies invariably dispensed with a tug in entering port.

Captain Davies handed over the command to Captain R. B. Watts in 1910.   A year or two later we find the *Birkdale* out on the Pacific coast in charge of Captain Walmsley.   In May, 1912, she was sighted by the French steamer *Felix Touache* near Philippeville. She was almost out of provisions and had been drifting for 52 days, after being badly damaged by the weather. Thanks to the Frenchman's help, she eventually made her port.

During the war the *Birkdale* was kept out of the submarine zone, being mostly employed in the Pacific, but she arrived at Cork from Australia soon after the Armistice. Her next work was taking sulphur from the Sabine Pass, Texas, to the Cape. In 1919 she went from Barry to the Sabine Pass in 33 days. To the southward, however, she received a bad dusting, and took 21 days in making the run between Port Elizabeth and Cape Town.

In 1924 she was sold to G. Ronald of Callao, after having been laid up for some time in that port. Loading guano at Don Martin Isles she cleared from Callao for Hull on August 31. On September 28 she put into Valparaiso with rigging damaged. Finally she took 134 days from Valparaiso to her port, arriving on March 9, 1926.

The length of her passage from Valparaiso drew the attention of newspaper correspondents to the nationalities composing her crew, and questions were even asked in the House of Commons as to why she was allowed to sail under the British flag with a Peruvian master and second mate, an American mate, and a crew consisting of seven Germans, two Finns, one Briton, one Swiss, one Italian, one Peruvian, one Argentino, one Norwegian, and one Swede. Sir P. Cunliffe-Lister, answering for the Board of Trade, assured the House of Commons that as long as the ship was in British territory his Department would see that Section 5 of the Aliens Restriction Amendment Act, 1919, would be complied with, whereupon a facetious member jumped up and said: "Will the right honourable gentleman ask the dye-makers if they can produce colours to make a suitable national flag for this crew." (Laughter.)

After lying some time in the Humber she loaded a cargo of coal and sailed again on February 19, 1927, for Callao. After 25 guineas per cent. had been paid at Lloyd's for re-insurance, a message was received from Punta Arenas stating that, after being on fire, the *Birkdale* had been totally wrecked on Lobos Island. The captain and 13 of the crew were rescued by a Chilian gunboat, but one life-boat with six of the crew was missing.

"GRETA"

Lent by Captain W. D. Cassady

[See Page 210

"GRETA"

[See Page 210

"BENICIA"

[See Page 211

The Rock Line.

James Cornfoot's Rock Line sailing ships consisted of the full-rigged ships:

Gantock Rock ex *Macleod*	..	built by MacMillan in 1879.
Inchcape Rock	..	..	„	Russell in 1886.
Beacon Rock ..	..	..	„	Rodger in 1892.
Castle Rock	..	..	..	„	Connell in 1892.
Red Rock	..	..	..	„	Hamilton in 1894.

The firm also owned the iron ship *Lismore*, built by Connell in 1885. This vessel came to grief on Santa Maria Island on June 1, 1906.

None of the "Rocks" were celebrated for their speed, and the earliest was probably the fastest of the fleet.

The *Inchcape Rock* is said to have loaded the first cargo of silver ore from New Caledonia to the Clyde. She made the run from Tchio to Greenock under Captain Armour in 129 days. This ship was wrecked in the great gale at Algoa Bay, 1902.

The *Beacon Rock* made one or two fair passages, such as— Wellington to the Lizard, 91 days in 1902. In 1900 she sailed from Port Pirie in ballast for Wellington, New Zealand; 88 days later, when 90 guineas per cent. had been paid on her, she turned up off the coast of Chile. Unable to face the westerly gales, she had been driven right across the Pacific, and after re-fitting was compelled to re-cross that ocean in order to complete her charter.

The only notes I have of *Castle Rock* is a passage in 1898 from Kobe to Tchio, New Caledonia, of 60 days. She went "missing" when bound from Sydney to Seattle in 1908.

The *Red Rock* in 1897-8 made the longest passage of the year— 193 days from San Francisco to Queenstown. In 1903 fifty guineas was paid on her, a boat and wreckage being picked up when she was on a passage from Victoria, B.C., to London. This time she was 176 days at sea.

The *Beacon Rock* was sold to the Norwegians and renamed *Komet*; later the Finns bought her and changed her name to *Cate*. She was broken up in Germany, 1924. I saw *Gantock Rock* in

Southampton Water under Norwegian colours in 1921. She too has been broken up. *Red Rock* was abandoned on fire January, 1907.

Mackay's "Saints."

The three sister ships, *Saint Mungo, Saint Enoch,* and *Saint Mirren,* which were launched in 1892 from Connell's yard for A. Mackay & Co., must not be mixed up with the older "Saints" of Rankin, Gilmour & Co.

Mackay & Co. will be remembered as the owners of two very beautiful iron clipper ships, the *Charlotte Croom* and the four-master *Wendur.* Their three "Saints" were not clippers by any means. They were 1950-ton full-built carriers.

The firm of Connell had started life building a number of beautiful tea clippers such as the *Wild Deer, Taitsing, Spindrift, Windhover,* and Skinner's "Castles." Their last sailing ships, however, were the reverse of speedy, their lines being entirely sacrificed to carrying capacity. As regards the three "Saints," though they did not figure in the yearly list of best passages, they managed to keep off the overdue list. The *Saint Enoch* has been missing since June 1902. The *Saint Mungo* was abandoned on fire, October, 1906, but the *Saint Mirren* was, I believe, still owned by Mackay's when 1914-18 war began.

"Balasore."

This big steel four-mast barque was the last ship built for Eyre, Evans & Co., the owners of the fine iron ships *Barcore, Indore,* etc. *Balasore,* like all vessels built by Barclay, Curle & Co., had a very good turn of speed for a modern ship. She was well known in the San Francisco grain trade until about 1910, after which she gravitated to the nitrate trade. As late as 1909 she made a passage of 109 days from San Francisco to the Start.

In her old age she was sold to the Americans and renamed *Monongahela.* She became an oil-carrying stump topgallant barge.

The "Lawhill."

The *Lawhill,* which was last reported under the Portuguese flag was rather an exceptional vessel. She was built for Captain

Barrie of Dundee by W. B. Thompson & Co.   As will be noticed in the illustration she was a bald-header with lower and topmasts in one, and topgallant masts fidded abaft the topmasts, which is a reversion to the earliest double topsail rig invented by R. B. Forbes of Boston.

Captain K. C. Carey, who was mate of the *Lawhill* under Captain Thomas Coss during the nineties, wrote as follows in praise of this innovation to the magazine *Sea Breezes*:—

When first I was shipmates with the rig, it being so unorthodox, I was quite a while before getting the hang of it.   We never experienced any difficulty in taking in the lower topgallant sails, and could always snug them up with the gear.   The topgallant yards, both upper and lower, had parrels and trusses, which kept the yards well forward of the masts, more so than usual.   The masts were certainly handy for sending up or down, no topmast fore and aft stays to come up, no lower yards to haul clear.

The appearance of the ship was not so trim, giving one the impression that she was clumsy and heavy, but really the *Lawhill* was not, although so squarely rigged.   The watch could always manage to handle two topgallant sails at the same time, clew up and furl, and on numerous occasions tackled three.

Captain Coss also praised them, his comment being:

Masts so fitted are stronger, because the strain does not come on the head of the topmast and cap, the same as it would if the topgallant was on the fore part.

The late Captain Erikson gave *Lawhill* a good name both for speed and seaworthiness   I have notes of two passages when she was owned by Captain Barrie, but they are both long ones:—

1893	Penarth to Colombo	.. ..	90 days
1899	Chittagong to the Isle of Wight	.. ..	156 ,,

This last was a very long passage, but the *Juteopolis*, which arrived at Falmouth a month later on August 27, took 165 days.

Lawhill was then sold to the Anglo-American Oil Co. and under Captain J. C. Jarvis she figured as an oil sailer until 1911, when she was sold for £5500 to G. Windram & Co.   Three years later she was bought by A. Troberg of Mariehamm for £8500.   Then in 1919 she became a member of Captain Gustaf Erikson's fleet.

Under the Finns the *Lawhill* did some very good sailing, such as the following consecutive passages to Australia:—

La Pallice to Port Lincoln	.. ..	78 days
Bordeaux	,, ,,	.. ..	74 ,,
Bordeaux	,, ,,	.. ..	70 ,,

On February 2, 1926, she arrived at Queenstown 103 days out

from Iquique. She discharged at Bruges, and crossing from Flushing to Campbeltown, N.B., in ballast, arrived there on July 30, 1926, 44 days out. Loading lumber, she sailed from Campbeltown on August 28, and arrived at Melbourne on December 10, 104 days out.

In 1927 she formed one of the grain fleet from Australia. Leaving Geelong on February 28, she was the seventh ship to arrive, anchoring in Queenstown 120 days out. Her passage was a light weather one, except for a terrible four days off the Horn, when she was in company with the *Greif*. The latter lost two men overboard, but the *Lawhill* only lost two boats and had her charthouse damaged.

She was employed in the South Australian grain trade until the last war, when she was seized as a prize by the South African Government. After the war she was sold to private interests in South Africa and then resold to Portuguese owners.

The "William Mitchell."

This big 2000-ton full-rigged ship was the last and biggest of the Foyle Line, being built in Bigger's Londonderry yard. In 1900 she was sold to Potter Bros., then in 1913 she came under the house-flag of Stewart & Co., of London, and she had the distinction of being the last full-rigged ship to fly the Red Ensign. This, indeed, is her only claim to fame, for she hardly ever made a good passage and has always been noted amongst sailormen as a "workhouse."

During the war she escaped the submarines, but was never very long in the danger zone. Her last years were chiefly notable for causing anxiety to the underwriters.

Here are a couple of her early passages:—

1893	Newcastle, N.S.W. to San Diego	..	99	days
1900	Caleta Buena to Rotterdam	..	..	160	,,

Soon after the war she nearly foundered on her way out to the River Plate with a cargo of coal. Then on her return passage she was 40 days battling with bad weather in the North Sea. She was in such a bad way at the last that, after the assistance of a German trawler had been declined, two British trawlers took her in tow. The *William Mitchell* did her best to sink one of these, and in the end they received £3000 for salvage. On her next passage out to the River Plate she was 266 days from Gulf Port to Buenos Ayres,

60 guineas per cent. being paid for re-insurance.   At the end of this voyage she was laid up for a time at Gravesend.

She next loaded a full cargo of lumber at Frederickstadt for Melbourne, and whilst she was off the Torungen light near Arendal on the Norwegian coast, running 8-9 knots before a strong N.N.E. wind, she crashed into the three-masted schooner *Leif*, which immediately sank, taking down her whole ship's company with the exception of a young seaman who managed to scramble aboard the *William Mitchell*.   In this disaster, besides the *Leif's* crew, the master's daughter-in-law and granddaughter were drowned.   This was in January, 1924.

The owner of the *William Mitchell*, Mr. Young of Billiter Street, was determined that the last British square-rigger afloat should be one of his ships.   During the war he had a fleet of fifteen deep-watermen of which the *William Mitchell* was the only one left. She was therefore sent out on her last voyage in the summer of 1925.   This voyage lasted for two years and nine months, during which time she shipped three different crews and carried six cargoes.

She arrived at Campbeltown, N.B., 45 days from Rotterdam on July 8, 1925.   Here she loaded lumber for Melbourne.   From Melbourne she went up to Newcastle and loaded coal for Callao, where she arrived on April 12, 1926, 59 days out.   Her next cargo was guano, loaded in Independencia Bay.   Leaving Independencia Bay on July 2 she went to Carolina, U.S.A., *via* the Panama Canal. On October 8 she sailed from Wilmington in ballast for Port Lincoln where she arrived on February 24, 1927, 139 days out.

Her next passage was from Melbourne to Callao.   From Callao she went up to Tocopilla in July and loaded a cargo of nitrate. Before sailing from Tocopilla on August 30, her officers, who were old West Coast traders, went through the time-honoured ceremony of cheering ship.   However, there were only steamers at Tocopilla with the *William Mitchell*, and not one of them took the slightest notice of the old "has-been."

The *William Mitchell* had a very uncomfortable run home *via* the Panama Canal, during which there was a good deal of unpleasantness between her officers and her crew.   The officers were short-tempered, being anxious about the future, the grub was bad and running low, and both crew and apprentices had many just grievances. Probably the owner was no better pleased than the ship's company, for goodness knows what the *William Mitchell's* last voyage cost him in hard cash. She sailed from Cristobal on September 25 and arrived at Ostend on November 25, 1927. She was then sold to Messrs. Sterne, the Dortmund shipbreakers, for about £2100.

"Madagascar" and "Mozambique."

These two Russell-built four-mast barques were managed by J. Boyd of Glasgow, the owner of the well-known ships, *Mid Lothian, East Lothian* and *West Lothian*. Neither of the two were considered slow sailers in comparison with other full carriers of their date, but they were criticised as being rather lightly built. In January, 1912, *Madagascar* arrived Melbourne only 42 days out from Monte Video, having averaged 220 miles per day for the trip.

This ship, which was launched in April, 1888, was afloat after the 1914-18 war as the Russian ship *Katanga*. The *Mozambique* was sold to the Germans in 1912 and renamed *Ulrich*. On October 20, 1914, she was captured by H.M.S. *Venus*, and in the spring of 1915, being condemned in the Prize Court, she was sold to the Norwegians, who renamed her *Sydnaes*. On March 5, 1920, whilst on a passage from Norfolk, Va., to Monte Video, she was abandoned in a sinking condition. One of her boats and its occupants were picked up by the Norwegian steamer *Vaarli*, and taken to New York, but thirteen of her crew were missing.

"Manchester" and "Lydgate."

The steel four-mast barques, *Manchester*, launched by Doxford in 1892, and *Lydgate* by the Palmers Co. in 1893, were the last two ships built for John Joyce of Liverpool. The *Manchester* proved herself to be a very fast ship, but the *Lydgate* was rather the reverse.

Unfortunately the *Manchester* went "missing" at the end of 1900. On her previous voyage she had run from New York to Shanghai in 127 days, and then broken the record from Shanghai to Tacoma. Leaving Shanghai on August 22, she was only 23 days to Puget Sound. Her master on this passage was Captain S. Forrest. It will be remembered that Joyce's *Galgate* made the run from Shanghai to the Columbia River that year in 27 days.

My only notes of the *Lydgate's* passages refer to her being overdue; for instance, in 1898 she left Portland, Oregon, on March 30 and did not reach Taku until June 27, taking 89 days to cross the Pacific. In 1901 she was 134 days between Barry and Adelaide, and in 1902 took 180 days coming home from San Francisco to Queenstown.

The *Lydgate* was sold to Norway 1915, and renamed *Skansen I*.

Haws' "Alcides."

This ship will always be remembered for her wonderful passage of 83 days between Hongkong and New York. She sailed from Hongkong on December 18, 1894, and arrived at New York on March 11, 1895. Her homeward passage of the previous year was also very good. On November 25, 1893, she arrived at Dover only 105 days out from San Francisco. On these passages she was commanded by Captain L. C. Dart, who took her from the stocks.

This ship was sold to J. MacDonald, of the Anglo-American Oil Co., about 1902 and became an oil sailer.

"James Kerr" and "Fannie Kerr."

These big four masters were built by Royden for E. R. Peel and G. McAllester. The *Fannie Kerr*, which was commanded through the nineties by Captain C. Gibbons, was destroyed by fire on May 29, 1902, but the *James Kerr* was afloat until the year 1926. She will be remembered as the last command of the celebrated Captain Thomas Yardley Powles, whose ships were noted as the happiest, not only for officers and apprentices, but for foremast hands as well, throughout the whole Mercantile Marine.

Sailors love music, and Captain Powles was a great musician. Sailors love sport, and Captain Powles was a devotee of every sport. Those who served aboard the *James Kerr*—and they included William Gordon Bennett, the apprentice nephew of the millionaire owner of the *New York Herald*—were actually taught music by their enthusiastic captain, and their memories of the *James Kerr's* main deck were not confined to hard work at the braces, or dreary hours on their knees with sand and canvas or holystone, but included exciting games of cricket, in which the captain's famous St. Bernard dog, "Klon," played her part, being both an expert fielder and catcher.

Captain Powles retired from the sea in 1902, and the *James Kerr* was then sold to W. Thomas & Co. Eight years later she was bought by Knohr & Burchard of Hamburg and renamed *Isebek*.

When war broke out she was lying at Valparaiso, and there she remained until the Armistice, being allocated to France. Eventually the Chilians bought her, and renamed her *Maria*.

On January 19, 1926, she was driven ashore at Chanaral and became a total loss.

Briggs' "Fords."

This fleet consisted of the sister ships *Gifford* and *Gunford*, built by Scott in 1892, *Chiltonford* and *Chelmsford* built by Fairfield in 1892 and 1893 respectively, and the *Belford*, launched from McMillan's yard in October, 1894.

The first four were steel four-mast barques, but the *Belford* was a full-rigged ship. I think that the *Chiltonford* had the best sailing record, the following being the pick of her passages:—

1893	Newcastle, N.S.W., to San Francisco	55 days
1894	Holyhead to Calcutta	84 „
1900	Start Point to San Francisco	115 „
1902	San Francisco to Kinsale	108 „

This ship was sold to the Norwegians in 1915. Her sister ship *Chelmsford* was for a time, about 1900, managed by Aitken, Lilburn & Co. of the famous Loch Line.

The *Gunford*, when bound from Hamburg to Santa Rosalia, was wrecked on the Fogo Reef near Cape San Roque in December, 1907.

The *Gifford*, which in 1900 made a passage of 109 days between San Francisco and Liverpool, was stranded on the Mussel Rock, near San Francisco, when under the management of Andrew Weir &

FIGURE-HEAD AND BOW OF "BIRKDALE"

Lent by H. E. Earp   [See Page 215

"GANTOCK ROCK"

Lent by F. G. T. Dawson   [See Page 217

"LAWHILL"

[*See Page* 218

"ALCIDES"

[*See Page* 223

Co. in 1903.   As so often happened in making the Golden Gate, the *Gifford* had to make her landfall in thick weather, without sights for some days, and in uncertainty as to the strength and set of the current.

Belford, which was a very handsome full-rigger, was nearly lost on her maiden passage.   She was towing round from Dumbarton to Swansea, her loading port, in November, 1894, behind the tug *Flying Serpent*.   Whilst close inshore under Garroch Head, Isle of Bute, a squall struck the tug and her tow which was so violent that it rendered the tug helpless, with the result that the *Belford* stranded. She was, however, refloated.

Belford was sold to R. Thomas & Co. a few years before the war.   Her last commander was Captain William Davies, who, it will be remembered, died at Rio in 1926 when he was bringing the *Monkbarns* home on her last voyage.   Captain Davies was in command of the *Belford* when she was sunk by a German submarine.

"Tonawanda."

This fine Russell-built full-rig ship was first of all the *Lita*, and belonged to the Germans.   Later on she became the *Indra*.   After the war she came under the control of the U.S. Shipping Board, and her name was changed to *Tonawanda*.

In 1922 she sailed from Newport News *via* the Panama Canal to Astoria in 72 days.   After this she had a few seasons as a salmon cannery ship, her main deck being blocked with big wooden houses for the fishermen.   In 1927 she had a bad time in a Pacific hurricane.   She had sailed from Astoria on March 26, and had rough weather the whole way across the Pacific.   She was bound for Melbourne, but, provisions running short, she put into Sydney at the beginning of August, being nearly 150 days out.   She finally arrived at Melbourne on August 19.   She was later sold to go to New Caledonia as a hulk.

Hamilton's Big Full-Riggers.

Messrs. W. Hamilton & Co. of Port Glasgow, who were one of the last shipbuilding firms to build sailing ships, launched seven very fine 2000-ton full-riggers between 1891 and 1894.   These were

Q

the *Dunsyre, Durbridge,* and *Blackbraes* for Potter Bros.; the *Bar-dowie* and *Barfillan* for Hamilton, Harvey & Co.; *Hyderabad* for W. & J. Crawford; and the *Riversdale,* launched in January, 1894, for R. W. Leyland & Co.

I have already described the *Dunsyre.* The others were much like her, and given favourable conditions, were capable of very good passages. For instance, the *Durbridge* made the run from Shanghai to Tacoma in 26 days, which is within a day or two of the record; and the *Blackbraes* on her maiden passage took only 37 days between Cardiff and Rio de Janeiro. This ship will be remembered for the length of her passage between the Tyne and San Francisco in 1899-1900. She sailed from Tyne Dock on June 3, and going north about, sighted Madeira on June 27. On August 3 she was abreast of Trinidad, and lost a flying jib, fore royal, and fore lower topsail, in some very heavy squalls. By September 5 she found herself off the pitch of the Horn, under the usual canvas for an outward bounder, three lower topsails and fore topmast staysail. The following day it was blowing so hard that the fore and main lower topsails went to ribbons, but the ship was hove to under a goosewinged mizen lower topsail and a tarpaulin in the weather mizen rigging.

The weather off the Horn this year was unusually bad, and ship after ship of the outward bound fleet turned tail with decks damaged and sails in tatters, and ran for Port Stanley. The *Blackbraes,* after a fight of weeks, during which her cabin skylight was carried away, and the cabin flooded, her boats stove in, deckhouse door smashed, and all her storm sails blown out of the bolt ropes, at last gave up for the reason that her fresh water gave out. In Port Stanley she found Roop's *Balkamah,* the old Frederickstadt barque *Langstone,* which had been built by Pile of Sunderland in 1869, Thomas's *Pengwern,* the Danish ship *Wilhelmina,* and Weir's *Beechbank,* which brought in the crew of a foundered ship.

The *Blackbraes,* with the notorious Port Stanley carpenters and blacksmiths aboard repairing damages to her decks, was not ready for sea until January 30. Her crew had spent most of this time in making new sails, while the boys in the half-deck did the boat work between ship and shore. She finally got away from Port Stanley on February 6, 1900. This time she had better luck off the Horn, and getting a favourable slant, passed Diego Ramirez with every sail set on March 4. She eventually arrived in San Francisco Bay on May 24, 356 days out.

She left San Francisco with a cargo of grain on July 23, rounded the Horn on October 21, 90 days out; crossed the Line on November 28, 128 days out; and arrived in the Mersey on January 6, 1901, 166 days out.

In February, 1910, when bound from London to San Francisco, the *Blackbraes* stranded near Dungeness, but was refloated, her salvors being awarded £3450.

All Hamilton's full-riggers lived to a good old age, the first to go being the *Bardowie*. She was wrecked in October, 1910, when owned at Sarpsborg, Norway. *Dunsyre*, as already stated, was laid up in 'Frisco Bay in 1926. The *Durbridge* was sold to Knohr & Burchard of Hamburg in 1909 for £4250, and was renamed *Steinbek*. *Barfillan* was sold to the Italians for £6000 in 1908, and was henceforward known as the *Caterina F.* The *Hyderabad* was sold to the Norwegians in 1911 and renamed *Audny*. She became a coal hulk at Casablanca. *Blackbraes* was sold to Hamburg and renamed *Luna*, then she became the *Kassai*; finally she was abandoned on fire in June, 1921, as the *Monte Bianco* of Genoa. *Riversdale* became the *Harvestehude*, belonging to Hamburg.

Clink's Slow-coaches.

The last three ships of Clink's fleet were the *Samoena*, *Yarana*, and *Zinita*. The first two were full-riggers, but the last was a three-mast barque. I am afraid these three ships did not emulate the yachts after which they were called in the matter of speed. They were in truth real slow-coaches.

Yarana only had a short life, as she has been missing since June 30, 1900, but *Samoena* and *Zinita* were eighteen and sixteen years respectively under the British flag before they were sold. *Samoena* was commanded by Captain J. L. Boyce from the date of her launch until 1906. Captain J. Thompson then took her until she was sold in 1910.

Here are just one or two examples of her lengthy passages:—

1898	Nagasaki to Astoria	62 days	
	(65 guineas was paid for re-insurance.)		
1903	United States to Buenos Ayres		
	(When 114 days out put into Barbados after 25 guineas had been paid on her.)		
1908	Caleta Colosa to United Kingdom	132 days	
1910	Iquique to the Channel	143 „	

After this she was sold to the Russians for £3250.

The *Zinita* even outdid these passages.   In 1907 when bound out to Astoria she put into Bahia owing to trouble with her crew. She then took 155 days between Bahia and Astoria.   In 1908-9 she beat this record by taking 276 days between the Tyne and Seattle, 40 guineas being paid on her.   Before she was well clear of the Channel she put back to Falmouth owing to stress of weather. Then she got caught in a pampero off the Plate, and jettisoned 100 tons of fire bricks.   Finally she failed to round the Horn and squared away for the long run round Australia, arriving at Seattle in August, 1909.   At the end of this voyage she was sold to the Norwegians for £2300, and henceforth was disguised under the name of *Sorknes*.

Hardie's " Corunna."

The next ship to be launched for J. Hardie & Co. after the *Pyrenees* and the *Vimeira* was the steel four-mast barque *Corunna*, which was built by Henderson in 1893.   Her first master was Captain Robson.   He was succeeded by McMillan in 1896, then came McNeil in 1898, and her last passage was made under Captain Mason.

The following are a sample of her passages:—

1893	Glasgow to Rio de Janeiro	40 days	
1894	Rio de Janeiro to Melbourne	55 „	
	Melbourne to London	89 „	
	(87 days to the Lizard.)		
1895	Cardiff to Mauritius	65 „	
	Mauritius to Newcastle, N.S.W.	33 „	
	Newcastle, N.S.W. to San Francisco ..	52 „	
	San Francisco to Falmouth	124 „	
	(Was partially dismasted when north of the Equator, and sailed into Falmouth under jury rig.)		

1896	Barry to Monte Video ..	..	..	..	43 days
	Monte Video to Philadelphia ..	..	..	41	„
1896-7	Philadelphia to Hiogo ..	..	..	..	136	„

This was a very good passage considering that the *Corunna* had very light winds in the North Atlantic, being 37 days to the Line.   Her best runs to the southward were 308 and 307 miles on the 23rd and 24th March, 1897.   During that week she logged 1982 miles, which gives an average speed of nearly 12 knots.   On April 19 in 10° 42' S., 164° 26' E. the *Corunna* overhauled the *Brodick Castle* (New York to Shanghai) which was considered a fast ship, and ran her hull down astern on the following day.   The *Corunna* hove to outside of Narrows at 2 a.m. on March 16, when 135 days out, the weather being too thick to pick up the light.   Next day she spent drifting about in the Osaka Gulf a few miles from port, and she did not reach the anchorage until 10 p.m.

1897	Hiogo to Port Townsend	..	..	..	37 days
	Tacoma to Havre	..	..	..	..	149	„
1898	Barry to Nagasaki	..	..	..	..	136	„
	(Both this passage and that to Hiogo were made by the long route round Australia.)					
1899	Nagasaki to Port Townsend	..	..	27	„
	(17 days from soundings to soundings.)					
	Tacoma to Iquique	..	..	..	..	68	„
	Iquique to Dunkirk	..	..	..	..	126	„
1900	Tyne to San Francisco	..	..	..	159	„
1901	San Francisco to Antwerp	..	..	121	„
	(Passed Kinsale 115 days out.)					
	Liverpool to Sydney	..	..	..	..	94	„
	(81 days to Tasmania.)					
1902	San Francisco to Queenstown	..	..	133	„
1903	London to Sydney	..	..	..	..	100	„
	(89 from Scilly.)					
	Newcastle, N.S.W., to Junin ..	..	..	52	„
1904	Pisagua to Antwerp	..	..	..	..	112	„

It will be noted from this list that the *Corunna* was a good passage maker under all three masters, and there is no doubt that she had a very good turn of speed for a modern steel barque. She was also a magnificent sea boat besides being able to carry a deadweight of 3800 tons.

On June 24, 1904, she sailed from Antwerp bound to Port Townsend under Captain Mason. On August 30 she stranded about 3 miles west of Miramar, South America, during thick and squally weather, and immediately began to fill up with water. Owing to her exposed position, and salt water having got into the fresh water tanks, **Captain Mason** abandoned the ship on September 2, the only casualty being the drowning of a seaman named Hanson whilst he was trying to swim ashore.

The *Corunna* was refloated on October 12, and taken to Monte Video, where she was dismantled and made into a coal hulk.   In the war she was refitted and sent to sea, disguised under the name of *La Epoca*, and was sunk by a U-boat on October 29, 1917.

The Lovely " Queen Margaret."

This four-mast barque was considered by experts to be one of the fastest and most beautiful of the carriers of the nineties. Indeed, many seamen declared that she was the equal in speed to that wonderful pair, *Muskoka* and *Oweenee*.   Like them she had the clipper rig for a four-mast barque, namely, three skysails over royals and single topgallant sails.

Her reputation for smartness and good treatment was equal to that of her sailing powers.   I have a vivid memory of her in San Francisco in 1899, when the officers and crews of every other sailing ship in port were envious of her beauty, and told tall yarns about her speed, whilst the apprentices of hungry ships told one with bulging eyes that her "hard bargains" actually had eggs and bacon for breakfast.

Her first commander, Captain D. F. Faulkner, was a splendid type of a windjammer seaman.   He was a Blue-nose from Nova Scotia, a giant of a man who stood 6 ft. 4 ins. in his socks.

Although the *Queen Margaret* had such a reputation for speed she was a large carrier, as we shall see from the following epitome of her first seven voyages, which I have taken from the office books kindly lent me by Mr. A. A. Stuart Black of John Black & Co., her owners.

FIRST VOYAGE.

Left Greenock   April   8, 1893 arrived Philadelphia Aug. 22, 1893 ..   45 days
(In ballast)
„ Philadelphia   Sept. 12, 1893 arrived Calcutta   Jany. 24, 1894 .. 134 „
Cargo 87,000 cases petroleum
Rate   16 cents
Freight (less commission and brokerage £120) £2780*
* Neglecting shillings and pence.

Left Calcutta   April 8, 1894 arrived Boston   Aug. 6, 1894 .. 120 days

        Cargo   2052 bags saltpetre (150 tons)

                15,331 bales jute (4027 tons)

        Rate   4rs. 75 per 40 cubic feet

        Freight (less commission £242) £3764

(*Queen Margaret* had 100 tons of iron kentledge as ballast in her hold.)

Analysis of Voyage.

        Insurance (ship valued at £18,000)

        Wages   £1358 (Captain's wages were £20 a month)

        Running expenses and management £250

        Profit on voyage £1500.

SECOND VOYAGE.

Left Boston   Aug. 30, 1894 arrived New York   same day

 ,, New York   Oct.   1,   ,,   Shanghai   Mar. 8, 1895 .. 158 days

        Cargo   87,000 cases petroleum

        Rate   21 cents

        Freight (less commission and brokerage £312) £3478.

Left Shanghai   Mar. 25   arrived Hongkong Mar. 31   .. 6 days

       (Bottom scraped and painted in dry dock at Hongkong)

 ,, Hongkong   May 28   arrived San Francisco July 26   .. 59 ,,

        Freight 10,000 dollars

 ,, San Francisco Sept. 20.   ,,   Liverpool   Feb. 7, 1896 .. 140 ,,

        Cargo   1084 tons wheat

              503 ,, barley

             1751 ,, general

        Rate   26/3

        Freight (less commission and claims £343) £4041

        Profit on voyage £2754.

THIRD VOYAGE.

Left Liverpool   Mar. 9, 1896 arrived Cardiff   Mar. 12   .. 3 days

 ,, Cardiff   Mar. 30   ,,   Nagasaki   July 27   .. 119 ,,

        Cargo   3390 tons coal

        Rate   15/6

        Freight £2627

 ,, Nagasaki   Aug. 7   ,,   Yokohama Aug. 18   .. 11 days

 ,, Yokohama   Sept. 14   ,,   San Francisco Oct. 16   .. 32 ,,

                 (In ballast)

 ,, San Francisco Nov. 21   ,,   Queenstown Mar. 12, 1897 .. 111 ,,

 ,, Queenstown Mar. 18   ,,   Fleetwood Mar. 19   .. 1 ,,

        Cargo   3365 tons wheat

        Rate   27/6

        Freight (less commission and claims £358) £4268

        Profit on voyage £1134.

FOURTH VOYAGE.

Left Fleetwood	April 9, 1897	arrived Barry	April 11	..	2 days
„ Barry	April 30	„ Nagasaki	Aug. 12	.. 103	„

(Was dry docked and had bottom painted at Cardiff.)

Cargo   3360 tons coal
Rate   20/6
Freight   (less commission and brokerage £246) £3198.

The abstract log of this fine passage will be found in the Appendix.

The *Queen Margaret* was in the Straits of Sunda with about a dozen large sailing ships all crowding sail to the eastward. The only one of these ships which could stay with her was the well-known Shire liner *Cromartyshire*. The two ships sailed neck and neck up the China Sea for 10 days. They were separated by bad weather off the south end of Formosa. *Cromartyshire*, which had left Barry on April 26, also arrived at Nagasaki on August 12, though a few hours behind the *Queen Margaret*, which anchored at noon.

Left Nagasaki	Sept. 13	arrived Portland, Or.	Oct. 20	..	37 days

(In ballast)

The *Cromartyshire* left Yokohama on September 27, and reached Portland, Oregon, on November 4, 38 days out.

Left Astoria	Nov. 12	arrived Dunkirk	Mar. 16, 1898	..	124 days

Cargo   3339 tons wheat
Rate   26/9
Freight   (less commission and brokerage £335) £4131
Profit on voyage   £1813.

It is interesting to note that the speedy *Cromartyshire* left Astoria on December 2, also for Dunkirk, where she arrived 152 days out.

Whilst rounding the Horn on her passage to Dunkirk the *Queen Margaret* passed close under the stern of the outward bounder *Springburn*. Mr. Forbes Eadie, who was an apprentice aboard the latter, has given a vivid pen picture of this incident, which I have taken the liberty of transcribing from the P.S.N. Co. magazine *Sea Breezes*. He writes:—

In the winter of 1897 the writer's ship was lying hove to, weathering out an exceptionally heavy Cape Horn snorter. The long grey seas were running high and with

"TONAWANDA"

[See Page 225

"LAURISTON"

Lent by Captain L. R. W. Beavis

[See Page 236

"QUEEN MARGARET"

"QUEEN MARGARET"

From a Painting in possession of Messrs. Black & Co.

[*See Page* 230

such irresistible momentum that all one could see of the old ship was four masts sticking out of the water. We were under a mizzen lower topsail only (the weather had to be bad when we were snugged down to such a spread) and were making very heavy weather of it.

It was about noon when *Queen Margaret* came into view, out on our starboard beam. What a magnificent sight she made! Flying six topsails, a reefed foresail, and a big main topgallant sail, she seemed as if she were daring the savage hail-laden blasts to take the sticks out of her. The amount of sail might seem small, but when one takes into consideration the extensive fury of the frequent squalls, it seemed to us to be verging on foolhardiness. Closer and closer she came, a smother of spray from fo'c'sle aft to her mainmast. In a very short time she was up to us, and easing off a point or two to round under our stern we read her name, *Queen Margaret*, without the need of binoculars. She passed not more than forty yards from us. The thought that came uppermost in my mind was the magnificent steering witnessed. Two men were at her wheel, and the one on her weather wheel grating was indeed a master helmsman.

It was thrilling to watch the mountains of water chase the ship, just falling short of pooping her, then suddenly divide and rush alongside, gaining in height and bulk until momentum was exhausted. As the sea ran past her, down would go her stern into an abyss from which one thought she would never emerge. Up to the heavens raked her jibboom, and her fore-foot and keel showed clear almost aft to the foremast. It was difficult to estimate her speed, but if any ship ever topped sixteen knots the beautiful *Queen Margaret* was doing it then. Despite the shriek of the gale we could hear the thrash of her as she swept past. Two oilskin-clad figures (presumably her commander and mate) were on the weather side of her poop, and they must have pitied us lying wallowing "outward bound."

Mr. Eadie goes on to declare that it was the greatest example of "cracking on" that he had ever seen, and that the wonderful sight of the great white ship steeple-chasing over the Cape Horn greybeards so impressed the crew of the *Springburn* that it was the talk of that ship for months afterwards.

FIFTH VOYAGE.

Left Dunkirk	April 3, 1898	arrived Cardiff	April **6**	..	3 days
		(Dry-docked at Cardiff)			
,, Cardiff	June 17	arrived New York	July 29	..	42 days
		(In ballast)			
,, New York	Sept. 17	arrived Hongkong	Mar. 5, 1899	..	169 days

Cargo   88,000 cases oil
Rate   23 cents
Freight (less commission and brokerage £340) £3963.

The *Queen Margaret* put into Cape Town on December 1,

when Mrs. Faulkner and her child were landed, the vessel leaving again on December 5.

Left Hongkong   June 16   arrived San Francisco Aug. 2   .. 47 days
             Freight   £1882
 ,, San Francisco Sept. 8   ,, Antwerp   Jany. 19, 1900 .. 133 days
             Cargo   3338 tons barley
             Rate   30/9
             Freight   (less commission £260) £4743
             Profit on voyage   £3074.

SIXTH VOYAGE.

Captain Robert Logie took over the command on January 28, 1900.

Left Antwerp   Feb. 24, 1900 arrived New York   April   4   .. 39 days
             Cargo   687 tons cement
             Rate   1/-
 ,, New York   May 15   ,, Hongkong   Oct.   3,   .. 141 days
             Cargo   87,000 cases oil
             Rate   24 cents
             Freight   (less commission and brokerage £344) £3980
             (Dry-docked and bottom scraped and painted at Hongkong)
Left Hongkong   Oct. 31   arrived Port Towns'd Dec. 21   .. 51 days
                                 ,, Tacoma   Dec. 24
 ,, Tacoma   Feb. 8, 1901   ,, Antwerp   June 24   .. 136 days
             Cargo   3327 tons wheat
             Rate   37/6
             Freight   (less commission and brokerage £468) £5770
             Profit on voyage   £3208

SEVENTH VOYAGE.

Left Antwerp   July 22, 1901 arrived New York   Aug. 31   .. 40 days
                           (In ballast)
 ,, New York   Oct. 14   arrived Shanghai   Feb. 28, 1902 .. 137 ,,
             Cargo   87,000 cases oil
             Rate   27 cents.
             Freight   (less commission and brokerage £388) £4482
Left Shanghai   Mar. 22   arrived Taltal   June 26   .. 96 days
                           (In ballast)
 ,, Taltal   June 27   arrived Caleta Buena June 30   .. 3 ,,
 ,, Caleta Buena Sept. 5   ,, Marseilles Dec. 30   .. 116 ,,
             Cargo   3324 tons nitrate
             Rate   25/-
             Freight   (less commission and brokerage £207) £3913
             Profit on voyage   £1543.

Captain Logie gave up command at the end of this voyage and was succeeded by Captain T. F. Morrison, who had the *Queen Margaret* until 1905, when he handed over to W. J. Scott. Scott remained in command until 1910, when R. Logie took the ship again for a voyage. Her last master was Captain Bousfield, and the dates of the *Queen Margaret's* last passages were:—

Left Barry	July 25, 1912	arrived Monte Video Sept. 18	..	55 days
„ Monte Video	Oct. 16	„ Sydney Dec. 11	..	56 „

On January 17, 1913, the *Queen Margaret* left Sydney with 4500 tons of wheat for the Channel. After a very fine passage the ship arrived off the Lizard at daybreak on May 5, being 108 days out. Here Captain Bousfield received orders to go to Limerick for discharge. As there was a head wind blowing the captain sent a telegram to ask if he might engage a tug, and took the ship close in to the Lizard in order to be able to read the signals.

At 8 o'clock, when it was about half-tide and the *Queen Margaret* was about a quarter of a mile off-shore from the lighthouse, there was a slight jar and the ship stopped, having evidently struck on an outlying rock. Captain Bousfield threw all aback and tried to work the ship off stern first, but it was no use, and the sails were hastily clewed up.

Soon after this the water was reported to be up to the 'tween decks in the forepeak, and Captain Bousfield immediately ordered the crew to swing out the boats. The weather was clear and fine, and there was no danger of life. Nevertheless, the Lizard life-boat came out and took the captain's wife and little boy ashore. She was followed by the ship's company in their own boats.

The poor old *Queen Margaret* gradually listed over to port until her rail was level with the water. By this time there was a French steamer standing by as well as the Lizard lifeboat and the Falmouth tugs *Victor* and *Triton*. Captain Bousfield remained on board the wreck until she had listed so far that he was able to slide down an oar into the lifeboat from the deck.

The rocks round the Lizard have accounted for a number of beautiful sailing ships in their day, and the only one which I can remember being salved was the French ship *Socoa*, a few years before.

From the first it was seen that the *Queen Margaret* was done for.

In fact, by May 8 all her masts had disappeared, the deck was gaping open, and she was fast breaking up.

There can seldom have been a more stupid and unnecessary end to a ship than that of the beautiful *Queen Margaret*.

"Tovarisch" Russian Training-Ship ex "Lauriston."

In October 17, 1892, Messrs. Workman & Clark launched the four-mast full-rigged jute clipper *Lauriston* for Galbraith & Moorhead of London, who at that time owned the *Bay of Bengal*, *Bay of Naples*, *Cave Hill*, *Lindores Abbey* and *Middlesex*. The *Lauriston*, which was a lofty ship, with a big sail area, carried 3600 tons of deadweight on a tonnage of 2301, and could shift berths with 300 tons of stiffening. Her early years were spent in the Eastern trade, and the following are an example of her passages:—

1897	Liverpool to Rangoon	arriving July 20	..	95 days
1899	Holyhead to Calcutta	,, May 26	..	96 ,,
1901	Liverpool to Rangoon	,, Sept. 6	..	106 ,,

By this date the name of her owners had been changed to Galbraith, Hill & Co., and she was the only ship left out of the six.

In 1905 she was bought by George Duncan & Co. of London. It was under their flag that she made the long passage of 198 days from Tamby Bay to Falmouth in 1908-9. By this time she had been reduced to a four-mast barque.

In June, 1910, Messrs. George Duncan & Co. sold the *Lauriston* to Cook & Dundas of London for £4000, and from them she went to the Russians. She seems to have been laid up in the Baltic for a great number of years, but in 1925 she was given an extensive overhaul, and re-fitted as a Soviet training ship under the name of *Tovarisch*.

Her first effort to make a passage ended in failure. With sixty cadets on board and a British captain, she arrived at Port Talbot. The captain then deserted the ship, and she was eventually navigated back to Leningrad by a woman.

Her second attempt to get to the southward was little better than her first. She sailed from Sweden with a cargo of paving stones for Rosario, but after being knocked about in the North Sea for 17 days by a succession of gales, the unhappy ship was towed into Vardoe. Here she proved of great interest to shipping people and was considered more or less of a joke. Although there was a beautiful grand piano in the fo'c'le for the use of the crew she possessed no charts, and it was proposed to navigate her to Rosario by means of a general map of the world.

After some little delay she again sailed for Rosario, but this time she put into Southampton. This was in August, and at first it was stated that she only intended to remain a few days, but after lying off Netley, where her red flag with its white Russian lettering mystified most of the seaside visitors, for a week or ten days, she went into dock for sundry repairs.

Leaving Southampton Docks in September, she then went and lay at Spithead for a while. At last her captain made up his mind to proceed on his voyage, and taking his departure from Ventnor, arrived at Monte Video 98 days out. His passage between Sweden and Rosario had occupied exactly 12 months. The *Tovarisch* left Buenos Ayres on April 20, 1927, for Leningrad, and put into Dover on July 6 after a 77 days passage. At Dover her crew and cadets, numbering 83 souls all told, spent money freely whilst the ship replenished her stores. Amongst the crew's purchases were bicycles, attache cases and mackintoshes. After these happy days at Dover, the Soviet training ship proceeded to her destination, where she finally arrived on July 26, 1927.

The next voyage of the *Tovarisch* began disastrously. Whilst proceeding down-Channel, being bound from Holtenau in ballast to Buenos Ayres with a full complement of cadets, the *Tovarisch* collided with the Italian steamer *Alcantara* off Dungeness. According to the evidence of Captain Ernest Friedman, the master of the *Tovarisch*, at the inquest, the *Alcantara's* red light was sighted on the Russian's port side. The captain heard his third officer give the order "Hard a-port," and at the same moment the steamer gave one short blast on her siren. A few minutes later the *Alcantara* struck the *Tovarisch* on her port bow, and apparently swung across the latter's stem and sank in the darkness, taking all her crew down with her except one man, an engineer, who was found clinging to one of the *Tovarisch's* back ropes.

The bow of the Russian was stove in for about 15 feet above the waterline. Her captain at once sent out an S O S and had his life-boats swung out and lowered half way down. He has been criticised for not sending his boats away in search of possible survivors in the water, but according to Southampton gossip his crew, consisting mostly of cadets, were such raw sailors that he was afraid of sending them away in the darkness, fearing that they would not be able to get back to the *Tovarisch*.

The curious part about this collision was that there was no fog at the time, the weather was quite clear, and the moon was shining. The *Tovarisch* was under all sail before a nice breeze. She must have sailed right over the Italian steamer, for the sole survivor, who was hanging below the Russian's bowsprit, declared that he felt the deck of his own ship sink beneath his feet. The coroner, in returning a verdict of "death from drowning" on the victims of the collision, remarked as follows:—

I won't go so far as to censure anyone, but I feel very strongly that something more should have been done by those on the Russian vessel. If they had thought a little more of others and less of themselves I think it would have been better.

There was one other matter connected with this collision for which the Soviet ship was severely criticised. As soon as Captain Friedman discovered that his ship was only holed above the water-line and was not likely to sink, he cancelled his S O S by wirelessing that he was not in need of help, and thus caused the Dungeness and Rye life-boats to stop putting to sea, and it was not until after a message had been received from the P. & O. *Moldavia* saying that she had picked up a man in the water and sighted a lot of wreckage that the life-boats were finally launched.

Meanwhile the *Tovarisch* made for Southampton, and when off the Nab was picked up by a couple of Southampton tugs, which had been sent off to meet her. The Soviet training ship towed past my windows at 4 o'clock on Saturday afternoon, and with the aid of a telescope I noticed that the fore royal mast was carried away above the sheave hole of the royal halliards, the mast hanging down in the rigging alongside the topgallant mast. Her stove-in bow was also very noticeable.

The *Tovarisch* was anchored at Netley, and afterwards taken in to the docks, where she was berthed about 9 p.m. The first man to board her was a representative from Arcos, who had travelled post haste from London, and he played the part of buffer between the tall bald-headed captain and the journalists.

After being in the docks for about a week the Russian came out and dropped her anchor off Calshot, right in front of my windows, and at the present moment as I sit writing these words she presents a most picturesque appearance with all her sails loosed to dry in the hot sun.

NOTE.—She was later towed back to Hamburg. After repairs she sailed from this port on July 21, and passed Gibraltar on August 13, 1928, on her way to the Black Sea.

"Ancona" and "Bermuda."

These two remarkable sister ships were considered to be the forerunners of the turret-decked steamers. They were bald-headed four-mast barques fitted with all the latest gadgets in the way of labour-saving appliances, such as patent topsail and topgallant halliards; but their chief peculiarity was the carrying of the half-round of the poop for the whole length of the ships, which gave them a strange appearance but a flush deck fore and aft. On this half-round they lashed their spare spars. The top of the half-round came 7 feet above the main deck, and on this level there was an awning or hurricane deck surrounded by an iron railing.

Below, the two ships were fitted with water ballast tanks amidships capable of carrying 1350 tons of water. The holds, also, were so bulkheaded off that the ships were considered practically unsinkable. There was a 60 h.p. engine to do the pumping for the ballast tanks. This also worked the patent windlasses and capstans. Both ships were handsomely fitted with wonderful accommodation, their crew having well-finished lavatories, baths, etc., whilst aft, besides a large saloon handsomely furnished in teak and birdseye, there was a separate dining-room for the officers. These ships cost £26,000 each, and they could lift 4250 tons of deadweight.

The *Bermuda* was launched by Russell in June, 1893, for P. Denniston & Co., and the *Ancona* in October for G. T. Soley & Co. The *Bermuda*, under Captain Kohn, sailed on her maiden passage with 4100 tons of Cardiff coal for Colombo, and apparently pleased her crew by logging 14 knots with fresh quartering winds. From Colombo she went on in ballast to Melbourne, where, after having her bottom cleaned of barnacles and grass 6 inches long, she loaded wool for London.

The *Ancona*, on her maiden passage, sailed under Captain Long to Rio, and then came on to Melbourne in ballast. At Rio sand ballast cost 7s. 6d. a ton, and the *Ancona*, by being able to fill her ballast tanks from the sea, saved quite £500. Whilst lying off Rio her bottom got very foul and she therefore made a longish passage to Port Phillip.

This ship will be remembered for a disastrous passage from Shanghai to New York, when, for the greater part of the time, her officers and crew were out of action through sickness, the ship arriving in charge of her apprentices and carpenter.

The *Ancona* and *Bermuda* made some longish passages with grain from the Pacific coast. In 1895 *Ancona* was 185 days from Astoria to Queenstown, and in 1900 *Bermuda* took 165 days from the same port to Falmouth.

The *Ancona* was lost by fire in November, 1906; *Bermuda* was sold to Norway and re-named *Nordhav*. She was sunk by U-boat, August, 1918.

" Clan Graham " and " Clan Galbraith."

These two Russell-built four-mast barques were the last members of Dunlop's "Clans." With a gross register of just under 2200 tons, they were of a tonnage that was easy to handle, and could also carry a good deadweight at a good speed. In the last days of sail they were amongst the barques which gave Russell such a reputation for combining carrying power with speed.

After a successful career under Dunlop's house-flag both ships were sold to the Norwegians in 1909. The *Clan Graham* was sunk by a German submarine in July, 1917. The *Clan Galbraith* was nearly lost by stranding in 1916. This was in July, near New York, but she was successfully refloated. This ship in 1900 crossed the Pacific from Newcastle to San Francisco in 55 days, and two years before sailed from Liverpool to San Francisco in 118 days, arriving on January 25, 1898.

"BERMUDA"

[See Page 239

"CLAN GRAHAM"

[See Page 240

"NORMA"

[*See Page* 242

"HENRIETTE" EX "ROYAL FORTH"

Lent by Captain L. R. W. Beavis
Photo by H. H. Morrison

[*See Page* 244

" Kilmallie."

The steel barque *Kilmallie*, which was built by Russell for Kerr, Newton & Co. in 1893, had the honour of being one of the last four British deep-watermen

After surviving the war, the *Kilmallie* sailed from Swansea with a cargo of patent fuel for Melbourne in 1920 under the flag of John Stewart & Co. of London, but she was not five days out before a fierce gale in the Bay of Biscay dismasted her. The main topmast went at the lower cap, and masts and yards crashing against the ship's side in the heavy sea threatened to sink her. However, Captain Henry, who was a very experienced sailing ship man, quickly braced his foreyards aback and stopped the ship's way. Then for two days the *Kilmallie* tossed about in a helpless condition, till the steamer *Elzasier* of the Royal Belge Line came along, and after a tremendous struggle managed to get a tow line fast; but the line parted three times and it took four hours after each break to make it fast again. Finally the mate of the *Kilmallie* jumped overboard and swam to the steamer's side with a lifeline round his shoulders. By means of this a towing hawser was at last made fast, and the *Kilmallie* was towed into Lisbon. Here she was five months being repaired. Besides sending up new spars, she had sundry leaks to stop. She then took her cargo to South America, and finally went on to Melbourne in ballast.

She made the passage home from Melbourne to Bordeaux in 96 days, not at all a bad performance for a modern barque.

At Bordeaux the *Kilmallie* was laid up alongside the *Falkirk* from June, 1921, to May, 1925, when a Dutch tug towed her to Liverpool. Here she loaded salt for Sydney, and sailing on June 18 made the run out in 125 days. She then crossed from Newcastle, N.S.W., to Pisco, Peru, with the usual coal cargo in 59 days.

Her last passage was from the Pescadores Island with guano *via* the Panama Canal to London. Leaving the West Coast on June 19, 1926, she passed through the Canal with the *Penang*, also guano laden, and beat the latter home by one day, making the run in 68 days. After discharging at London the *Kilmallie* was towed to Bo'ness and broken up.

R

Walker's " Kings."

In 1894 the two Russell-built full-rigged sister ships, *King David* and *King George*, were added to Walker's fleet, which already consisted of the iron barques, *King Alfred* and *King Malcolm*, the iron ship *King Arthur*, and the steel ship *King Edward*.　Another of the fleet, the *King James*, had been abandoned on fire on March 31, 1893, when 200 miles from San Francisco with Newcastle coal. Captain Drummond was saved, but eleven of his crew, including his son, were drowned through one of the boats capsizing.　This *King James*, I am told, was a most peculiarly rigged vessel; indeed many sailors affirm that her upper yards were longer than her lower ones, so that it was necessary to send a dozen men aloft to stow her main royal.

The *King Edward*, which was built by Russell in 1891, distinguished herself by making the run from Newcastle, N.S.W., to Valparaiso in 31 days.　Another good passage of hers was from London to Mauritius in 78 days, arriving July 26, 1902.

The *King George* also distinguished herself as a sailer when commanded by Captain John Burnett, making two record passages. The first was from Cape Town to the Delaware Capes in 47 days.　In 1902 she sailed with 1,800,000 feet of timber from Port Blakeley to Iquique in 65 days.　This ship afterwards became one of the Anglo-American oil sailers.

The *King David*, whilst still under Walker's house-flag, was wrecked in December, 1905, on Vancouver Island.

Of the old ships, *King Edward* was sold to the Russians in 1910 for £3400.　The *King Alfred* and *King Malcolm* both went to the Italians.　The *King Malcolm* was totally lost off New Zealand in 1914; the last survivor of Walker's fleet being the *King Alfred*, which was broken up in 1924 as the *Generosita*, having previously borne the names of *Lucia* and *Provvidenza*.

"Norma".

Built by Barclay, Curle & Co. for M. J. Begg of Cardiff, the *Norma* was a stump topgallant four-mast barque with a tremendous spread of canvas : she was built of the best mild steel and designed to carry an enormous cargo.　Her first commander was Captain

D. McDonnell, who had formerly had the *County of Antrim* and the *Moreton* in the Colonial trade.

The *Norma* was launched in May, 1893, and on her maiden passage took 3500 tons of coal to Rio de Janeiro. Here she was busy discharging when the revolution broke out, and she had a very nasty experience, her hull being marked all over with bullet splashes. Her crew had constantly to take refuge under hatches to escape the flying bullets, and on one occasion a shell burst overhead and a piece weighing 2 lbs., which fell on the *Norma's* deck, was preserved as a curio. The ship's company had many miraculous escapes, but the only casualty was a ballast lighterman, who was killed by a rifle bullet. The *Norma* went on from Rio to Melbourne in ballast.

An interesting reference to this ship will be found in Captain Clements' *Gipsy of the Horn.* In 1903, during a hard gale, the *Norma* attempted to run into Newcastle, N.S.W., under her own canvas without the help of a tug, but failing to weather the reef to the northward of the entrance she had to let go both anchors to save running on the rocks. Luckily her cables held though she was within a stone's throw of the reef and in the backwash of the tremendous surf which was breaking over it.

The Newcastle life-boat went out and made fast alongside, but the *Norma's* master, Captain McLaughlin, refused to abandon his ship and signalled for a tug.   Several tugs went out, and hawser after hawser was made fast to the *Norma*, but she was a heavy ship, and none of the towing lines could be got to hold, each one in turn parting, according to Captain Clements, like rotten thread.   However, her cables held, and with the life-boat alongside of her she lay in the broken water of the reef all through the night. The next day the *Champion* arrived from Sydney. She was the most powerful tug on the coast. A $4\frac{1}{2}$-inch steel hawser was then passed aboard the *Norma*, upon which the *Champion* took hold, and after a very hard fight managed to drag her out of the surf and towed her to a berth up the dyke, all the shipping in port cheering as the two ships went by.

Whilst the *Norma* was lying at the Semaphore anchorage on April 20, 1907, she was run into and sunk by Crawford & Rowat's *Ardencraig.*

"Royal Forth."

This mighty 3000-ton four-mast barque was built by **Ramage & Ferguson**, and managed by J. Ferguson of Leith.

At the beginning of the twentieth century she was sold to Schmidt of Hamburg, and renamed *Henriette*. After the war she was allocated to the Italian Government and was broken up in 1924.

"Centesima."

One of the largest four-mast barques launched in 1893 was the *Centesima*, which was built and owned by R. Williamson of Workington. She was a powerful ship, but I remember in 1899 the *Ross-shire* seemed to have the legs of her in both light and strong breezes, whilst the two ships were making their way down the Pacific when homeward bound with grain from San Francisco. There was certainly not much in it, but we in the *Ross-shire* were quite satisfied that we had had the best of it on each occasion that the ships were in company.

The two ships were in company in 21° S., 127° W., on September 26 and 27, and again for a short time on November 8 in 23° S., 16° W. so the *Centesima* was evidently making a pretty good race of it.

This fine ship was sold to Bremen owners in 1901, and renamed *Nauarchos*. She was lost by fire in April, 1908.

R. Williamson & Son in 1895 built a sister ship to the *Centesima* for their own use, which they named the *Iranian*. This ship was lost by stranding on April 3, 1900.

"Belford's" Sisters.

Amongst the full-riggers built by McMillan of Dumbarton were the four sister ships *Marechal Suchet*, *Vincent*, *Belford* and *Conway*. *Belford* we have already mentioned amongst Briggs' "Fords." The *Marechal Suchet*, which must not be confused with the French ship of the same name, was owned by A. Ruffer & Sons, of London, until 1904, when she was bought by W. Thomas & Co. and renamed *Marshal*, but was wrecked two years later in February, 1906.

The *Vincent* and *Conway* were built for R. N. Smith of Liverpool. The *Vincent* came under the flag of J. Joyce in 1900, and the *Conway* went to the Germans in 1905, being renamed *Walkure*.

The Skysailyarder " Lynton."

The *Lynton* was one of the handsomest barques ever built in the Mersey. She had the same sail plan as the *Queen Margaret, Muskoka* and *Oweenee*, three skysails over royals and single topgallant sails. On her jigger she had two monkey gaffs for signalling purposes which gave her a very distinctive appearance. She was beautifully fitted and finished off with lots of carved teak, and was always very smartly kept up. Her accommodation also, both fore and aft, was excellent. Although a full model lifting 3800 tons of dead-weight, she was a good sailer, particularly when close-hauled; with all sails set and the yards on the backstays she easily logged 11 knots. She was also a very easy ship to steer, even with the wind aft.

The *Lynton* was not often passed at sea, though I know of two occasions when she was bested. One of these occurred to the westward of the Horn, when the famous *Wendur* proved the faster vessel. On the other occasion the *Lynton* was passed by the *Queen Margaret* off the Lizard.

The *Lynton's* first owners were Johnston, Sproule & Co., and Captain T. G. Fraser took her from the stocks and commanded her until 1899. For the first seven years of the twentieth century she was owned by W. Montgomery of London, and commanded by Captain E. G. James, a lieutenant in the Royal Naval Reserve.

Thomas A. Shute gave £11,000 for the *Lynton* in 1906. This was by far the highest price for a British sailing ship paid that year and goes to prove that the *Lynton* was a most superior vessel. Captain W. Jones then took over from Captain James. After the former's death off the Horn in 1908 Captain Morrell was put in charge on the West Coast. Finally, in 1914, the old ship was sold to the Russians. She was sunk by a U-boat off the south coast of Ireland, May 21, 1917.

As regards her passages, in her early days she was in the Calcutta jute trade, and I find the following good runs:—

1894-5 Calcutta to Philadelphia   ..   .. 94 days
     (Race with *Thirlmere*, which arrived New York March
     15, same day that *Lynton* arrived Philadelphia.
     Thirlmere was 95 days out)
1897   Liverpool to Calcutta   ..   .. 93 „
1897-8 Calcutta to New York   ..   .. 97 „

During her time in the Eastern trade the *Lynton* experienced a very bad cyclone, in which she had every sail blown to ribbons.

Here is an example of her later work. On June 28, 1907, she left Port Talbot under Captain W. Jones, and made the run out to Iquique in 87 days, being beaten by one day by the *Rowena* from Newport. At this time Mr. Hanna was her mate and she had an uncertificated American as second mate.

Loading nitrate at Caleta Buena the *Lynton* sailed for Falmouth on January 26, 1908. Off the Plate a S.E. gale was picked up, and the ship tore by a big four-masted barque which had her mainsail and crossjack stowed, whilst the *Lynton* was carrying everything except her skysails and gaff topsail. The wind increased steadily, and before noon the royals had to be furled. That evening, at the change of the watch, 8 p.m., all hands furled the crossjack. During the night the *Lynton* constantly put her whole lee rail under as she tore through it heavily pressed. At 4 a.m. the wind freed a bit, and an attempt was made to check in the yards. This resulted in all hands being swept away from the weather main braces, both mates and six men being badly knocked about. Shortly after this a sea smashed the starboard life-boat on the forward house, and swept the hencoop containing all the potatoes off the midship-house. At 8 a.m. next morning the mainsail and fore and mizen topgallant sails went to pieces. Soon after this the *Lynton* ran into a dead calm, which lasted for three weeks and completely spoilt her passage, so that she did not reach Falmouth until the 105th day out.

On July 4, 1908, she left Port Talbot for Mollendo. This time Mr. Denwood was mate, and Jones second mate. She had a terrible time off the Horn, during which Captain Jones was taken ill and died. After several weeks fighting against a succession of westerly gales, the ship was head-reaching off the pitch of the Horn when a kick of the wheel sent the helmsman flying. Luckily he landed on the taffrail and fell inboard. The wheel took charge and was soon smashed to pieces. However, a racking was put on the relieving tackles, and the carpenter managed to turn out a jury wheel. Some time after this the second mate was washed up against the main rigging and was so badly bruised that he was laid up for a week.

The next trouble was a leak, 19 inches being discovered in the well; and for the rest of the time until she reached port most of the watch on deck had to spend their time pumping. Later, when the ship was dry-docked at Sydney, the butt of a plate right aft in the run was found to be cracked, and only the cement inside had prevented the leak from being fatal.

The *Lynton* finally arrived at Mollendo after a passage of 119 days. Here Captain Morrell, a Nova Scotian, took over the command, Mr. Denwood left, and Jones became chief officer. The ship sailed across to Sydney in 61 days, on one of which she made a run of 288 miles under six topsails and mainsail.

Her next passage was 50 days from Newcastle, N.S.W., to Talcahuano. Here her officers again changed, Mr. Titterington joining as mate from the *Eudora*. The *Lynton* loaded nitrate at Iquique, and sailing on September 17 arrived off the No. 1 lightship at the mouth of the Elbe, 95 days out, having beaten the French barque *Cap Horn* by one month.

Coming up Channel with a fair wind on that passage, the *Lynton* caught up and passed every steamer that was going the same way.

She continued in the West Coast trade until sold to the Russians.

"Kinross-shire" and "Inverness-shire."

These two bald-headers were the last four-masters built for the Shire Line, the *Kinross-shire* being launched in May, 1893, from Russell's slips, and the *Inverness-shire* in April, 1894, from Duncan's yard. The *Kinross-shire* was put in charge of Captain W. Cooper, whilst Captain Peattie took over the *Inverness-shire*. Tremendously squarely rigged with lower yards of 88 feet long, both ships could sail when given the chance. The sailing reputation of a vessel is, of course, greatly in the hands of her captain, and as regards the *Kinross-shire*, old Captain Cooper was a sail carrier, but Angus McKinnon, who succeeded him in 1898, never seemed to be in a hurry.

Like so many ships in the early nineties, the *Kinross-shire* went out to Australia on her maiden passage *via* Rio de Janeiro. The following are a selection of her passages :—

1893	*Maiden voyage*—Left Greenwich May 29 arrived Rio de Janeiro July 20 52 days						
	Left Rio	Oct. 16	arrived Adelaide	Dec. 15	..	60	,,
1894	,, Geelong	Feb. 9	,, Channel	May 26	..	105	,,
	,, Sharpness	Aug. 4	,, Sydney	Nov. 8	..	95	,,
1895	,, 'Frisco	June 13	,, Falmouth	Oct. 25	..	133	,,
1896	,, Barry	Jan. 8	,, Iquique	Mar. 31	..	82	,,
	,, Iquique	July 19	,, Hamburg	Nov. 17	..	120	,,
1897	,, Frederickstadt	Mar. 9	,, Melbourne	July 5	..	118	,,
	(95 days from the Channel)						
	,, Melbourne	Aug. 26	,, Portland, O.	Oct. 26	..	61	,,
1897-8	,, Portland, O.	Nov. 25	,, Havre	April 4	..	130	,,
1898-9	,, Philadelphia	Sept. 7	,, Hiogo	Feb. 8	..	154	,,
	,, Kobe	Mar. 26	,, New Caledonia	May 11	..	46	,,
	,, Noumea	July 15	,, Rotterdam	Nov. 23	..	131	,,
	(Put into Barry Nov. 9; sailed Barry Nov. 13, put into Penzance Nov. 16)						
1900	Left Antwerp	Feb. 1	,, 'Frisco	June 26	..	145	,,
1900-1	,, 'Frisco	Sept. 3	,, Channel for				
			Hull	Mar. 4	..	182	,,
1901	,, Frederickstadt	May 13	,, Melbourne	Aug. 29	..	108	,,
1909	,, Pisagua	Feb. 23	,, Channel	May 5	..	71	,,

On her next passage Captain Purdie succeeded McKinnon in the command, and took the ship out to Santa Rosalia from Hamburg in 133 days.

Kinross-shire was eventually sold to the Norwegians, and under the name of *Fiorino* she has been "missing" since December, 1920.

The *Inverness-shire* was considered by many people to be a faster ship than the *Kinross*; however, my readers can draw their own conclusions from the following, her first four voyages:—

1894	*Maiden voyage*—Left Greenock May 15, arrived Buenos Ayres July 25				68 days
	Left Buenos Ayres	Sept. 18	arrived Newcastle, N.S.W.	Nov. 14	57 ,,
1894-5	,, N'castle, N.S.W.	Dec. 4	,, Portland, O.	Feb. 21	.. 78 ,,
1895	,, Astoria	April 20	,, Liverpool	Aug. 15	.. 116 ,,

"LYNTON"

[See Page 245

"INVERNESS-SHIRE"

[See Page 247

"KINROSS-SHIRE"

[*See Page* 247

"GRENADA"

[*See Page* 250

1895-6	Left	Liverpool	Nov. 2	arrived	Portland, O.	April	2	..	152	days
1896	,,	Astoria	June 6	,,	Liverpool	Oct.	26	..	141	,,
1897	,,	Liverpool	Jan. 1	,,	Sydney	April	9	..	91	,,
		(Put into Holyhead: left Holyhead Jan. 7)								
	,,	N'castle, N.S.W.	June 16	,,	'Frisco	Aug.	31	..	76	,,
1897-8	,,	Frisco	Nov. 21	,,	Liverpool	April	4	..	134	,,
1898	,,	Liverpool	May 4	,,	New York	June	9	..	35	,,
1898-9	,,	New York	July 16	,,	Kobe	Jan.	5	..	172	,,
	,,	Kobe	Feb. 25	,,	Port Towns'd	April	4	..	38	,,
	,,	Tacoma	June 14	,,	Sydney	Aug.	20	..	67	,,
1899-1900	Left	Sydney	Nov. 22	,,	Honolulu	Jan.	10	..	49	,,
1900	Left	Honolulu	Mar. 5	,,	Astoria	Mar.	23	..	18	,,
	,,	Portland, O.	May 2	,,	Queenstown	Sept.	30	..	151	,,

The *Inverness-shire* was sold to the Norwegians after being dismasted off the Australian coast in 1915. She had come out from Liverpool with phosphates to Fremantle, W. Australia, in 124 days. She had a very mixed crowd, both fore and aft, this voyage, and I have a letter from one of her apprentices describing all sorts of trouble at Fremantle, including daily fights between the mates and the men.

At Fremantle sand ballast was taken in for the run across the Pacific to San Francisco. Soon after rounding the Leeuwin *Inverness-shire* ran into bad weather, and one Monday during the first dog watch the fore topgallant mast carried away. Two days later the fore topmast, with the topsail yards, crashed down on to the fo'c'sle-head. In spite of every kind of lashing and preventer staying, the main and mizen masts only held up for two more days, then the mizen broke off a yard above the deck and fell over the side, followed by everything on the main above the lower mast. The main braces carried away and left the mainyard swinging perilously at every roll of the ship. Twenty-four hours later the dismasting was completed in the most astonishing fashion. During the violent plunging and rolling of the ship the main lower mast jumped out of its step and clean over the side without touching the maindeck or bulwarks. This left the jigger mast with its jib-headed spanker alone rising above the debris. In an effort to get sufficient sail set to give the *Inverness-shire* steerage way, a wire was taken from the jigger masthead to the end of the broken bowsprit. On this wire

three small staysails were set.   They proved of little use and were
soon hauled down.

For the next three weeks the *Inverness-shire* drifted helplessly
about with her decks a mass of wreckage, her rails twisted and
broken, and her jigger mast threatening to come down at any
moment.   At last she was sighted by two Japanese cruisers which
were bound to Hobart.   They reported sighting her as a derelict.
The *Carteela* and the *Dover*, two ferry steamers, were at once
sent out to look for the lame duck, and after three days' search
they picked her up.   Then came a very hard tow before the anchor
was dropped in Sandy Bay, Hobart.

After this terrible knocking about the poor old *Inverness-shire*
was sold to the Norwegians and renamed *Svartskog*.   She has been
"missing" since October, 1920.

"Loch Nevis."

The last ship built for the famous Loch Line of Glasgow was
the *Loch Nevis*, launched June 5, 1894, by J. Reid & Co.   The
Loch Nevis was a very big carrier, lifting 4000 tons of deadweight
on a gross register of 2431 tons.   She was commanded by Captain
Colin McLeod, but only had a short life, being burnt at Iquique
after being some six years afloat.

"Grenada."

This ship was another of Russell's water ballast tank four-
masters.   Like many of the latter day big carriers, she was able
to make good running in strong fair winds.   As late as 1912 the
Grenada did the following good work under Captain Jones:—

Channel to Newcastle, N.S.W., in water ballast   ..   ..   ..   86 days
      (Best run 320 miles; 900 miles in 3 days; Cape to Leeuwin in 17 days)
Newcastle, N.S.W., to Valparaiso, Sept. 20-Oct. 26   ..   ..   36 days

At the end of the nineteenth century the *Grenada* was owned
by P. Denniston & Co. with a German in command.   She was then
bought by Lang & Fulton, who ran her until 1910, when she was
sold to Roberts, Owen & Co.; and she was still afloat when the
war started, but was sunk by U-boat, November, 1916.

Barrie's "Dudhope."

This big 2000-ton full-rigger, which was launched from Connell's yard in August, 1894, for C. Barrie & Son of Dundee, was still afloat and owned by Thomas Shute when war broke out, after which her ominous name proved too much for her and she was sunk by U-boat, July, 1917.

On her maiden passage she sailed from the Clyde to Philadelphia in 24 days—not bad work for a vessel of her type.   In 1913 we find her taking 109 days between Liverpool and Sydney under Captain Bright, which represents her average work, for, like all Connell's later ships, she had no pretensions to speed.

" Caithness-shire" and " Duns Law."

The last two ships to be built for the Shire Line were the sister barques *Caithness-shire* and *Duns Law*, the first of which was launched by Russell in June, 1894, and the second in November, 1896.

Registering 1640 tons, these two barques were an example of the most economical sailing ships that could be built.   They carried a large cargo, yet did not sail badly, and could be managed by a very small crew.

Here are the first few passages of the *Caithness-shire*, which was commanded by Captain David Stott, late of the *Linlithgowshire*.

1894	Left	Glasgow		Aug. 28	arrived	Sydney	Nov.	29	..	92 days
1894-5	,,	N'castle, N.S.W.	Dec. 25		,,	Valparaiso	Feb.	5	..	42 ,,
	,,	Taltal		May 8	,,	Rotterdam	Aug.	24	..	108 ,,
1895-6	,,	Rotterdam		Oct. 13	,,	Port Pirie	Jan.	7	..	85 ,,

The *Caithness-shire* was wrecked on Watling Island, Bahamas, on February 4, 1911, when bound from Wilmington, North Carolina, in sand ballast for Port Arthur, Texas.   She apparently struck on a quiet night, when abeam of the San Salvador light.   Captain Hatfield tried to back her off, but it was no use, and she only drifted further inshore and struck again.   The crew stood by on Watling Island for about a month, but the ship eventually had to be abandoned about the beginning of March.   In the inquiry it was discovered that the rocks on which the *Caithness-shire* struck were not properly marked, either in the Admiralty charts or in the American charts which Captain Hatfield was using.

The *Duns Law*, which was taken from the stocks by Captain Robert Greig, had a very short life, being burnt and sunk at Iquique in November, 1904, when commanded by Captain John Nichol.

Amongst the Shire Line fleet during the years before the war were two or three bought ships, such as the well-known four-mast barques *Falls of Halladale* and *Jordan Hill*. They also bought the 1900-ton steel full-rigger *Aspice* from R. J. Swyny of Liverpool. The *Aspice*, which was launched by Mackie & Thomson in February, 1894, was sold to the Genoese in 1900 and renamed *Sant' Erasmo*. She was re-sold in 1905 to Hamburg and then received the name of *Sea-Rose*. Finally in 1909 she went to the Norwegians and became the *Aggi*. The *Aggi* was wrecked in May, 1915.

The Family of Law and the Shire Line Captains.

After writing so much about the various ships of the famous Shire Line, I think it is only fair that I should say a few words about the Laws and their captains.

The family of Law came from the county of Fifeshire. which has the reputation of breeding a "pawky, langheided" people, who waste little time and less sentiment. Thomas Law, the founder of the firm, was a very able and far-seeing man, and it has always been said in Glasgow that he would have been a man of the "Inverforth" and "Inchcape" type had he lived. To show his business acuteness I will give the following anecdote: The Laws had chartered and were loading a ship on their Glasgow berth with general cargo for Australia. At the last moment a shipper sent down a consignment of bricks, but there was no room for them and there was not another sailing for at least a month. The shipper kicked up a row because he had been told to send them down. Thomas Law, who did not want to lose the shipment, thought for a bit and then went to the skipper of the chartered ship. After a few casual remarks he asked the latter whether it was true that the ship was stored in excess of B.O.T. requirements for that particular passage. The captain innocently admitted that this was the case, whereupon the astute Law told him that he must take out his excess stores to the weight of the short-shipped bricks. The furious skipper could do nothing but obey, but he did not fail to air his opinion of Thomas Law in a voice that would have reached the foretop.

Thomas Law was followed as head of the firm by James Law, and then William Law, later senior partner. David Law, senior, the father of Thomas Law, was the owner of several ships, such as the unfortunate *Cowden Law*, but he was never a partner of the firm.

In the Appendix I give a list of the best known commanders in the Shire Line. Many of these have already been alluded to, especially the older men, such as Peattie and McGibbon. Amongst the younger commanders one of the most interesting characters was Captain C. C. Dixon, who commanded the *Arctic Stream* and the *Elginshire*. Small and wiry of build, he was a second Captain Kettle without the pointed beard, and possessed all that intrepid little man's love of adventure.

The captain's gig, when Dixon was in command, was constantly in use, for he was a great sportsman in every way, and he was also a naturalist and geologist, besides being a keen surveyor. If a tropical island happened to be on the course of Dixon's ship, and the weather was favourable, he would sling his Winchester and a camera into the gig, and with a crew of four apprentices set out on a voyage of exploration. He always inspected derelicts or any wreckage floating on the water at close range, and he was a great ship visitor, passing windjammers and even steam tramps being stopped and visited.

As regards his surveying, any little known island or seldom visited bits of coastline were always of great interest to the little captain, and he rarely failed to take a running survey. Particular attention was paid to Kerguelen Island, and he rectified many of the details of its coastline as given in the charts.

Most navigators steered a wide course to avoid such obstructions as the Crozets and Prince Edward Islands, but Dixon always passed them close to and kept a sharp lookout for shipwrecked mariners. He had 1000 fathoms of wire on his sounding machine, and was always taking deep sea soundings and examining samples of the ocean bed   As an inventor of scientific instruments he was full of ingenuity.   In his saloon he kept a large chest full of assorted wheels, springs, rods, etc., from which he used to construct such instruments as anemometers, wind pressure gauges, deep sea pressure gauges, etc.   With the help of these his meteorological logs were packed with interesting observations.

Captain Dixon was a keen fisherman and ornithologist, a splendid shot, an enthusiastic photographer and cinematographer, and last but not least, a splendid sailor and navigator.

Captain Dixon commanded the *Arctic Stream* from 1904 until 1912, and the *Elginshire* from 1912 to 1919.   The *Arctic Stream* was a fast ship and her passages were always above the average, even with captains who were not carriers of sail; but the *Elginshire* was not considered a flyer.   Nevertheless she made some splendid runs under Captain Dixon, such as:

Santos to Cossack (N.W. Australia)   ..   42 days

On this passage the *Elginshire* made a run of 318 miles, and averaged 224 miles a day for 36 days.

To show Captain Dixon's daring navigation, in 1917 he sailed the *Elginshire* right into Durban harbour without a local chart, without any sailing directions, and without a pilot on board (owing to some misunderstanding about the pilot boat).   The little skipper had never been to the port before, and the shipping fraternity of Durban, which is a large and knowledgeable one, made much of him for this exploit.

As an up-to-date, highly intellectual shipmaster, it would be hard to find Dixon's equal.   All those who sailed with him became his devoted admirers, and I am not exaggerating when I say that the boys in the half-deck worshipped him as their hero.

Another of Law's later captains of whom I should like to say a few words was John Nichol.   He was by far the youngest master in the fleet at the time when he gained his first command.   Nichol served his time in the new *Inverness-shire* under John Peattie, who declared that he was a splendid boy, first in everything, and bound to get on.   In May, 1898, he passed for second mate, and joined the *Ross-shire* at Hamburg in that capacity when only 20 years old.   I was in his watch, and a better leader I never want to serve under. Being as strong as a bull he was a tremendous hard worker and allowed no malingering, but he was always cheery and good-tempered.

On leaving the *Ross-shire* in 1900 he joined the *Agnes Oswald* as mate. He left her in April, 1901, to pass for master, and then joined the *Duns Law* as chief officer. The *Duns Law* left Cardiff on August 27, 1901, with coal for Hongkong, but was obliged to put into Funchal with her captain sick. Nichol was then appointed master of the *Duns Law* when he was only 23 years of age. All went well until November, 1904, when the *Duns Law* took fire and sank whilst lying in Iquique. Nichol was then given the command of the old Allan four-mast barque *Glencairn*. This was in July, 1905. Two years later on July 25, 1907, whilst on a voyage from Rochester to Seattle, the *Glencairn* stranded in attempting the Le Maire Straits. After the vessel had struck the starboard life-boat was launched, but it capsized and two of the men in it were drowned. A little while later the rising tide floated the *Glencairn*, but she was leaking so badly that Captain Nichol was obliged to beach her. The remainder of the crew, along with Mrs. Nichol and her two young children, were safely landed in the other boats, and it was owing to Nichol's fine leadership that there were no further casualties.

At the Court of Inquiry it was suggested that it would have been more prudent if Captain Nichol had shaped a course outside Staten Island rather than making a daring attempt at Le Maire Straits. However, the Court refrained from dealing with his certificate owing to his past good character and seamanlike conduct after his ship had stranded.

Messrs. Law gave Captain Nichol the command of the second *Fifeshire* in January, 1908, but his luck was still out, for on August 21 of that year his ship was stranded on an uncharted reef off the Gilbert Islands on a fine clear night with a smooth sea and moderate breeze from E.N.E. This time poor Nichol was done for, and his certificate was suspended for twelve months for reckless navigation, the Court contending that he had set a dangerous course. His career in Law's was, of course, finished, but he rose above misfortune and worked his way up to master in Maclay & McIntyre's steam tramps. Then at the end of 1914 he came ashore in bad health, and died of consumption, the scourge of his family, in October, 1915.

John Nichol was a splendid seaman and a grand shipmate. His bad luck seems to have been due to his keenness to make a passage, which led him to cut corners and take risks. However, he was not to be beaten, and took his ill-fortune with the same old happy smile and unconquerable spirit.

John Nichol must not be confused with David Nicoll, a much older master, but one who was almost as unlucky. David Nicoll commanded the *Hannah Landles* way back in 1884. In 1893 he succeeded Captain Peattie in the command of the *Sutherlandshire*, and at once distinguished himself by sailing her from Astoria to Falmouth in 98 days.

Tragedy overwhelmed Captain Nicoll on July 25, 1900, when he lost his beautiful ship on Java Head. Here we have another example of the fatal malignity of the sea against captains' wives. In the wreck of the *Sutherlandshire* Mrs. Nicoll was the only person drowned. Besides having his leg badly hurt, Captain Nicoll was knocked out for about a year. Then in 1902 he was given another famous Shire liner, the *Cromartyshire*. After making a number of outstanding passages in this vessel, David Nicoll's luck again deserted him, and he lost her near Antofagasta in October, 1906. After this he was given the command of the *Gulf Stream*.

In 1911 Captain Nicoll sailed from Glasgow for Vancouver, but never arrived, the *Gulf Stream* being posted "missing" on February 21, 1912. It is probable that the little barque and her aged commander fell victims to the fury of Cape Horn.

After a careful inspection of the passages listed in Messrs. Law's voyage books I should say that John Peattie, Andrew Baxter, C. C. Dixon, David Nicoll and David Roberts were the best passage makers amongst the Shire Line captains. My old commander, Andrew Baxter, never made a bad passage from 1884, when he took over the *Kirkcudbrightshire*, until 1900, when he gave up the command of the *Ross-shire* and retired from the sea. The passages of the *Ross-shire* under Captain Baxter have already been mentioned, but the following were the best of those made by the *Kirkcudbrightshire* whilst he was her master:—

CAPTAIN DAVID STOTT

CAPTAIN WILLIAM WRIGHT

CAPTAIN T. C. FEARON

CAPTAIN DAVID ROBERTS

[See Page 256

CAPTAIN R. H. FURNEAUX

CAPTAIN JOHN PEATTIE

CAPTAIN O. H. HENDERSON

CAPTAIN JOHN NICHOL

[*See Page* 257

1884-5	Port Glasgow to San Francisco	..	..	115 days
1885	San Francisco to Queenstown	..	..	106 „
	Liverpool to Rangoon	..	..	95 „
1886	Liverpool to Chittagong	..	..	95 „
1887	New York to Melbourne	..	..	86 „
1888	Newport to Albany (W. Australia) ..	..	73 „
1888-9	Calcutta to Dundee ..	..	..	101 „
1889	Montrose to Melbourne	..	..	83 „
1889-90	Lyttelton to London ..	..	..	86 „
1891	Astoria to Queenstown	..	..	104 „

The longest passage made by the *Kirkcudbrightshire* while under Captain Baxter was 133 days from Maryport round the Horn to Tonala, Mexico. The longest passage made by the *Ross-shire* whilst under Captain Baxter was 149 days from Philadelphia to Kobe, Japan, in 1898. Neither of these was a slow passage by any means, and taking all his passages to every part of the world, I think it would be hard to find a record which had greater freedom from accident or a better average per passage.

The veteran Captain Peattie excelled in San Francisco passages when in command of the *Sutherlandshire*. The *Sutherlandshire* was undoubtedly one of the fastest ships in the Shire Line, and her record in the grain trade is truly amazing, the outward passages round the Horn being specially good. Captain Peattie took command of the *Sutherlandshire* in 1885, and the following is a complete list of his passages in the grain trade from 1885 to 1893:—

1885	San Francisco to Queenstown	..	..	104 days
	(Captain Peattie took command in San Francisco)			
	Liverpool to San Francisco	..	..	115 „
1886	San Francisco to the Lizard	..	..	105 „
	Tyne to San Francisco	..	..	136 „
1887	San Francisco to Queenstown	..	..	107 „
1889	Antwerp to San Francisco	..	..	138 „
1889-90	San Francisco to Liverpool	..	..	114 „
1890-91	San Francisco to Queenstown	..	..	108 „
1891	Tyne to San Francisco	..	..	126 „
1891-2	San Francisco to Dunkirk	..	..	134 „
1893	Astoria to Antwerp ..	..	..	134 „

Captain Peattie then took over the *Inverness-shire*, but she was not a ship that could emulate the performances of the

s

Sutherlandshire, his best grain passage in her being Astoria to Liverpool, 116 days in 1895.

Captain Dixon was probably the next best passage maker, but Roberts ran him close   Captain D. Nicoll had a splendid chance to make passages when he commanded the *Sutherlandshire* and the *Cromartyshire*.   Here are a few of the *Sutherlandshire's* grain passages whilst under his command:—

1893	Antwerp to Portland, Oregon	..	..	134 days
1894	Astoria to Falmouth ..	..	..	98 „
	Antwerp to San Francisco ..	..	..	137 „
1895	San Francisco to the Channel	..	..	106 „
1896	Astoria to Liverpool ..	..	..	114 „
1897-8	Portland, Oregon to Falmouth	..	..	131 „

In the records of Captain Baxter and Captain Nicoll I have given a complete list of the *Sutherlandshire's* outward and homeward passages from Europe to California, and I much doubt if many of the famous clippers of the fifties made a better average, taking it all round.   It may be contended that the best passage makers always had the fastest ships.   This, to a certain degree is, of course, the case, because naturally an owner would pick a good passage maker to put into a ship which had a reputation for speed to keep up. Baxter, however, made some splendid passages in the *Ross-shire*, which certainly could not be considered in the same class as the *Sutherlandshire* or the *Kirkcudbrightshire* as regards her sailing powers.

The fastest ships in the Shire Line were undoubtedly the full-riggers *Cromartyshire*, *Sutherlandshire*, *Arctic Stream*, and the sister ships *Kirkcudbrightshire* and *Clackmannanshire*.   To these must be added the beautiful little barque *Selkirkshire*, which was probably as fast as any of them.   No doubt there are many men who will declare that several others of the Shire fleet were as fast as the six mentioned.   If this is so, I can only say that they were not as lucky in their captains or their voyages.

The pretty little full-rigged ships *Agnes Oswald* and *Linlithgow-shire* ex *Jeanie Landles* certainly possessed a very good turn of speed, but they were not always sailed hard, so that the length of their passages varied a good deal.   The *Linlithgowshire*, however, when commanded by Captain Stott, who was afterwards Law's marine superintendent, made the following fine voyages in the Cape Horn trade:—

1884-5	Glasgow to San Francisco	.. .. ..	113 days
1885	San Francisco to Queenstown	.. ..	125 „
1887-8	Antwerp to San Francisco	.. .. ..	105 „
1888	San Francisco to Queenstown	.. ..	95 „
1889-90	London to San Francisco	.. .. ..	112 „
1890	San Francisco to Hull	.. .. ..	101 „
1890	London to Tacoma	.. ..	141 „
1891	Tacoma to Queenstown	.. .. ..	117 „

The smartest voyage of the *Agnes Oswald* was probably her New Zealand voyage under Captain Henderson in 1888, when she went from London to Lyttelton in 78 days, and from Lyttelton to Falmouth in 81 days.

Taken all round, the Shire Line fleet were very consistent passage makers, and except for their last few carriers Messrs. Law did not possess a slow ship.

"East Indian," "East African," and "Australian."

These three ships of Lang & Fulton's were well known in Melbourne during the few years previous to the war. *East Indian* and *East African* were Duncan-built 1750-ton steel barques, but the *Australian* was a full rigger of 2100 tons of Russell's build. All three were meant to carry large cargoes rather than make record runs, but they were no slower than other ships of their date.

In 1901-2 the *Australian* took part in a race home round the Horn from San Francisco, the times of which were as follows:—

Manydown	left 'Frisco	Oct. 16, 1901	arrived Hull		Mar. 3, 1902	138 days
Celtic Chief	„ „	„	„	Falmouth	„ 4 „	139 „
Australian	„ „	„	„	Queenstown	„ 8 „	143 „
Brussels	„ „	„	„	„	„ 10 „	145 „

It was agreed between the captains that the master of the last vessel to arrive should pay for a dinner. The captain of the *Brussels*, therefore, had to provide a feast for the other three.

The *Australian* went "missing" in 1909 when bound from Mazatlan to Sydney.

The *East Indian* was sold to the Germans in 1910-11 and renamed *Hans*; and the *East African* was sold to the Norwegians for £3600 in 1911.   Both were still afloat when war broke out.

"Cambuskenneth."

In December, 1892, Russell & Co. launched the steel full-rigger *Cambuskenneth* of 1925 tons gross.   She was followed in 1894 by the *Cambuswallace*, and in 1895 by the *Cambusdoon*, all three ships being managed by R. Russell & Co.

The *Cambuswallace* was wrecked on September 3, 1894, on her maiden voyage.

I have a note of the following passages made by the *Cambus-kenneth*:—

1893	Clyde to Rio de Janeiro	36	days
1901	New York to Sydney	137	,,
1901-2	Prawle Point to Melbourne	77	,,
1902	New Caledonia to Greenock	138	,,
1903	Newcastle, N.S.W., to San Francisco ..	60	,,

The *Cambusdoon*, which only registered 1522 tons net did not make any crack passages, my only notes concerning her being:—

1897	San Francisco to Queenstown	169	days
	(The worst passage of the year)		
1898	New York to Melbourne	130	,,

This ship was condemned in February ,1904.

The *Cambuskenneth* sailed from the Columbia River on February 13, 1915, for Liverpool and was captured before being sunk by U-boat.   She had been under Norwegian flag since 1909.

"Kynance."

This bald-headed full-rigger, which was built in 1895 by A. Rodger & Co. for Gordon Cowan, and managed by Lang & Fulton, was named after the famous Kynance Cove in Cornwall, a painting of which place used to hang in her saloon.

The *Kynance* was of course a carrier pure and simple, but whilst under the command of Captain Alex. Auld between 1903 and 1909 she made some very fair passages.   Captain Auld was a very experienced shipmaster.   Previous to taking over the *Kynance* he had had the *Algoa Bay* since 1891.   His first command had been one of Smith's famous "Cities," the *City of Delhi* which he had taken over at the age of twenty-one.

In 1903 the *Kynance* was laid up in San Francisco for two years and nine months, after which she took a grain cargo to London. In 1906 she loaded at Antwerp for San Francisco and sailed on July 8.   On this passage, after being battered off the Horn for seven weeks, she reached San Francisco 149 days out.   Three days behind her the *Leyland Brothers* arrived.   This ship had been spoken off the River Plate 17 days before the *Kynance* left Antwerp.   In February, 1907, the latter crossed the Pacific in ballast from 'Frisco to Newcastle, N.S.W., in 41 days.   Her next passage was from Newcastle with coal to Caldera, Chile, in 46 days.   Finally she loaded nitrate at Taltal and reached Falmouth just under 100 days out, her passage being spoilt by north-easterly gales after passing the Western Isles, to which point she had only taken 65 days.   After discharging at Glasgow the *Kynance* sailed from Liverpool on April 6, 1908, for Vancouver.   This time she had a five weeks' struggle off the Horn, and when she arrived off Cape Flattery, 150 days out, was held up by fog and did not anchor at Vancouver until 12 days later.

Captain Auld's last passage in the *Kynance* was from Bellingham Bay, Puget Sound, with heavy squared timber to Liverpool, and the *Kynance* made the run in 148 days.

On her last voyage the *Kynance* was commanded by Captain Barham, and she made the passage from Liverpool to Sydney in about 100 days.   During the passage she had considerable deck damage when running the Easting down; and at Sydney one of her apprentices fell down the hold and was killed.   The luck of some ships seems suddenly to peter out until they are overwhelmed in a final disaster.   From Sydney the *Kynance* crossed to Valparaiso. She made a very fair run, but lost her fore topmast.   After discharging she sailed for Iquique in ballast, and on July 29, 1910, drifted ashore in a calm at Punta Blanca, near Tocopilla, and became a total loss.   All hands were saved, but a few days later an apprentice off the *Vimeira* was drowned whilst salving gear from the wreck.

"Largiemore" and "Arranmore."

These two Russell-built steel full-riggers were the largest vessels belonging to Thomson, Dickie & Co.'s Maiden City Line of sailing ships. In 1890 Russell had built the sister ships *Culmore* and *Edenballymore* of 1640 tons for Thomson, Dickie, and the *Largiemore* and *Arranmore*, 300 tons bigger, were improvements upon these 1890 ships. The *Culmore*, by the way, foundered at sea on November 14, 1894, whilst the *Edenballymore* was sold to Lang & Fulton in 1902 and renamed *Edenmore*.

The *Largiemore* was considered one of the finest of Russell's full-riggers. Though a large carrier she was very heavily rigged. One of her sail makers, writing to the P.S.N. Co. magazine *Sea Breezes* in 1922, gives the following interesting information about her rigging plan:—

Her masts and yards were all of steel, and of the hundreds of ships I have had connection with in my business as sail maker and rigger she was the squarest I have had through my hands. Her fore and main yards were 98 feet long, and fore and main royal 50 feet, and weighed 25 cwts. Her mainsail had 750 yards of canvas in it, and the dimensions were: head 94 feet, leaches 49 ft. 6 ins., and foot 102 feet—some sail! She had six topgallant yards, and I say without fear of contradiction that she was as strong a ship and as well found as ever sailed.

As regards her carrying capacity, the *Largiemore* lifted 3300 tons on a gross register of 1938 and net 1786. Throughout her existence under Thomson, Dickie's house-flag she was commanded by the late Captain G. J. Spencer, and under him she gained a great name for being a smart all-round ship in the last days of sail. Here are a few of her best passages:—

1897	Barry Dock to Rio de Janeiro	..	..	42 days
	Rio de Janeiro to Adelaide	..	..	43 ,,
1898	San Francisco to Falmouth	..	..	117 ,,
1898	Barry to Algoa Bay ..	..	..	57 ,,
1900	Barry to Rio de Janeiro ..	..	..	41 ,,
1901	Dover to San Francisco ..	..	..	119 ,,
1902	San Francisco to Falmouth	..	..	103 ,,

The Rio to Adelaide passage was said to be a record at the time. She was in ballast, and whilst running her Easting down before a westerly gale under royals, with her main and mizen courses hauled up, she made the remarkable 24-hour run of 360 knots. Her passage would have been even better if she had not been hove to in three days of furious weather off Cape Leeuwin and afterwards becalmed for five days.

Owing to the coal strike at Newcastle, N.S.W., the *Largiemore* was ordered across to San Francisco from Port Adelaide. After a passage across the Pacific of 72 days Captain Spencer found on his arrival (September, 1897) that grain freights were down to 30s. His owners ordered him to await better times, so the *Largiemore* was laid up off Mission Bay until September, 1898, when she was forced to take a cargo of grain at 27s 6d. Amongst the ships loading in San Francisco at the same time as the *Largiemore* was the famous *Muskoka*, and Captain Crowe was offering to wager that he would be first ship home of the fleet. The *Muskoka*, as we have already noted, arrived on January 25, 1898, and reached Queenstown 98 days out. *Largiemore* sailed 10 days behind the crack four-master and made a remarkable run as far as the Equator in the Atlantic, where she was 70 days out. Unfortunately she did not find any N.E. trades until she was in 6° N., and then they were very scant. This spoilt what should have been an unusually good passage.

On his next voyage from Algoa Bay Captain Spencer sailed from Algoa Bay for Newcastle, N.S.W., ballasted with dry sand. When five days out from Port Elizabeth the *Largiemore* was nearly capsized in a cyclone off Mauritius. For three days she lay on her beam ends, with her lower yards dragging in the water on the lee side and her hatches covered. However, she came out of this trouble with only the loss of some of her canvas, and she reached Newcastle 43 days out. Instead of crossing to San Francisco this year she took coal to Valparaiso, and it was whilst she was lying in Valparaiso Bay that Beazley's *Falstaff* came to grief in a norther by dragging across the bows of the P.S.N. Co. steamer *Victoria*. The *Largiemore's* crew distinguished themselves by taking off some of the *Victoria's* native crew. The *Largiemore* was lying to windward of the steamer, and it took the men in her volunteer boat three hours of desperate pulling to get back to their ship from the *Victoria* with the rescued Chilenos. Her homeward passage that year was 92 days with grain from Punta de Lobos to Plymouth.

Her Cape Horn voyage in 1901-2 was perhaps the best round voyage made by the *Largiemore*. She took her departure from Dover on June, 27, 1901, and arrived at Falmouth March 31, 1902.

As crews became less and less efficient, and freights less lucrative the *Largiemore's* passages gradually lengthened, and her stays in port were longer. Her career under the British flag came to an end in 1910, when she was sold to the Norwegians. Four years later, in 1914, she was posted as "missing."

The *Arranmore*, which was launched in October, 1893, was one of the few ships salved after a S.E. gale off the Cape. Algoa Bay has been a veritable graveyard for sailing ships. On September 1, 1902, no less than 17 sailing ships, 2 steam tugs, and several lighters, were driven ashore by a furious south-east gale. On this occasion 63 lives and 12,500 tons of shipping were lost. The ships were literally torn to pieces and piled on top of each other in the terrific surf. To the eastward of the sea wall the following wrecks lay along the shore. I give them in their order from west to east.

Steam lighter *Scotia*, a complete wreck		*Limari*		
S.S.	*Clara*	*Agostino Rombo*	in one confused heap of	
	Gabrielle	*Waimea*	wreckage.	
	Arnold	*Hermanos*		
	Constant	*Inchcape Rock*		
	Iris	*Hans Wagner*		
	Oakworth	*Coriolanus*		
	Emmanuel	*Nautilus*, a complete wreck		
	Content	*Sayre*		
Tug	*Countess Carnarvon*	*Thekla*		
	Cavaliere Michele Russo, a complete wreck			

A few days previous to this the man-of-war anchorage in Simon's Bay had been visited by a tremendous blow from the northward, in which H.M.S. *Gibraltar*, flagship of Rear-Admiral Moore, and *Penelope*, depot ship, had all they could do with both bowers and sheet anchors down to ride it out. On this occasion the well-known *Principality* was nearly lost. At 10-45 a.m. there was a tremendous squall from N. by E. which came down the valley past Elsey Peak and hit the anchorage in a series of furious gusts. This started the anchors of the *Principality* and she commenced to drive so fast

CAPTAIN ANGUS MACKINNON

CAPTAIN HUGH BRABENDER

CAPTAIN ANDREW BAXTER

[*See Page* 257

CAPTAIN ANDREW BAXTER AND CAPTAIN DAVID BONE

[*See Page* 258

that it seemed certain that she would go on the rocks to leeward. However, the mate quickly hoisted his fore topmast staysail with the sheet to port, and thus paid the ship's head off to starboard. Soon after this her starboard anchor hooked up in the moorings on to which H.M.S. *Penelope* was hanging.   The *Principality* then veered cable and dropped down alongside the *Penelope*, but her anchor held and she was saved.

The *Arranmore* came to grief in Algoa Bay on the night of November 14, 1903, during which a terrible gale raged along the Cape coast.   The following ships stranded at Port Elizabeth:—

British barque	*Arranmore*	Norwegian barque	*Elda*
,,	*County of Pembroke*	,,	*Wayfarer*
Italian barque	*Sant' Antonia*	,,	*Two Brothers*

Whilst at Mossel Bay the Norwegian barque *King Cenric* was blown high and dry.

The *Arranmore* had just arrived in Algoa Bay with a cargo of wheat from Portland, Oregon.   During the gale she and the s.s. *Mashona* were in collision, and at the inquiry it was found that this collision had rendered her helpless and was the chief cause of her going ashore, no blame being attached to master, officers or crew.

After five months the *Arranmore* was refloated, but her fore and main masts had gone by the board, and it was found too expensive to send out masts from England, so a Dutch tug, the *Zwartezee*, was sent out to the Cape, and she was successful in towing the *Arranmore* from Algoa Bay to the Clyde.   This must be one of the longest tows on record, being 6800 miles.   Including time occupied in coaling the tug at Dakar, this remarkable piece of towage was accomplished in 54 days, or at the rate of 130 miles a day.

In 1910 the *Arranmore* was sold to Hamburg owners and renamed *Waltraute*.   In 1913 the renamed *Arranmore* was converted into a sailors' hostel belonging to the Hamburg Harbour Mission, but soon after the outbreak of war she was commandeered and turned into a submarine depot ship at Heligoland, being fitted with electric light and every convenience for housing the crews of the submarines whilst they were in port.   Soon after the Armistice she was taken to Leith under the name of *Vindicatrix* in order to house the crews of the surrendered German ships.   Here she was nearly lost, for she dragged her anchors and stranded at Inchkeith. A later service was during the shipping strike in 1925, when she was taken to the West India Dock, London, and used by the Shipping Federation as a floating hostel for seamen.

The Queerly Rigged "Falklandbank."

Besides the two magnificent four-mast barques *Olivebank* and *Cedarbank*, Messrs. Mackie & Thomson built one other ship for Andrew Weir & Co. This was the full-rigger *Falklandbank* of 1780 tons.

There was nothing very remarkable about the *Falklandbank's* sailing or build. Launched in April, 1894, she was just a steady-going, large capacity, round the world deep-waterman. But wherever she went she had sailormen gazing at her in wonder owing to the unusual way in which she was rigged. Her lower masts and top-masts were in one steel tube, and she had extremely long topgallant doublings. Instead of the upper topsail yards being parrelled to the topmast, or, when topmast and lower mast are in one, to that mast, they were parrelled to the heel of the topgallant mast and hoisted to the cap. Over these she had single topgallant and royal yards, which were very square. I do not think there was any advantage in this rig, and it certainly spoilt the look of the ship aloft, the thick doubling when the yards were on their lifts filling up the space between the upper topsail and topgallant yards, and giving a very clumsy appearance. Many sailormen declared that the *Falklandbank* had stump topgallant yards, but the squareness of her sail plan, and the almost equal depth of her topgallant sails and royals, gave her the appearance of a bald-header when she was under sail.

On November 9, 1907, the *Falklandbank* sailed from Port Talbot with Welsh coal for Valparaiso and went "missing." Some believed that she foundered in a pampero which raged off the River Plate just about the time that she would have been passing. Others suggested that she had been destroyed through her coal lighting by spontaneous combustion, but it is more probable that she, along with the big *Toxteth*, was overcome by the terrible weather dealt out by Cape Stiff that year.

The *Invermark*, which followed the two big full-riggers from the coal port, was six weeks off the Horn, and had a fearfully hard struggle to survive, and her officers declared that the weather they went through was enough to sink any vessel except an Inver barque.

"Thornliebank's" Trying Passage.

The last sailing ship built for the Bank Line was the 2100-ton full-rigger *Thornliebank*, which was launched from Russell's yard in September, 1896.   This was the second *Thornliebank*, the first, a 1500-ton barque, having been burnt in February, 1891.

Thornliebank II was just a large economical carrier with no pretensions to speed.   For instance, in 1900 she was 174 days coming home from Astoria to Queenstown.   In 1903, however, she had a worse passage than this.   She sailed from Philadelphia in August of that year, bound for Sydney.   After weathering out a series of heavy gales in the North Atlantic, the *Thornliebank* began to leak badly, and on September 9 it was discovered that a number of her rivets had started.   The donkey engine, as was often the case with machinery aboard a sailing ship, was not in working order, and so it was spell and spell at the hand pumps for the rest of the passage. The *Thornliebank's* next trouble was the shifting of her cargo, which rolled from side to side so that the ship was sometimes sailing with her starboard rail under, and at others with her port rail in the water.   In such a case the captain kept his boats fully provisioned and all ready for lowering, but the *Thornliebank* must have had a fine crew who stuck to their work most gallantly, for after 165 days the Bank liner was brought into Sydney safely, in spite of leaks, bad weather, and shifting cargo.

The *Thornliebank* was wrecked in November, 1913.

"Monkbarns" The Last of the Flying Horse Sailers.

During the nineties four big carriers of just under 2000 tons gross were launched for Corsar's Flying Horse Line.   These were:—

Almora, steel three-mast barque	Built by	Hamilton	Launched	June, 1893
Monkbarns, steel ship	,,	McMillan	,,	June, 1895
Fairport, steel ship	,,	Russell	,,	Mar., 1896
Musselcrag, steel barque ..	,,	Hamilton	,,	May, 1896

The best known, and I think the best sailer, of these four ships was the *Monkbarns*.

There were very few large three-mast barques that possessed any speed, but the *Almora* was noted wherever she went for the extraordinary length of her passages, and I do not think that *Musselcrag* was any more of a clipper.   *Fairport* will be remembered for her dismastings.

The *Monkbarns*, by rights, should have been mentioned amongst *Belford's* sisters, for she was one of McMillan's standard 1900-ton ships.

Like all Corsar's ships, as will be seen from the illustration, she had the famous flying horse figure-head.

During her long life, for the *Monkbarns* was one of the last sailing ships under the Red Ensign, she had many adventures.   Many old windjammer apprentices of the nineties will remember the race at Crockett in 1896 between the gigs of the *Monkbarns*, the *Buteshire,* and a German barque, which was won by the lads of the *Monkbarns* after the German boat had led most of the way, the *Buteshire's* crew coming in second.

Of her grain passages, the best I know of was 110 days from 'Frisco to Falmouth in 1904, when her time was better by two days than that of such famous flyers as the Loch Line clipper *Loch Carron*, and the French barque *Marguerite Molinos*.

Whilst outward bound to San Francisco in 1906 she was caught in field ice to the southward of the Horn, during the depths of the winter, and frozen in for 63 days of bitter Antarctic weather, during which time her veteran skipper, Captain Robinson, died.

In 1910 the *Monkbarns* had a very unpleasant passage out to Melbourne from Hamburg.   Leaving Hamburg on February 14 she was held up for 17 days in the North Sea by furious gales. Then on May 1, when off the Leeuwins, she weathered out another heavy gale.   Unfortunately, as so often happens, the wind went down before the sea, and left the *Monkbarns* rolling rail under. It was a marvel that she did not roll all her masts out of her, but her gear held, except on the fore, where the topgallant mast was carried away though it luckily fetched clear of everything.

The *Monkbarns* arrived at Port Phillip 116 days out, and Captain

J. Parry heaved a sigh of relief as his anchor went down, for the passage had been an anxious one for him owing to the fact that the *Monkbarns* had 750 cases of dynamite and 300 kegs of gunpowder in her hold, which, in the heavy pitching and rolling of the ship during her passage, might have blown up at any moment.   At this date Corsar's ships were being managed by Hardie & Co.

In 1910-11 the remaining ships of the flying horse fleet were dispersed, *Almora*, *Fairport* and *Musselcrag* going to the Norwegians, and the *Monkbarns* being bought by Stewart for £4850.

In the few years before the war, under Stewart's house-flag, the *Monkbarns*, commanded by Captain Donaldson, went the usual round of sailing ships at that date.   This was Europe to River Plate; River Plate to Newcastle, N.S.W.; Newcastle, N.S.W., to nitrate port; and nitrate port to U.K. or Continent.

As regards the *Monkbarns's* sailing on these **passages** I find the following times:—

1912	Newcastle, N.S.W., to Taltal	..	..	58 days
	Taltal to London	..	..	95 „
1913	London to Buenos Ayres	..	..	60 „

After successfully running the gauntlet of mine and torpedo the *Monkbarns* turned up in the Mersey in the spring of 1923, being then commanded by Captain William Davies, who, it will be remembered, had the *Belford* when she was sunk by a German submarine. She was the first sailing ship to load at Liverpool for 18 months, her cargo being rock salt for Sydney.

On her passage out, whilst running her Easting down to the westward of the Cape, the *Monkbarns* very nearly foundered in a gale of wind, which her crew described as of hurricane force.   It appears that on May 8 the wind suddenly increased from the south whilst Captain Davies was in the act of bringing his ship to the wind.   It was pitch dark and a torrential rain was falling.   The *Monkbarns* seems to have been hit by something like a tidal wave, and as she fell over into the trough her cargo shifted to leeward and held her down with her fair-leads in the water.   Captain Davies gave the order to cut away the fore and mizen lower topsails. This was done, but owing to the cargo having shifted the ship remained on her beam ends throughout the night.   As soon as it was light all hands were turned to trimming cargo. Whilst this was going on her decks continued to be looted by the angry seas. Her boats had been stove in, the galley funnel and skylight washed away, so that the galley was filled up with water, and the cabins also flooded out. Besides this one of the apprentices had fallen overboard from aloft before daybreak and been lost. But the *Monkbarns* had always been well kept up and was a sturdy well-built ship, and she came through this struggle successfully. As soon as the weather moderated Captain Davies determined to put into Cape Town, which was about 600 miles to leeward. Here the necessary repairs were quickly made, after which the ship continued her passage and arrived at Sydney 35 days out from the Cape.

From Sydney the *Monkbarns* proceeded across the Pacific to the West Coast *via* Newcastle, N.S.W. Twice she returned to Newcastle for a further coal cargo, and her last Pacific passages were:—

Iquique to Sydney arrived May, 1925 .. .. 89 days out
Newcastle, N.S.W., to Callao .. .. .. 60 „

After this, her third passage from Newcastle, the *Monkbarns* went to Valparaiso and took in the cargo of the *Queen of Scots*, which ship had been condemned as unseaworthy. Sailing from Valparaiso on January 20, 1926, she put into Rio de Janeiro on March 28, in order to land her captain, who was so ill that he died in Rio hospital shortly afterwards. After landing Captain Davies the ship proceeded on April 1 in charge of her first officer, and made a long run home, arriving at Gravesend on July 10, 1926, 99 days out from Rio.

She was then sold to the Norwegians for £2500; and they moored her at Corcubion to do duty as a coal hulk, post 1914-18 war.

The Dismasting of "Falkirk."

Another post-war member of Stewart's fleet was the barque *Falkirk*. The *Falkirk* and the *Wynford*, steel barques of 1980 tons gross, were built by Hamilton & Co. in 1896 and 1897, the former for Potter Bros. and the latter for Hickie, Borman & Co., of London.

The *Wynford* was sold to Norway, 1911, was renamed *Storegrund* and converted into a lighter in 1921; and when the Potters sold their ships the *Falkirk* came under Stewart's flag.   In her last days she was commanded by the well-known Captain Stainton Clark, who will be chiefly remembered as the master of the *Loch Carron* during the last years of the wool clippers.

After being laid up for some time at Bordeaux the *Falkirk* sailed from that port on January 6, 1924, in ballast for New York. The Bay of Biscay in January is not a pleasant spot for a sailing ship, especially when she is flying light, and from the first day the *Falkirk* had a very hard time of it.   It is probable that the ship's gear, after her long lay up, was in none too good a condition, and with her crew kept busy by the elements from the moment that sail had been made it was not possible to replace the rigging that was defective.

On the evening of January 12 the poor old *Falkirk* was almost overwhelmed by a tremendous cross sea, which hurled her about in such a way that Captain Clark must have spent most of his time gazing anxiously aloft.   At 8.20 p.m., in the midst of a storm of hail, thunder and lightning, the expected happened—the foremast came down with a crash.   Twenty minutes later this was followed by the main.   It was lucky that no one was killed, for much of the wreckage fell on the deck; but with the ship rolling wildly, the broken masts and yards, with their tangle of wires and ropes, were soon tipped over the side by the violent motion.   As usual the spars, held to the side of the ship by the lower rigging, began to act as battering rams and threatened to break in the steel plates both above and below the waterline.

It was a time when the best seamen, and the bravest, show up, for big risks had to be taken in cutting the gear clear of the ship. This, however, was done without more than a few minor injuries to the gallant crew.   With both fore and main gone it was dangerous to venture aloft on the mizen, whose stays had been cut adrift from the main.   The mizen topmast swayed perilously with every roll of the ship, and at last it too carried away, and in its fall broke the lower rigging adrift from the screws.   Again it was a wonder that no one was hurt.   The second mate had the luckiest escape, for he just had time to jump clear before the spanker boom dropped down on the top of the chart house.   The ship was also very lucky in that her wheel and binnacle, standard compass, and **two after** life-boats, were left undamaged.

At the time of the dismasting the *Falkirk* was in 48° N., 9° W. The French steam trawler *Gamin* came to her assistance, but owing to the heavy sea running could do no more than stand by whilst the dismasted ship drifted to the N.N.E. at the rate of three miles an hour. On January 15 the steamer *Somerset* made several tries to get a towing hawser aboard the *Falkirk*, but failed, and proceeded on her voyage on learning that the crew of the *Falkirk* refused to leave their vessel. Soon after this, a wireless message having been sent out for a tug, the Dutch ocean tug *Roodezee* appeared on the scene, and, getting hold of the *Falkirk*, brought her into Falmouth on January 17.

After this disastrous attempt to cross the Atlantic in mid-winter the *Falkirk* was not re-fitted, but was sent to the shipbreakers whilst Captain Stainton Clark retired from the sea after being 50 years afloat in sailing ships.

The " Glens" of Glasgow.

Between 1893 and 1897 Messrs. A. Rodger & Co. of Port Glasgow built the following stump topgallant yarders for Sterling & Co., of Glasgow:—

			Tons gross		Tons net		Launched	
Glenbank	steel barque	..	1481	..	1359	..	Aug.	1893
Glenard	,, ship	..	1937	..	1786	..	Sept.	1893
Glendoon	,, ,,	..	1981	..	1824	..	Oct.	1894
Glenelvan	,, ,,	..	1919	..	1756	..	Apr.	1895
Glenfinart	,, ,,	..	1963	..	1802	..	May	1895
Glenholm	,, ,,	..	1968	..	1804	..	June	1896
Glenpark	,, ,,	..	1959	..	1799	..	Jan.	1897

These bald-headers really came too late in the day, and were all sold soon after the end of the nineteenth century.

The *Glenard* was the last of the fleet to survive. She became a Finnish cadet ship, and with the yards stripped from her mizen carried about twenty cadets, and was maintained in excellent condition and very smartly kept up until the autumn of 1925, when she was broken up. None of these latter-day "Glens" were

"LARGIEMORE"

Photo by Adamson

[*See Page 262*

CAPTAIN WM. COUPER ABOARD THE "MORAYSHIRE"

Lent by R. C. Todd

"MONKBARNS" LOOKING FORWARD

Lent by W. P. Austin

[*See Page* 267

fast sailers, and the *Glenard's* last passage was 146 days from Iquique to Hull.

The *Glendoon* went to the Anglo-American oil fleet.

The *Glenfinart* was sold in 1899 to R. Thomas & Co., and was renamed *Harlech Castle,* she was wrecked July, 1905. The *Glenelvan* became very well known under G. M. Steeves' house-flag. This ship must not be confused with the *Glenafton,* an 1100-ton ship built by Hamilton in 1887, which was later in the blubber oil trade under the Uruguay flag and the name of *Ba.* Nor must we mix up the *Glenelvan* with the *Glenalvon,* which belonged to De Wolf.

The *Glenholm* was sold to the Prices of Liverpool in 1901. She was sunk by a U-boat in 1915.

Glenpark, the last of the fleet had a very short life, being wrecked on Gambia Island on February 2, 1901, when bound from Port Germein to Algoa Bay with a cargo of wheat.

"Glenalvon's" Record.

My mention of *Glenalvon* reminds me that I should correct what I said on page 336 of Volume I. about her record run. This was made under Captain W. Frank Andrews, and not under Captain King. Captain Andrews, writing to me from his home in Yarmouth Co., Nova Scotia, states that the *Glenalvon* made the following runs in 42° S. latitude when on a passage from Philadelphia to Kobe in the month of September—354, 354, 359, 355 and 379. These distances were computed from observations. The dead reckoning showed that the westerly set was 24 miles for each 24 hours during the five days. The late Captain D. H. Andrews, who succeeded Captain W. F. Andrews and later died in Rangoon, was then first officer of the ship, whilst the second mate was only an apprentice just out of his time, so the two brothers, Frank and Dan Andrews, sailed the ship watch and watch. Throughout the time they had northerly winds with clear weather. The crossjack and mizen royal were furled all the time, and the fore and main royals and mizen topgallant sail were constantly lowered to squalls but mastheaded again directly the wind eased.

As regards the list of passages given on page 335, Volume I., that from Kobe to Los Angeles should be from Kobe to Port Angeles,

T

Washington. This was made under Captain Frank Andrews. The *Glenalvon* left Kobe noon of the 1st and arrived 3 p.m. of the 22nd, which must be a record for this run.

As regards the captains of the *Glenalvon* I have received the following information from Captain W. F. Andrews: Captain Jones had the ship for her first two voyages and was then relieved by Captain W. F. Andrews in 1891. In 1898 Captain W. F. Andrews handed over the *Glenalvon* to his brother, Dan Andrews, in order to take command of the *Engelhorn*. On his first passage in command Captain Dan Andrews took the *Glenalvon* out to Rangoon in 92 days, but on his second passage to this port died during the smallpox epidemic. Walter Chamberlain, the chief officer, brought the ship home, when Captain W. F. Andrews took command again and Chamberlain continued as chief officer.

Altogether Captain W. F. Andrews was sixteen years in the *Glenalvon*. When he retired at Tacoma in order to go into business and take over De Wolf's agency there, Captain Oscar Henderson brought the ship home. Henderson was then relieved by Captain W. J. King, who had the *Glenalvon* for three voyages. It will thus be seen that Captain W. F. Andrews had the ship longest, and most of her records were made under his command.

The *Glenalvon's* record of 1801 miles in five days of $23\frac{1}{2}$ hours each has never been beaten, so far as I know. In commenting upon it Captain Andrews says that the ship could never log 17 knots, her best being about $16\frac{1}{2}$, but she possessed the merit, like many another iron clipper, of being able to carry her canvas under almost any strength of wind short of a hurricane.

Hardie's Sister Ships "Nivelle" and "Hougomont."

These two four-mast barques were launched in April and June, 1897, respectively from the Greenock yard of Scott & Co. The *Nivelle* had a short life, but the *Hougomont*, under those sturdy supporters of the square-rigger, the Finns, remained afloat until she was dismasted in 1932 when outward bound to Australia. She was condemned on arrival and her hull was sold for use as a breakwater.

The *Nivelle* was lost on Point Grande near Antofagasta on June 30, 1906, after a 45-day passage from Newcastle, N.S.W.

The following is *Nivelle's* record:—

1897	(Captain Williams) Penarth to Monte Video	56 days
	Monte Video to Sandy Hook	40 ,,
1897-8	New York to Shanghai	162 ,,
1898	Shanghai to Astoria	42 ,,
1898-9	Astoria to Liverpool	143 ,,
1899	Liverpool to Calcutta	108 ,,
1900	(Captain Stephen) Calcutta to Dundee	137 ,,
	Dundee to New York	46 ,,
1900-1	New York to Hongkong	154 ,,
1901	Hongkong to Astoria	58 ,,
	Astoria to Queenstown	128 ,,
1902	(Captain McMillan) Hamburg to 'Frisco	132 ,,
1903	San Francisco to Chemainos	17 ,,
1903-4	Chemainos to Cape Town	84 ,,
1904	Cape Town to Melbourne Heads	27 ,,
	Melbourne to Queenstown	109 ,,
1905	Liverpool to Victoria, B.C.	154 ,,
1905-6	Port Townsend to Sydney	74 ,,

On her maiden voyage the *Hougomont* sailed from Barry to Rio under Captain McNeil in 54 days, then Captain Lowe took command and went up to New York from Rio in 56 days, arriving January 16, 1898. From New York the *Hougomont* made the run to Yokohama in 142 days; then crossed to Astoria in 40 days, and came home from Puget Sound to Falmouth in 135 days.

These passages are a good example of her sailing powers. Like the *Nivelle*, she not only kept off the overdue list but, when given a chance, was capable of excellent work. For instance, on her second voyage she left Antwerp on June 28, 1899, and arrived San Francisco on November 6, after a passage of 131 days. Her homeward passage that year was also a good one. Leaving San Francisco on January 5, 1900, she arrived at Falmouth on May 4, 119 days out.

In the spring of 1901 she took 121 days from San Francisco to Falmouth. Then in 1903 she arrived home from San Francisco in 136 days to Point Lynas, where she arrived on February 22. Her cargo on this occasion consisted of 2000 tons of wheat and barley in bags, and just under 2000 tons of tinned fruit and salmon in cases.

The *Hougomont* had orders to discharge at Liverpool, but it was blowing hard from the southward and Captain Lowe was unable to get a tug or a pilot. As the ship was drifting to leeward he at length squared away, and on February 25 brought up in Maryport Roads. On the afternoon of February 26 the tug boat *Brilliant Star* was sent after the *Hougomont* by her owners. That night a furious sou'west gale screamed over the British Isles. The *Brilliant Star* hung on to the heavy *Hougomont* until her tow rope parted, and after being badly knocked about by the furious seas succeeded in reaching Maryport harbour. Meanwhile the *Hougomont* was driven up the Solway Firth before the wind and sea. Captain Lowe, who had his wife aboard, at once started to send out distress signals, but on such a night of storm no help could be given, and the ship went ashore in Allonby Bay at 6 o'clock the following morning.

Whilst the *Hougomont* was bumping in the surf her fore topgallant mast came down, and this was followed by the main topgallant mast. All hands took refuge on the poop, and, with the rising of the tide, were compelled to take to the jigger rigging, as the seas swept the ship from stem to stern. Soon after daybreak the northwest shift occurred, and this, together with the flood tide, drove the *Hougomont* up until she was close to the Grapes Inn, lying broadside on to the surf, which speedily gutted the main deck. Fo'c'sle, midship-house, and cabin were washed out and stripped of everything movable by the raging seas, and presently the hatches were stove in, and the cases of tinned fruits and salmon soon began to come ashore, where a crowd of people were watching the doomed ship. It was not until high tide and 11 a.m. that the life-boat from Maryport reached the *Hougomont*, and the ship's company were pretty well at their last gasp from exposure when they were brought ashore, where, however, they were quickly supplied with food and warm clothing by the kind inhabitants of the district.

The salvage of the *Hougomont* was placed in the hands of the late Sir Frederic Young, of the Liverpool Salvage Association. With the aid of two 10-inch pumps he managed to refloat her by March 15, when she was anchored in Maryport Roads. Bad weather, however, set in before anything further could be done, and in order to prevent the ship from again being driven up on the beach

Captain Young determined to take the bold course of bringing her into Maryport.

Even at high tide there were only a few inches between the ship's keel and the bottom of the harbour. It was blowing a whole gale from the W.N.W. Two tugs, the *Cruiser* and *Wrestler*, had the job of keeping the heavy *Hougomont* in the channel. However, the operation was performed successfully, although the harbour-master and deputy harbour master of Maryport, Captains Nelson and Dawson, had an anxious time of it until the ship was berthed and clear of the channel.

Finally, on March 31, the salved four-master was towed to Liverpool by the salvage steamer *Ranger*. Here she discharged the remainder of her cargo and afterwards proceeded to Greenock to re-fit.

Her first passage after the stranding was a very fine one. Sailing from Liverpool on October 18, 1903, she arrived at Victoria, B.C., on March 8, 1904, 139 days from Holyhead. That year her homeward passage was a long one, being 161 days from Tacoma to Dublin. At the end of this passage Captain McNeil took command of the ship, and in 1904-5 took her out to Antofagasta from Port Talbot in 99 days.

Other passages made by Captain McNeil were:—

1905	Pisagua to San Francisco		51 days
1905-6	Tacoma to Hull		142 „
	(138 days to the Lizard)		
1906	Hull to Philadelphia		45 „
1906-7	Philadelphia to Melbourne		125 „
1907	Melbourne to Queenstown		85 „

In the autumn of 1907 Captain J. McMillan succeeded Captain McNeil for a voyage. He took the *Hougomont* out to Sydney in 102 days from Liverpool, crossed from Newcastle, N.S.W., to Coquimbo in 43 days, and was then ordered to Tocopilla.

Tocopilla is some 500 miles to the northward of Coquimbo. A week after sailing from the latter port the *Hougomont* drifted past Tocopilla on the current, and, owing to the calm weather and the depth of water right in to the shore, was unable to anchor. With nothing but light airs, which hardly gave steerage way, Captain McMillan presently found himself 400 miles to the northward of his port. He thereupon threw up his charter and sailed away to Sydney, where he arrived on September 27, 1908, 80 days out from Coquimbo.

This instance of a sailing ship being carried past her port was by no means unusual on the West Coast of South America. In 1903, the *Lindisfarne* arrived off Antofagasta from Australia, but before she could make the anchorage she drifted past on the northerly current and was compelled to sail 1300 miles to the sou'west, and then up the coast again before making her port. This cost her a month's delay.

The *Hougomont* sailed from Sydney on Christmas Eve, 1908, and made a very long passage home. She was off the Lizard on May 20, 1909, and eventually arrived at Rotterdam on May 26, 153 days out. After this Captain McNeil took command again.

Her next adventure occurred during the war. On December 22, 1914, she sailed from London for New York, ballasted with chalk. Forty-six days later, on February 6, 1915, she went ashore on Fire Island during a dense fog, but was refloated without much trouble. She then took general cargo from New York to Melbourne in 104 days.

Messrs. John Hardie & Co. held on to the *Hougomont* until the end of 1924, when they sold her to Captain Gustaf Erikson who already had bought the *Archibald Russell* and the steel barque *Killoran* from Captain Hardie.

The *Hougomont's* first passage under the Finns was from St. Nazaire to Callao, where she arrived on July 9, 1925, 119 days out. Loading guano at the Lobos Islands she sailed from Peru on October 26, and reached London *via* the Panama Canal on January 18, 1926, being 56 days out from Colon. From London she went to Loderitz Bay, and from there to Port Loncoln, where she loaded grain.

On May 4, 1927, the *Hougomont* arrived at Falmouth 120 days out after a close race with the *Archibald Russell*. Her passage was the second best in the grain fleet. Her cargo was discharged at London.

Her next passage was from Gefle and Hernosand to Melbourne. Captain Hagerstrand sailed from Hernosand on August 26, 1926, and, after a bad time in the Bay, was dismasted off the Portuguese coast, being towed into Lisbon on October 27.   Here the *Hougomont* was refitted, and after a month's delay resumed her voyage on November 28.   She reached Melbourne on March 3, 1928—96 days from Lisbon.

"Ben Lee" and "Ben Dearg."

These two big full-riggers were the last of the famous Ben Line belonging to Watson Bros.   The *Ben Lee* was launched by Barclay, Curle in September, 1893, and the *Ben Dearg* by Connel in February, 1894.   When the Watsons sold their sailing ships the *Ben Lee* went to J. J. Rae & Co., of Liverpool, whilst the *Ben Dearg* was bought by Hamburg owners and renamed *Lasbek.*

Ben Lee came to grief in January, 1916.   After loading a general cargo for Australia in the Liverpool Docks, her captain decided to dispense with the services of a tug owing to the wind being fair, or perhaps because there was a scarcity of tug boats. Weighing anchor in the Sloyne he managed to get clear of the Channel under his topsails, but he was no sooner outside the North-West Lightship when the wind veered to the westward and started to freshen.   After beating to and fro for a couple of days the *Ben Lee* was run into off Bardsey by the American liner *St. Paul.*

As the ship seemed likely to sink at any moment, her crew abandoned her and were taken back to Liverpool by a Cork steamer. However, the *Ben Lee* did not sink as was expected, and was reported still afloat by a coaster at Holyhead, whereupon two mine-sweepers were sent out, and towed her into Refuge Harbour, Holyhead, where she was anchored.   On the following morning there was nothing to be seen of her except her topgallant masts sticking up above the water.   She seems to have gone down suddenly in the night and taken the shipkeeper with her, for he was never seen again.   She lay at the bottom until the war was over, when she was raised, repaired temporarily, and towed to Liverpool.   Here she was reconditioned as a hulk.

The *Ben Dearg* was allocated to the French Government at the end of the war.

CHAPTER VI.

THE SQUARE-RIGGERS OF THE TWENTIETH CENTURY.

The master, the swabber, the boatswain, and I,
  The gunner, and his mate,
Lov'd Mall, Meg, and Marion and Margery,
  But none of us car'd for Kate:
  For she had a tongue with a tang,
  Would cry to a sailor, go hang:
She lov'd not the savour of tar nor of pitch,
Yet a tailor might scratch her where'er she did itch:
  Then to sea, boys, and let her go hang.

(The Tempest.)

The Old Sea Song.

SHAKESPEARE with his supreme genius has caught the full flavour of the old "tarpaulin's" coarse and captious stave, but he has not given us the rant and the roar, the swing and the swank of the "Come-all-ye" of Nelson's time.

The dog-watch sea song came to its zenith with the glory of Trafalgar, after a series of fleet and single ship victories, which were without parallel in the history of the world.

The pig-tailed quid-chewing mahogany-cheeked shellback of our wooden walls had a simple childlike nature which delighted in professional songs strongly dashed with patriotic fervour—such as "Spanish Ladies," "The Saucy Arethusa," "Black Colours under her mizen did fly," "Will ye go to Cawsan' Bay, Billy Boy, Billy Boy?" Some of the tunes came from the playhouse. Of such was "Heart of Oak," to which many a doggerel account of a glorious sea fight was set. The words of "Heart of Oak" were written by David Garrick, and the music composed by Dr. Boyce as far back as 1759.

How the old-time seaman must have roared out such inspiriting and swinging choruses as "Heart of Oak are our ships," or "From

FIGURE-HEAD OF "MONKBARNS"

[*See Page* 267

"LOCH NEVIS"

[*See Page* 250

"HOUGOMONT" IN TOW

Photo by Cooper

[*See Page* 274

Ushant to Scilly is 35 leagues." How the gruff sea-broken voices must have cracked over "And it's oh, the bold blades of Old England" or "We'll go no more to Greenland in a ship that has no guns."

Glascock in 1834, like Boultbee Whall fifty years later, lamented that the old naval song was being supplanted by the music-hall ditty. But not only songs, but all kinds of sounds, were changing aboard ship as machinery slowly vanquished rope and canvas.

The Reef-Topsail Voice.

In Nelson's time the shouted commands of the officers resounded through all parts of a ship, and a strong voice in a watch-keeping lieutenant was greatly prized. Lord St. Vincent, that admiral of an iron-hard nature, had one weakness: he was inordinately proud of the power of his lungs, and it was his delight, when a band of thirty musicians was in full blast on his flagship, to hail the main-top and drown their instruments with his tremendous voice.

Another famous sailor, Sir Henry Blackwood, Nelson's frigate captain, had a voice that easily carried a mile. With the peace came the fashion for silent ships. A son of Sir Henry Blackwood was brought up under Admiral Hercules Robinson, and used to say that the silence aboard Robinson's ship during every manœuvre was "death-like." In the Merchant Service only the well-manned Blackwall frigates could be worked semi-man-of-war fashion by pipe and whistle; all-round-the-world cargo-wallahs were commanded by strength of voice, aided in a few cases by fist and belaying pin.

The Speaking Trumpet.

Few people have seen an old naval speaking trumpet used. Apparently there were watch trumpets and war trumpets, for we find Commodore Truxon before a night action ordering "the battle lanthorns to be lighted and his war trumpet to be placed in the lee gangway." Though this speaking trumpet has given way to the bridge telephone and the pea-whistle, the bosun's pipe remains as a relic of the old sea life.

With the last of the windjammers not only the chanty but the queer minor notes of the hauling cry are become extinct. The modern A.B. does not know how to sing out on a rope; the peculiar rhythm and yodelling howl are beyond him, and he contents himself generally with short quick grunts when tailing on to rope falls or hauling lines.

The Thunder of Canvas.

In the modern steamship the chief noises that assail the ears, besides the usual creaking of her internal fittings and the dull steady crash of an irresistible steel hull forcing its way through angry seas, are the pant of giant engines, the hum of motors, and in bad weather perhaps the howl of racing screws suddenly increasing their shuddering vibrations.

Numbers of sailors have never heard the thunder clapping of shaking canvas, nor have they ever listened to the grand oratorio of rope and wire singing, booming, humming and whining, to the twanging of those two mighty musicians, the East and West winds.

The tyro can gain some idea of the bang and clatter that canvas can make when it shakes if he can get handy to a big racing yacht when she goes about. You could hear the flogging of the sails and the cracking, like so many pistol shots, of the head sheets at a good deal over a mile to leeward when such a vessel as the glorious *Britannia*, or the great schooner *Westward*, put her helm down to change tacks in a hard breeze. And if close enough you can hear the hauling cries of the racing crew as they rapidly purchase the sheets whilst the yacht gathers way on the new leg.

Increase the thunderous flogging of canvas, the sharp cracks of the sheets, and the working cries of the crew some four-fold, and you get somewhere near the noise aboard a big square-rigged sailing ship when wearing or in stays.

The Beautiful Sister Ships "Eva Montgomery" and "Ladye Doris."

These two 1950-ton full-riggers, which were built by W. Hamilton & Co. in 1901 for Montgomery of London, were considered by many sailing ship men to have been the fastest ships launched in the twentieth century. They had very fine lines for modern square-riggers, and no doubt could sail, but I have not found any unusually good passages credited to either ship.

As a proof of their worth I need only say that both ships were bought by the Rhederei Aktien Ges. von 1896 of Hamburg, the *Eva Montgomery* in 1909, and the *Ladye Doris* in 1910, the purchase price of each being in the neighbourhood of £5500 or over £3 a ton. Both were renamed; the *Eva Montgomery* became the *Orla*, and the *Ladye Doris* the *Oliva*.

Whilst bound from Newcastle, N.S.W., to Coquimbo under Captain Ringleben, the *Orla* ex *Eva Montgomery* was posted "missing" on April 3, 1912.

Her sister ship was caught in Valparaiso by the outbreak of war, and remained there without paint or attention until the Armistice, when she was allocated to France. The French Government, however, did not think it worth while to spend money in reconditioning her, and she was sold to the Chilians about 1923 and renamed *Dharma*.

Whilst under the Red Ensign the *Eva Montgomery* was commanded by Captain G. Harrison from 1901 till 1904, when he was succeeded by Captain H. Doherty, who remained in the ship until she was sold.

Captain C. G. Wood had the *Ladye Doris* throughout her career under Montgomery & Co.

"Fitzjames."

A third sister ship was launched by Hamilton in March, 1902. This was the *Fitzjames*. She was commanded throughout her existence under the British flag by the well-known Captain Fearon.

On her maiden passage she sailed from Glasgow on May 29 for Sydney, and Captain Fearon had an interesting race with the *Derwent* from London, *Kilmeny* from Sharpness, and the *Achnashie* from Liverpool, which three ships had sailed five days ahead of him. After very stormy passages all four ships anchored in Port Jackson on September 9, within a few hours of each other. The *Fitzjames* had therefore beaten the others by five days.

This splendid modern full-rigger was snapped up by F. Laeisz in 1909, the purchase price being £8000 or £4 7s. per ton. The *Fitzjames*, under the name of *Pinnas*, was dismasted and abandoned in 1929 when outward bound to Chile.

In July, 1923, she turned up at Southampton, and whilst

she lay in the docks was much admired. She had been most efficiently rigged by the Germans with all wire running rigging.

The Cadet Ship "Medway."

This splendid cadet ship was specially built by A. McMillan & Son in 1902 for Sota & Aznar of Monte Video, and her first name was *Ama Begonakoa*. On a gross tonnage of 2516 tons she could lift a deadweight cargo of 4000 tons.

A big house was built on the main deck abaft the mizen mast in order to accommodate a large number of cadets. Besides this house there was the usual midshiphouse, and the two were connected to the poop and topgallant fo'c'sle by flying bridges. Messrs. McMillan were able to give the new cadet ship a big sail plan with the knowledge that she would always be well manned. Though she never had the speed quite of the *Port Jackson*, she could make good passages if she got enough wind, being able to bear sail well, especially with the wind abaft the beam.

Devitt & Moore bought the *Ama Begonakoa* in 1910, and the chief officer of the *Port Jackson*, Robert Jackson, was placed in command, the ship being renamed *Medway*. Under Devitt & Moore's house-flag she was kept in the Australian trade, and her passages were very steady, except in 1912, when she got a bit out of her beat, and crossing from Lisbon to New York made a long passage out to Australia *via* the Cape.

Her homeward passages from Australia were very consistent, the first being 95 days, and the second, when she raced the *Loch Etive*, 101 days from Sydney. In 1912 she raced the *Howard D. Troop* from Sydney, both ships leaving on January 16. On April 4 the P.S.N. Co. liner *Orissa* spoke the two ships in 2° N., 31° W., both being 79 days out. As the *Howard D. Troop* had a great reputation for speed, this speaks well for the *Medway*, which was evidently making a very level race of it, though their time was a poor one.

In 1914 the *Medway* sailed from Sydney just a fortnight before war was declared. Whilst under low canvas in the neighbourhood of the Horn the *Medway* was ordered to heave to by a German steamer, but Captain Jackson immediately crowded sail to topgallant sails, and speedily left his pursuer behind. After this the *Medway* arrived at Falmouth on November 13, 116 days out. Shortly after her arrival Captain Jackson died, and the *Medway* was sent round to Liverpool in charge of the veteran Captain McKay, who was eighty years of age. In December Captain David Williams was appointed to the command, and on April 22, 1915, the *Medway* left Liverpool with 3630 tons of rails for Hobart, where she arrived on July 27, 96 days out, having safely escaped enemy cruiser, mine and torpedo.

From Tasmania the *Medway* crossed to Portland, Oregon, in water ballast with 500 tons of road metal as extra stiffening. On the run across the Pacific Captain Williams declared that she behaved splendidly, which is not always the case with a big four-master in ballast. Portland was reached on December 18, 79 days out. Here the *Medway* loaded grain and sailed on January 5, 1916, under Admiralty instructions for the Channel. After an average passage she arrived at Falmouth, where all her cadets were landed, and those who had completed 12 months' service were at once sent off to the Grand Fleet as temporary midshipmen R.N.R.

The *Medway's* cargo, having been bought by the French Government, had to be discharged at Bordeaux. Messrs. Devitt & Moore at once asked for an escort for this dangerous passage. The Admiralty offered a tug armed with one 4.7 gun, which had recently returned from the Rufigi River, where she had aided in trapping the *Konigsberg*. The owners of this tug, however, demanded an outrageous sum to tow the *Medway* round to Bordeaux, and rather than put up with the extortion Captain Williams offered to sail round without an escort.

Shipping a crew of runners, he sailed from Falmouth on July 2, 1916, and picking up a splendid slant from the nor'west, went foaming through the danger zone, and reached Bordeaux on July 5. The return journey was equally lucky. The *Medway* sailed from Bordeaux without escort on July 19 with a cargo of pit props for Barry Dock. This time she was becalmed for several days in the neighbourhood of the Lizard, and Captain Williams and his runners actually bathed over the side in waters where they might well have expected a torpedo at any moment. However, nothing was seen, and the *Medway* reached Barry on July 31. By this time Great Britain was one vast training camp, and the Admiralty were hard put to it to train sea officers. Thus Devitt & Moore were told to take every possible cadet they could accommodate in their training ships, and to keep the vessels as much as possible out of the war zone.

On Tuesday, September 12, 1916, the *Medway* was once more ready for sea. Her cargo consisted of 202 tons of general, 1906 tons of cement, and 1543 tons of coal. In her cadet house 26 eager boys had stowed their gear. The ship's company consisted of the following:—

Commander	.. ..	Captain D. Williams
Chief mate	.. ..	R. O. Harris
1st mate	.. ..	H. L. Marshall
2nd mate	.. ..	T. B. Latchmore
3rd mate	.. ..	T. W. Beauchamp
Carpenter	.. ..	A. G. Trail
Sailmaker	.. ..	E. Lawson
Boatswain	.. ..	G. B. Massey
Surgeon	.. ..	F. H. Douglas
Instructor	.. ..	C. F. Adamson

16 A.B.'s, 2 O.S.'s, 2 stewards, and 2 cooks

The ages of the executive during this voyage of the *Medway* are significant. Captain Williams was 40 years of age, and his chief mate 42, but the other three officers were very young, the first mate being 23, the second 19, and the third 17. The instructor also was under 30 years old. As a set-off to these youths, the carpenter and sailmaker were old hands, the carpenter, who hailed from Peterhead, being 71, and the sailmaker, a Lerwick man, 57. The boatswain was younger, being a Newport man of 34 years of age.

After Mr. P. H. Devitt had visited the ship and inspected the cadets, the *Medway* was towed out of the basin of No. 1 Dock and anchored in Barry Roads. At 9.30 a.m. on September 14 permission was received to proceed to sea. With a fresh north wind the ship was soon hurrying out of the danger zone at the rate of 10 knots, and by September 16 we find her in 49° 36′ N., 9° 20′ W. with two other outward bound barques in company.

After her ship's company had been tested in a heavy sou'west gale during September 24, Porto Grande, St. Vincent, was reached on October 6. The cadets seem to have had a very good time in port under the genial command of Captain Williams; for instance, one finds entries such as the following constantly in the ship's log:—

October 8.—Sunday, 2 p.m., three divisions of cadets on shore.
October 11.—Port watch cadets entertained by friends on shore. Commander and 2nd officer in attendance.
October 12.—10.30 a.m., cadets left ship for picnic.
October 14.—a.m., cadets boat exercises, school ashore, and deck duties. p.m., cadets boating and bathing on the beach.
October 15.—Sunday, 10.15 a.m., cadets mustered and inspected. 2.15 p.m., cadets leave party. Returned 5.30 p.m.
October 16.—All cadets left ship for picnic. Returned 6 p.m.

The *Medway* sailed from Porto Grande on October 19 and had an uneventful passage to Santos, where the anchor was let go on November 10, 1916. From Santos the ship was ordered to Tocopilla, which meant that the budding sailors would receive the usual severe baptism from Cape Stiff. At the present day the turbulent waters of the Horn are deserted, and that most difficult of all traverses is quite unknown to the modern generation of seamen. I have therefore been tempted to quote the full log of the *Medway* between 50° S. in the Atlantic and 50° S. in the Pacific, which log consists of 20 days of typical Cape Horn weather. The *Medway* left Santos on December 19, 1916, and on the 29th crossed 50° S., and here we will begin quoting the log:—

December 29, 1916.—Lat. 49° 57′ S., long. 64° 38′ W. S. 38° 60′ W., by account. Wind N.E., light smooth sea. 6 a.m., heavy bank to S.W. 6.20, furled royals. 6.30, wind suddenly shifted to southward, heavy squall, hail, rain, thunder, lightning. 7.45 a.m., clearing, wore ship to westward. 11 a.m., furled upper topgallant sail, moderate breeze, threatening appearance. 1.45., tacked ship to S.E., set crossjack, light and moderate sea. 5 p.m., set upper topgallant sails. 11 p.m., furled outer jib and jigger staysail.

December 30.—53° 5′ S., 65° 36′ W. S. 11° W. 191 miles. Wind west, W. by N., fresh. 9 a.m., furled upper topgallant sails. P.M., moderating; set fore and main upper topgallant sails. 5.30 p.m., sighted west end of Staten Island. 8.30 p.m., Cape Diego S. 17° W. by standard compass. Error 16° E. 10.35 p.m., Cape Bartholomew S. 40° E.

December 31.—54° 14′ S., 64° 59′ W.   Dist. 160 miles.   Wind S.W. and var.   2.30 a.m., tacked ship to N.W., furled crossjack.   5.54 a.m., tacked ship to southward. 6.30 a.m., wind hauling to S.W., increasing rapidly to fresh gale with heavy squalls; wore ship and bore away to N.W.; furled mainsail and upper topgallant sails.   8 a.m., ship clear of Le Maire Straits; fresh gale, squally, rough sea.   P.M., falling, light to calm, N.W. swell.   2 p.m. wore ship to southward.

January 1, 1917.—54° 36′ S., 65° 2′ W.   Dist. 22 miles.   Light airs and calm.   5.45 a.m., set mainsail.   7 a.m., Cape Diego bearing S. 32° W.   Middle peak of Three Brothers S. 63° W. true.   9 a.m., set royals; gentle breeze N.W.   4 p.m., ship clear of Le Maire Straits; set course S. 22° W.; moderate unsteady breeze north-westerly.

January 2.—56° 58′ S., 66° 15′ W.   Dist. 148 miles.   Wind N.N.E., light airs, continuous rain.   5.15 a.m., increasing to moderate gale S.W. by W., squally.   5.30, furled fore and main upper topgallant sails.   7 a.m., furled lower topgallant sails.   11.30, fresh; stowed crossjack and mainsail.   2 p.m., furled foresail and lower staysails; fresh gale, high sea, squally; ship labouring heavy. 4 p.m., wore ship to N.W.   5 p.m., set foresail, mainsail and lower staysails; fresh gale.   10 p.m., gale moderating.

January 3.—57° 0′ S., 68° 0′ W.   Dist. 183 miles.   S.W. fresh.   2.30 a.m., wore ship to southward.   7 a.m., set fore and main lower topgallant sails.   P.M., gale moderating.   5 p.m., furled crossjack.   7.30, furled lower fore and main topgallant sails; moderate gale, misty.   9.30, furled mainsail.   11 p.m., wore to northward; moderate gale, threatening.

January 4.—56° 37′ S., 68° 30′ W.   Dist. 178 miles.   Fresh gale W. to W.S.W., S.W. high sea; ship labouring heavy.   P.M., gale increasing, violent snow and hail squalls, high sea; ship labouring heavily; furled fore, main and mizen upper topsails.   6 p.m., sighted Il Defonso Island W.N.W.; wore ship to S.E.   8.30 p.m., set foresail.   10.30, set main upper topsail and jigger staysail, frequent casts with sounding machine; strong gale, heavy squalls.

January 5.—56° 11′ S., 67° 0′ W.   Dist. 159 miles.   Wind S. by W., S.W., strong gale, very high sea.   8 a.m., wore ship to westward.   10 a.m., set fore and mizen upper topsails; gale moderate; set mainsail, crossjack and lower topgallant sails.   1 p.m., wore ship to S.E., set outer jib.   P.M., strong breeze; rough sea, hail squalls.   9 p.m., stowed outer jib.

January 6.—58° 10′ S., 66° 3′ W.   Dist. 158 miles.   Wind S.W.W., moderate high swells. 8 a.m., set main upper topgallant sail.   8.30, set fore upper topgallant sail. Noon, wore to N.W., wind increasing; furled upper topgallant sails; compass error 25° E.   8 p.m., moderate gale, heavy squalls, high sea, ship labouring and pitching heavy.

January 7.—56° 36′ S., 67° 30′ W.   Dist. 180 miles.   Winds S.W.ly, set fore and main upper topgallant sails; moderate to strong, squally, high swell.   6 a.m., furled upper topgallant sails, wind increasing to moderate gale; misty, squally

"FITZJAMES": Logging 11 knots off Cape Hatteras

Lent by Captain Fearon

"EVA MONTGOMERY"

[*See Page* 283

"MEDWAY" LEAVING NEW YORK

Lent by Captain J. Fitzpatrick

[*See Page* 284

weather, high sea, ship labouring heavy. 8 a.m., wore ship to southward. Cape Horn bearing N. 45° E. true, distant 10 miles. 11.15 a.m., French four-mast barque *Marthe* of Dunkirk passed homeward bound. Compass error 22° E. 8 p.m., wore ship to westward, moderate breeze S.S.W., heavy swell.

January 8.—56° 57′ S., 68° 0′ W. Dist. 104 miles. Light S.W. breeze, moderate sea. 6 a.m., wore ship to southward, set upper topgallant sails.

January 9.—58° 36′ S., 71° 14′ W. Course S. 46° W. 143 miles. Wind westerly, moderate. Compass error 27½° E. Strong to moderate breeze. Noon, wore ship to N.W.; fine clear weather. 11 p.m., wore to S.W.; light westerly breeze.

January 10.—58° 40′ S., 74° 10′ W. Dist. 161 miles. W. by N., W.N.W., N.W. by W.; moderate to strong, heavy head swell, hazy. 7.30 p.m., furled upper topgallant sails and outer jib; ship pitching and straining heavily. 11 p.m., furled mizen lower topgallant sail, moderate gale, high head sea.

January 11.—59° 31′ S., 80° 14′ W. Course S. 75° W. 194 miles. Wind north-westerly, strong. 4.30 a.m., decreasing, set crossjack and mizen lower topgallant sail. Compass error 37° E. P.M., strong to moderate gale, high sea; ship pitching and straining. 6.30 p.m., furled upper topgallant sails and outer jib. 7.30, furled mizen lower topgallant sail and crossjack; heavy squall; mizen upper topsail sheet carried away, same immediately repaired. 10.45 p.m., wore to northward; moderate gale, high sea.

January 12.—58° 29′ S., 80° 50′ W. Dist. 212 miles. Wind W.N.W., strong, sea rough, heavy snow squalls. Compass error 22½° E. 6 a.m., set mizen lower topgallant sail. 9 a.m., furled mizen lower topgallant sail and jigger staysail; moderate gale, high sea; ship labouring and straining heavily. Leeway 10°. Course N. 10° E.

January 13.—56° 22′ S., 77° 30′ W. Dist. 215 miles. Wind W.N.W. Furled crossjack and lower topgallant sail; moderate gale and rough sea; wore ship to S.W.; hands working ship and standing by. P.M., moderating set crossjack and lower topgallant sails. 5 p.m., set fore and main upper topgallant sails. 11 p.m., barometer falling rapidly; furled fore and main upper topgallant sails; light breeze, N.W. swell, overcast and misty.

January 14.—55° 12′ S., 80° 30′ W. Dist. 146 miles. Wind N.E. to S.W.; barometer falling rapidly to 28.73; furled lower topgallant sails, crossjack and mainsail. 4 a.m., light wind, continuous rain. 4.30, wind hauling to S.S.W., increased to moderate gale. 9.30, weather clearing; set mainsail. 10.30, set crossjack. 11 a.m., set fore and main lower topgallant sails; barometer rising rapidly, moderate gale, high sea. P.M., moderating; set mizen lower topgallant sail and fore and main upper topgallant sails; strong wind, high sea, squally. Compass error 26½° E. 10 p.m., wind increasing to fresh gale; furled upper and lower topgallant sails.

January 15.—51° 35′ S., 77° 40′ W. Dist. 242 miles. Wind W. by N. 1.30 a.m., inner jibstay carried away at the bar; got sail on board and temporarily set up

U

stay with tackle; furled fore and main lower topgallant sails.   Noon, wore
ship to southward.   9.30 p.m., hauled crossjack and mainsail up; strong
wind, rough sea.

January 16.—52° 0′ S., 79° 0′ W.   Dist. 158 miles.   Wind westerly.   4 a.m., set mainsail
and furled crossjack.   6 a.m., wore ship to northward.   Compass error 24° E.
P.M., frequent heavy squalls to moderate gale, high sea; ship straining and
labouring heavy.

January 17.—49° 7′ S., 77° 44′ W.   Course N. 15° E.   180 miles.   Wind westerly; 7 a.m.,
gale moderating; set lower topgallant sails.   1 p.m., set fore and main upper
topgallant sails.   8 p.m., set upper mizen topgallant sail.   Compass error
23½° E.

From January 17 the *Medway* had the usual weather up the
coast, and finally anchored at Tocopilla on January 30.   Here again
we find Captain Williams giving his cadets a good time, sandwiched
in between school, deck duties, and navigation classes.   For instance,
we find such entries as these:—

February 3.—First officer and six cadets boat sailing.   P.M., cadets' cricket team ashore
playing Tocopilla eleven.

Meanwhile the crew carried on the ship's work.   Captain
Williams was a smart officer, and he saw to it that his mate and
boatswain regularly inspected the rigging from the trucks to the
deck, and from the spanker boom to the shark's tail on the bowsprit.
Whilst in Tocopilla he had the mizen royal yard sent down, and
condemned it as unfit for further service.   A few days later we find
the fore royal yard sent on deck for repairs to the starboard yardarm,
and whilst the cargo of nitrate was coming aboard all defective
running gear, especially gaskets, was overhauled and renewed.

By 8 a.m. on February 19 there were 3700 tons of nitrate in the
hold.   Whilst the last bags were being taken aboard from two
lighters the ship began to unmoor and weigh her anchors.   This
is a big job at Tocopilla, and it was not until just before noon that
the stern anchor showed above water, when it was found that one of
the arms was broken off.   At 3.30 p.m. the tug *George* made fast
ahead, the starboard anchor was broken out, and the *Medway*
proceeded to sea on a passage to Cape Town.

With a fine powerful ship and a strong crew, Captain Williams
had a splendid chance to make a quick run, and he did not miss it,
for the *Medway* arrived at Cape Town on April 3, 42 days out, which

was good work for a full-built ship. With strong fair winds the log has not much to record, except the usual making and reducing sail, and occasional unbending and repairing of split sails. A good deal of ice, however, was sighted between South Georgia and the Cape. From March 20 to the 22nd the ship averaged 12 knots, during which time the log has the following ice entries:—

March 20.—5 p.m., sighted South Georgia Island. 5.30, Cape Disappointment abeam 7 miles. 5.55, passed iceberg 3 miles north. 7.0 p.m., iceberg ahead. Passed it safely. 7.30, large iceberg 3 miles north. 8.0 p.m., lookout doubled.

March 21.—7 a.m., fog set in; lookout doubled. 1 p.m., passed large iceberg 300 feet high, distant 3 miles. 2 p.m., passed large iceberg 150 feet high, distant 2 miles.

March 22.—7 a.m., passed a berg 2 miles south. Noon, passed a berg with several growlers. 2.30 p.m., passed a very large berg about 10 miles north. 3.20 p.m., passed a large berg 8 miles south. 4.20, passed a low berg 2 miles south. 5.20, passed a large berg 3 miles north; lookouts doubled.

The best run on the passage was made on March 25, in 48° 37′ S., 7° 34′ W., the wind being nor'west, strong to moderate gale with a rough following sea. The run was 280 miles by account. The best speed logged was 13 knots.

After discharging her nitrate at Cape Town the *Medway* proceeded east about to Tocopilla for another load. Captain Williams took his departure from Green Point at 10.55 a.m. on May 1, 1917, and running his Easting down on a course which took him as far south as 54° 20′, he made the run in 62 days, thus circling the world round the Horn and the Cape from Tocopilla to Tocopilla in 104 sailing days. The *Medway* made a splendid average running her Easting down, her best 24 hours being 285 miles on May 27 in 53° S., 150° E. Other runs worthy of record were:—

May 10 ..	.. 273 miles	June 2 ..	.. 285 miles
May 12 ..	.. 282 „	June 3 ..	.. 265 „
June 1 ..	.. 270 „	June 17 ..	.. 265 „

The westerlies gave the sailmaker plenty of work, for there are constant references to split canvas; for instance:—

May 12.—Strong wind and high sea; unbent and sent main lower topgallant sail on deck for repair; splice drawn in leach.

May 30.—Fresh gale; hail, rain and snow squalls. 6 p.m., heavy squall struck ship carrying away foresail; hauled up and furled same.

May 31.—7.20 a.m., heavy snow squall; wind suddenly shifted to S.S.E., whole gale; furled
    fore and main upper topsails, both sails split.
May 31.—Antipodes Day. 1 a.m., fresh gale, violent squalls; fore topmast staysail
    carried away.
June 1.—4 p.m., S.W. gale; unbent main lower topsail, seam adrift.

And so the fight goes on between wind and canvas.

The *Medway's* second run from Tocopilla to South Africa was
not so favoured by the winds as the first.   Sailing from Tocopilla on
July 21, 1917, she reached Durban 61 days out on September 20.
This time she rounded the Horn in mid-winter, and was iced up
almost as high as her tops with frozen spray.   For several days her
main deck was like a skating rink.   The weather, too, was wild,
with the usual violent squalls and mountainous seas; but the old
Medway weathered it out without anything worse than the usual
wear and tear.

From Durban the *Medway* was ordered back to the West Coast,
and she made the run to Iquique in 65 days, arriving on January 24,
1918.   This time the globe had been circled in 126 days.   For the
third time she loaded nitrate for the Cape, and sailing from Iquique
on February 14, 1918, she arrived in Table Bay on April 12, 57
days out.   By this time the Ministry of Shipping were seeking in
every direction for suitable oil carriers, and with money no object
they hit upon the expensive plan of converting sailing ships into
Diesel engine tramps.   The poor old *Medway* was one out of a
dozen fine sailing ships which were changed into those hideous
monstrosities.   The *Port Jackson* had been torpedoed in April, 1917,
and Devitt & Moore fought their hardest to avoid losing their last
cadet ship.   In this they had the full support of the Admiralty,
who were anxious that the *Medway* should continue her good work
of training cadets.   Although Devitt & Moore refused to sell,
the Ministry of Shipping used their war-given power and took
possession of the *Medway* on her arrival at Cape Town.   The
cadets were landed with scant ceremony, and the ship sent in
ballast to Hongkong, where she was converted into an oil carrier, with
her masts cut down and Diesel engines blocking up half her hold.

Needless to say, the *Medway* was not ready in time to do any
war work, for the Armistice came before her transformation from a

beautiful four-mast barque to a hideous oil tanker was completed. The poor old ship under the name of *Myr Shell*, after service as depot at Singapore, went to Japanese scrappers in 1933.

"Colonial Empire."

This fine four-mast barque was the last of George Duncan's Empires, being built by Reid & Co. in 1902. Like all Reid's ships, she was not a bad sailer, though of course a large carrier. On her maiden voyage she went from Cardiff to Mauritius in 79 days, and from Newcastle, N.S.W., to Valparaiso in 39 days.

Other good passages made by the *Colonial Empire*, given in order of date, were as follows:—

Antwerp to San Francisco	134 days
San Francisco to Melbourne	62 ,,
Newcastle, N.S.W., to Tocopilla	37 ,,
Melbourne to Newcastle, N.S.W.	4 ,,
Tocopilla to Sydney	7 ,,
Newcastle, N.S.W., to Coquimbo	46 ,,
Coquimbo to Sydney	69 ,,
Sydney to Falmouth	102 ,,
Monte Video to Sydney	58 ,,
Newcastle, N.S.W., to Talcahuano	29 ,,
Tocopilla to Falmouth	98 ,,
Cardiff to Iquique	104 ,,
Iquique to Falmouth	88 ,,
Swansea to Iquique	99 ,,
Iquique to Fayal	90 ,,

The illustration shows her wrecked on Thunderbolt Reef, Algoa Bay, on September 27, 1917, at which time she was under the flag of Cook & Dundas, who had become her owners in 1910.

"Speedonia."

This big four-mast barque was built by McMillan in 1902 for the well-known Hamburg firm of Wencke & Co. under the name of *Urania*. She had the reputation at one time of being a very fast ship, and was also credited with a 120 ft. main yard. She was one of the first German ships interned in Australia at the outbreak of war, after which she came under British colours, and her name was changed to *Speedonia*, her owners being the Anglo-Saxon Petroleum Company, and her captain Walsh, who had been in command of the *Port Jackson* when she was torpedoed.

The *Speedonia* had a narrow escape from being destroyed by fire just before she was converted to a steamer. The captain had both his legs broken, and the ship was actually abandoned by her crew, though the mate afterwards picked her up again.

She sailed the seas under the name of *Scala Shell* as an oil tanker driven by engines instead of sails. Her master was Captain John Baxter, who had been skipper for so many years of the old *Dolbadarn Castle* ex *Earmount*, which also carried oil about the East as the *Dolphin Shell*. The *Dolphin Shell* was scrapped in 1931.

The *Speedonia*, by the way, had a sister ship, launched by McMillan in May, 1902, two months after the former had been sent afloat. This was the *Alsterberg*, belonging to the Hamburg Alster Line. This ship also had a good reputation for speed, and holds the record from Monte Video to Port Townsend. This was made on her maiden voyage when she arrived at Port Townsend on December 16, 1902, being only 68 days 12 hours out from the River Plate.

Hardie's "Saragossa."

This steel four-mast barque was the only vessel built for Captain Hardie by the Dundee Shipbuilding Company. Unfortunately she had a very short life. On January 8, 1903, she sailed from Liverpool to Sydney, and was then kept in the trans-Pacific trade for over a year, being lost on Mangaia Island in the South Pacific on August 15, 1904, when bound from Newcastle, N.S.W., to San Francisco. She seems to have been unlucky in her passages, and actually took 42 days coming round from Dundee to Liverpool before sailing for Sydney. Perhaps a few dates may be of interest:—

She sailed from Dundee on October 29 for Liverpool under Captain Steven. On the following day she put into Long Hope, and did not up anchor again until November 20. Two days later she put into Loch Siziot, Skye, and stayed there for six days. Her next anchorage was in Loch Bracadale, where she remained until December 3, when she once more up anchored, only to put into

Tobermory. Tobermory was left on December 8, the Calf of Man passed on December 9, and Liverpool reached on December 10, 42 days out from Dundee.

The following are the times of her few passages:—

Liverpool to Sydney	.. ..	115 days
Newcastle, N.S.W., to 'Frisco ..	.. ..	70 „
'Frisco to Port Townsend	.. .. ..	8 „
(Captain Duncan having taken over the command)		
Port Townsend to Port Pirie ..	.. ..	74 days
Port Pirie to Newcastle, N.S.W.	.. ..	19 „

She sailed from Newcastle on July 26, 1904, and was wrecked as already stated.

" Bay of Biscay" and " Castleton."

These two 1800-ton full-riggers, which were built by A. Rodger in 1902 and 1903 respectively for T. Beynon & Co., of Cardiff, have already been noticed in Volume I. They were powerful bald-headers. In July, 1913, some splendid photographs of work aloft and on the main deck in bad weather which were taken aboard the *Castleton*, were published in the *Town and Country Journal*, Sydney, N.S.W., and later in *Country Life*.

The *Bay of Biscay* was sold to the Norwegians in 1915 and renamed *Svendsholm*. In March, 1917, she was sunk by the Germans.

The *Castleton* was also bought by the Norwegians about the same time, and renamed *Svalen*. Later she became the *Skaregrom*, and my last note of her states that she was dismasted in the Bay of Biscay when bound from Frederickstadt to Adelaide in the winter of 1926. After discharging her cargo at London she was sold to Dutch scrappers.

"Ormsary."

This four-mast barque, which was launched in December, 1902, by Russell & Co., was the last ship built for Lang & Fulton. Unfortunately she had a very short life, being posted "missing" in 1907, when bound on a passage from Caleta Colosa to Antwerp.

"Kildalton."

This 1800-ton steel barque was built by the Ailsa Shipbuilding Co., for J. Brown of Glasgow. On December 12, 1914, when 96 days out from Liverpool for Callao, she was captured and sunk by the *Prinz Eitel Friedrich*. Her crew were deposited on Easter Island, where they had to remain until February 26, 1915, when they were rescued.

The Inver Line.

In October, 1902, McMillan & Son launched the 1900-ton steel barque *Inverness*; this was the last ship built for George Milne's Inver Line, which was undoubtedly one of the finest fleets of windjammers sailing the seas in the twentieth century. As I have not touched upon these fine little barques before, I propose now to give some account of them.

Except for the 1600-ton *Inverclyde*, the already mentioned *Inverness*, and the three bought ships *Inveravon*, *Inverlogie*, and *Inverlyon*, the "Invers" were all three-mast barques with a gross register of between 1400 and 1500 tons. With the exception of the *Inverurie*, which was the first of the Line, and was built by Hall of Aberdeen in 1889, they were either built by Russell or McMillan, and many of them, as we shall see, were sister ships.

The "Invers" were very pretty little vessels, painted French grey with a thin white line running along the sheer strake, and with white figure-heads, and their masts and yards painted mast colour. Being very well looked after and extremely well found and victualled, they were very popular amongst seamen. Though large carriers with snug sail plans their passages were very regular, but they were not fast enough to gain places in the yearly lists of best passages.

During the eighties George Milne's fleet consisted of a number of small wooden ships such as the *Argosy*, 1061 tons; *Donegal*, 693 tons; *Dunrobin Castle*, 545 tons; *Gettysburg*, 1025 tons; *Giovanni*, 710 tons; *Hindostan*, 674 tons; *Java*, 948 tons; *Martha Birnie*, 832 tons; *Nirvada*, 674 tons; and *Star of China*, 794 tons.

The first of the steel barques, the *Inverurie*, was commanded for some years before the war by the well-known Captain Holmes, who had made a great reputation for good passages in the wool clipper *Cimba*. Captain Holmes was one of the advocates of holes in the clews of staysails and along the foot of courses; these, he

"COLONIAL EMPIRE"

Lent by Captain Bailey   [*See Page* 293

"COLONIAL EMPIRE"
Wrecked on Thunderbolt Reef, Algoa Bay

Lent by H. E. Earp, Esq.

"INVERSNAID"
Built by Robert Steele & Co., 1882

"INVERNEILL"

[See Page 298

argued, released the dead wind which acted as a cushion and took off a great deal of the effect of the true wind on a sail.

In 1905 the little *Inverurie* had an exciting race with the barques *Iredale* of Liverpool and *Esto* of Hamburg.   All three ships sailed from Melbourne on the same day, and arrived at Queenstown on the same day 99 days out, yet they had not sighted each other at all during the passage.   Although only a few hours behind, the *Inverurie* had the luck to be third, the German arriving first and winning the wager.

The *Inverurie* was wrecked at Ballyferis Point, County Down, in November, 1914.

The second ship of the Inver Line was the *Invermark*, launched by Russell in 1890.   This ship in 1913 beat the *Elfrieda, Dowan Hill* and *Metropolis* in a race from Monte Video to Melbourne, her time being 44 days.   She was posted "missing" when bound from Fremantle to Iquique in 1916.

The *Invercauld*, Milne's third ship, besides being the first of those built by McMillan, was one of the fastest ships in the Line. Her best passages were made under Captain A. G. F. Kebblewhite, such as the following:—

> Liverpool to Valparaiso   ..   ..   ..   78 days
> (On this occasion the little *Invercauld* beat several of
> Laeisz's famous "P" Line nitrate clippers)
> Buenos Ayres to Wallaroo   ..   ..   ..   42 days
> (This time she beat the *Inverlyon* by 18 days)

The *Invercauld* was sold in 1916 for £13,000, or at the rate of £10 a ton, only to be torpedoed shortly afterwards.

The *Inveresk*, which, with the *Invergarry*, was a sister ship of the *Invercauld*, after several changes, was sold to the Greeks in 1931, and finally scrapped at Genoa, 1937.   She was converted into a steamer at Londonderry in 1919. and trades regularly to Sweden from Hull as one of the Glen Line.   It may be of interest to note that the fitting of engines took 1200 tons off her deadweight capacity. In January, 1923, she was in dry dock on the Clyde, being repaired from the effects of a collision in which her clipper bow had saved her from being sunk.

The Dismasting of "Garthgarry."

The *Invergarry* was bought at the end of the war by Sir William Garthwaite, along with the *Inversnaid* and the *Inverneill.* Sir William's enterprise in trying to keep the British flag flying amongst the few sailers that remained to us was not rewarded with the best of luck. We have already described the wreck of the *Garthwray* after the longest passage in history. His *Garthforce* ex *Celtic Glen* ran into an iceberg off the Cape in 1921, was towed into Durban with all her headgear gone, and there sold for £500 and turned into a hulk. A few years later she was condemned, towed out to sea and sunk. The *Garthpool* ex *Juteopolis* became the only ship of the fleet sailing the seas.

The *Garthgarry* was dismasted on March 22, 1924, in 22° 16′ S. 25° 30′ W. when homeward bound under Captain David Roberts. This well-known commander had had the *Garthgarry* since 1922, at which date his previous command, the *Elginshire,* had been delivered over to the ship-breakers.

The following account of the *Garthgarry's* dismasting comes from the pen of Captain Roberts, and gives one a very clear idea of a modern dismasting and jury-rigging:—

Saturday, March 22, 1924.—Lat. 22° 16′ S., long. 25° 30′ W. 0.15 p.m. Ship struck by strong gust of wind, heeled over suddenly and the fore topmast carried away about 12 ft. above the lower cap. The topgallant mast, part of topmast, topgallant and royal yards, crosstrees and headsails trailing alongside attached to backstays and head gear. Gooseneck of upper topsail parrel snapped, and yard hanging halfway down the lower rigging ripping the foresail to ribbons. Rove off 4-inch manila 3-fold purchase and hung yard, and managed with much difficulty to cut adrift, unparrel and take on board the topgallant yard. All hands employed clearing wreckage until midnight. Moderate N.E. wind with passing squalls, and nasty sea throughout. Wreckage pounding heavily alongside all night.

Sunday, March 23, 1924.—Lat. 21° 8′ S., long. 26° 00′ W. Crew employed throughout the night cutting away wreckage in endeavour to save topgallant mast, sails and gear. At 2 p.m. finding it impossible to make any headway at saving gear and fearing damage to ship's hull, decided to slip everything. At 4.30 p.m. all wreckage was clear of ship, everything lost or destroyed from lower topsail yard up. The fore hatch being stove in and tarpaulins ripped, donkey engine knocked out of position and badly damaged, also starboard dinghy and spare fresh water tank damaged by flying backstays and gear. All sails on foremast destroyed or lost, also three jibs, fore topmast staysail, main topmast staysail, and topgallant staysail. Fore lower cap fractured and badly twisted and bent. Crane of lower topsail yard bent. All backstays and fore and aft stays lost, lower topsail yard strained and bent and jackstays twisted. Foretop destroyed and bowsprit fractured. Wind E.N.E. moderate confused sea. Landed upper topsail yardarm on forecastle head and lashed yard outside lower rigging; yard badly dented and bent and parrel lost. 5 p.m., bent No. 2 foresail and No, 2 lower topsail. Sounded well and found an increase from 4 ins. to 10 ins. since noon. Rigged pumps. Crew pumping throughout night watches and steadily gaining on water. Guide on starboard spar broken.

Monday, March 24, 1924.—Lat. 19° 32′ S., long. 25° 23′ W. Day begins with gentle E.N.E. breeze and rough confused sea, cloudy and passing showers. Upon examination found that main topmast head was strained and working considerably, this was caused by excessive pressure put on it by fore and aft stays, braces, etc., leading forward when fore topmast went. After chain plate of main topmast carried away starboard side. Mushroom ventilator over forecastle smashed, head pump and W.C. damaged. Galley funnel and skylights on house broken. Stream anchor shifted from position and bed smashed. Port lower rigging strained and badly chafed and battens lost, forecastle head ladder and rails broken, fish tackle cut up and lost whilst shipping wreckage. Castings on wheels of donkey broken, injector and steam gauge broken off, barrel warped and gauge cocks broken. Port forward mooring pipe broken. Four hands kept working pumps throughout. Bulwarks stanchion broken and six stanchions started from main rail. Stretched length of mooring chain from mooring bits to midship scupper holes, cut 4-in. wire hawser and fitted preventer backstays on both sides to main topmast head, setting up same with 2½-in. wire 3-fold purchase to mooring chains. 4 p.m., water in well down to 3 in. Upon examination found rivet had dropped out from ship's bottom in well chamber on starboard side. Found several leaky rivets in fore lower peak. Drove wooden plug into hole, and tommed it down with strong wooden tom. Bailed out chamber and cemented around play.

Tuesday, March 25, 1924.—Lat. 17° 57′ S., long. 26° 24′ W. Day begins with moderate east wind and sea. Cloudy and fine. Crew on ordinary sea watches during the night. 6 a.m., sent down remaining portion of fore topmast. Sent down mizen topmast, and sent it up the fore as jury fore topmast, to enable this to be done, 10 ft. had to be cut from it. Mizen topmast backstays and fore and aft stays fitted to fit jury topmast. Bent jib and rove off new halliards, all jib halliards having been lost overboard with head stays Soundings taken every four hours and ship found to be making no water. Cut 3-in. steel hauling wire, and fitted stay from mizen lowermast head to mainmast and set extra staysail on mizen. Also fitted double stay of same from fore lowermast head to bowsprit, and bent and set fore staysail.

Wednesday, March 26, 1924.—Lat. 16° 13′ S., long. 26° 30′ W. Sent topgallant yard up
on jury fore topmast, fitting lifts with 2½-in. wire. Sailmaker altering
upper topsail to fit topgallant yard on head and sheet home on lower
topsail yard.

Thursday, March 27, 1924.—Lat. 13° 47′ S., long. 27° 00′ W. Sailmaker finished altering
upper topsail and same sent aloft and bent on fore topgallant yard, lashing
clews to lower topsail yard. Crew fitting new wire sheets, clew lines, etc.,
for altering upper topsail and reeving off all new buntlines and leachlines
for foresail and fore lower topsail in place of those destroyed.

Friday, March 28, 1924.—Lat. 11° 59′ S., long. 27° 30′ W. Put strong lashings round main
topmast cap to main topmast preventer backstays and frapping turns
tightly as possible to strengthen mast from cap, and as preventer below
band where rust is seen coming through.

The *Garthgarry* reached Queenstown on June 6, 1924, and after
a week at the port of call sailed to her discharging port, Barrow-in-
Furness, where she arrived at 10 p.m. on June 15. She was then
broken up.

The Two "Inversnaids."

George Milne's *Inversnaid* must not be confused with an
earlier vessel of the same name, the beautiful main skysail yard
iron clipper which was built by Robert Steele in 1882, and of which
I give an illustration. Robert Steele was noted not only for the
beauty of his models, but for the perfection of his workmanship
and the care which he gave to each of his productions. On the
Clyde it was said that Steele could only build a first-class ship, and
that it was because he could not cut down his price per ton, or rather
he could not be induced to use material that was not of the very best,
that his shipbuilding ceased to pay, and the famous firm was forced
to go into liquidation.

The 1882 *Inversnaid*, a ship of 1550 tons net, was one of the
last ships built in Steele's yard at Greenock, the last being the
Inveruglas, now known as the *Tusitala*. In 1886 the *Inversnaid*
and the *Inveruglas* were bought by Thompson, Anderson & Co., of
Liverpool, the founders of the famous Sierra Line. The *Inveruglas*
became the *Sierra Lucena*, but the *Inversnaid* was lost before she
could be renamed. On October 15, 1886, she sailed from Penarth
for Singapore under Captain James Dodds, with four other ships in
company. That night there was a furious storm in the Bristol

Channel and all five ships were lost with all hands. The only evidence to prove that the *Inversnaid* had foundered in the Bristol Channel was discovered about a fortnight later when her figure-head and part of a life-boat were washed up on Lundy Island.

Milne's *Inversnaid* and her sister ship the *Invercoe* were built by McMillan in 1892. The latter was captured by the German raider *Prinz Eitel Friedrich* on February, 1915, and sunk by the explosion of bombs placed on board. Her crew were taken prisoners, but afterwards landed in the United States. The *Inversnaid* survived the war and was bought by Sir William Garthwaite, along with the *Invergarry* and *Inverneill*. In 1922, having been renamed *Garthsnaid*, this little barque was dismasted when bound from Iquique to Melbourne. The White Star liner *Zealandic*, from Sydney to Geelong, found the *Garthsnaid* lying in a helpless condition with her mainmast gone, her fore topmast hanging over the side, her mizen topmast missing, her decks a tangle of twisted and broken gear, and all her boats stove in.

Captain Jones of the *Zealandic* at once decided to tow the lame duck into port, but the weather was bad, and it was only after four unsuccessful attempts that a steel hawser was at last got aboard the *Garthsnaid*. Her crew had been without sleep and with scarcely any food for three days, and were so weak that it took them three hours to heave in the hawser by their capstan and make it fast round the base of the foremast.

The two ships were off Gabo when the *Zealandic* started her tow, but she brought the *Garthsnaid* into Melbourne all safe, after a good long tussle.

"Inverlyon"-"Khorasan" Collision.

The next two sisters in the Inver fleet were the Russell-built *Inveramsay* and *Inverlyon*. The *Inverlyon* was sunk in lat. 2° N., long. 26° 30′ W., in January, 1904, through collision with the German barque *Khorasan* whilst on a passage from Port Pirie to Antwerp with an ore cargo. The *Khorasan*, which, by the by, was a beautiful iron barque which had been built by J. Reid & Co. as far back as 1864, was criticised for not standing by the sinking *Inverlyon*. Had she done so, those lost in the *Inverlyon* would probably have been saved, but the master of the *Khorasan* declared that his own ship was in danger of foundering and he was fully occupied in saving the lives of his own men.

To replace the *Inverlyon* George Milne & Co. bought the *Gostwyck* in 1906, which they renamed *Inverlyon*. The *Gostwyck* was a steel barque of 1827 tons gross, launched by McMillan & Son in March, 1904. Messrs. George Milne & Co. paid £9750 for her, which was at the rate of £5 15s. per ton. This second *Inverlyon* was captured by U-boat on April, 1918, and sunk by gunfire when bound into Limerick.

" Inverkip"-" Loch Carron" Collision.

A still more disastrous collision in the same year was the *Inverkip-Loch Carron* collision. This *Inverkip*, however, did not belong to George Milne, but to W. Walker & Co., of Greenock. She was 50 tons larger than the *Inverlyon*, though launched by Russell in the same year.

This was a very sad case, for Captain Jones of the *Inverkip* and his wife and the whole ship's company except two men were drowned. To add to the tragedy, the captains of the two ships were very great friends, and the affair so affected Captain Stainton Clark that his health was quite broken for a time, and he had to hand over his ship for a voyage to another man.

The collision occurred at 11.20 p.m. on August 13, 1904, about 60 miles to the south and east of the Fastnet light. The night was pitch dark, heavy rain was falling, a high sea was running, and it was blowing hard from the sou'west. The *Inverkip*, loaded with wheat from Australia, was making for Queenstown, whilst the *Loch Carron* was outward bound from Glasgow to Sydney with general cargo. The latter was close hauled on the port tack, going about 7 knots under a press of canvas, when the red light of the *Inverkip* was seen close ahead. Before there was even time to alter her helm the *Loch Carron* was into the other ship, striking her a tremendous blow with her stem just abreast of the foremast.

The *Loch Carron* had three passengers aboard, and the following is a statement made by one of them, Mr. W. P. Watson of London, to the newspaper reporters:—

The *Loch Carron* left Greenock last Wednesday, bound for Sydney. The crew numbered 30 hands, and there were three passengers. Captain Clark was in charge. All went well until Saturday night at 11.45. When south of the Fastnet in thick weather a strong wind and heavy sea prevailed. I was in my stateroom under the poop when I heard and felt a terrible crash as if the ship had struck violently on a rock. I jumped out of my berth and rushed on deck in my nightshirt. When I got on the deck the crew were busy getting out the life-boats. I was directed to put a life-belt on at once, which I did, as the forward part of the ship was all battered in, and water was getting into the fore compartment.

My attention was then directed to the fact that we had been in collision with another ship, and that she had apparently gone down. Two of her crew were on our deck. One man, who spoke English imperfectly, was in great torture. Three of his fingers were cut off, and he was covered with blood about the head and face. It appears that he was in the rigging of the *Inverkip*, and when the collision occurred he was pitched on to the deck of the *Loch Carron*. The other rescued man scrambled up the bowsprit of the *Loch Carron*, and thus saved himself. All our boats had meanwhile been got out and provisioned, as we did not know how long our own vessel would keep afloat.

No trace of the *Inverkip* was seen after the collision, and she must have sunk within two minutes. All night we kept in the same position in the hope that something might be seen of the crew of the *Inverkip*, but we saw no trace of them, and doubtless 20 men, with Captain Jones and his wife, all went down in the ship.

According to other reports the *Inverkip* was locked with the *Loch Carron* for a few moments before going down head foremost. The crew of the latter said that the screams on the *Inverkip*, amongst which those of the wife of Captain Jones could be distinguished, were heartrending. One of the two men of the *Inverkip* who were saved, named Stewart, made the following statement:—

The *Loch Carron* struck us between the foc's'le-head and fore rigging. The impact was terrible. The *Loch Carron's* foc's'le rail was level with my position, and I scrambled on board her. I then saw the *Inverkip* swing round and fall off to about 10 yards. Two of the crew made an effort to spring on board from the poop, but they fell in the water between the two ships. I also saw the captain's wife in her nightdress on the poop, screaming and praying, and the captain was also there. The *Inverkip* then went down, stem foremost. It all occurred in about three minutes.

The *Loch Carron* was judged to blame for this collision, and her owners had to pay £30,000 damages.

The Sister Ships "Inverneill" "Inverlochy" and "Invermay."

When George Milne disposed of his ships the *Inverneill* was bought for £13,000 by Sir William Garthwaite, who renamed her *Garthneill*. This ship will always be remembered for her amazing

passage under Captain Shippen.   In 1919 the *Garthneill* arrived at
Melbourne from Cape Town.   From Melbourne she was ordered to
Bunbury, West Australia, but owing to heavy westerly gales was
forced to leeward, and when the weather moderated found herself
off Sydney.   Captain Shippen, after putting into Sydney,
again set sail for Bunbury, but after experiencing a further
succession of westerly gales determined to go east about the
whole way round the world in order to reach his port, which was not
much over 1000 miles from the longitude of Sydney.   By pushing
the *Inverneill* along he reckoned to circle the world in 95 days, but
the ship actually did the 14,500 miles in 76 days.   From Sydney she
averaged 240 miles a day for five days, which carried her to the north
end of New Zealand.   It took another 28 days to round the Horn.
In her long spell of running the Easting down the *Inverneill's* best
distance for the 24 hours was 266 miles, and her average for the
76-day passage was 192 miles a day.

Captain Shippen, by the way, was one of the many mercantile
seamen who were both shelled and torpedoed by German submarines.
He and his wife and crew spent three days in an open boat in mid-
Atlantic before being rescued.

During her last six years of active service the *Garthneill*
was commanded by the well-known Captain Thomson, later
commander of the *Garthpool*.   Her last passage was from Grangemouth to Melbourne in 1925, when she arrived at Melbourne on
November 6, 122 days out.   After being laid up at Melbourne for a
while she was sold very cheap to the Yorke Peninsular Co., who
use her as a hulk for the storage of lime, salt and gypsum at Adelaide.

The second of the three sisters, the *Inverlochy*, only had a short
life, being lost on the Ingoldsby Reefs, Split Point, Victoria, in
December, 1902, when bound from Liverpool to Melbourne.   Apparently the master made a mistake in his navigation, for he carried
on for nearly half an hour on a N.E. by E. course whilst within the
white light danger sector of the Split Point lighthouse, and so ran
his ship on the rocks.

The *Invermay* was one of the three Milne ships which were
bought by Sir William Garthwaite.   He paid £14,000 or £10 9s. a
ton for her in 1916.

"KHORASAN"

[See Page 301

"ARCHIBALD RUSSELL"

Lent by Captain L. R. W. Beavis

[See Page 307

"FAVELL"

[See Page 333

"R. C. RICKMERS"

[See Page 310

"Inverclyde."

The *Inverclyde*, which was built by Russell in 1898, was 200 tons larger than the rest of the Milne barques. She was sold to the Finns in 1919, and finally scrapped at Wilhelmshaven in 1924.

In her early days this ship carried away her fore royal mast under Captain Milne. This and the royal yard were never replaced, and her stumpy appearance forward rather spoilt her looks.

She was one of those ships which were continually escaping disaster by a narrow margin. I have described her narrow escape from a capsize in 1914 on page 14, Volume I. In August, 1910, she was nearly destroyed by fire. After arriving in Buenos Ayres roads with a cargo of coal and coke from the Clyde, a fire was discovered in the after hold. The usual methods of smothering a coal fire were taken by Captain King. The hatches were battened down, and water was poured through holes cut in the deck over the seat of the trouble; but as the fire showed no signs of decreasing the tug *Gladiator* was called in, and for a day and a night she pumped water into the ship without any apparent effect. A thick black smoke of a most poisonous description warned the *Inverclyde's* crew that things were not improving, and the following night the hatches were blown off in an explosion of coal gas, which shot flames as high as the mastheads; but the plucky ship's company continued to fight without resting. After several further explosions of coal gas the decks began to buckle up. It was then that the boats were lowered into the water. By midnight the sides of the ship were red-hot, the decks were smouldering and in places on fire, and a huge cloud of steam rose as the water which was being pumped into the ship came to the boil. Soon after midnight it was noticed that the *Inverclyde* was sinking, and she settled so rapidly that she was down on the muddy bottom of the River Plate before there was any time to save even the ship's papers and money; but 30 feet of water on top of the burning coal eventually smothered the fire. A few days later the ship was raised and towed to Buenos Ayres, where she was refitted. After discharging the remains of her cargo at Ensenada she sailed in ballast for Liverpool.

In the winter of 1915-16 the *Inverclyde* was badly dismasted off

v

the Cape, arriving at East London with the loss of her mainmast and mizen topmast.

Captain King remained in command of the *Inverclyde* until 1917, and she was sold to the Finns two years later.

"Inverness."

The last ship to be built for the Inver Line was the *Inverness,* which was launched by McMillan & Son in October, 1902. This vessel was a good deal larger, registering 1959 tons gross, and also I should say a good deal slower, than the rest of the "Invers," being a very large carrier. For instance, in 1916 she took 212 days between New York and Brisbane.

Messrs. George Milne & Co. were very conservative shipowners, and had no use for steam in any form. Thus the *Inverness* was not given a donkey boiler and had no handy winches as an aid to man power. She was therefore a heavy handling ship.

She was commanded by Captain J. A. Lewis until 1911, when he was succeeded by Captain R. Rendell.

Captain Lewis was a very superstitious man and he would on no account allow an albatross to be killed. As the albatross wing pipe stem and web foot tobacco pouch were in great demand amongst apprentices it is not surprising to find that on one occasion the boys broke Captain Lewis's rule.

It happened that in 1908, whilst the ship was becalmed off the Cape, the boys managed to catch an albatross from the foc's'le-head unknown to the "old man." For the next week the ship lay in a heavy westerly swell with scarcely steerage way, and before the week was up one of the helmsmen was thrown over the wheel and killed.

That was the first albatross caught in the *Inverness* and the first man killed or lost aboard her. Though a slow sailer and a heavy worker, she was neither an unlucky ship nor a man killer.

On the passage out the voyage before the albatross incident, whilst the ship was lying under bare poles off the Horn in the grip of a westerly gale, a man was blown off the main royal yard and fell into the sea to leeward. As the vessel was being blown to leeward, lying almost in the trough of the sea, he speedily found himself swimming about in the lee scuppers more scared than hurt, having been scooped in over the lee rail as the ship rolled.

The *Inverness* was abandoned on fire at sea in 1918, and it was after her loss that George Milne sold his few remaining ships and retired from business.

Besides the *Gostwyck* George Milne bought two other ships, the *John Cooke*, which he renamed the *Inveravon*, and the *Chelmsford*, which was renamed *Inverlogie*. After being bought for £3500 in 1909 the *Inveravon* sailed for Melbourne from London on Christmas Day. From the first she had to encounter severe westerly gales, but she thrashed her way down Channel until she was to the southward of the Lizard. Here the squalls came down on her with hurricane force. At last the main topmast backstays carried away, and with the next roll the topmast came down, dragging in its train the mizen royal mast and yard. Five days later a tug picked up the drifting ship off the Lizard Head and towed her into Falmouth. Here the *Inveravon* was refitting for a couple of months. She sailed on March 5, and eventually reached the anchorage off Williamstown on the 196th day out from London, having actually been nearly a week beating up the bay from Port Phillip Heads.

"Archibald Russell."

This four-mast barque was not only the last vessel built for Captain Hardie, but was one of the last square-rigged sailing ships to be built on the Clyde. The Scotts of Greenock did not build many modern sailing ships, but those they built were all outstanding vessels. To look at, the *Archibald Russell* was a typical Clyde four-mast barque, English rigged, with a fine sheer, high topgallant foc's'le, from which a flying bridge led to the midship-house; whilst aft she had what was never a usual feature in a British ship—a wheelhouse. In appearance she resembled the *Ross-shire* forward, though she was given more overhang aft than that ship.

The *Archibald Russell's* most interesting innovation in the design of her hull was her bilge keels, which her owners declared were a great success. They lessened the heavy rolling which was such an unpleasant characteristic of many modern heavily rigged ships, and thus saved a great deal of wear and tear of gear. The

Archibald Russell lifted 3930 tons of dead weight on a mean draught of 21 ft. 7½ inches.

On February 28, 1905, she left Greenock in tow for Port Talbot, where she arrived on March 2, having taken 42 hours towing round. On March 21 she sailed from Port Talbot under Captain Lowe, and made the run out round the Horn to Iquique in 103 days. She then crossed from Iquique to Sydney in 91 days.

On February 25, 1906, she sailed from Sydney to the Channel and arrived at Falmouth on May 29, 93 days out. On the same day six ships from Australia arrived at Queenstown, all of which had been well beaten by the *Archibald Russell*, their times being as follows :—

Invermay	left Wallaroo	Jan. 3, 1906	arr. Queenstown	May 29—146 days
Lucknow	,, Sydney	,, 18 ,,	,, ,,	,,	131 ,,
Loto	,, Melbourne	,, 20 ,,	,, ,,	,,	129 ,,
Notre Dame d' Arvor	,, Port Pirie	,, 27 ,,	,, ,,	,,	122 ,,
Marechal de Villars	,, Wallaroo	,, 30 ,,	,, ,,	,,	119 ,,
Queen Elizabeth	,, Sydney	Feb. 6 ,,	,, ,,	,,	112 ,,
Archibald Russell	,, ,,	,, 25 ,,	,, Falmouth	,,	93 ,,

On her second voyage the *Archibald Russell* went out from Hamburg to Sydney in 100 days from Prawle Point, and sailing from Sydney on February 21, 1907, arrived at Falmouth on June 6, 105 days out. After discharging at Antwerp she loaded at Hamburg, and made a long passage out to Santa Rosalia under Captain Swinton, arriving on February 24, 1908, 145 days out.

Her passage home in 1908 was equally lengthy, being 175 days from Tacoma to Dublin.

On her next voyage she was commanded by Captain McMillan, and made the fine passage of 87 days from Port Talbot to Tocopilla, arriving on December 1, 1909. Since then she has made the following fine passages:—

Liverpool to Taltal	..	..	..	81 days
New York to Melbourne	..	..	92 ,,
Melbourne to New York	..	..	90 ,,
New York to Fremantle	..	..	92 ,,
Fremantle to Cape Town	..	..	52 ,,
Cape Town to Melbourne	..	..	40 ,,
Cardiff to Rio	..	..	..	45 ,,
Barry to Buenos Ayres	..	..	60 ,

The *Archibald Russell* kept out of trouble during the war, and gave underwriters very little anxiety until 1920, when she made a long passage out to Melbourne and was put on the overdue list, her rate for re-insurance going up to 20 guineas.

On her return home Messrs. Hardie laid her up at Milford Haven. Here, in September, 1923, during a severe gale, the Elder Dempster ship, *Monarch*, breaking adrift from her moorings, fouled the *Archibald Russell* and did her some damage.

In February, 1924, the *Archibald Russell* was bought by Captain Erikson, her first voyage under the Finns being as follows:—

Milford Haven to Callao in ballast	114 days	
Lobos de Tierra with guano to Savannah *via* Panama	19 ,,	from Panama to Savannah
Savannah to Port Lincoln	123 ,,	
Port Lincoln to Queenstown	130 ,,	

After discharging at Dublin in September, 1925, the *Archibald Russell* went into dry dock and had some new steel plates put into her forefoot, after which she returned to Finland, where she was re-fitted as a cadet ship, and, taking on board a large number of Lithuanian cadets, loaded a lumber cargo at Sundsvaal for Melbourne. Unfortunately she was frozen in just when she was about to sail, and did not get free of the ice until May 25, 1926. Her passage out to Melbourne, where she arrived on September 8, 1926, was 126 days from Sundsvaal, and 102 from Dungeness.

In 1926-7 she formed one of the grain fleet from Australia. Loading at Geelong she had an exciting race with the *Hougomont*, which sailed from Port Lincoln. The two ships were in company on several occasions, but in the end the *Hougomont* had the best of it, arriving at Falmouth on May 4, 120 days out, whilst the *Archibald Russell* arrived at Queenstown on May 15, 124 days out.

After discharging at Antwerp the *Archibald Russell* returned to the Baltic and loaded for Melbourne. On April 19, 1927, she sailed from Ornskoldsvik, and was spoken off the Outer Hebrides on September 7, from whence she was 99 days to Melbourne, where she arrived on December 15, 1927. Loading at Geelong, she sailed from that port on Feb. 21, 1928, and reached Queenstown June 19, 119 days out. Very bad weather was experienced off the Horn, two seamen being washed overboard.

Archibald Russell discharged at Barry. She remained in the grain trade until the last war, when she was seized by the British authorities and used for storage purposes on the Tyne. Latest report is that she is refitting for further service.

"R. C. Rickmers."

The family of Rickmers were not to be discouraged by the unfortunate end of their enterprise in building the *Maria Rickmers*, and in 1906 they launched the huge five-masted auxiliary *R. C. Rickmers*. As this vessel was a very interesting attempt to combine sails and engines I will give her passages until the outbreak of war.

On her maiden voyage the *R. C. Rickmers* crossed from Bremen to New York under Captain August Walsen. At New York she loaded 189,976 cases of petroleum, and made the passage out to Saigon in 83 days. At Saigon Captain H. Bandelin took over the *R. C. Rickmers* and she sailed to Bangkok, where she loaded 6942 tons of rice and made the run home to Bremen in 91 days (85 days to the Channel, where she signalled on February 5, 1907).

Her next cargo was 7006 tons of cement, her freight being 21s. 6d. from Hamburg to San Pedro, the passage being made in 97 days. From San Pedro she sailed and steamed to Sydney in 40 days, loaded 6668 tons of coal at 21s. in Sydney, and crossed to San Francisco in 58 days. Her last passage this voyage was from Tacoma to Antwerp with wheat. She loaded the largest cargo of wheat ever shipped from Tacoma. This amounted to 7181 tons or 267,626 bushels, valued at 240,800 dollars. Her freight on this occasion was 30s., and she made the run home round the Horn to Antwerp in 122 days.

It was reckoned that the profit on this voyage was from £7-8000. The *R. C. Rickmers* had cost £75,000, and her running expenses per day, including provisions, wages, insurance interest, plus 5 per cent. depreciation on ship and 10 per cent. on machinery, came to £50 a day. In two years and seven months the ship had covered 100,310 miles in ten passages, 603 days being spent at sea and 334 days in port. Altogether Messrs. Rickmers had reason to congratulate themselves on the success of their huge five-master.

Captain Schwetmann now took over the command and taking

7256 tons of coke on board, sailed from Antwerp to San Francisco in 92 days. The rest of her passages until the beginning of the war were as follows:—

1909	Moji to Singapore	15 days
	(7150 tons of coal)	
	Bassein to Bremen	87
	(6718 tons of rice)	
	Newcastle-on-Tyne to San Francisco	103 „
	(6464 tons of coke)	
1910	Moji to Singapore	16 „
	(7161 tons of coal)	
	Rangoon to Bremen	97 „
	(7117 tons of rice)	
	Newcastle-on-Tyne to 'Frisco	96 „
	(6283 tons of coke)	
1911	Newcastle, N.S.W., to Valparaiso	32 „
	(7490 tons of coal)	
	Taltal to Hamburg	57 „
	(7300 tons of saltpetre)	
1912	Philadelphia to Kobe, Japan	100 „
	(2114 cases of petroleum)	
	Portland (Oregon) to Antwerp	101 „
	(7225 tons of wheat)	
1913	Philadelphia to Hiogo	111 „
	(199,984 cases of petroleum)	
1914	Vladivostok to Hull	98 „
	(6880 tons of beans and hemp seed)	

The outbreak of war caught the *R. C. Rickmers* in a British port, and owing to the scarcity of shipping, she was fitted out and sent to sea under the name of *Neath* and the British flag. We next hear of her stranded off Beachies Head, Alexander Bay, Newfoundland, when on a passage from Gambo, Newfoundland, to Cardiff. She was, however, refloated without suffering much damage. She did not last long, however, for a German submarine caught the ex-German five-master and sent her to the bottom.

" France II."

This tremendous five-mast barque was the largest sailing ship ever built. She was launched at Bordeaux on November 9, 1911, from the yard of the Ch. & Atel. de la Gironde, and took the water amidst a scene of great enthusiasm.   She was intended for the French ore trade from New Caledonia, and was fitted with every modern invention to save labour, as well as wireless and an electric lighting plant.   She also had twin screws driven by internal combustion engines, which, it was calculated, when added to the sails, would give her a speed of over 17 knots.   In many ways her equipment resembled that of the giant oil tanker *Quevilly*.

Like all well designed ships, the *France* did not look her size at a distance, but close to she was truly enormous for a sailing ship, and when you got on board her size was still further accentuated. One of her chief characteristics was a tremendous sheer, her figure-head being 40 feet above the waterline, and it was like walking up a steep hill going forward from the break of the bridge deck.   The accommodation was very good, being placed amidships along with the machinery, but it is evident that the engines were not much of a success, for they were taken out before her last voyage. She was a stump topgallant mast barque, but even so her spread of canvas was an impressive one, consisting of 32 sails altogether. The captain reckoned that she had 38 miles of manila rope and 42 miles of wire rope in her standing and running rigging.

I went aboard this ship when she was in London in the winter of 1921-2, and the captain, over a glass of wine, showed me her log books in her spacious saloon.   These recorded some very fine bits of sailing in strong fair winds, when the ship very easily topped the 14 knots.

The *France* was a long time completing, and did not actually sail on her maiden voyage until the summer of 1913, when she went out to New Caledonia.   During the war she was armed, and made several trips across the Atlantic, when she was lucky enough to escape both submarine and mine.

I think it was just at the end of the war that the *France* caused considerable anxiety by breaking away from her tugs during a strong gale in the North Sea.   She had left the Tyne bound for Baltimore in tow of several tugs.   As soon as an offing had been made all these left her except one, which was engaged to tow her as far as the Lizard.   However, this tug turned up in the Tyne and stated that she had left the *France* at midnight off the Yorkshire coast, and that

"FRANCE II"

By Courtesy of Photographer C. C. Knobeloch

[See Page 311

THE MAIN DECK "BELLPOOL"

[*See Page* 314

the big ship was then on her beam ends and making bad weather of it. However, the *France*, which had a crew of over fifty hands, managed to come through this North Sea blow in safety.

In the spring of 1921 we find her loading 7000 tons of Welsh coal at Newport, Monmouth. She sailed from Newport under Captain A. Leport on March 7 and reached Lyttelton, New Zealand, on June 25, 110 days out. Her best run on this passage was 285 miles. The *France* weathered out 12 hours of hurricane weather off Goff Island, when she lost several sails. She was chartered to load wool at Lyttelton and Wellington, and took the largest cargo ever shipped from New Zealand, consisting of 11,000 bales of wool and 6000 casks of tallow.

The big sailing ship left Wellington on September 5, 1921, for London, and her passage took 90 days. On the way to the Horn she made the following runs on consecutive days: 266, 240, 276, 322, 286 and 243 miles. When asked if 322 was the best 24-hour run the ship had ever done, Captain Leport declared that she had actually averaged over 17 knots, and totalled 420 in a day's work. It was blowing very hard at the time. In fine weather with moderate winds, he said that she had averaged 14 knots for six consecutive days. The little captain, who was a sturdy, bearded Breton, evidently was not afraid to drive his big ship, and that he was a thorough all-round seaman is proved by the fact that he cut out all his sails himself. He was a believer in flat sails and in hand stitching in preference to machine sewing. Thus all the *France's* sails, to the number of 32, were made aboard.

On her way up from the Horn the *France* struck some very bad weather, and one big sea created havoc on her main deck, besides carrying two of her crew overboard. I have already mentioned that previous to this voyage her motors had been taken out of the ship.

On February 5, 1922, the *France* left London with a cargo of cement, steel rails, and trucks, for the ore mines in New Caledonia. Captain Leport made the good run of 21 days to the Line, and arrived out at Tchio in 103 days. From Tchio the *France* sailed in ballast for Pouembout in order to load 8000 tons of nickel.

Whilst proceeding along the coast she was drifted by the current on to the coral reef near a place called Coya, about 60 miles from the entrance to Noumea. This was on July 12, 1922. Apparently a big surf was running, and all night long the *France* bumped on the reef with the seas breaking over her. Early on the following morning her S.O.S. signals were picked up by the steamer *Canadian Transporter*, which was 220 miles away. The latter immediately replied "Keep a stout heart. Stokers doing their damnedest," but by this time the crew of the *France* had already abandoned the wreck, which was hard and fast. According to the photographs of the wreck the poor old *France*, sitting high up on the reef, was badly bilged. When the Australian Salvage Company appeared on the scene they found two holds full of water; but there is no doubt that the *France* could have been salved without very much difficulty if her wreck had not occurred at a time when shipping was in a very low state.

That autumn all her sails, cabin fittings, and wireless were sent home to Bordeaux, and the hull sold for £2000. My latest news of the ship in December of that year was that she was nearly dry at low water, and leaked very little. It therefore seems certain that only a little enterprise was needed in order to float her. But the enterprise, or at any rate the incentive, was evidently non-existent, and so the largest sailing ship ever built has been left to rot on that New Caledonia coral reef.

" Bellpool" and " Bellco."

For a few years after the war Messrs. James Bell & Co., of Hull, ran a few sailing ships which were all given names beginning with Bell. Amongst these was the *Bellpool*. This 1900-ton steel ship was known before the war as the *Wellgunde*, having been built in 1904 by A. Rodger & Co. for H. Folsch & Co., of Hamburg. James Bell & Co. also owned the *Bellands* ex *Forteviot*, which we have already described, the *Bellco*, originally the Dutch-built *Dione*, and others.

Although the *Bellpool* had a deadweight capacity of 3200 tons she was considered a smart sailer, and in 1914 made the passage from Mejillones to Falmouth in 60 days. She was lucky to find herself in Hamburg at the commencement of the war. There she was laid up until 1919, and was one of the German ships which escaped being allocated to one or other of the Allies. Her original owners, however, sold her to a Bremen firm, who renamed her *Hansa*.

Her first passage for six years was from Hamburg to Kotka, and she remained under the German flag until 1922, when she was bought by James Bell & Co. and renamed *Bellpool*. For the short time that she was under the Red Ensign she was employed in the timber trade from the Baltic to Australia. In 1922, whilst on her way to Adelaide from Bjorneborg, she put into Port Natal in distress having lost most of her deck cargo. She was by this time owned by the Norwegian, Monsen of Tonsberg.

Her last voyage was from Skelleftea, Sweden, to Adelaide in 119 days, and from Adelaide to Falmouth in 113 days. She was then laid up at Belfast in the Musgrave Channel for nearly two years. Her end came in 1926, when she was sold to British shipbreakers.

The *Bellco* was built by Rijkee & Co., of Rotterdam, for Wachesmuth & Krogmann, of Hamburg, and was one of the last sailing ships built in Holland. With a deadweight capacity of 3250 tons on a gross tonnage of 2103, she was given a large sail plan with double topgallant yards, and made a name for herself in the nitrate trade. Her good sailing attracted the attention of F. Laeisz, who bought her in 1912 and renamed her *Pelikan*. Under the "P" flag she made some very smart passages between the nitrate ports and Hamburg.

At the outbreak of war she was caught at Valparaiso. After the Armistice her crew did their best to render her unserviceable when they learnt that she was to be taken over by Chile. Besides playing havoc aloft, they wrecked her steering gear; then a norther came along and she dragged ashore. However, in 1920 she was salved and sailed for the United Kingdom.

James Bell & Co. then renamed her the *Bellco*. After some months at Hull in 1921 she crossed the Atlantic to Campbelltown, N.B., in 37 days. Soon after this she came under the ownership of Mr. A. Monsen of Tonsberg.

In 1923 journalists suddenly became interested in the *Bellco* owing to her race with the German ship *Landkirchen*, both vessels being homeward bound with nitrate. The *Bellco* sailed from Taltal just four days after the *Landkirchen* had sailed from Antofagasta, and they signalled within a few hours of each other at St. Michael's in the Azores. From there to their discharging ports they each took a fortnight, the *Bellco* going to Granville, and the *Lankirchen* to Rotterdam. The *Bellco*, unfortunately, was badly damaged about the bow by colliding with the quay at Granville on her arrival. After this she was laid up in the port until the summer of 1924, when she was towed across to Plymouth and repaired. She then went back to the West Coast.

In the autumn of 1924 the *Bellco* again had an interesting race when homeward bound with nitrate. On her way up the Atlantic she fell in with the three-mast barque *Anitra*, and the four-mast barques *Lawhill* and *C. B. Pedersen*. *Anitra* and *Lawhill* soon dropped astern, but the *C. B. Pedersen* and the *Bellco* kept together for five days, the latter eventually reaching Fayal first out of the four ships, 106 days out from Caleta Buena.

The *Bellco* was put up for auction in 1926, and has since followed the *Bellands* and *Bellpool* to the shipbreakers, being broken up in Italy.

A Plea for Sail Training.

The finest square-rigged deep-water sailing ships afloat to-day are the foreign training ships. The Dutchmen and Dagoes, the Souwegians and Finns, and even the Greeks, all recognise the value of sail training, and have sailing ships going deep water for this special purpose. It is only the British who allow steam trained apprentices to become officers in their Mercantile Marine.

Most of the shipowners, and even some of our shipmasters, pretend that steam trained apprentices are good enough for the job of navigating our present-day ships, but our modern shipowners are nothing more or less than financial wizards, masters of organisation who, with but very few exceptions, have fought their way to the top of vast business combines from the office stool of the poorly paid shipping clerk. Those shipowners who have had a sea training can be counted on the fingers of one hand, and it is only they who can appreciate the necessity for a harder training than that given to an apprentice in a well found steamer.

This harder training, as is recognised by the Germans, and all other seafaring nations, can only be found in the ship of masts and yards. I do not think that the all-round seamanship, nor even the invaluable sea-sense, which are obtained by a training in sail, are by any means the most important advantages gained over a training in steam, but it is the splendid character-making traits of self-reliance, presence of mind, alertness of brain, quickness of decision, and endurance of physical stress and nerve strain which are the priceless fruits of the hard times and knocking about experienced in life at sea under sail.

My contention is that the safe, easy life of a steam trained apprentice is no testing of a boy likely to become an officer, who in future years may have thousands of lives in his charge, and who, by a want of decision, a lack of grit, or a breakdown of nerve, may sacrifice those lives in a few moments of heartrending tragedy.

No man knows how he is going to behave until he is tested. The most promising material often turns out to be straw when the critical moment arrives. If it is hard for a man to tell himself how he will behave under certain strains and stresses, it is still harder for his employer to know, and the only safeguard for that employer can be the knowledge that the man has come through a training which has thoroughly tested out the qualities necessary to fight those grim opponents, wind and sea.

The most experienced judgment is often at fault. The man who gives every indication of being white turns out to be yellow. Everyone who has commanded men, whether at sea or in war, on the trail or in the bush, has to ward against being let down by the weakness of one single unit in his command. It is in this way that a panic starts, for men are like sheep and are as quick to follow the man who turns back as the man who goes forward. In a time of danger and crisis the man who is sure of himself does the right thing; the man who has led a sheltered life and has had no experience does not know what to do, and has an overpowering inclination to do nothing or to follow the lead of someone else, however senseless that lead may be; and finally the man with the yellow streak in him runs away from the trouble.

I have experienced all three types on many occasions. I

remember once in the South African War, when my job was to capture a Boer Cossack post stationed on a ridge as an outpost of a commando, that one or two men infected a whole troop with panic.

It was about 1 a.m. on a bright moonlight night. I had managed to reach a kraal wall within a quarter of a mile of the Boer post, but that quarter of a mile was a bare grassy slope. There was no hope of getting at the post unperceived, and the only chance was to gallop at them. Riding out from behind the wall I gave the order to trot and then canter by means of the hand signals. Before we had gone twenty yards the post opened fire, as I expected them to do. I then quickened up into a gallop with my sergeant riding close behind me. I was thinking of whom I should put in charge of the Boers when I captured them, when my sergeant suddenly cried out, "My God, sir, they've all gone back!" A panic had taken the men, who, being a scallywag corps, were of all nationalities, though enlisted mostly as Canadians—the corporal, for instance, was a Spaniard, thus we two found ourselves charging the post alone. When we got in amongst the Boers they tried to knock us off our horses, but we rode over them, and in some extraordinary way escaped to the main body of our men. This panic, so far as I was able to find out, was caused by two men who so lost their heads that they rode straight into a donga, and leaving their horses and rifles in the donga ran for about 30 miles on their own feet back to the railway line. This experience shows the danger of panic.

On another occasion in the same war my corps received a new officer, a hard looking South African, who spoke Dutch and several Kaffir dialects perfectly. We naturally looked upon him as an invaluable addition. It so happened that his first little fight with us was against General Botha's outposts. At that time several columns were trying to catch the wary Botha, and our corps were scouting for one of these columns. Sneaking out before daybreak, about half a squadron strong, we ambushed ourselves on the ground that the Boer outpost was accustomed to take up. As soon as it was light the Boers, some fifty or more, were perceived approaching. Unfortunately for us our new officer and his troop happened to be nearest. He was ordered on no account to fire until he received the command. The Boers came on at a slow walk, with no scouts out, and evidently quite unsuspecting our presence, but they were fully 300 yards away when our new man, who had been causing us no little anxiety by his evident excitement, could contain himself no longer and started firing at them. This entirely spoilt this little fight, though a few Boers were knocked off their horses. They retired, were quickly reinforced, and we presently found ourselves fighting a rearguard action against an overwhelming force, and only extricated ourselves with difficulty and loss of life.

The man who gets excited in the face of danger is useless and even more harmful than the man who gets frightened. Neither the frightened man nor the excited man is capable of the right judgment at the right moment And the man who lacks experience, though he may be no coward, may give way either to excitement or to the apathy of a numb brain just when he ought to be calmly but vigorously taking hold of things and bossing his job. No boy who has had four years training in sail could escape, at some time or other in the four years, finding out whether he is fitted to be a leader of men or not; but the steam trained apprentice has no such chance, and his battle with himself has to be fought later on, when, as officer of the watch, he is in charge of the ship and the lives of all on board.

A training in sail means a training in endurance, which certainly cannot be said of steam. It was endurance more than brains, more than any skill in fighting or mechanical devices that won the Great War.

Many reasons have been advanced for the result of the 1914-18 war, but if the truth were told, it was really won by doggedness— by the sheer power of sticking it—possessed by the British Tommy and the British subaltern as they clung to their mud-filled, rain-swept, or frost-bound trenches in the face of bombs, gas, pip-squeaks, shrapnel, and high explosive. It was won by the power of unconquerable endurance possessed by the field artillery driver, who steered his horses night after night along shell-torn roads and slippery plank tracks, or led his protesting pack mules through acres of bog-like ground that reeked of poison gas. It was won by the stubborn grit of the signallers, who were often shot down faster than they could be replaced in the desperate work of mending their telephone wires.

At sea also the war was won by endurance, the steady, dull, never-ending work of mine-sweeping, of patrolling, of transporting troops, food, and ammunition in spite of all that enemy submarine and mine could do.

It is this endurance which the hard life of the old sailing ship can grind into a boy. Then there is the work aloft, which is of the very greatest value in developing a boy's character. I remember that my first essay above the sheer pole was to clear the flag halliards at the main truck—this meant shinning up the chain of the royal halliard, and then up the mast itself, which, long-legged and long-armed as I was, I could not quite encircle. I did not know when I started to carry out this order, what sort of a head I had for heights, or whether I could succeed in making my muscles perform a duty which they had never been called upon to do before, and I can assure those who read this that it took all my determination and will-power to force both nerves and muscles to the task and to carry it out. Afterwards I always loved work aloft.

Sail handling in bad weather is nothing more or less than a fight between man and the elements, a fight that used often to continue through a whole watch or longer without the chance of a breather. As all sail trained men will tell you, one cannot help but gain strength of wind and muscle, as well as strength of spirit, in such a contest.

There is one other great advantage that sail training has over steam training, and that can be described in the one word—health. In a sailing ship a weak and weedy youth is speedily transformed into a burly, hard-muscled athlete, with a cool head for heights and a perfect organ of balance. There was no need for physical jerks in the days of sail. One had more than enough of natural exercise, and the continual muscle work, both on deck and aloft, with spells in bad weather that tested one's physique to the limit of its endurance, kept one every bit as fit as the trained athlete. The safe, easy drudgery which makes up the life of the steamship seaman can always be suddenly overset by the breath of the storm wind, by the unforeseen accident, or by such enemies as fire and ice, and

"HERZOGIN CECILIE"

[See Page 322

Courtesy of Nautical Photo Agency

"BEATRICE"

[*See Page* 324

then the qualities of resolution, resource and endurance, which can only be produced by sail training, are badly needed.

It may be argued that the training given to an apprentice in steam is sufficient for his needs, but what is this training beyond ship cleaning, bridge work and perhaps navigation? Here is a letter which I take from the *Nautical Magazine*:—

Ten months ago, my son joined a cargo steamer belonging to a Liverpool firm as a cadet. It was agreed that he should not receive any salary for the first year, but that at the commencement of the second year he should receive £1 per month. He made three voyages in the vessel, during which time he was put to work washing boats, driving winches, cleaning brass work, sweeping up holds, and doing odd jobs along with the men. At sea he was kept on watch four hours on and four hours off duty. He learned nothing whatever about navigation or seamanship, and what he did learn he picked up from the men in the forecastle. The vessel only carried two officers and as they had other duties to attend to, which kept them going from fifteen to sixteen hours per day, they had little time to devote to teaching my son anything.

Since the above letter was written there is another duty which is sometimes trusted to the steamship apprentice, and that is standing by "Iron Mike," as the latest steering device has been called. What a contrast to steering a sailing ship with all its grind of muscle, test of nerve, and delicacy of touch!

The reason usually given for the abandonment of the training squadrons and the brigs in the Royal Navy was that it was impossible to give every officer and rating a course in them, and the same argument has been put forward by shipowners to explain why they have made no attempt to preserve sail training in the Mercantile Marine. But the fact is that it is entirely a matter of expense. Rather than put their hands in their pockets our shipowners are ready to put up with officers who, although they may be scientific navigators and very knowledgeable on such subjects as mechanics, are not full-fledged seamen in the real sense of the word, nor yet in a great number of cases, A1 subjects in the matter of health.

I fear I have probably wasted space in making this plea for sailing ship training, but one cannot help feeling a bit sore when one sees that even Russia recognises the value of sail training. The fleet of training ships, both naval and mercantile, is now a very fine one indeed, but not a single one of them hoists the British flag.

W

German Training Ships.

Most seafaring nations refuse to grant officers' certificates except to candidates who have done their four years in a sailing ship. This training, for a small Mercantile Marine, can be provided by two or three ships, but it is a different matter when one comes to a large seafaring nation like the Germans.

The first German cadet ship was the pretty little flush-decked, steel full-rigged ship *Grossherzogin Elisabeth* of 1260 tons, which was built by Tecklenborg in 1901, and ever since that date has served as the school ship of Oldenburg. Painted white, beautifully kept up and perfectly sparred, the *Grossherzogin Elisabeth* is an example of what a small cadet ship should be.

In 1901 the North German Lloyd decided to provide sailing ships for the training of their own officers, and the result of this decision was the building of the four-mast barque *Herzogin Cecilie* of 3242 tons gross in Rickmers' yard at Bremerhaven.

This vessel was built to sail and was therefore given very fine lines. As she was to carry from 90 to 100 cadets no aids to man power were provided such as steam capstans and halliard winches. It was lucky, however, that a double wheel was fitted to steer her by, as it often took four strong men to keep her near her course in heavy weather.

The *Herzogin Cecilie* was a lofty ship, and a full suit of sails, numbering 36 in all, took up over 37,000 square feet of canvas. Before the last war a suit of canvas for her would cost £4000, and her captain reckoned that he used up £400 worth of canvas every voyage in keeping her sails in repair.

The *Herzogin Cecilie* was the pride of the German Mercantile Marine, and up to the time of the war she had never made a bad passage. On her maiden voyage she made the following runs:—

Lizard to Monte Video	.. .. ..	53 days
Monte Video to Portland, Oregon ..	..	66 ,,
Astoria to Falmouth ..	.. .. ..	105 ,,

Her complement at this time consisted of captain, four officers, surgeon, two schoolmasters, cook, 14 paid hands, who were mostly idlers and stewards, six third-year apprentices rated as able seamen, and 59 other apprentices.

Another good passage was made in 1904, when she went out round the Horn from Dungeness to San Francisco in 112 days.

In 1908 she went from Beachy Head to Adelaide in 78 days, and in 1910 from Mejillones to the Scilly Isles in 63 days.

When war broke out she was outward bound within a few days of her nitrate port. She was interned at Coquimbo for the four years and was kept in far better condition than most of the German ships caught on the West Coast. After the Armistice she was allocated to the French, and sailed from Antofagasta in October, 1920, for Ostend. On her arrival in the latter port she was somewhat damaged by running into the quay.

Captain Gustaf Erikson then bought her for £4000. Under the Finnish flag she was at first commanded by Captain Reuben de Cloux, her passages including:—

Frederickstadt to Melbourne	..	..	..	92 days
Frederickstadt to Cape Nelson		..	..	84 ,,
Channel to Australian coast	..	..	..	67 ,,
Melbourne to Taltal (in ballast)		..	..	35 ,,
(21 days from Campbell Island)		..	..	
Mejillones to Falmouth	..	..	..	92 ,,
Grangemouth to San Antonio	..	..	..	102 ,,
San Antonio to Caleta Buena	..	..	..	6 ,,
Caleta Buena to Falmouth	..	..	..	97 ,,
Ostend to Mejillones	..	..	..	112 ,,
Mejillones to Dunkirk	..	..	..	107 ,,
Dunkirk to Albany (in ballast)		..	..	100 ,,
Albany to Port Lincoln	..	..	..	6 ,,
Port Lincoln to Callao	..	..	..	51 ,,
(4500 tons of wheat)				
Callao to Port Lincoln (in ballast)		..	..	62 ,,
Port Lincoln to Falmouth	..	..	..	136 ,,

With only 19 hands all told Captain de Cloux tried the Cape route, but the *Herzogin Cecilie* could not weather the Leeuwin owing to fierce head gales, and was finally obliged to head away for the Horn, which was not passed until she was 58 days out.

When she arrived at Falmouth her crew were about dead beat after experiencing a tremendous sou'west gale in the Bay.

On her next passage she sailed in ballast from Hamburg to Port Lincoln in 96 days, being only 19 days from the Cape of Good Hope.

On May 2, 1927, the *Herzogin Cecilie* arrived at Queenstown only 88 days out from Port Lincoln, having beaten the rest of the Australian grain fleet by a whole month.

Her next outward passage was from Sundsvaal to Melbourne in 96 days. On this passage she was only 79 days from Beachy Head. She then distinguished herself by covering the 600 miles between Melbourne and Port Lincoln in 45 hours, an average of 13½ knots.

Race Between "Herzogin Cecilie" and "Beatrice."

After making this record *Herzogin Cecilie* was engaged in a desperate race with the Swedish four-mast barque *Beatrice*, which was originally Shankland's *Routenburn*, one of the last ships built by the famous firm of Robert Steele & Co., of Greenock.

Before describing the race between the *Herzogin Cecilie* and the *Beatrice* the latter deserves a few words of description.

Like all Steele's ships, the *Routenburn* was beautifully built. She had been splendidly kept up, and when dry docked at Melbourne in December, 1927, her plates looked as good as new. The only sign of weakness that she has ever shown was the sinking of her foremast some 5 inches in 1927, owing to the heel having rusted away. This was put right, and no other defect could be discovered after the closest examination. Unfortunately her old sail plan has been replaced by the economical but ugly stump topgallants.

The following are a few of her best passages during the four years to 1928:—

Gothenburg to Melbourne	92 days
Melbourne to London	86 ,,
Gothenburg to Adelaide	96 ,,
Adelaide to Falmouth	102 ,,
(Beat the French cadet ship *Richelieu* by a day)	
Sundsvaal to Melbourne	94 ,,
Melbourne to London	116 ,,
Frederickstadt to Melbourne	94 ,,
Melbourne to Port Louis, Mauritius	39 ,,
Mauritius to Seychelles	4 ,,
Seychelles to Bluff, New Zealand	56 ,,

In her early days under Shankland's house flag the *Routenburn* crossed main and mizen skysails above her royal yards. As she had a very short hoist to her upper topgallant yards it will thus be seen that her sail area had been considerably reduced. The *Herzogin Cecilie* still had her original sail plan, crossing three royals over double topgallants, and in this had a considerable advantage over her rival. Both ships were manned by boys and their officers were also very young.

The master of the *Beatrice*, Captain Harold Bruce; her mate, David Ohlson; her second mate, Sam Svennsen, who was a real sailing ship enthusiast, and her crew took a tremendous pride in their ship, and I do not suppose that there was a better kept vessel sailing the seas at that time.

Captain de Cloux and Mr. Harald Lindfors, the chief officer of the *Herzogin Cecilie*, were equally keen, but with a total crew of only twenty-five they had a harder task with their big sail spread, although the *Herzogin Cecilie* was a wonderfully dry and stiff ship and carried her canvas well. She had a further handicap in this short race with the *Beatrice* in that she had not been docked for some months, whereas the *Beatrice* had just come out of dry dock; also the ballast of the *Herzogin Cecilie* had been badly stowed, and as a result she steered very wildly.

In the race round to Port Lincoln the Finn sailed eleven hours before the *Beatrice*, but this did not help her much as she was becalmed outside for those eleven hours. The *Beatrice*, sailing out from the Heads the following morning, brought the breeze along with her, and the two vessels practically remained together throughout the passage.

On the first night out the *Herzogin Cecilie* was some seven miles to windward at nightfall, and weathered Cape Otway some hours before the *Beatrice*. On the following day, a Saturday, the *Beatrice* was sighted on the port quarter 15 miles further out to sea. That night a strong beam wind came along and both ships started sailing very fast, the taffrail log of the *Beatrice* recording 59 miles for the forenoon watch on Sunday. During all this time the *Herzogin Cecilie*, which was further inshore hugging the land, had kept abreast of the Swede, and she passed Cape Borda with a lead of 3 miles, having sailed a shorter distance through cutting corners. By midnight, however, both ships were abeam, and according to the *Beatrice's* log she had covered 312 miles since midnight on Saturday. Both ships now shortened down to topsails in order to avoid reaching the anchorage before daylight.

In the end the *Herzogin Cecilie* anchored off Port Lincoln just 17 minutes before the *Beatrice*, her time being 81 hours from where she dropped her pilot off Port Phillip Heads at 10 o'clock on Thursday evening, December 15, whilst the *Beatrice*, dropping her pilot at the same spot eleven hours later, had made the run in 70 hours.

The rivalry between the two ships was continued on the passage home. On January 18, 1928, both vessels completed loading their wheat and were moved out to the anchorage. The *Herzogin Cecilie* had stowed 51,409 bags, whilst the *Beatrice* had 37,015 in her hold.

On January 19 *Beatrice* sailed at 9 a.m., and the *Herzogin Cecilie* at 2 p.m., the wind being fresh from ahead. *Herzogin Cecilie* was up with the *Beatrice* off the Allthorpes. Captain de Cloux, who knew the coast well, then proceeded to beat through the Backstairs Passage, whilst the more cautious *Beatrice* went round Kangaroo Island. The *Herzogin Cecilie* saw the *Beatrice* for the last time when two days out. The latter was then hull down to leeward on the beam.

On this same day great excitement was caused on the *Herzogin Cecilie* by the discovery of a woman stowaway. On the night before sailing, a farewell dance had been given, at which this girl had been present. She had previously tried to ship as stewardess, and it appears that in despair at being refused she asked one of the officers of the ship chaffingly where was the best place aboard to stow away. Without thinking that his information would be acted upon, he gave her his opinion, and taking her courage in both hands she seized the opportunity of the dance to sneak into the hold, where she remained hidden for 70 hours without food or light and in terror of rats.

The *Hergozin Cecilie* had very poor winds to the latitude of New Zealand, and this spoilt her run to the Horn, which was rounded on February 21, 1928, 33 days from port and 17 days from the latitude of New Zealand.

The first really bad weather was encountered on the thirtieth day out. After the fore royal, mizen upper topgallant sail, and main lower topgallant sail had blown away, Captain de Cloux considered that it was about time to shorten sail. It took all hands 36 hours to shorten canvas down to six topsails and foresail. Except for the four men who were needed at the wheel and even then could hardly hold it, every soul aboard was required in clewing up a topgallant sail and stowing it, and no sooner had the worn-out men crawled down from aloft when the weather sheet of the fore upper topsail carried away.

Let me now quote from the account written by A. J. Villiers in the *Blue Peter*, as it gives a very good idea of the strenuous life aboard a windjammer as compared with that in a steamer:—

Then we learnt that so far we had been only playing, for when we tried to clew that upper topsail up before we lay aloft, every bit of its gear carried away, except the lee clew-line. We stared up in dismay, though we could see nothing. We were pretty far gone then, and tired, and worn out.

"Aloft and furl it," said the mate, and led the way himself. We followed; and the morning broke before we came down again.

It looked madness to go on that yard; and maybe it was. It looked madness to try to reach it; and maybe it was. But we went, just the same. It is impossible to imagine the job that handful of tired out and sorely tried boys faced that night—and did. The whole foremast was shaking and quivering with the furious thrashing of the sail; the great steel yard quivered and bent; the rigging shook violently as if it wanted to shake us off into the sea boiling beneath. The loose ends of the broken sheet and the wire buntlines were flying around through the air, writhing like steel and chain snakes; if any had been touched by these it would have been the end.

Laying out along that yard, with the whole area of the sail flying back and over it, looked like facing death. Maybe it was, in a way; but nobody thought of that as, inch by inch, we fought our way out. The wet sail, which was over a thousand square feet of best storm canvas, was banging back over the yard; every now and then we had to drop beneath the yard, and lie balanced along the foot-ropes. I have not the faintest idea how we got that sail fast. I don't think anyone who was there has. We fought it times without number, and lost; but there came a time when we fought it, and won. But that was not before our bare hands—you cannot fight wet canvas with gloves—were red with blood and blue with cold.

A flying buntline end touched one of the German seamen in the head once, and brought the swift blood. He reeled a bit, but carried on. Then he fainted, after a while, and because we could not take him down we had to lash him there. When he revived he carried on again.

The *Herzogin Cecilie* had a weary time from the Horn to the Line, experiencing nothing but calms and light airs with heavy downpours of rain. The Equator was crossed on March 27, 35 days from the Horn. In the Doldrums the *Herzogin Cecilie* was in company with the *C. B. Pedersen*, Swedish four-mast barque, which had left Sydney on January 8. Captain Dahlstrom of the Swede and his mate rowed over to the *Herzogin Cecilie* one calm morning and were being shown over the ship when a sudden squall caught her aback. The Swede's boat's crew came in handy to haul the yards round.

Meanwhile the other ship was hidden from view by the falling rain. Captain Dahlstrom, however, had every confidence in his second mate, and when the squall cleared off there was the *C. B. Pedersen* within signalling distance. That afternoon the Finns returned the visit of the Swedes.

Soon after this the Trades were picked up and the two vessels parted. *Herzogin Cecilie* took 89 days to the Western Isles, and finally arrived at Falmouth on April 24, 96 days out. The *C. B. Pedersen* arrived at Queenstown 104 days out, and the *Beatrice* did not reach Falmouth until 18 days after her rival, having taken 114 days. Captain Bruce complained that he had had a light weather passage, which did not give his vessel, with her cut-down rig, a chance.

The *Herzogin Cecilie* discharged at Cardiff; *C. B. Pedersen* went to Shields, and the *Beatrice* went to London.

"Herzogin Sophie Charlotte" and "Deutschland."

Besides building the *Herzogin Cecilie* the North German Lloyd bought the *Albert Rickmers*, which had been built by the Rickmers at Bremen in 1894, and renamed her *Herzogin Sophie Charlotte*. This vessel was also very well known before the war, especially in the Australian trade, when she distinguished herself on more than one occasion in racing home from the Dominion against British vessels.

Her run from Hiogo to Portland, Oregon, is considered a record. She arrived on December 12, 1900, only 21 days out.

Another smart passage was from Honolulu to Bremen, 103 days to the Lizard and 36 hours on to the North Sea.

After the war the *Herzogin Sophie Charlotte* was handed over

"RICHELIEU"

[*See Page* 331

"KOBENHAVN"

to the British Shipping Controller. In 1923 he sold her on the Baltic Exchange without reserve for £1500 to the enterprising Captain Erikson. She remained on offer for some time before being acquired by Finnish interests, who intended to refit her for deep-sea work. But in 1928, after a long spell of idleness, she went to the scrappers.

Of the three training ships mentioned above the *Grossherzogin Elisabeth* is the only one still under German colours, but in 1926 the German Training Ship Union placed an order with Tecklenborg of Geestemunde for a ship of the same size and style as the *Grossherzogin Elisabeth,* which was to be built at the cost of 885,000 marks,

This vessel was launched on June 14, and christened *Schulschiff Deutschland* by Mrs. Heineken, the wife of Dr. Heineken, the general director of the North German Lloyd. The *Schulschiff Deutschland* had accommodation for 180 cadets. Not content with this vessel and the *Grossherzogin Elisabeth,* the Training Ship Union and the Association of German Shipowners made arrangements with the firm of Laeisz by which four of the latter's vessels would be fitted with accommodation for 40 cadets apiece. By this means the Germans reckoned to turn out 300 sail trained cadets every year.

The "Af Chapman."

The Swedes, like the Germans, have always held stoutly to the sailing ship tradition, and will only grant certificates to sail trained seamen.

In July, 1926, I was sailing across from Hamble to Ryde in order to race. It was a beautiful day and a nice southerly breeze was blowing. To my astonishment I noticed a white painted full-rigged ship running up the west channel under full sail. She passed the Thorn Knoll Buoy and it was not until she was abreast of the North Thorn that she made any attempt to take in sail, although she would shortly have to round the Calshot lightship and head up the narrow channel of the Southampton Water.

Suddenly, as I was looking, a crowd of black figures appeared in her rigging, and as they swarmed aloft her royal, topgallant and topsail halliards were let go, and the sails hauled close up by the spilling lines. In another moment her yards were black with men, and, as it seemed to me watching, in less than five minutes her upper sails were furled, her courses hauled up, and she was all ready to receive the hawser of an attendant tug.

This smart ship turned out to be the Swedish Government training ship *Af Chapman*, which had once been the British *Dunboyne*, launched at Whitehaven in 1888. The *Af Chapman* was purchased for the Swedish Navy from the Trans-Atlantic Company at Gothenburg in November, 1923, and carried no less than 200 boys. Finally in 1948, she was converted into a floating hostel at Stockholm for the Swedish Tourist Association.

The Argentine Cadet Ship "Presidente Sarmiento."

In the summer of 1925 the British ports received a visit from the Argentine naval cadet training ship *Presidente Sarmiento*, whose appearance gave us a hint of what our men-of-war looked like during the transition period between sail and steam. This full-rigged ship had crossed single topsails and set a full suit of stunsails. She also had fore and main spencers as well as main topmast and mizen staysails. All her square sails were clewed up to the quarters and showed the pig's ears, as they used to be called, hanging on each side of the bunt. When stunsails were done away with and square sails were first clewed up to the yardarm, the old sailors snorted with indignation at the innovation as being most unseamanlike. I remember a modern square-rig seaman criticised the *Presidente Sarmiento* when she appeared in the Mersey for her slovenly fashion of clewing her sails up to the quarter. This is a proof of how custom rules our eyes and influences our opinions in this world.

The *Presidente Sarmiento*, by the by, was launched at Birkenhead in 1897. She was built of steel, but sheathed and coppered. She had the old-fashioned quarter gallery and the heavily ornamented bow of the old sailing man-of-war; but in the matter of guns and machinery she was right up to date. Her speed under steam was 15 knots, but she was fitted with a Bevis feathering propellor, and did most of her cruising under sail alone. Her displacement was 2750 tons, and she had accommodation for 400 boys.

Presidente Sarmiento was replaced as a training ship in 1937 by a cruiser built for the purpose. She has since been converted into the Argentine Presidential yacht.

The Norwegian "Sorlandet."

To show the public spirited enterprise of the seafaring community of other nations I have only to mention the beautiful little Norwegian training ship *Sorlandet,* which in 1927 paid a visit to the Thames. This specially built cadet ship was presented to the Norwegian Training Ship Association by Mr. Skjelbred of Christiansand.

The *Sorlandet* is a full-rigged ship of 600 tons, and in appearance reminds one very much of the famous yacht *Valhalla.* She is built of steel and carries no cargo, her lower hold being given up to ballast and stores, whilst her boys sleep in hammocks in the 'tween decks. The lads undergoing training have a five months' course on the *Sorlandet,* after which they are drafted to one of the deep-water-men of the Norwegian merchant fleet. Aboard the *Sorlandet* the boys are divided into two watches of forty, plus two boys from each watch who serve in the galley. All the ship's work is done by the boys, and they all have their stations and duties. For instance, eight boys are told off for the furling of a course, six to a topsail, four to a topgallant sail, and two to a royal.

Captain G. S. Pedersen was in command of this up-to-date training ship. The *Sorlandet* is still in service, but Captain Pedersen gave up command some years ago.

The French Training Ship "Richelieu."

The *Richelieu* represented the French effort to maintain a training ship with masts and yards. She was built by Blohm & Voss of Hamburg, in 1916, as the *Pola,* a steel four-mast barque of 3100 tons, and when taken over by the French was turned into a training ship under the name of *Richelieu.* Unfortunately this fine cadet ship did not last **very** long, her end being something of a mystery.

In August, 1925, the *Richelieu* arrived in the Mersey to discharge a cargo of grain from Australia, her passage having been about the best out of eight ships, being 102 days to a position 120 miles west of Land's End. Whilst in the Mersey she was very much admired by the Liverpool shipping people, who, with their sailing ship traditions, are particularly severe critics.

After discharging at Liverpool the *Richelieu* was laid up at Brest for a year, then on November 7, 1926, after being thoroughly re-conditioned, she sailed for Baltimore, where she arrived on December 16, 39 days out from Brest *via* Madeira.

Whilst loading 3200 tons of pitch for L'Orient an explosion occurred in her No. 3 hold which killed two negro stevedores from burns and injured no less than thirty. After this the ship began to sink, and only floated long enough to give her crew and cadets time to get away.

At first it was thought that the explosion was due to foul play, as soon after the *Richelieu* was handed over to the French a bomb was found in her hold, but an investigation showed that the explosion was really due to the ignition of pitch dust either by means of an electric spark from a mechanical trimmer or from a naked lamp used by the railway trimmers.

The *Richelieu* was very badly damaged, the telegraphed report saying "Lying aground, angle of 40 degrees, listed outwards from jetty with hatch-ways two-thirds submerged; main and mizen masts destroyed, hanging over side; fore and jigger masts intact. Decks very seriously damaged, full length, and bridge erection destroyed, also damage to side plating. 3134 tons of cargo aboard. Divers' report indicates cargo a good deal consumed judging by space in hold."

The *Richelieu* was managed by the Societe des Navires-Ecoles. She had been handed over to France in accordance with the Treaty of Versailles, and this French training organisation, which had been founded by the leading shipowners, chartered her from the French Government at the nominal price of one franc per year. It was hoped that the Societe des Navires-Ecoles would be able to replace this magnificent but unfortunate cadet ship, but this proved impossible.

The Belgian "L'Avenir."

The Belgians had two sailing ships to train their budding seamen. One of them, the old Shire liner *Linlithgowshire*, was called the *Comte de Smet de Naeyer*. She was broken up in 1934. Cadets were given a preliminary course on her before being drafted to the seagoing four-mast barque *L'Avenir*.

The *L'Avenir* was specially built at Bremerhaven by the

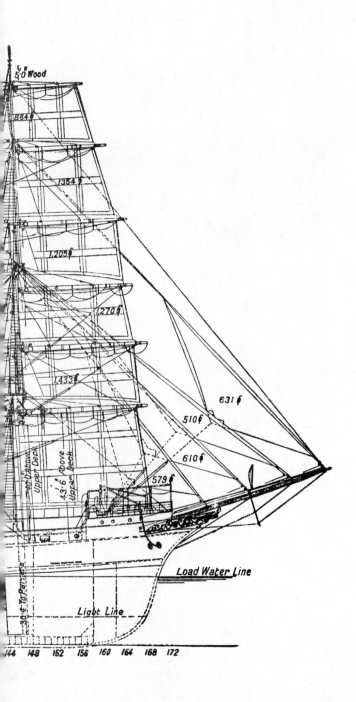

5'0"Wood

.864 ₵

1.354 ₵

1.205 ₵

.270 ₵

.433 ₵

631 ₵

510 ₵

610 ₵

579 ₵

43'6" Above Upper Deck

Load Water Line

Light Line

144 148 152 156 160 164 168 172

[See Page 332.

Rickmers in 1908, and was a steel barque registering 2738 tons gross, and 2074 tons net, with a deadweight capacity of 3400 tons.

She was one of the fastest of the foreign cadet ships, having made the following outstanding passages:—

Wallaroo to Falmouth ..	..	..	..	101 days
San Francisco to Sunderland ..	..	..	105 ,,
Port Talbot to Antofagasta	..	..	..	68 ,,
New York to Melbourne	..	..	..	94 ,,
Bahia Blanca to Antwerp	..	..	..	56 ,,

In July, 1925, she arrived at Antwerp only 38 days out from Tampa. According to the well-informed shipping periodical *Syren and Shipping*, the *L'Avenir* has covered 337 miles in the twenty-four hours. She was sold to Erikson when replaced by the specially designed auxiliary barquentine *Mercator*, 770 tons gross, built 1932 by Ramage & Ferguson of Leith.

The Finnish Training Ships "Fennia" and "Favell".

Of these two training ships, bought by the Finnish Steamship Company of Helsingfors, the *Fennia* was formerly the French four-mast barque *Champigny*, 3230 tons gross, built 1902. She was bought by the Finnish Co. in 1923. The *Favell* was a three-mast barque of 1334 tons. She was interesting as being the last of the great fleet of ships launched from the famous Bristol yard of C. Hill & Sons. She was built in 1895.

In January, 1926, both *Fennia* and *Favell* arrived at Melbourne in the hopes of a grain charter for Europe. The *Favell* was able to get one, having made the crack passage out of 80 days between Copenhagen and Melbourne, but the *Fennia* waited in Hobson's Bay in vain for four months, and eventually on May 1 sailed away for the West Coast. After drifting about on the coast for over a week in her endeavour to make Taltal, the *Fennia*, after reaching the anchorage of Nuestra Senora Bay, was informed by the pilot boat that her destination had been changed to Antofagasta. After some more drifting she managed to reach Antofagasta on June 23, 54 days out. Here she loaded nitrate for home, and leaving on August 3, rounded the Horn on September 6, crossed the Line on October 17, and arriving at the mouth of the Ems on December 7 moored alongside the quay at Delfzijl, 128 days out.

Her next passage, Cardiff for Valparaiso, ended disastrously, for she was dismasted off the Horn in April, 1927, and after drifting about for some time managed to anchor in a dangerous position in the neighbourhood of the North Cape, Falkland Islands. From here she was towed to Port Stanley by a coasting steamer. Although her hull and cargo were undamaged, it was found on survey that besides her main and mizen masts, which, with all yards except the crossjack, would want renewing both her fore and jigger masts were badly sprung. The expense of procuring the new masts and yards and the re-fit was evidently considered prohibitive, and after some delay the *Fennia* was sold and converted into a hulk.

On her last outward passage the little *Favell* left Gefle, October 21, 1927, for Melbourne, passed Dungeness November 13, and arrived out on February 13, 1928, 92 days from Dungeness. She was finally broken up in 1934.

The Danish Training Ships "Viking" and "Kobenhavn."

In 1907 the United Steamship Company, the largest shipping organisation in Denmark, commissioned Burmeister & Wain of Copenhagen to build the four-mast barque *Viking* as a training ship for their young officers. Being specially built, the *Viking* had her poop deck extended well forward of the mainmast, giving splendid accommodation to the cadets and their instructors. Then there was a small well deck corresponding to the height of the usual main deck, through which was stepped the foremast. Forward of this came the topgallant foc's'le. This short well-deck round the foremast rather spoiled the flush decked appearance of the *Viking*. From aesthetic considerations it was a pity that the upper deck was not carried the whole length of the vessel.

The *Viking* registered 2952 tons gross and 2541 tons net, and was handsomely sparred with royals over double topgallant yards, and wireless aerial between the main, mizen and jigger masts.

During the bad times for shipping which followed the Armistice the *Viking* was laid up. However, in 1926 she once more received a crew of 32 budding officers, and sailed on October 31 for Peru. On her passage out, the training of the cadets being her chief object, visits were paid to several West Indian and North American ports.

Then 4000 tons of guano was taken on board, and the ship sailed from Pachacamac, Peru, on July 8, 1927, cleared the Panama Canal on July 28, and reached London on October 27, 1927.

Viking was sold to Erikson in 1929; survived the last war and has since been employed in the South Australian grain trade.

Although few nations had a finer training ship than the *Viking*, the Danes were not content, and early in 1914 placed a contract with Ramage & Ferguson, of Leith, for a still bigger vessel. The work on this new Danish training ship was pretty well advanced when war broke out. However, she was then taken over by the British Admiralty and fitted out as an oil fuel tender. The East Asiatic Co., of Denmark, who had given the order to Ramage & Ferguson, were still determined to persevere with the sail training of their officers at the termination of the war, with the result that they gave Ramage & Ferguson a second commission for a training ship, and this vessel was the celebrated *Kobenhavn*, the largest sailing ship ever built in the British Isles.

The *Kobenhavn* was a five-masted barque like the *Potosi*, but she also had a four-cylinder Diesel engine capable of driving her about 6 knots. As a speciman of what a British yard is still able to do in the way of building an up-to-date sailing ship, the *Kobenhavn* is of particular interest, and deserves being described with some detail.

She was built under special survey to class 100 A1 at Lloyd's, and to conform with all the special requirements of the British Board of Trade and the Danish. The following are some of her main dimensions:—

Gross tonnage	3965 tons
Load displacement	7900 ,,
Deadweight capacity	5200 ,,
Length overall from shark's fin on bowsprit to taffrail	430 ft.
Length on deck	390 ,,
Length between perpendiculars	354 ft. 2 in.
Breadth moulded	49 ft.
Depth moulded	28 ft. 7 in.
Draught loaded	24 ft.

As regards her deck plan, the *Kobenhavn* has a poop which extends almost to the jiggermast, being 112 feet long. Under this poop is the accommodation for the captain, officers and doctor, together with hospital, dispensary, bathrooms, pantry, and main saloon, all finished off in polished hardwood and white enamel. The apprentices are housed just aft of the mizenmast, whilst under a large midships bridge deck surrounding and aft of the mainmast, is accommodation for crew, a large sail room, galley, water tanks, etc. Then forward there is the usual topgallant foc's'le over the windlass. All these erections are connected by flying bridges. The two holds of the ship are divided by a large water ballast tank amidships with a capacity of 1245 tons. These holds are bulkheaded fore and aft and athwartships into four partitions.

Throughout, the ship is lighted by electric light and warmed by electric heaters. She is steered from a wheelhouse on the bridge deck, but she has the usual stand-by steering gear aft. For working cargo there are oil driven winches for each of the four hatches. These operate 3-ton cargo derricks, and the engines are 10 h.p. crude oil starting on petrol. The windlass forward can be either worked by hand or driven from No. 1 winch by a gipsy. The labour-saving appliances for working the ship consist of two capstans on the after deck, specially placed for warping, in addition to which the *Kobenhavn* has four brace winches and eight halliard winches. These winches, which automatically take in and pay out, can each be worked by one seaman.

As regards her sail area, the *Kobenhavn* spreads 56,000 sq. ft. of canvas. This, at any rate in the case of her first suit, was made of American cotton and not flax.

Her spar plan is a moderate one, her four square-rigged masts being 197 ft. from keel to truck. The yards are of the same measurement on all four masts:—

Lower yards	.. 90 ft.
Lower topsail yards	.. 88 ft. 6 in.
Upper topsail yards	.. 79 ft.
Lower topgallant yards	.. 74 ft. 6 ins.
Upper topgallant yards	.. 63 ft.
Royal yards	.. 49 ft.

In her original sail plan, she was fitted German fashion with two gaffs on the pusher mast, but has since done away with the lower

"WILLIAM"

                    [See Page 341

"KESTREL"

                    [See Page 344

"ORCHID"

Lent by Jas Randall, Esq.

[*See Page* 352

gaff, preferring to set a jib-headed spanker to upper and lower gaff topsails. Her present gaff is 44 ft. long, and the spanker boom 52 ft. In her masting the *Kobenhavn* has her lower and topmasts in two pieces in the old way, the doubling being 16 ft. 6 ins., whilst that of the topgallant mast is 14 ft. Her lower masts weigh 23 tons, whilst the lower yards weigh 4½ tons.

For those who like these statistics the *Kobenhavn* is reckoned to have about 4½ miles of standing rigging weighing about 27 tons, 23 miles of running rigging weighing 23 tons, 1200 blocks, and 8 tons weight of sails in two complete sets.

Whilst crossing from Leith to Copenhagen in ballast after being taken over, the big ship logged a speed of 10½ knots under canvas in light winds, and since then she has sailed over 16 knots. Her engines seem to have been of more use than those of most large auxiliaries. I know nothing about engines, and I give the following particulars, taken from an article in the *Shipbuilder*, for those to whom they may be of interest:—

The engine consists of a four-cylinder Diesel of the Burmeister & Wain 4125 L type; the cylinders have a diameter of 480 mm. and a stroke of 730 mm. and develop 500 B.H.P. at 180 revs. per minute. Pumps are directly attached to the engine for cooling water, forced lubricating oil, and bilge purposes. The engine is of the enclosed, forced-lubricated trunk-piston type and is non-reversible; the two-bladed bronze feathering propeller is fitted with reversible blades, for giving the vessel stern way. The *Shipbuilder* writes as follows regarding this screw:—

Reversal of the blades is accomplished from the motor room by means of a reversing clutch of the Zeise make, by which arrangement the pitch of the propeller can also be varied so as to adapt it for efficiently assisting propulsion at various speeds when the vessel is under sail power. The propeller is a fixture, *i.e.* it cannot be hoisted on board when the vessel is under sail only, as in some auxiliary-powered sailing ships. The propeller blades when vertical are in a fore and aft position, so as to present the minimum resistance when the vessel is under canvas alone, and the engine stationary.

The *Shipbuilder* goes on to state that the consumption of the engine is about 2.7 tons of oil per day, and that 204 tons of oil fuel can be carried in the cellular double bottom. The exhaust from the engine is carried up the outside of the pusher mast. The

x

owners of the *Kobenhavn*, by the way, after considerable discussion, decided that the five masts of their magnificent ship should be called fore, main, mizen, jigger and pusher

In the motor room there are two Bolinder motors, one for working the ballast pump and the other for the electric dynamo. The staff of the motor room consists of two engineers and a greaser.

The *Kobenhavn* is beautifully finished with something very special in the way of gingerbread work on bow and stern. Her figure-head, which was carved at Copenhagen, consists of a teak representation of Absalom, the warrior priest who founded Copenhagen. The initials of her owners, together with the house-flag, are sewn on to her fore lower topsail in the style of the old Atlantic packet ships.

Baron Juel-Brockdorff of the Danish Royal Navy superintended the completion of the *Kobenhavn*, and took command of her from the stocks. During her first stay at Copenhagen, before loading for her maiden voyage, the ship was visited by over 12,000 people, including the King and Queen of Denmark.

The Danes, following the fashion of the other northern nations, carry very few foremast hands in their foc's'le. On her maiden voyage I believe the complement of the *Kobenhavn* consisted of captain, four mates, schoolmaster, doctor, two engineers, one greaser, cook and cook's mate, baker, steward, two boatswains, one carpenter, one sailmaker, one wireless operator, 28 seamen, and 18 apprentices; but my latest news about her is that she now carries no boatswain or A.B.'s, their work being done by the leading boys, who now total 60 instead of 18, and occupy all the crew space under the midships bridge deck.

The Danes are very proud of their beautiful training ship, and well they may be. More than one keen Englishman has attempted to sign on aboard her under any capacity, but her owners will not allow a man aboard who is not of Danish nationality. I only hope that some public-spirited British shipowner will follow the splendid example set by the Danes, and build a British training ship something on the lines of the *Kobenhavn*.

The *Kobenhavn* has considerably finer lines than the usual cargo carrier of the present day, and it was expected that she would prove a good passage maker with the help of her engines. I do not know how much she uses these engines, but the following are the times of some of her passages:—

1925	London to Bangkok *via* the Suez Canal	64 days
1925-6	Plymouth to Melbourne	81 „
	(The *Kobenhavn* sailed from Danzig timber laden on October 12, 1925, but put into Plymouth on October 28 with her officers' quarters gutted by a fire. Repairs were executed by Messrs. Willoughby in the Great Western Docks)	
1926	Banjowanji to Copenhagen	86 days
	Copenhagen to Adelaide	78 „
	(On this passage the *Kobenhavn* was only 67 days from the Lizard and averaged 11 knots for 21 days between the Cape and Semaphore, Port Adelaide. Her best 24-hour run was 305 miles.	
	Her dates between points were :—	
	September 19.—Sailed from Copenhagen.	
	September 29.—60 miles south of Land's End.	
	October 5.—Passed Madeira.	
	October 12.—Passed Dakar.	
	November 10.—Passed Meridian of the Cape.	
	December 6.—Arrived Adelaide.	
1927	Adelaide to Falmouth (discharged Liverpool) ..	109 days

On July 31 the *Kobenhavn* left Liverpool for Chile *via* the Panama Canal. The Canal was cleared on August 30, but when 300 miles south of Callao on September 15 the ship lost a propeller blade and was ordered into Callao for repairs.

On her homeward passage *Kobenhavn* sailed from Caleta Coloso on October 18, and arrived at Danzig on January 7, 1928, 81 days out. She was commanded by Captain Christiansen, and her chief officer was Mr. Andersen.

This vessel left Buenos Ayres December 14, 1928, for Melbourne with Captain Andersen in command and 15 officers and ratings and 45 cadets on board. She became overdue and finally, after many searches, was regarded as "missing", closing entries at Lloyd's being made January 1, 1930.

CHAPTER VII.

SMALL FRY.

"I desire no more delight than to be under sail and gone to-night."—

(Merchant of Venice.)

IN the last two chapters of Volume I., I attempted to give an account of the numerous fleets of small fry, ships of under 1000 tons, barques registering scarcely 300, and brigs, brigantines, and schooners of even less than 100, which had ventured to the most distant coasts, snatched a living from the most dangerous seas and put up sailing records which were worthy to be compared with those of the smartest clippers.

In the following chapter will be found a few more notes on these gallant little craft.

The Harbour Grace Fish Carriers.

In my description of the Newfoundland fish carrying fleet in Vol. I., I omitted to mention any of the ships owned by the well-known firms of Munn and Bennett. The first Munn was in the trade in partnership with William Punton as far back as the early forties, whilst the Bennetts were carrying cod to Bristol from Newfoundland at an even earlier date. The two firms were closely allied in business, the Munns having their headquarters at Harbour Grace, Newfoundland, whilst the Bennetts had their head office in Bristol.

One of the fastest of Munn's little flyers was the *William Punton*, a brig built by Hall of Aberdeen in 1843. This vessel must have been one of the earliest of the famous Aberdeen clippers, for the first Aberdeen model, the schooner *Scottish Maid*, was only sent afloat by Alexander Hall in 1839.

During the fifties the barque *Rothesay* was not only considered to be the smartest ship in Munn's fleet, but the best sailer and finest ship in the trade. At this time Munn had two other barques, the *Queen* and the *Fleetwing*. The *Fleetwing*, under Captain Jim Pike, arrived at Lisbon on one occasion with her decks swept clean, and the stern knocked out of her, but with her fish cargo undamaged. The *Queen* distinguished herself in 1860 by making the round trip from Harbour Grace to Pernambuco, and from thence to Liverpool, including stay in port, unloading her fish and taking on sugar and cotton, in 71 days.

The brigs and brigantines of J. Munn & Co. must have been happy ships, if one may judge by the way in which their men stayed by them year after year. For instance, Captain Joyce, who commanded the brigantine *Clutha* for over thirty years, and claimed that he never discharged a stained drum of fish in all that time, carried his steward, Lorenzo Martin, and his bosun, Joe Barrett, for twenty years.

Captain Jim Pike, when the *Fleetwing* had been condemned at Lisbon after the passage when her decks were swept, sailed the brigantine *Flora* for fourteen years without an accident of any sort.

One of the most remarkable records ever made in the New-foundland fish trade was that of Captain Charles Layton, who, in nine years, in the *Charles W. Oulton*, made seventy-two trips across the Atlantic and in one season actually landed five cargoes in British ports.

In 1872 Cox of Bridport built two famous brigs for J. Munn & Co. These were the *William* of 207 tons, and the *Trusty* of 163 tons.

The first commander of the *William* was Captain Bailey. Later Captain Jim Pike had her for a time; then Captain O. Foote, and finally Captain John Tizzard. The *William* was heavily sparred, and, some said, over-masted. On September 30, 1889, she sailed from Emily Harbour, Labrador, with 5000 quintals of cod in bulk for Gibraltar under Captain Tizzard. When thirty-six hours out, and bowling along before a fresh W.S.W. wind, the mainmast, without any warning, broke in three pieces, and all the heavy gear came tumbling down on deck.

The accident happened a little before daylight. All hands

were immediately called, and Captain Tizzard kept both watches on deck until the *William* was jury-rigged. Strong westerly winds continued, and the lame duck arrived off Gib. on the night of the sixteenth day out. Here orders were received to proceed to Genoa for discharge, but the Board of Trade surveyor would not allow the ship to continue her passage until a new mast was fitted. Captain Tizzard was lucky in getting a mast and rigging from a condemned brig. After some hard work by all hands this was got in place: a new mainsail was borrowed from the schooner *Sea Lark*, another fish carrier: and in twenty-four hours the *William* was on her way to Genoa. After being held up outside that port by light head winds for five days the brig arrived on the October 29, thirty days out from Emily Harbour, which was considered a wonderful performance for a jury-rigged ship.

The *William* was re-rigged at Genoa as a barquentine, and for the next twelve years sailed the Atlantic under that rig. She was then sold, and entered the British coasting trade. Her end came in the winter of 1906, when she was lost with all hands in the English Channel.

The *Trusty* was sold by J. Munn & Co. to H. J. Stabb & Co. about the end of the nineteenth century, and it was at this date that the yards were stripped off her mainmast and she became a brigantine. In 1904 she was bought by Captain J. G. Coode. This fine old ship was sunk by collision in January, 1909.

Messrs. H. J. Stabb, by the way, owned the Exmouth barquentine *Belle of the Exe*, which, under Captain Randell, made some very smart passages across the Atlantic. Another vessel commanded by Captain Randell which was famous for her good sailing was the barque *Olinda*, which was built by Robert Steele in 1859.

The following crack passages are also worthy of mention:— Captain S. Fogwill drove the little schooner *Fruit Girl* from Bowring's Wharf, St. John's, to Pernambuco in 19 days: whilst Captain William Hennesey sailed the Prince Edward Island brigantine *Belle* from Harbour Grace to Lisbon in a week, sailing on a Wednesday and arriving on a Wednesday. This little ship was condemned at Queenstown in 1878 after having had a bad battering on a passage from Labrador.

Of earlier passages, that of the brig *Charles*, owned by Bennett & Co., should be mentioned. The *Charles* was built by the Newhooks of New Harbour, Trinity Bay. In the year 1836 she sailed from St. John's, Newfoundland, under a Captain Hart for Bristol. The sailing day was a Friday, and she had her owner's wife aboard. The superstitious amongst her crew prophesied all sorts of disaster from the fact of her sailing on a Friday with the owner's wife on board, but the little *Charles* had a very favourable passage, and, on the second Sunday after leaving, Mrs. Bennett was able to attend Holy Communion in Bristol Cathedral, the *Charles* having made the run across in under ten days.

The " Devil" Breaks the Atlantic Record.

On July 29, 1872, a rakish looking topsail schooner arrived at Harbour Grace. This schooner was painted black from truck to keel, whilst on either bow and on her stern, in large gilt letters, the strange and ominous name of "Devil" stood out. I described in Vol. I. how this beautiful schooner came by such a name. She is still well remembered in St. John's and on the coast of Labrador. The boys who played on Munn's Wharf in those days are now old men, but they can still remember the schooner's life-size figure-head representing His Satanic Majesty, with cloven hoofs, forked tail, horns, and pointed beard complete. Not even the most reckless of these boys dared to loiter near Munn's Wharf after dark as long as the *Devil* remained in port.

Although the schooner was a little beauty, of handsome model and graceful lines, and built and finished regardless of cost, she was a vessel of ill omen and ill repute. There always seemed to be some sort of trouble on board. Her crew of six men were always quarrelling and drinking. They even used firearms and knives in their constant fights, and the police of Harbour Grace were kept busy escorting them backwards and forwards between the schooner and the town lock-up.

This ill-named schooner was also a weather breeder, and whilst she lay at Harbour Grace she dragged her anchors during a sou'west gale, and battered her stern and quarter to pieces against Godden's Wharf. She was, however, repaired and loaded, and, under the command of Captain Tulloch, sailed from Harbour Grace on August 2, and Punch Bowl, Labrador, on August 26, 1872, for Liverpool. The people of Harbour Grace had hardly got used to the absence of the notorious schooner before news reached Munn's office that she had arrived on the other side after a passage of 6 days and 18 hours.

At this distance of time it is impossible to verify this extraordinary run. Presumably the time was counted from Labrador to Queenstown, where she probably called for orders. Unfortunately there is no trace of her arrival date in Messrs. Munn & Co.'s voyage books, but the clerk who opened the cable announcing the time of her passage is still alive.

The news of the *Devil's* record aroused still further interest in the vessel, both in Newfoundland and along the Labrador coast, and many a superstitious seaman declared that she owed her extraordinary passage to the Devil himself.

Curiously enough, this was not the first visit of the *Devil* to Newfoundland, for she was at Harbour Grace in 1870 under a Captain Hannah.

It was after her record passage in 1872 that the name of the schooner was altered to *Newsboy*. In 1873 she sailed from Liverpool under the flag of Knotts Bros., of London, bound for South America, and according to Lloyd's news was wrecked in the following year.

The schooner *Sheitan*, which was built at Preston in 1869 for P. Miller, the owner of the *Devil*, remained in the Newfoundland trade for many years. She seems to have had all the sailing qualities of the *Devil* without her bad reputation. She had also an equally terrifying figure-head. This was a lifesize effigy of a female devil—Sheitan, in Chinese demonology, being the Goddess of Evil.

There is not space to describe all the beautiful brigs, brigantines, and schooners in the fish trade, but amongst the many outstanding vessels not already noted, the following should have an honourable mention:—

Tessier's *Petunia* and *Silver Sea.*

Munn's *Atlanta, Kestrel, Islay,* and *Rose of Torridge.*

Bennett's *Sunbeam, Sea Breeze, Rosevear, Maud,* and *Muriel.*

And of the later ships, J. E. McDonald's Brazil trader, *Stella,* afterwards *Amy Louise,* the three-master *Olwen,* built in Pembroke

"AUGUSTA"

[See Page 352

"FLOWER OF THE FAL"

"ELIZABETH McLEA"

Lent by Jas. Randall, Esq.

"RONA" EX "POLLY WOODSIDE"

Photo by Captain Schutze

[*See Page* 356

Dock, the Lunenburg schooner *Minto*, and the Mahone Bay schooners *Clara* and *Harold*, the Irish schooner *James O'Neill*, and the *Royal Lister*, one of the numerous Portmadoc three-masters.

C. T. Bennett's brigantines and schooners were mostly built in the West of England; they were all flyers and usually made steamer time between Newfoundland and the Bristol quay.

Shipshape and Bristol Fashion.

To every old sailor the words "shipshape and Bristol fashion" denoted everything that was seamanlike and good in the old trade of the sea. The expression is rarely heard nowadays, but right up to the early nineties quite a fleet of sailing craft hailing from Bristol gave the world an example of what the words really meant. In the seventies and eighties these Bristol traders were principally wooden vessels of two types. The first type were big full-riggers, nearly all built in the United States or Canada, and were engaged in the coal, guano, and timber trades. The second type were all British-built vessels, mostly small barques of from 200 to 500 tons register. These either sailed in the West African barter and palm oil trade or the West Indian sugar and rum trade.

Most of these little vessels were the product of Bristol shipyards —staunch hardwood craft built in the fifties and sixties.

Perhaps it would be of interest to give a few notes on the big American-built ships before turning to the Guineamen and West Indiamen.

American-built Bristol Traders.

The biggest of these American-built vessels was the *Chancellor* of 1971 tons net register, which was built in Maine in 1855. Her usual round was coal out to Rio, then in ballast to a guano port, where she loaded for home.

The *Chancellor* was driven hard in her earlier days under the U.S. flag, and in spite of constant work upon her in Messrs. Hill's dry dock whenever she was home, she became very leaky. On her homeward passage with guano from the Chincha Isles in 1885 the leaks became so bad that Captain McNair prudently put back to Valparaiso. Here she was condemned. Some months later some

Chile lumber people bought her, repaired her, and sent her up to Puget Sound in ballast disguised under the name of *Domingo Santa Maria*. After making two or three trips lumber loaded on the Pacific Coast she was finally condemned in 1887.

The *Eagle*, of 1715 tons net, which was built at Thomaston, Maine, by Edward O'Brien in 1859, was a much tighter vessel than the *Chancellor* if not quite so fast. She was brought into the Bristol floating harbour in the early seventies after being badly ashore. Messrs. Hill & Son bought her for a song, and after repairing her in their Albion dockyard sent her to sea all "shipshape and Bristol fashion," with the old red duster flying at her monkey-gaff.

The *Eagle* was a handsome, well-kept vessel with painted ports, and under Captain Fairweather voyaged steadily in the guano trade. In 1884 she was laid up at Bristol for a couple of years, and was then sold to go to Gibraltar as a coal hulk, and there she could be seen swinging to her moorings amongst a dozen historical vessels.

The third of Hill's big coal and guano ships was the *Saint George* of 1499 tons net, built by Pierre Valin at Quebec in 1872. She was a typical St. Lawrence carrier, heavy looking and powerful. The most striking feature about her appearance was a massive figure-head consisting of our national patron saint spearing a ferocious dragon. This figure-head was kept most carefully by the *Saint George's* carpenter, and as soon as the ship was safely berthed in the Cumberland Basin after perhaps a trip from St. John's with deals, "Chips" brought out all the spare parts of the figure-head, such as St. George's weapons, and carefully shipped them into place. There they were no doubt surveyed with much satisfaction by the late Colonel Sir Edward Hill, M.P., the military member of the firm.

Another Quebec ship owned by the Hills was the *Saint Vincent* of 1377 tons net, which was launched by Dunn in the same month as the *Saint George*. Both the *Saint George* and the *Saint Vincent* were bought on the stocks, and came over to Bristol to be fastened and coppered, being practically completed by the Hills in their own dockyard.

The *Saint Vincent* was commanded by Captain Evans, later

Hill's shore captain, who was known all over Bristol as "Stuttering Bob." The *Saint Vincent* was reduced to a barque about 1880. Her last passage under the Blue Star flag was in 1884. On her arrival at Bristol from Quebec she was laid up along with the rest of the sailing fleet. She was finally sold to Swedish owners, who ran her until 1898, when, after being in trouble off the Plate, she was bought by Montevideo owners, and for several years sailed under the Uruguayan flag as the *Maristany*; she was broken up 1907.

Other vessels which should be noticed amongst the American and Canadian built ships of Hill's fleet were the *Ida & Emma* and *Her Royal Highness*. The *Ida & Emma* was a 1393-ton vessel built at Searsport, Maine, by McGilvery. After being damaged by getting ashore in 1882 she was bought by the Hills and repaired at Bristol. Then for a couple of voyages Captain Jones, who was afterwards in the *Palgrave*, sailed her for the Hills, after which she was sold to Bremen owners.

Her Royal Highness was built at Quebec in 1865 and registered 1245 tons. Captain George commanded her in the coal, guano, and timber trades. Her last passage under Hills' house-flag was made in 1885.

During the seventies and early eighties Messrs. C. Hill & Sons owned several small American or Canadian built ships and barques, such as:—

Transit ..	.. wood ship	886	tons built at	Nova Scotia,	1849
Conference	.. ,,	967	,,	,,	New Brunswick	1856
Marie ..	.. wood barque	1107	,,	,,	Baltimore	1857
Southern Belle ..	,,	1120	,,	,,	Quebec	1862
Moss Rose ..	,,	760	,,	,,	New Brunswick	1863
British American	wood ship	1208	,,	,,	,,	1863
Avonmore ..	,,	1260	,,	,,	U.S.A.	1863
Adria ..	.. wood barque	836	,,		Quebec	1868

Charles Hill & Sons.

At the offices of Charles Hill & Sons there are two large rooms whose walls are entirely covered with the half models of sailing ships built by the firm, and going as far back as that of Dibden's *Saucy Arethusa*, which was built by Messrs. Hillhouse, the predecessors of the Hills in the ownership of the Albion dockyard.

Unfortunately the firm has no records of all these vessels, for when they started iron shipbuilding all the office records, log books, etc., of the old wooden fleet were consigned to the flames, and with them I fear has gone most of the material for writing a history of Bristol shipping.

When the Hills abandoned their sailing ships and gave up wooden shipbuilding in 1885, they started building steamships. Then, just before the end of the nineteenth century, they launched some pretty little steel barques, the last of which was the well-known *Favell*.

The wooden, glass-roofed building sheds which covered the three slips on which the Hills built their sailing ships for a hundred years have long since been demolished, and their space has been taken by up-to-date berths, where the firm turn out New York liners, British India motor ships, etc.

The Bristol Guineamen.

From the days of the Tudors Bristol merchants have traded with the West Coast of Africa. Outward cargoes consisted mostly of obsolete firearms, cheap and flashy jewellery, cloth and cotton, household utensils, and last but not least, what was listed on the ships' manifests as "Geneva." This word, of course, in plainer language spelt "alcohol."

The Bristol Guineamen went out to such ports as Half Jack, the Cameroons, Bonny, Cape Lahon, etc., and moving up and down the coast from anchorage to anchorage sold off their outward cargoes piece by piece, the chief commodity taken on in exchange being palm oil.

This method of trading along the coast was a slow one, and it often took from eighteen months to two years collecting a homeward cargo

The chief Bristol firms in the West African trade during the eighties were:—R. & W. King—Lucas Bros. & Co.—Cummins & Co.—Rider, Son & Andrew.

These four firms all lost their identity towards the end of the nineteenth century when they transferred their interests to the African Steamship Co., of Liverpool

The largest fleet was that of R. & W. King, who, during the eighties, owned no less than 20 of these little Guineamen. The largest ship listed in their fleet was the *Queen of England*, a full-rigger of 876 tons, which was built on the Thames as far back as 1842; the smallest was the beautiful little barque *Laughing Water* of 223 tons, which was built at Plymouth in 1858. Nearly all their vessels were wooden barques of from 250 to 400 tons. They did, however, possess four iron vessels—

Ribbleton (ex *Manolo*)	iron barque	402	tons	built at	Preston	1865
Mervyn	,,	318	,,	,, ,,	Sunderland	1866
Charlotte Young ..	,,	302	,,	,, ,,	Hartlepool	1867
Leonor Troncoso	iron brigantine	330	,,	,, ,,	Glasgow	1875

Two or three of King's older ships were hulks on the West African coast.

The very last of the Bristol Guineamen to remain in commission as a sea-going vessel was King's beautiful composite barque *Elvira Camino*, which had been launched by Connell in November, 1872, for A. Martinez of Havannah as the *Dona Juana*.

The *Elvira Camino* was eventually sold to South of Ireland people, though she still hailed from Bristol until the end of her days. Her new owners converted her into a stump barquentine and put her into the coastwise coal and general trades. She was finally broken up in 1926.

The firm of Lucas Bros. & Co. owned about a dozen little barques and brigantines from first to last, most of which were built in the forties, fifties and early sixties. The earliest of which I have any note was the *Ann Hood*, a wooden brig of 199 tons, which was built at Glasgow in 1847.

Another old-timer was the snow *Watkins*, built at Newhaven in 1848 and broken up at Bristol in 1890. The *Daisy*, built at Sunderland in 1862, was also a snow. The rest of the fleet were all wooden barques with the exception of the little *Look Out*, a brigantine of 197 tons which was built at Workington in 1858.

Probably the Jersey-built brig *Amber Nymph*, which was originally owned by Scrutton of London and later came under the flag of Rider, Son & Andrew, was the smartest sailer in the whole West

African flotilla. She was one of the most beautiful and graceful brigs ever sent afloat.

Cummins & Co., besides the Quebec built barque *Eleonore* and the Norwegian-built *Souvenir*, owned three very fine Sunderland built barques. These were the *Charmian, Jane Lamb*, and *Gift*. The *Charmian*, which was launched in February, 1866, was a very fine composite barque of 575 tons. She was still afloat in 1927 acting as a grain hulk in the Bristol docks. As she towed up and down the float many an old sailing ship man would stop to admire her graceful lines.   The dainty little *Jane Lamb*, which was launched in July, 1866, and the still smaller, but no less beautiful *Gift*, which was launched in October, 1870, were about the last sailing ships to remain in the West African trade.

Not very long ago visitors crossing Bristol Bridge, in the busiest part of the old city, would have passed right under the jibboom of the *Jane Lamb*, for she lay there for about a couple of years before going to the shipbreakers.

Daniel's "Duff and Dough Boys."

Bristol's trade to the West Indies dated almost as far back as her trade to West Africa.   In the palmy days of the sugar planters towards the end of the eighteenth century, when a man who had estates in Jamaica was considered the great catch of the London season, and was only rivalled by the fabulously rich Nabob from India, Bristol's fleet of West Indiamen almost equalled that of London itself.

The great western port maintained her trade until the collapse of West Indian sugar in the late eighties.   The last firm which took out general cargoes from England and brought home sugar and rum from Jamaica and the other British islands was that of Thomas Daniel & Sons, whose offices were in that stately old Clifton centre, Berkeley Square

At the beginning of the eighties Daniel's fleet consisted of twelve clipper barques, all of them built of wood and ranging from 216 tons in the case of the little *Dora*, up to 614 tons in that of the oldest ship, the *Sylph*. During the sugar season four other vessels were usually chartered. These were the Salcombe brigs *Okenbury* and *Beatrice*: a smart little Blyth brig, *Waterloo*, which is mentioned by Sir Walter Runciman in his book on the colliers; and a large Russian brig called the *Novi Molodez*.

These smart ships were known as the "Duff and Dough Boys" on account of their house-flag, which had a large "D" in the centre, and a ball, which their crews declared was meant to represent a lump of dough, in each corner.

It must not be supposed that this fine-weather trade in staunch hardwood fast-sailing barques was any more comfortable and easy-going than the rest of the old-time trades when sail reigned supreme. Daniel's commanders, who were mostly Bristol men, had Bristol's reputation to maintain. Everything aboard one of Daniel's West Indiamen had to be "shipshape and Bristol fashion," and this meant never-ceasing work for the foremast hands and boys; and old Bristol seamen will recall, too, memories of gruelling work on the cargo winches in the blazing tropical sun up the Demerara River, or stowing huge tierces of sugar or puncheons of rum at Barbados. Kedging down a steamy tropical river in order to get to sea was another job which raised muscle aboard the "Duff and Dough Boys." The passage home was generally accomplished in from 25 to 35 days, every bit of muslin being piled on and dragged through the strength of the Trades.

One of the best sailing performances was that of the *Frances* in the summer of 1884. She left Bristol on June 7 with general cargo for Barbados; arrived there in 28 days; discharged and returned to Bristol sugar laden; loaded again for Demerara, where she discharged and again re-loaded for Bristol, at which port she arrived on August 15, having been out and home twice in 69 days. She was commanded at this time by Captain Henry Pretty, a very religious man, who combined sail carrying with regular prayers and Sabbath services for all hands.

Towards the end of her career the *Frances* worked a good deal and needed pretty constant pumping, but she maintained her reputation for speed until the end. When the firm gave up, the *Frances* and the *Dora* lay together tied up in Bristol for a long time; then the *Frances* became a dock hulk and she was only broken up in 1920.

The smartest ship in the whole West Indian fleet was the

beautiful little barque *Orchid*, which had a dusky Indian maiden for a figure-head, holding in her hand a carved representation of a West Indian orchid. Captain William Cooke, who was afterwards dock master at Bristol, kept the *Orchid* like a new pin. Her sails, when in port, were always harbour stowed under the most brilliantly painted sail covers; her bright work was always shining; and turk's-heads, graftings, ornamental knots, and pointed ropes paid testimony to the fine marlinespike seamanship aboard her.

When the "Duff and Dough Boys'" flag was hauled down the *Orchid* was bought by Captain J. K. Thomas of Bristol, who commanded her throughout the nineties. In 1901 her rig was changed to that of a barquentine, and she was bought by J. Philpott. Finally, in 1906, she was sold to the French to be broken up. During these later years she seems to have voyaged mostly to the stormy latitudes of the Falkland Islands.

The little *Dora* rivalled the *Orchid* in the smartness of her appearance and the care with which she was kept up. During her last few years in the West Indian trade she was said to be the smallest barque-rigged craft afloat. After being sold she was converted into a barquentine and put into the coasting trade, only to be lost with all hands a year or two later.

Her last commander when she was a barque was Captain George Cowlislaw, who, a few years afterwards, took charge of the Standard Oil Company's *Brilliant,* one of the largest four-mast barques ever built. It must have been a change for Cowlislaw to tramp the spacious poop of the mighty *Brilliant* after being used to the "two steps and overboard" which made up his quarter-deck walk aboard the little *Dora*.

The *Augusta* went to the Norwegians, who ran her for some years afterwards in the Baltic and lumber trades; built as she was of picked oak and teak, she was considered too tight and solid a ship to rival the *Frances, Orchid* and *Dora* in sailing. Her last commander was Captain Young, who left her in order to take Hill's steel barque *Favell* from the stocks.

The *Gwendoline* was sold to Turner, Edwards & Co., who, after keeping her for a few years, disposed of her to the Spaniards. She was renamed the *Josefita,* and was broken up 1911.

"ALICE WILLIAMS"

Photo Amos   [*See Page* 356

"WATERWITCH"

Photo Amos   [*See Page* 357

"NELLIE FLEMING"

Lent by Jas. Randall, Esq.

[See Page 357

"KATE"

Photo Amos

[See Page 358

Turner, Edwards & Co., of Bristol, also possessed a number of smart little craft in the eighties, such as the *Annie Fisher, Lady of the Lake, Light of the Age, Payta, Santa* and *Lota*. These were mostly engaged in the South American trade. The *Santa* lasted until 1923, when she was scrapped.

Sunderland Barques.

During the sixties, when wooden shipbuilding may be said to have reached its high-water mark, a number of very beautiful little teak barques and brigs were built at Sunderland by such firms as Blumer, Mills, and Adamson.

Old East Coast sailors may remember the following vessels which traded out to India and China under the management of William Adamson:—*Claro Babuyan—Sooloo—Guam—Bussorah—Loochoo—Valkyrien—Evangeline—Fluellin—Stanfield—Ching-too.*

These had all been dispersed owing to the competition of steam by the end of the eighties.

Another fine little Sunderland-built fleet was that of F. & W. Ritson, whose pioneer ship was the small brig *John Ritson*, commanded by Captain Francis Ritson. This enterprising skipper was, I believe, the founder of the firm of F. & W. Ritson. His largest ship was the barque *Phaeton*, which, under Captain Matthews, was a steady passage maker without putting up any remarkable records. For instance, in 1870, she went from Liverpool to Chittagong salt loaded in 124 days, and came home from Akyab to Antwerp in 133 days.

The *Phaeton* was destroyed by fire in the Andamans soon after the Ritsons sold her.

The *T. B. Ord*, under Captain John Allen, was one of the fastest sailers in the fleet. In 1871 she was only 71 days from London to the anchorage in Valparaiso Bay. Her time to the Equator was 21 days, and she arrived off Valparaiso on the 69th day, but was unable to get into the Bay for 48 hours owing to calm.

The *T. B. Ord* went "missing" in the early eighties when bound from Hamburg to the West Coast. It was foggy weather in the North Sea when she sailed and as she was never reported in

Y

the Channel it was concluded that she had been run down and sunk by a steamer in the North Sea.

Ritson's barques voyaged to every part of the world and penetrated to many little known ports; for instance, on one of her voyages the *T. B. Ord* took general cargo from Liverpool to no less than six ports in Central America, namely:—Punta Arenas, La Union, Realejo, Acajutla, La Libertad, and San Jose. For her homeward cargo she loaded logs of cedar and mahogany, which were found lying on the beach on the coast of Guatemala. These logs were either rafted or towed off to the ship, which, after calling at Falmouth for orders, finally discharged them at Bremerhaven.

Besides their barques, the Ritsons had a brig called the *Sunium* in the West Indian trade, and three collier brigs, *Mazeppa*, *Maida*, and *Reindeer*, which took coal either to London or Hamburg.

British Coasters.

Up to the outbreak of the 1914-18 war there was hardly a port in the British Isles which did not own a smart little coasting schooner, and it was no unusual sight to see more than a dozen of these vessels crowded together in one of the Cornish China clay ports.

Many of these little coasters played an heroic part in the war, which accounted for quite a few of them, though there must have been hundreds waiting to take up their old work at the end of 1918; however, their owners soon found that they were not only unable to compete with the hideous steam coaster, but that even in the trades still open to them they could not make both ends meet. They are thus becoming daily more scarce, and amongst all lovers of ships an interest in this very able and seaworthy type of small trader has been steadily growing for some time.

The landsman's eye, after one casual glance, wanders from the carefully patched grey flax sails of the British topsail schooner to the bristling outline of some monstrous tramp steamer, and one would probably overhear some such statement as the following:— "That dirty old coaster doesn't interest me, but look at that fine big steamer!"

But the sailor sees with different eyes. He notes the good

lines of the schooner, and recognises many signs about her rigging
which tell him that she is a well-kept ship with good seamen aboard.
He probably passes over the tramp steamer with some such remark
as "Look at that rusty tramp, all amuck with oil and coal dust.
There'll be no rest aboard her."

The sailor can tell the age of the spritely topsail schooner to
within a year, and some of these coasters are a good deal more than
half a century old. The sailor, also, can form a pretty shrewd
guess as to the old-timer's age by the cut of her figure-head. Figure-
heads, like sailing ships, are growing scarcer and scarcer, and
many of the more modern coasters were content with a mere scroll
or fiddle-head. However, there are still a few real old time figure-
heads hanging out over the Channel seas and all aglow with the
crudest colours from the paint locker.

Most often a coaster's figure-head is that of an elegant lady
clad in a sailor hat with her hair tied up in a net, for most coasters
are called after the wives and daughters of their owners. Occasionally one will see the effigy of the original owner himself under the
bowsprit of some ancient brigantine. Then the figure-head will
sport a bell topper and perhaps drooping whiskers. The more
artistic figure-heads were generally sturdy bare-armed Amazons
with flying tresses and flowing draperies, in the classical style which
was so popular in the days of Tenniel and Tennyson.

In every particular trade one will always find that a type of
craft has been developed that exactly fits that trade. It may
therefore be of interest to see how the rig of the British coaster has
come about.

The first vessels which voyaged from port to port around our
coasts were all brigs and snows, hoys and ketches. Then gradually
the brigantine began to supplant the brig as it became evident
that the former sailed just as well, if not better than the latter,
besides being more economical in gear. The topsail schooner only
differed from the brigantine in that she set her lower square sail
flying, and preferred a gaff foresail to staysails between the masts.

From the early thirties until the end of the seventies heavily
sparred brigantines and topsail schooners with raking masts and
long stunsail booms sailed under the Red Ensign in every part of

the world, for these were the favourite rigs of the fruiter, the opium clipper, the South Sea Island trader, and pretty nearly every other kind of small craft which needed a clean pair of heels.

The three-master which, at the beginning of the twentieth century, was as common around our coasts as the two-master, was a rig of economy and safety, being very snug and handy for any vessel of from 150 to 300 tons. Most of the Mediterranean and Western Island fruiters were cut down into three-masters when their racing days were over, and there were two of these famous little craft still earning a living as three-mast schooners until quite recently. These were the *Susan Vittery* and the *Jane Slade*. The *Susan Vittery*, disguised under the name of *Brooklands*, survived the last war and has recently been sold and given back her original name of *Susan Vittery*. This little vessel was kept in excellent condition by her owner, H. Parker of Grimsby. The *Jane Slade* was broken up 1929.

It is impossible in this chapter to do more than note a few vessels out of the many hundreds of British coasters which were built during the last seventy or eighty years. Every port that boasted a building slip seems to have contributed its quota of coasting tonnage.

Though in their main characteristics these handsome two and three-masters bore a close resemblance to each other, it was, of course, quite easy to distinguish a Welshman from a West Country-man, or a Jerseyman from a Scot.

One of the oldest schooners to be seen afloat after the war was the Falmouth owned *Alice Williams*. She was built at Llanelly as far back as 1854. This vessel was wrecked in February, 1928.

Amongst other old-timers that were afloat within recent years may be noted the Bristol brigantine *Elizabeth McLea*, which was built by the famous Robert Steele of Greenock in 1860. The Whitstable Shipping Co. used to own a three-mast schooner named the *Resolute*, which was built by Duthie of Aberdeen in 1869. This vessel was noted for her speed. After being converted to power with twin screws and renamed the *Mary C. Soppit* she was lost off the French coast.

Iron was never popular amongst the builders of British coasters, but there were two rather notable vessels which were iron-built. These were the brigantine *Margaret Sutton*, which was built at Cork, in 1866, and the barquentine *Iron Queen*, built at Newport in 1865. This latter began her career in the West Indian fruit trade. She was a very smart vessel, but over sparred, and I believe came to her end in a capsize. During her last days she ran as a Tyne and Dover collier under the flag of Sir William Crundall of Dover.

There was another Dover and Folkestone collier which had a great reputation for speed, and this was the *Friendship*, owned by Smith Bros. of Colchester. This schooner was very flat-bottomed. She once grounded on a buoy in Folkestone harbour, and the buoy broke through her planking and landed in her hold. She was run into and sunk by a steam collier off Spurn Head in 1911.

One does not hear of many fast sailing records put up by coasters of the present day, but the three-master *Nellie Fleming* sailed from Youghal to Bristol in twenty-four hours. This ship was built at Carrickfergus in 1884. She went missing March, 1936.

Whilst racing at Ryde I passed close by the St. Malo topsail schooner *Flying Foam*, which was beating to the westward over the tide and going like a train. She was wrecked 1936.

I must not forget to note the *Waterwitch* of Fowey, which was built at Poole as far back as 1871. This vessel at one time carried out the curious duty of training candidates who wish to qualify as Thames pilots. Every Thames pilot had to serve a year as an officer in a sailing vessel, but this sail training for pilots has now been abolished. Before the war the *Waterwitch* was commanded by a skipper who had a wooden leg. Some years before the 1914-18 war she lay at the bottom of Newlyn harbour; she was, however, raised and re-conditioned at Par in 1918. *Waterwitch* was sold to Estonia in 1939 and survived the 1939-45 war.

Another old-timer run by the same owner as the *Waterwitch*, namely, Stephens of Fowey, was the *Lydia Cardell*, which was built at Appledore in 1873. She was sunk by collision in March, 1929.

Amongst the Folkestone and Hartlepool colliers may be mentioned the three-master *Cumberland Lassie*, built at Amlwch, Wales, in 1874. She was considered a very fast vessel in light winds. She came to her end in heavy weather off the Start.

The last of Sir William Crundall's Dover colliers was the *Coppename*, which was built at Sunderland in 1880. This three-mast schooner sailed at one time under the Portuguese flag in the Oporto trade.

Another of Crundall's colliers was the *James Simpson*, now a hulk at Falmouth.

The illustrations of the *Kate* and the *Pet* are good examples of handsome two-masters. The *Kate* was a Manxman built in 1872, and the *Pet*, which belonged to Chester, was built at Kingston in 1876.

As a contrast between the real old-timer and the more modern type, the illustrations of *Mary Ann Mandall* and the *Elsa* will be of interest. The *Mary Ann Mandall* was built by Wilson at Ulverston in 1868, whilst the *Elsa* was built by Shilston at Plymouth in 1891.

There is one more vessel which I should like to mention before leaving the British coasters, and that is the three-master *Margaret Murray*, which was built of steel at Grangemouth in 1885. In 1912, when loaded with China clay, she had a narrow escape from being sunk in the Channel through collision. During the war she was commandeered for service as a mystery ship, but her name does not figure amongst the Q-boat records, though it is possible that it may have been changed for that service.

The Ranterpikes.

There was a query in a shipping newspaper not long ago as to the Clyde coasters which rejoiced in the curious name of ranterpikes. These vessels were built to carry iron ore, and were very sturdy craft. At the same time they were heavily rigged and carried a big sail plan. They sported very long topmasts, which were fidded abaft the lowermasts.

The first of these schooners was the *Sapphire*, built at Greenock in 1846; then came the *Onyx*, 30 tons bigger, in 1847. The last of the ranterpikes was the *Jasper*, an iron schooner built in 1867.

The *Sapphire* and *Onyx* were sold to Walker of Maryport during the seventies. The first was wrecked in the Channel about 1884, and the *Onyx* was broken up soon afterwards. The *Jasper*, re-rigged as a barquentine, ended her days on the New Zealand coast. In 1894-5 she made what is considered a very smart round trip. Leaving Lyttelton in ballast on December 23, 1894, for Surprise Island, she there loaded guano, arriving back at Launceston, Tasmania, on January 31, 1895, being only 39 days out.

The New Zealand Timber Trade.

Twenty years ago there used to be hundreds of smart schooners and brigantines employed in the timber trade round the New Zealand coast and between New Zealand, Tasmania and Australia. Before the war it was no uncommon sight to see a dozen of these small fry lying at Lyttelton at one time. In size these New Zealand coasters averaged just under 100 tons, some of them were very smart vessels and they never seemed to wear out, especially when built in Tasmania.

The *Ronga*, which was built at Auckland in 1900, was considered the clipper of the fleet. In September of that year she ran from Lyttelton to Wellington, a distance of 180 miles, in nineteen hours, which is very good work for a little 98-ft. schooner.

Soon after making this record she capsized in Pelorus Sound. All her ballast had been dumped out of her when a squall struck her, and over she went. All hands were saved, and the ship was afterwards righted, but it was recognised that she was over hatted, and 9 feet were cut off her masts.

Four years later the *Ronga* left Lyttelton in ballast bound for Havelock. She sailed away before a hard sou'west gale in company with the American four-mast barquentine, *Addenda*, which was bound for Newcastle. The *Addenda* ran right up on the beach in Palliser Bay and could not be refloated. The *Ronga* was found floating bottom up off the coast and was towed into Wellington. No trace of her master, Captain Ned Peterson, and his crew of five hands was ever found. After this the little vessel was again cut down, and also given an engine. She went soon after the 1914-18 war under the name of *Wairau*.

Of all the hundreds of schooners on the New Zealand coast only about a dozen are left. The oldest and fastest of these was the *Aratapu*, which was built at Auckland in 1878. For some years she was named the *Zita*, but got her old name back, and ran between Waitara and Lyttleton. She went before the last war.

Here are a few others of these timber schooners worthy of mention:—*Enterprise—Lily—Jessie—Nicoll—Eliza—Firth—Falcon.*

The following are some of the best sailing records made on the coast:—

1876	*Kenilworth*	schooner	Lyttleton to Auckland—5 days
1878	*Wild Wave*	barque	Hobart to Port Chalmers—6 days
	(She is said to have beaten this record in 1880, but I have no details)		
1894	*Thurso*	barque	Newcastle to Lyttleton—6 days

A New Zealand correspondent informs me that the record round trip between New Zealand and Australia was made by the *Quathlamba* in 1899. She sailed from Nelson to Kaipara in ballast, being two days on the passage. She then crossed from Kaipara, loaded with Kauri pine, to Sydney in seven days. From Sydney she went to Newcastle, N.S.W., and loaded coal, and she arrived back in Newcastle on December 4, only seven days out from Auckland having made the round trip in the wonderful time of sixteen days.

I am pleased to hear that this beautiful little ship, although only a coal hulk, is still carefully looked after in her old age. In a letter received some time ago from a member of the firm who now own her I find the following:—

I was down in her cabin recently. The beautiful panelling is almost the same as it was in 1879: the old ship-keeper keeps the brass rails, etc., polished, and takes a great pride in her. One of our old pilots, Urquhart, who was A.B., mate and master, and had his honeymoon in her, asked our manager for the figure-head, and it now adorns his fernery, looking out over the Bay.

The record between the ports of Noumea and Bluff, N.Z., was held by the *Rothesay Bay*, which in 1915 covered the distance in ten days. The record between the Cape and New Zealand was, I believe, held by the pretty little *Lake Superior*, which arrived at Lyttleton in ballast on March 19, 1899, only twenty-eight days out from Cape Town.

"MARGARET SUTTON"

[*See Page* 357

THE "PET" OF CHESTER

[*See Page* 358

"MARY ANN MANDALL"

"ELSA"

[See Page 358

"RAUPO" EX "LOUISA CRAIG" EX "PERU"

Photo by Captain Schutze [*See Page* 361

"ALEXA"

Photo by Captain Schutze [*See Page* 363

"WHITE PINE" EX "QUATHLAMBA"

[See Page 360

"ROTHESAY BAY"

[See Page 360

Here are a few more notes and corrections on the "Craig" family of inter-coastal clipper barques.

The *Joseph Craig* was never converted into a hulk as I stated in Volume I., but was wrecked near Hokianga, N.Z., on August 7, 1914.

The *Alexander Craig*, commanded by Captain Airey for three years, after lying as a hulk in Auckland until 1924, was then condemned and burnt to the water's edge.

One of the "Craigs" which I failed to mention in Volume I. was the *Constance Craig* ex *Margarita*, late of the British and Mexican Shipping Company. She went "missing" on a passage from Gisbourne, N.Z., to Hokianga in 1907.

The smartest of the fleet, next to the *Quathlamba*, was undoubtedly the *Louisa Craig*. During the war she was sold to G. H. Scales, Ltd., of Wellington, and put into the 'Frisco-New Zealand run. Towards the latter part of the war she ran from Auckland to San Francisco in thirty-one days. She was off the Sandwich Islands twenty-five days out, and averaged 213 miles per day for the whole passage, truly a splendid performance. Her name, by the way, was changed to *Raupo*. Her active service came to an end in March, 1922, when she was converted to a hulk at Lyttelton.

The Pacific Island Trade.

The island schooner, which figures so prominently in the romantic writings of Stevenson and Louis Becke, was rarely a vessel worthy of the admiration lavished upon her, and the average cockroach-infested copra carrier would have drawn a snort of disgust from the foremast hand of the aristocratic fruiter. She was in most cases slovenly and unkempt, overrun with every kind of unpleasant insect, and full of disagreeable tropic smells.

The *Equator*, an American-owned schooner of about 70 tons, in which Stevenson made a prolonged trip, was one of the fastest vessels trading in the Gilbert Group. She was also one of the best kept.

The first auxiliary schooner, the *Hercules*, made her appearance in the islands towards the end of 1897. The island trade—up to the advent of steam and auxiliary engines—was carried on mostly by fore-and-aft schooners, but there were also a few sloops, topsail schooners, barquentines and barques, ranging in size from 30 to 300 tons.

Probably the smartest ship inside and out in the whole of the South Seas, as well as the handiest and best sailer, was the *John Wesley*, which was built by Hall of Aberdeen in 1867, and when she arrived out in the Pacific to take up her duties as a Wesleyan mission ship was rigged as a brig. Afterwards, when she was sold into general trading she was first of all rigged as a barquentine and later as a barque. When barque-rigged her officers described her as "the handiest little thing afloat."

The vessels of the island trade needed to be handy when being navigated through coral reefs, or when standing off and on at some of the islands which either had no anchorage, or where the anchorage was often dangerous to approach.

The Wesleyan Mission sold the *John Wesley* to H. P. Pulser of Sydney in 1887, and she was put into the Tonga and Samoa trade under Captain J. Mansell. Her last active service was under the Jaluit Company, a Hamburg firm. She was laid up as a hulk in 1899, and in 1903 was burnt to the water's edge and sunk at her moorings.

Another famous mission ship which ended her days in general trading was the Melanesian barque *Southern Cross*, which was bought by Captain W. Ross of Auckland, in the early nineties. She was built of kauri pine in 1875 and when first launched had an auxiliary engine. At that date she had single topsails with Cunningham's patent reefing gear. This vessel, which was renamed *Ysabel*, went down about 1926 while under the French flag.

The chief trader to the Caroline Islands in the eighties was the *Montiara*, a schooner of 80 tons. The schooner *Franziska*, of 90 tons, was a regular trader in the Marshalls, whilst the *Equator*, of Stevenson renown, worked in the Gilbert Group. Amongst the Samoan traders the following sailed under the house-flag of the so-called "Long-handle" firm:—The barque *Brasillera*, topsail schooner *Taviuni*, and the sloop *Atafu*.

Another well-known vessel was the *Flink*, a wood schooner of 198 tons, which was built by J. W. de Wolff at Parrsboro' in 1883.

This vessel was very heavily sparred, her lower masts being 85 feet long and 26 inches in diameter.   The Hamburg firm lost her in 1897 on Butaritari Island.

One of the fastest vessels owned by the Jaluit Company was the *Mercur,* a 75-ton schooner which was built in San Francisco in order to run as a mail boat between the Line Islands and Sydney. Her trips between Butaritari Island and Sydney were generally made in from 19 to 26 days.   This little vessel was lost on Jaluit Island in 1905.

Another Gilbert Island trader was the Chinese-owned bar-quentine *George Noble.*   She was wrecked on Nanouti Island in 1889, and was then replaced by the celebrated *Loongana,* which was wrecked at Butaritari Island in 1906.

The last sailing ship running out to the Line Islands from Sydney was the barquentine *Alexa.*

Another vessel which held her own against the auxiliaries for some time was the San Francisco-built schooner *Neptun,* of 150 tons.

The copra trade direct to Europe seems to have been almost entirely in the hands of the Danes, Norwegians and Germans, who sent out handy little barques of between 500 and 800 tons.

The End of the South Sea Pirate, Ben Pease.

It is not until one begins to pry into the history of the labour recruiting trade—the Blackbirders, as they were called—that one really leaves the ordinary, dull, humdrum trader for the romantic lawless adventurer.   There were, however, two lawless piratical gentlemen who roamed the South Seas in the sixties and seventies and who were known and dreaded not only in Micronesia but throughout the Pacific, and whose hands were far more bloodstained than the worst kidnapper amongst the Blackbirders.

I refer to the two captains, Bully Hayes and Ben Pease.   A great deal has been printed about Bully Hayes, and the details of his lawless life are pretty well known, but the career of his one-time partner, Captain Ben Pease, has never been published.   It would no doubt make lurid reading.

Ben Pease was known in the Pacific as the first man to recruit black labour for the Fijis.   Like Bully Hayes, he came to a violent end at the hands of his native crew. This happened about 1881 or 1882. Pease was then skipper of a little schooner called the *Lotos*, trading in the Marshall Group. He was exceedingly cruel in his treatment of his crew, and one day when bound from Jaluit to Ebon Island the hands rose upon him and threw him overboard.

There was a light breeze blowing at the time, and the schooner was making about 3 knots. Swimming in the wake of the vessel Pease sang out lustily ordering the crew to pick him up. Their only response, however, was to throw him his sea chest, telling him sarcastically to make his way back to Jaluit on that.

One of the Ebon boys who took part in the murder of Pease afterwards sailed as an A.B. in the German built schooner *Milly*, which was owned by the Jaluit Company until she was condemned and broken up at the end of the nineteenth century. The *Milly* was a very sharp but cranky schooner of 92 tons built at Hamburg in 1884. Her looks, however, were much better than her sailing qualities.

The Blackbirders.

Towards the end of the sixties it became necessary to find cheap black labour for the lately planted cotton lands of Queensland and the Fiji Islands. The first cotton plantation in Queensland was that of the notorious Captain Bobbie Towns, started near Brisbane in 1863. Three years later his crop of cotton amounted to 183,630 lbs., and when want of labour became a problem he immediately thought of the teeming islands of the New Hebrides, etc., where his vessels had been employed for some years cutting sandalwood for the Chinese market.

The first vessel to recruit South Sea labour for the Queensland cotton plantations was the notorious schooner *Black Dog*, probably the fastest vessel in Towns' fleet. The *Black Dog*, some ten years before, had been an opium clipper which had to make racing passages between Bombay and the Canton River

Captain Bobbie Towns had undoubtedly a greater knowledge of the Pacific Islands and their inhabitants than any other man of his time. There was no cannibal island in the whole of the South Seas which he had not dared to land upon, and he was quick to recognise that the most treacherous and the least amicable native, and therefore the most dangerous to deal with, would yet make the best labourer on a cotton plantation. Thus it came about that the recruiting schooners, commonly known as "the Blackbirders," were sent after the black woolly-headed but robust cannibals of the New Hebrides and Santa Cruz Islands, rather than to the more distant but more friendly islands to the north and east of the Fijis.

The men who officered the South Sea Island traders of the sixties were a reckless, hard-drinking, heavy-fisted crowd. Some of them were runaway men-of-war's men, others were merchant seamen who had come to grief or lost caste, whilst a few were undoubtedly ex-convicts. There were also a certain number of seamen amongst them who were attracted to the life through a sheer love of adventure.

These officers were paid so much a head for every native they were able to recruit, and it is not surprising, therefore, to find them ready to entice the men aboard by every kind of trick. From the very first they were opposed by the missionaries, who accused them in the public press of being nothing more or less than slavers and kidnappers.

Nor were the reports of the missionaries exaggerated. At first the chief method of the recruiters was undoubtedly that of kidnapping. One of their favourite tricks was to sink the canoes alongside as if by accident, sometimes by the lowering of a boat on top of them, sometimes by the vessel being given a sheer into them with the helm. Then when the natives clambered on deck they were easily enticed into the hold and made prisoners.

A very terrible case of this sort happened at the island of Florida in the Solomon Group. A canoe went off to a low black brig which had recently arrived. As the canoe passed under the stern of the brig the stern-boat was dropped on top of it, swamping it and throwing the islanders into the water. The brig immediately lowered two boats, as it was supposed, to pick up the men from the swamped canoe, but as the Solomon Islanders were pulled out of the water they were seized by the hair and held head down over the gunwale of the brig's boat. Then a fiend with a long knife proceeded to cut their heads off. In this way several of the natives were murdered, whilst their friends, watching from a distance in a couple of canoes, were too frightened to interfere.

This atrocious murder requires explaining. It was a general custom in the islands for enemies slain in battle to be decapitated, and the man who was able to exhibit the greatest number of heads as trophies was treated with the greatest respect in his village. There is no doubt that some so-called white men entered into a contract with the chiefs of some of the tribes to supply heads in return for living men, and the method of the black brig seems to have been one of the ways in which the whites carried out their contract.

In the early days of the Blackbirders Bishop Patteson was in the habit of cruising amongst the islands of the New Hebrides, Santa Cruz, and the Solomon Islands in his little 60-ton schooner *Southern Cross*. He was very popular on most of the islands, and even the wildest and shyest of Melanesians had learnt to trust him. The kidnappers took full advantage of this popularity of the Bishop, and even went to the length of painting and rigging their schooners so that they might be mistaken for the *Southern Cross*. The next act in the drama was the arrival of one of these disguised schooners at an island which had lately been visited by the Bishop. As soon as the anchor was down, the white recruiter would dress himself up in a clergyman's long black coat and wideawake hat, adding as a last touch to the deception a pair of spectacles in order to give his villainous countenance an air of respectability.

He would then be rowed ashore, where he would inform the crowd of natives which speedily collected round him that the good Bishop was too unwell to leave the schooner, but that he would be delighted to see all his friends on board.

Canoe loads of victims would then follow the boat back to the ship. The black-coated recruiter's next step was to entice the natives below with the excuse that the Bishop was too ill to come on deck; and directly the men were below they were at once seized and thrown into the hold. The canoes were then cast adrift, the anchor would be quickly tripped, and away the vessel would go for the next island.

The Death of Bishop Patteson.

The murder of Bishop Patteson on the island of Nakapu on September 20, 1871, was entirely due to one of these impersonations by a Blackbirder. It was his custom to land alone while his boat remained outside the reef. On the occasion of his murder the boat was driven off by a sudden discharge of arrows, several of her crew being wounded. Later a canoe was seen drifting towards the *Southern Cross*. In it lay the Bishop's body, which was slashed with a knife in five places, and had a palm leaf with five knots tied in it on the breast. The gashes and the knotted palm leaf denoted that five kidnapped or perhaps murdered natives of Nakapu had been avenged.

The killing of the Bishop drew the attention of the whole world to the South Sea labour traffic, and resulted in the passing of the Kidnapping Act of 1872. From this date the trade was strictly controlled. British men-of-war schooners cruised amongst the islands and looked into any doubtful cases, and such methods as swamping canoes alongside in order to kidnap the men struggling in the water could no longer be resorted to with impunity.

Murder on the High Seas.

There were, however, one or two bad cases of murder and kidnapping subsequent to the passing of the Queensland Labour Act. The most notorious of these cases were those of the *Carl* in 1871, and the *Hopeful* in 1884.

The brig *Carl* sailed from Melbourne on a labour recruiting cruise in June, 1871. Her captain's name was Joseph Armstrong, but the chief actor and prime villain in the tragedy was Dr. James Patrick Murray, who, from being a part owner of the brig, acted as the person holding the supreme authority on board. After visiting a few of the islands in the New Hebrides Group without success the *Carl* sent her recruiter ashore on Palmer Island dressed up as a missionary, but on this occasion the trick absolutely failed. After this failure Dr. Murray was reduced to the most common device of the kidnapper.

Let me give his account in his own words, as recorded in the Sydney *Morning Herald* at the time of the trial:—

We went on to several of the islands and captured the natives generally by breaking or upsetting their canoes, and by getting the natives out of the water into which they were plunged; we smashed the canoes by throwing pig-iron into them and then seized the natives in the water; the captain and crew used to be chiefly engaged in throwing the weights into the canoes, and the passengers, in their own boat, used to pick the natives out of the water, sometimes hitting them over the heads with clubs or slung shot as they were at times very hard to get hold of. Each man had his appointed duty and place. In this manner eighty natives have been collected. They were kept in the hold at night and allowed to go on deck during the day.

It was, of course, unlikely that the kidnapped natives would quietly give in without a struggle. On the night of September 12 the unfortunate islanders started to make a hullabaloo below, but were soon quietened by a pistol shot fired over their heads. On the following night the watch on deck were once more roused by the noise in the hold. This time neither pistol shots nor shouts were able to frighten the prisoners, who were apparently breaking down the fittings of the sleeping bunks. With the stanchions and posts of these they next tried to batter open the main hatchway, and when it was found that they were likely to succeed in breaking out orders were given to fire into the hold. This firing was kept up steadily for eight hours, until daylight in fact, by which time all seemed to be quiet below.

Here again Murray seems to have been the ringleader, and it was even stated by one of the witnesses, a seaman, that he kept singing the song "Marching through Georgia" in between his musket shots. Just before daylight, when, as Murray said in his evidence, "We thought they were quite subdued," Scott, another of the so-called passengers, volunteered to go down and see how things were below, but before he reached the bottom of the ladder a long pole sharpened at the end was thrust at him and slightly wounded him in the breast. He thereupon retreated and the firing began again. Another passenger, named Wilson, amused himself by throwing lights into the hold in order to direct the aim of the marksmen.

Dr. Murray, in his evidence, gives a blood-curdling account of the last act in this terrible bout of wholesale murder. At daylight the hatches were thrown open and those who were still alive were told to come on deck. Five only of the Kanakas were able to climb the ladder without help, the rest being all more or less

incapacitated by bullet wounds. It was then found that there were 50 dead bodies and 16 badly wounded men lying in the hold, which was swimming in blood. After some discussion between the white ruffians, who were now thoroughly scared and whose only thought was to hide all trace of the night's slaughter, it was decided to throw the wounded men overboard at once.

Let me again quote from Dr. Murray's evidence at the trial, which, according to the report, was given in a manner that created general horror and disgust in the Court.

Murray remarked:—

I saw that the men so thrown overboard were alive when they were thrown overboard: there were about 16 of them. We were at the time out of sight of land. It was impossible for the men in the state that they were to escape to the land. Some of the men thrown overboard were tied by the legs and by the hands.

After all this the hold of the ship was thoroughly cleansed and whitewashed, every trace of the late event being removed; we then proceeded on our voyage.

On her way to Api the *Carl* fell in with H.M. corvette *Rosario*, which was making a special cruise through the New Hebrides, Santa Cruz, and Solomon Groups in order to see that the Blackbirders observed the new recruiting regulations. The second lieutenant of the *Rosario* was sent on board the *Carl* and, after making a careful investigation of the brig, returned to the man-of-war and reported that he found nothing wrong, adding that the *Carl* seemed to be specially clean for a labour vessel, her between decks having been freshly white-washed.

Murray, as soon as he found that the whole horrible story was in danger of coming out, turned Queen's evidence, and as a result of his information Joseph Armstrong (the master of the *Carl*), and Charles Dowden (one of the crew), were indicted at the Central Court of Sydney on a charge of "murder on the high seas." Dowden, in his defence, stated that he only obeyed Murray's orders, and that the Doctor was wont to read prayers to the crew before giving the order to smash the canoes of his victims. He also took great pains to teach those of the kidnapped Kanakas who had not been butchered on the night of September 13 to hold up three fingers and say "three yam," which meant that they had agreed to give three years' service.

z

Armstrong and Dowden were both found guilty and sentenced to death, but for some reason or other escaped the extreme penalty of the law. Murray, the arch-fiend, got off scot-free.

The Case of the Barquentine "Hopeful."

The barquentine *Hopeful* of Townsville was the first vessel to recruit the islands of New Britain and New Ireland in the Bismarck Archipelago. This was in 1883, and on her first voyage her master was Captain Briggs, the name of the Government agent being Chayter, and that of the recruiter Neil McNeil.

Captain Briggs anchored in Blanche Bay in company with the brigantine *Fannie*, Captain Wawn. Neither recruiter had any success in this district owing to the opposition of the Roman Catholic mission and also the Samoan Protestant mission teacher. McNeil, however, enraged at his ill success, as his boat was being launched off the beach, seized a native by the wool and pulled him into the boat. On hearing of this piece of kidnapping Captain Wawn told the *Hopeful's* Government agent that if Chayter did not report McNeil to the Government for kidnapping, he, Wawn, would do so as soon as he got back. After this the *Hopeful* sailed for Nadup Beach, where McNeil kidnapped another man.

On her second voyage the *Hopeful* was commanded by Captain Voss, McNeil still acting as recruiter.

On her third voyage her master was a young man named Shaw, who had never had charge of a ship before and knew nothing about the Queensland labour trade. Her Government agent, Harry Scholefield, was a gentleman by birth and education, but a notorious drunkard, and the unscrupulous McNeil saw to it that Scholefield was always too fuddled with drink to realise what was going on both ashore and aboard the *Hopeful*.

The two chief villains in the *Hopeful* case were Neil McNeil (the recruiter), and his right hand man, Bernard Williams (the bosun). They were charged with both murder and kidnapping, whilst Captain Shaw, Scholefield, the Government agent; Freeman, the mate; and Able Seamen Preston and Rogers were only charged with kidnapping. Unfortunately the case was a political one, and therefore it is very difficult to get at the truth.

The Polynesian labour trade was the burning question of the hour. Sir Samuel Griffiths, the Prime Minister of the Queensland Government, was the most bitter opponent of the labour traffic, whilst the opposition were strongly in favour of it. Thus it came about that the Queensland Government tried to use the *Hopeful* case as a political lever, but in so doing they over-reached themselves, as we shall see.

The chief witness for the prosecution was the negro cook of the *Hopeful*, Albert Messiah. He only came forward after he had failed to blackmail the prisoners, and there is no doubt that the greater part of his evidence was invented in order to get back on the recruiter and the bosun, both of whom had ill-treated him. His spite against McNeil was due to many a kicking. It appears that the bosun, after a drinking bout, had lurched into the galley in a very quarrelsome state, and after abusing the cook had boxed his ears, whereupon Messiah snatched up his carving knife and struck at the bosun, but he was not quick enough and was knocked out by a nasty punch on the jaw.

Other members of the *Hopeful's* crew had also ill-treated the cook, and he was only too eager to vent his spite against every white man on board.

The other white witness for the prosecution was Dingwall, the carpenter, who had only come out of gaol a short while before shipping on the *Hopeful*. Men openly stated during the trial that both Messiah and Dingwall were being paid by the Government. The other witnesses were all Kanakas, whose evidence was taken through interpreters, the chief of whom was a rascal named Cago, who had been an interpreter during the cruise of the *Hopeful* and was involved up to the hilt in all the cases of kidnapping.

The *Hopeful* made her first stop at Milne Bay, off China Straits, near the eastern end of Papua. Here McNeil, Harry Scholefield, two white seamen, and two Kanakan interpreters, who were all, according to the cook, more or less drunk, pulled away for the shore. The bay was thickly wooded right down to the beach, which was deserted, not a native being in sight. The usual island trade such as beads, looking glasses, tomahawks, tobacco, etc., was placed on the beach, and the boat's crew retired to a distance in order not to frighten the natives. After some time a few boys crept down to the small heap of trade, and picking everything up ran away into the bush. This was too much for the drink-inflamed McNeil, and followed by the other white men he dashed after the thieves. Several shots were heard from the *Hopeful*, and presently the party returned accompanied by a number of recruits. One of the white seamen, however, had a spear wound in his arm, which seemed to point to a fight.

Those who visited Milne Bay during the next few months found the natives so shy that it was almost impossible to get into communication with them, and this seems to indicate that they had been badly scared and intimidated.

At the next place recruited there was another fight, another of the crew receiving a severe spear wound, and according to the cook 38 natives were shot. This was followed by other attempts at kidnapping, during which the recruiter was accused of killing four more natives.

Finally, whilst the *Hopeful* was lying at anchor at the island of Teste, south of China Straits, 21 of the new recruits, including several women, dived overboard and started to swim for the shore. The cook swore that McNeil and the bosun at once opened fire upon the swimming natives and killed several of them, but it came out afterwards that the men had only fired in the air in the hopes of frightening the boys into returning. One of the native interpreters, however, in his attempt to stop the recruits from jumping overboard, gave one of the women a terrible gash on the head and also wounded several of the men recruits.

From Teste Island the *Hopeful* sailed for Townsville, and on her way home she was overhauled by the gun-boat *Paluma*, which found everything aboard the Blackbirder in order.

The trial took place in Brisbane and aroused tremendous excitement throughout the colony. The Chief Justice, Sir Charles Lilley, presided, and a special amendment of the criminal law was passed by Parliament after the prisoners had been committed for trial in order to admit native evidence without oath. Much of this native evidence, it was found out afterwards, had been paid for and dictated by Messiah, who himself was in the pay of the anti-black labour party.

The accused were convicted, but the sentences were so fiercely vindictive that they defeated their object and brought down the Griffiths Government. McNeil and Williams were sentenced to death; Shaw and Scholefield were given life sentences, the first three years of which were to be served in irons; Freeman, the mate, was given ten years, the first two in irons; and Rogers and Preston, seven years, the first of which was to be served in irons. Scholefield, who was dying from an incurable disease, wrote a pathetic letter to Sir Samuel Griffiths whilst he lay on his death-bed asking that he might be allowed to die without irons on his limbs, but his request was refused.

As bit by bit the falseness of the evidence and the irregularities of the trial became known, public indignation became intense, meetings of protest were held in every township, and finally the Griffiths Government fell beneath the storm.

Six years later, in 1890, the convicted men all received free pardons, and were even given a public banquet in the Brisbane Town Hall. Nevertheless it was the *Hopeful* case which gave the enemies of the trade a great chance to blacken it in the eyes of the world.

Dangers of the Trade.

It must not be supposed, however, that all the killing was due to the recruiter's rifle. Here is a list of attacks made on Blackbirders:—

December, 1870.—English schooner *Marion Rennie*. Rae, recruiter; Durle, mate; the steward; four white A.B.'s, 6 Rotumah boys, and one Sandwich Islander all murdered at Cherry Island.

July, 1871.—Fiji schooner *Fanny*. The mate, white able seaman and one native seaman murdered at Nguna.

1874.—Sydney schooner *Zephyr*. Mate and son of the captain murdered by Three-fingered Jack at Duane Point, Api.

1874.—Fiji cutter *Loelia*. Master murdered at Narovorovo, Aurora Island.

1874.—*Donald McLean*, schooner, attacked by fleet of canoes in the Maskelynes.

1875.—Boats of schooner *Stanley* attacked at Lepers Island.

1875.—Boats of schooner *Stanley* attacked in Champion Bay, Ambrym Island.

1875.—Schooner *Dancing Wave*. All hands except one white A.B. murdered at Gala, Florida Islands.

June, 1876.—Schooner *Lucy and Adelaide*. Captain Anderson murdered at St. Bartholomew Island, New Hebrides.

1878.—Schooner *May Queen*. Mate and two of his boat's crew killed while recruiting at Pentecost Island.

1878.—Brig *Janet Stewart* of Maryboro' and schooner *Daphne* of Fiji. Boats fired on by natives of South West Bay, Mallicolo. One white man killed, several Kanakas wounded.

November, 1878. Schooner *Mystery*. Mate, Government agent, and four native boatmen killed at Lepers Island whilst recruiting.

1880.—Schooner *Annie Brookes*. Captain Foreman and his crew murdered at Brooker Island in the Louisiade Archipelago.

1880.—Fiji brigantine *Borealis*. Mate and crew killed off Kwai, Malayta Island, whilst captain and Government agent were away recruiting.

1880.—Schooner *Esperanza*. Crew murdered at Kulambangra Island, Solomons.

1880.—Schooner *Zephyr*. Crew murdered at Choiseul Island, Solomons.

1880.—Brigantine *Borough Belle*. Boatmen murdered at Gaua, Banks Island.

1881.—Brig *Janet Stewart*. Cut off by natives of Kwai and all hands massacred except one who hid himself.

1881.—Sydney schooner *Leslie*. Captain Schwartz murdered near Cape Marsh.

1881.—Fiji schooner *Isabella*. Boat attacked on Espiritu Santo Island. Mate and Government agent killed.

The above list, though very incomplete, gives one some idea of the dangers undergone by the crews of the recruiting vessels at the hands of the treacherous New Hebridean and Solomon Islanders; but there were many other dangers attached to the trade of Black-birding. The navigation, especially for a vessel without steam power, was often both dangerous and difficult. In the months of January, February and March hurricanes were common throughout the whole area worked by the recruiters, from the Bismarck Archipelago in the North to the Loyalty Islands in the South. These cyclonic storms generally travelled in a south-easterly direction, the centre passing as a rule to the westward of the New Hebrides.

Here is an incomplete list of recruiting vessels which were either stranded or lost in a hurricane:—*Bobtail Nag—Lucy and Adelaide—Charybdis—Asha—Northern Belle—Eliza Mary*.

A calm amongst the coral reefs, where tides and currents run strong, is almost as dangerous for a sailing vessel as a hurricane. In February, 1884, the labour schooner *Alfred Vittery*, which had once been a famous fruiter, drifted ashore on Kaan Island, New Ireland, during a calm, and was totally wrecked, her crew being rescued by the *Lochiel*.

The topsail schooner *Stanley*, which distinguished herself by weathering out two hurricanes, was very nearly lost during a calm. In 1875, on her second voyage, she was returning to Queensland with 90 recruits on board. One afternoon she was heading southward about 2 miles off the western coast of Erromanga with a light wind off the land. Suddenly the wind fell, veered round, and came out of the opposite quarter.

The captain was asleep in the deckhouse; the mate, being very busy on deck, after trimming the yards, paid no more attention to the vessel's drift. Suddenly the captain was awakened by a native hailing the schooner from the shore. Jumping out on deck he was astounded at the sight which met his gaze. A bare half cable's length away on the port quarter a line of surf was breaking against an 8-foot wall of coral. Back of this rose a 300-foot cliff which was crowned with dense forest. The schooner was gradually being drifted into the breakers broadside on by the ground swell Hardly a catspaw ruffled the surface of the water, which shone like a mirror. The trade wind, which was blowing overhead, was cut off by the high, precipitous cliffs of the island.

Captain Wawn instantly roared out "Down with the boats." He was only just in time. Luckily two towing lines were always coiled up on the jibboom in readiness for just such an emergency, and the boats, working their hardest, managed to get the ship's head pointing out to sea; but the danger was by no means over; a powerful current was drifting the schooner along the coast, and the swell was tending to set her in on to the coral reef. The square sails were taken in and the fore-and-aft canvas trimmed ready to catch the slightest zephyr, but most of the puffs of wind that came along only blew the schooner's head off. The eight oarsmen in the boats, and helmsmen, with their long steering oars, pulled for dear life, but all their efforts were powerless to keep the *Stanley* clear.

For half an hour the schooner drifted along the shore and was only prevented from striking by the most frenzied efforts on the part of the oarsmen. Then, just when it seemed that her days were done, the *Stanley* drifted over a short spit of sunken reef. Captain Wawn, a man of great experience in South Sea navigation, at once lowered his anchor and succeeded in hooking it under the point of the reef, and in this way brought the ship up. It was a very narrow escape, as the stern was in only 12 feet of water, and the taffrail was only just clear of the outer breaker.

For two hours the *Stanley* hung on to that spit of coral waiting for the clouds to clear off the land and the true Trade wind to reach her. During those two hours about fifty armed natives crowded on to the rocks close under her stern in the hopes that the vessel would be wrecked and so fall into their hands. Shouts and excited babbling between the cliff tops and the reef showed that many more natives were up above in the bush awaiting the moment when the *Stanley* would come ashore.

Her captain and crew knew well enough the danger which they were in from the natives, and when one of these asked if they meant to lie there all night the bluffing reply was made to him that the captain considered it a good place to buy yams and boys. It should be explained that the expression "buy a boy" meant to recruit a man.

At last, just about sunset, the wind came down and ruffled the glassy surface of the water. Once more the boats were sent ahead, but there was soon no need for them as the *Stanley's* sails filled and she headed away out to sea.

The schooner *Magnet* was not so lucky as the *Stanley*. On May 17, 1882, she drifted ashore on Tanna Island during a calm and became a total loss.

The " Fanny " in an Earthquake.

All through the islands worked by the recruiting schooners earthquakes and even submarine volcanic eruptions were by no means uncommon; usually the earthquakes raised the coral reefs 2 or 3 feet, though they nearly always subsided again after the third shock. An earthquake in 1877, however, so shoaled the harbour of Port Resolution, which used to be a safe anchorage during

"YSABEL" EX "SOUTHERN CROSS"

Photo by J. Kimear, Esq.   Lent by Captain Schutze

[See Page 362

FURLING THE MAINSAIL

[*See Page* 380

the Trade winds, that henceforward it could only float the smallest vessels.

The following experience of the brigantine *Fanny*, belonging to Messrs. Rawson & Co. of McKay, gives a very good idea of one of these disturbances.

The *Fanny* was lying at anchor in the channel between the south-west coast of Mallicolo Island and the tiny islet of Ura. The boats, with the Government agent and the bosun, who was also recruiter, had pulled away to the northward. It was just after midday. Captain Wawn was below at dinner with a mind at ease, for the brigantine was lying in smooth water with a clear blue sky overhead and only a very light easterly wind blowing.

All of a sudden the vessel began to shake from stem to stern. There was a shout on deck of "She's away!" The *Fanny* was, in fact, being whirled round in circles, and as her anchor dragged along the bottom it kept catching its flukes in the coral, so that she was continually brought up with a jerk as the chain cable surged on the windlass. At the first shock the *Fanny* had been lifted and slewed round on the top of a long swell. This wave, sweeping over the shallow reefs, broke high over the bush and small trees that lined the shore and went roaring away to the westward.

The wild cries of the natives as they fled towards the high ground of Ura could be heard on the *Fanny*. The steep hills and mountains of Mallicolo were speedily hidden in clouds of dust. For as far as those on the *Fanny* could see, the shores of the islands had subsided from 8 to 10 feet, so that the bush and all the low-lying villages were flooded.

For a while there were continual earthquake shocks at short intervals, then gradually the ground rose again. Out of the forest and over the shore reefs came a mighty torrent of water, carrying with it broken huts, tree trunks, canoes, and even livestock, such as squeaking pigs.

Then came the most marvellous sight of all. All along the shore the reef rose out of the water until it was 6 feet above sea level. The "live" coral, wet and glistening in the sun, showed all the colours of the rainbow—red, yellow, green, blue, and purple. The reef remained above water for about a minute, and then there came another subsidence, slowly the coral sank; then a second earthquake wave rolled majestically in from the westward. The *Fanny* rode over it successfully, although her windlass was nearly torn from its bed. Then there came a dull roar, and all along the shore the wave broke in clouds of foam, tossing gigantic tree trunks and other debris before it in its path. After this there came a second upheaval, but this time the reefs were only raised about 3 feet out of the water. Finally a third wave rolled in as the ground sank back to almost its exact level before the earthquake had attacked it.

The *Fanny* was safe, though she had dragged dangerously close to the Ura shore reef, and all around her the water and also the beaches were strewn with broken branches, etc.

All this time Captain Wawn had been worrying about his boats but they were soon seen pulling back towards the ship. Luckily they had been crossing a bay in deep water when the earthquake took place. Afterwards they had landed and half filled the boats with fish, which were lying everywhere, on the beach and in the forest behind.

Several of the New Hebrides such as Paama and Ambrym are nothing but the cones of volcanoes, some of which have been long extinct whilst others still throw out columns of smoke.

The natives of Mallicolo declare that up in the mountains, which run as high as 3000 feet, there are two holes in the ground inhabited by fiery devil-devils, one of which devours grass, and the other stones. These evidently are the craters of two small occasionally active volcanoes.

The Fitting out of a Labour Schooner.

A labour schooner, it must be confessed, was fitted up very much like a West African slaver. First of all a deck was laid on top of her iron ballast. On either side, for the whole length of the hold, ran a long shelf 6 feet wide, and above this was a second one, making an upper berth. These shelves were the sleeping quarters of the recruits. The hold was divided up by a bulkhead of 4-inch wooden battens, on the after side of which was the women's quarter. This could only be reached by means of a hatch in the deck.

This accommodation had to be passed by an immigration agent, who also had to see that the recruiting vessel had sufficient provisions, clothing, and blankets for the number of men and women she was licensed to take on board.

Cabin stores on a labour schooner consisted chiefly of drink, the lazarette being filled up with cases of champagne, whisky, gin, and beer. If ever there was a thirsty lot it was the captains and officers of the Blackbirders.

In the early days of the trade it was only necessary for the recruiter to have her name plainly painted upon her stern, but when the Polynesian Labour Act became law the Blackbirders found themselves in the grip of a whole host of tiresome regulations. One of these was that a vessel licensed to recruit Polynesian labour had to be painted a pale green peasoup colour, with a broad black band along each side, whilst a black ball 3 feet in circumference had always to be hoisted at the mainmast head. I believe that the stripe was sometimes red, at any rate on Queensland vessels.

In 1888 there was a French schooner, the *Lulu*, recruiting in the New Hebrides which was painted a pale slate colour with a dark red stripe and red boats. This vessel was so painted in order that she might deceive the natives into thinking that she was a Queensland recruiter.

Every Blackbirder had two boats and sometimes three. Each boat had four oars and a standing lug. Though rudders and tillers were provided she was generally steered by an 18-ft. oar. Each native boatman was armed with a smooth bore musket. The barrel of this musket was cut short so as to enable it to lie on the thwarts under the gunwale. A strip of painted canvas was nailed round the gunwale in order to protect these muskets from the salt water.

In the early days the white members of the boats' crews, who were usually the recruiter in the landing boat and the mate and Government agent in the covering boat, were armed with revolvers and Snider carbines. In the eighties the boatmen's smooth bores were changed for Snider carbines, the white men usually preferring Winchester rifles.

Besides these arms, on the thwarts amidships, along with the mast and sail, were some Brown Bess muskets in a painted canvas bag. These, however, were part of the trade. The men of the New Hebrides generally preferred the old Tower musket to the cheap German fowling piece. A musket was the most valuable present you could give a native, and they were always reserved for the special friends of the recruiting officer.

The rest of the trade was carried in a trade box, and consisted usually of twist tobacco, short clay pipes, black gunpowder in $\frac{1}{4}$, $\frac{1}{2}$, and 1 lb. flasks, percussion caps in boxes, coloured beads, some cheap printed calico, a dozen or so of knives, large and small, some Turkey-red twill, tomahawks, mirrors, fish hooks, and some Jew's harps. On some islands paint, especially red and blue, was highly valued.

All this trade was needed in order to compensate the different tribes for the loss of their fighting men when these latter were taken as recruits to the Fiji or Queensland plantations. In the early seventies a man or woman of the New Hebrides was valued by his or her chief at $\frac{1}{2}$ lb. of tobacco, a few pipes, a yard or two of calico, a necklace of beads, together with a long bladed knife and perhaps a cheap American tomahawk. A few years later it was necessary to add a Tower musket to this trade before a single recruit was allowed to get into the boat.

The master of a recruiting vessel and also the recruiting officer received head money until 1884, when this payment was stopped by the Pacific Island Labourers Act of that date. This head money used to be 5s. a recruit. When it was abolished the wages of both masters and recruiters had to be raised. Before 1884 the captain of a Blackbirder was paid from £15 to £20 a month plus head money. After this date his wages rose to over £30, whilst recruiters received another £5 a month. Owners received as much as £8 to £10 a head for adult recruits.

The captains of the labour schooners very often added to their income by taking a passenger or two who wished to see the islands and perhaps have a bit of excitement.

The Blackbirding Fleet.

The number of vessels employed in the Polynesian labour trade to Queensland and the Fijis between 1865 and 1890 probably did not exceed 100 vessels.   During the sixties and early seventies, when the regulations were not as strict as they were later on, there were perhaps a dozen regular vessels in the trade.   The best known of these were:—*Donald McLean*—*Jason*—*Dancing Wave*—*Petrel*—*Lytton*—*Helen*—*Cambria*.

The schooner *Donald McLean* got into trouble in 1871 for kidnapping an exceedingly hideous Albino woman from Nguna.

The *Jason* was also somewhat notorious, owing to her chief officer, Irving, accusing the missionary, the Rev. Peter Milne, on the island of Nguna, of inciting the natives to fire upon the *Jason's* boats.

The schooner *Dancing Wave*, which was a Fiji recruiter, when overhauled by H.M.S. *Rosario* in 1871, presented an extraordinary sight.   She had on board 41 natives from the Solomons, and at a distance looked as if she had a colony of rooks perched on her masts and yards, for the recruits, who were all naked, were clambering about aloft, some even at her mastheads, others on her crosstrees and yards, a row of them out on the jibboom, and one or two even hanging to the dolphin striker with their legs dangling in the water.

The *Petrel*, of 90 tons burden, was one of the largest vessels in the trade at that time.

The fore-and-aft schooner *Cambria* was suspected of kidnapping, and her master and mate were both killed on the Solomon Islands in revenge, it was said, for stealing men.

In 1876 the Blackbirding fleet consisted of nine vessels, and all those already mentioned had gone.   The *Lytton* was wrecked; the *Jason* was burnt; one or two of the others had been condemned, and the rest had left the fleet.

The names of the nine vessels in 1876 were:—*Stanley*—*Sibyl*—*Chance*—*Lady Darling*—*May Queen*—*Isabella*—*Bobtail Nag*—*Lucy and Adelaide*—*Flora*.

At the beginning of the eighties the fleet numbered about 30 vessels, consisting of topsail schooners, brigantines, and barquentines.   Unfortunately very few of these little Blackbirders were registered at Lloyd's.   A good many of them were built in the Colonies and were never classed.

"Stanley," the Clipper of the Fleet.

This 115-ton topsail schooner, which was built by Menzies at Granton in 1863, was considered to be about the smartest vessel in the trade. Besides being very fast she was a weatherly vessel and extremely handy, which was very necessary in South Sea work.

On her first recruiting voyage the *Stanley* sailed from Maryborough in May, 1875, for the New Hebrides. She was commanded by Captain William T. Wawn, a master mariner of great experience in the South Seas, who, both as a master of an island schooner and also as a resident trader, had already had ten years' experience of the Pacific from New Caledonia to the Solomons and from Papua to the Samoa, Caroline, Marshall, and Gilbert Groups.

Although Captain Wawn understood the treacherous native of the New Hebrides and was up to all their tricks, during the years that he commanded the *Stanley* he had several narrow escapes from being cut off and killed. He was a bold man and was not afraid to take his little schooner into the most dangerous localities. At one place where he anchored, Dillon's Bay, no less than five missionaries had been killed and eaten at different times. Whilst he was watering at Naravorovo, Aurora Island, and just at the moment when most of his people were bathing, including all the white men, fifty armed savages suddenly advanced upon the boats from the thick bush. However, Captain Wawn had taken the precaution of posting armed sentries on the edge of the bush, and when these suddenly stepped out of their hiding places with their muskets at the ready, the natives, who were all fully armed with bows and poisoned arrows, spears, clubs, and tomahawks, began to slink off again in the direction of their village. Suddenly one of them turned and let fly an arrow at one of the *Stanley's* boatmen. Luckily it missed its aim, and the natives were then chased back into the forest.

The recruiter had another narrow escape on the north of Mbangon. A crowd of 200 natives seized the boat as she touched the sand and pulled her out of the water. However, the ship was hove to within range, and the covering boat quickly pulled in to the recruiter's assistance, whereupon the natives, who evidently meant mischief, retreated without harming the occupants of the boat. If the recruiter or any of his crew had offered any resistance they would undoubtedly have all been massacred.

At Lepers Island, whilst the schooner lay becalmed under the lee of the land about three-quarters of a mile off the shore, the recruiter was suddenly attacked with clubs and tomahawks. He made good use of his fists but the doctor and the other white men were knocked into the bottom of the boat. The affray was a sharp one and nearly every one in the boat was wounded before the attackers were driven off. Tom Sayers, a Mare Island boatman, had his scalp laid open by a tomahawk; Bobbie Towns, another boatman from the same district, had both his thumbs cut off; Lahu, a Lifu boy, had several cuts and spear pricks; whilst Jack, an unlucky Tanna boatman, received the 8-inch bone head of an arrow right through his forearm.

The recruiter would have got off unharmed, but just as they were shoving the boat off he had one of his fingers pinned to the steering oar by an arrow. The natives did not give up their attempt until two had been killed and several wounded.

After a successful first voyage of four months' duration the *Stanley* arrived back at Maryborough at the end of August. Captain Wawn sailed again in October, 1875, and after wood and watering as usual at White Cliffs made Port Resolution, Tanna Island, his first port of call.

On this trip the recruiting boats were twice attacked. On the first occasion the recruiter was fired on from Paama Island as he pulled in, and on the second occasion, when off Merrabwei, the boats were actually attacked afloat, the Kanakas wading waist deep into the water brandishing tomahawks, clubs, and spears; whilst another party, hidden on the edge of the bush, let fly a flight of arrows. On each occasion there were no casualties.

The *Stanley* was back at Maryborough by December 1, 1875, and sailed again on December 20.

On his third voyage Captain Wawn did his own recruiting as his mate had had no previous experience of the South Sea Islanders.

Whilst the captain was giving out presents on the beach at Champion Bay, Ambrym Island, suddenly every man and woman round him rushed away yelling. The next moment there was a volley from the bush, and bullets came whizzing round Captain Wawn and splashing into the water round the two boats; but the New Hebridean is no marksman, and although it was some time before the boats could pull out of range no one was hurt.

Captain Wawn's nastiest experience was during his fourth voyage, in the summer of 1876. He was busy trying to get recruits on a narrow strip of beach near Bulhagh Bluff, Pentecost Island. About forty natives, led by a grey-headed chief, who were all armed with spears, clubs and poisoned arrows, crowded round the boat, which was drawn up on the shore. The women, however, kept their distance, and this was always a suspicious sign. Captain Wawn was already offering his trade and asking for yams, when all of a sudden the natives raised their spears and threaded their arrows so that every point was levelled straight at the *Stanley's* captain.

It was a tight corner but Captain Wawn kept his head. Raising his hand palm outwards as a sign of peace, and with a valiant attempt at a grin, he said to the chief, who understood a little English, "You darned fool, what for you want fight?"

Meanwhile the Government agent and the boat's crew were stealthily reaching for their guns, but Captain Wawn, with his hand behind his back, motioned to them to lay the guns down. This they did, and presently spear points and arrow heads were slowly lowered, whilst the old chief, who had been standing on a large boulder, came down and made peace.

It appeared that the natives had noticed the boat's crew handling their Sniders because a native had stolen a bag of tobacco out of the sternsheets of the boat and run off into the bush. When this was explained the chief had the thief caught and the bag restored, and the incident closed.

There is no doubt that if Captain Wawn had lost his head and allowed his boat's crew to take up their rifles the whole party would have been killed.

The schooner was back in Maryborough by the end of July, 1876, and sailing again in August arrived back on November 20, after her fifth successful recruiting trip to the New Hebrides.

"RIO LOGE"

Photo by Captain Schutze

[See Page 397

The "Stanley" in a Cyclone.

It was on her sixth trip that the *Stanley* made a great name for herself by weathering out the cyclone which swept through the islands in January, 1877.

Captain Wawn landed several returns on Moto Lava of the Saddle Group on January 15. Whilst the boats were at work the aneroid was falling fast and the wind was freshening in squalls, whilst the sky was covered with dull, heavy, torn-edged clouds. As it was the hurricane season Captain Wawn decided to take his chance in the open sea rather than trust to a doubtful anchorage, and he therefore headed to the eastward under double reefs.

All through the night it rained in torrents, with the wind slowly freshening and the glass slowly falling. About 2 a.m. the *Stanley* was once more headed in towards the land. Soon after day-break Captain Wawn stood in between Sugar Loaf Island and Saddle Island. A hard gale was now blowing from the nor'west. Ahead of the schooner, reaching up to the zenith from the horizon, lay a dense bank of lead coloured cloud, yet overhead and astern the sky was clear and the sun sparkled on the foaming seas.

Captain Wawn was hunting a safe anchorage and driving his schooner, which, lying down to it, was sending the sprays over her crosstrees. However, seeing that it was impossible to beat up to the anchorage, he kept away for the passage between Vanua Lava and the small islands of Pakea and Nivula.

Directly the *Stanley* got into the passage the wind was cut off by the high land. Then when she was about half way through, a sudden "williwaw" or whirlwind caught the schooner's square canvas aback and gybed the mainsail. Captain Wawn, who was conning the ship from the starboard boat in the davits, was almost smothered by the sheets of spray and narrowly escaped being capsized overboard.

Before the schooner was through the passage three similar squalls were experienced. As soon as she was outside she once more got the full force of the gale. Captain Wawn now decided to give the land a wide berth, and ran off to the eastward on top of a long regular swell.

Every preparation was now made to withstand the worst;

AA

boats were housed on deck and secured; hatches battened down; the topgallant yard set on deck; and sail shortened to a close-reefed topsail and inner jib. When the schooner was 2 miles off the island of Vanua Lava she suddenly plunged into a terrible sea, which was tossing wildly in every direction owing to cross currents. By noon the aneroid was down to 29.40; the wind was veering to the nor'west, and the black cloud seemed to be travelling south-east. Captain Wawn did his best to edge away with the wind on the port quarter, but this made ticklish steering as the following seas were very heavy and dangerous.

During the afternoon, whilst the centre of the cyclone was about abeam of the schooner, bearing S.W. to S.S.W., the sight from her deck was most awe-inspiring. To the north and east there was not a cloud in the sky. The *Stanley*, scudding like a wild thing under her topsail, was just under the edge of a monstrous cloud bank, which Captain Wawn declared was indigo blue in colour and of a lumpy, rounded appearance like a bunch of black grapes. The horizon to the north-east showed clear cut and bright whenever the ship rose on top of a sea, but to the south-west a solid wall of rain shut out everything. This deluge drew closer and closer until presently it swept over the ship.

The *Stanley's* people now began to experience the usual difficulty in a cyclone of breathing. The vessel was smothered fore and aft in a continual sheet of spray, and it was only when she was on the top of an extra high sea that her company were able to draw a breath. During the afternoon the aneroid fell to 29.10, where it remained steady.

Captain Wawn was now satisfied that the *Stanley* had won her race with the hurricane. The centre was approaching no nearer, and by sundown the wind had begun to ease up, as it slowly veered towards the west. After running all night Captain Wawn hove the *Stanley* to under a storm main trysail soon after daybreak. By 8 bells 8 a.m. the storm had passed away to the south-east, and the *Stanley*, under all plain sail, was beating back to the Banks Islands against a light sou-west breeze.

All through the cyclone the return natives were battened down with but very little ventilation, and must have had a hard time of it; but when they were allowed on deck on the morning after the storm and found that the *Stanley* had sustained no damage they expressed their admiration of the schooner in the most extravagant way, for every South Sea Islander dreads the hurricane or "big wind."

On this voyage the *Stanley* arrived back at Maryborough on March 23, 1877, when, owing to some disagreement with his owner, Captain Wawn resigned his command and was succeeded by Captain Kilgour.

In April, 1881, Captain Wawn once more took command of the *Stanley* and made two successful trips to the Solomon Islands. On December 6, 1881, when off the south-east end of Indispensable Reef, Solomon Islands, Captain Wawn experienced his second cyclone in the *Stanley*. All that afternoon the weather signs grew worse and worse; the barometer was unsteady and falling; the wind was also unsteady but mostly from the east; the sky was overcast and there were constant showers of rain. Just before sunset, during a heavy downpour, the bowsprit was almost torn out of the ship by a "williwaw." The gammoning carried away, but Captain Wawn unshackled his anchors and secured the spar with the chains. During the night the wind gradually freshened from the E.S.E. and the ship was kept on the port tack under her lower canvas. Soon after 8 o'clock the glass suddenly fell two tenths and the wind flew round to the north. With the wind increasing with every gust Captain Wawn lowered his mainsail, and bearing away, wore the schooner round on to the starboard tack.

During the execution of this manœuvre, whilst the ship was still scudding before the wind, a tremendous squall tore the topsail out of the bolt-ropes, and Captain Wawn was obliged to allow the ship to come to on her old tack. The order was now given to haul down the head sails, but directly the halliards were started the canvas began to flog itself to ribbons. Nor could the men get forward, as the schooner dipped her bows under to every sea. Luckily the fore trysail was a new one. This was reefed and set balanced, and under it the schooner rode out the night, making splendid weather of it. With her starboard rail just buried and her decks smothered in spray, she lifted to the seas like a duck, and no heavy water was shipped. The trysail, standing like a board, held on, but the wind tore every other rag of canvas off the spars. The starboard boat, which was still in the davits, was soon washed away, and the port boat, which had her gripes and tackles broken, had two holes knocked in her bilge.

On this occasion the barometer went down to 29.10 and did not begin to rise until 3 a.m., when the wind hauled to the W.N.W. By daylight the worst was over; at 7 a.m. the cyclone gave the *Stanley* a parting blow and then the wind lulled right away to a light sou'west breeze.

The little schooner reached Maryborough on December 24, and here Captain Wawn resigned his command owing to a difference with the Government agent, with whom he had been at loggerheads during the whole trip.

The Wreck of the "Stanley."

Three and a half years after the gallant little schooner had weathered out the cyclone off Indispensable Reef, she was wrecked on July 1, 1884, on the south-east spur of that same reef when homeward bound with recruits.

Her master at this time was Captain Davies, the Government agent being a man named McMurdo, and there were 116 souls on board.

On July 1 Captain Davies was cracking on before a strong breeze. During the afternoon the square sail blew away. The order was then given to shorten sail. Whilst the crew were busy with the canvas there came a sudden cry of "Breakers ahead!" but before the helm could be altered the schooner crashed on to the reef.

After pounding heavily the poor little ship lay down with her rail buried in the surf, whilst all was confusion aboard. The recruits, in a state of panic, clambered into the rigging and several of them jumped overboard on the weather side. They were, however, wonderful swimmers and managed to get back on to the schooner again. Then the night fell down as black as pitch and nothing could be done until daylight. The schooner bumped on the reef with every sea, but she was a stout little vessel and refused to break up.

At daylight it was found that although there was shallow water under the lee of the wreck there was not a foot of dry land to be seen anywhere.

One of the boats had been broken up by the sea, so it was decided to make a raft. This was completed in 24 hours. McMurdo then set his people to work to construct a breakwater of loose coral, 70 feet long, 3 feet wide, and 3 feet high. This was an unpleasant job as the water was very cold. In this the men had to work often up to their waists in a strong current. However, the breakwater was successfully finished. On July 5 a heavy surf broke it down and it had to be rebuilt. The raft also was washed away and had to be brought back.

On July 6 one of the fresh water tanks was discovered to be empty and McMurdo immediately put all hands on an allowance of one pint a day. On the 7th Captain Davies, leaving behind the Government agent, Moussue the mate, and Connell the cook, took the rest of the white men away with him in the boat in order to get help.

It was entirely due to the stout-hearted McMurdo that those who were left behind survived the six weeks which they spent on the reef before they were rescued on August 23 by the Sydney trader *Venture*. He kept the black people busy, flogging them when they disobeyed him or stole provisions, physicking them when they were ill, and cheering them up when they were inclined to lose heart.

His first action was to call all the people together as soon as the boat had gone. He then carefully explained the situation to the recruits by means of the interpreters, after which he turned to the native boat's crew consisting of eight men, and told them that he should regard them as white men, and if they acted as such he would see that the Queensland Government rewarded them.

The first trouble was caused by the New Ireland recruits, who refused to work at the breakwater. McMurdo, who believed in ruling by physical force, at once flogged these men with his own hands until they obeyed him. During the next few days the raft was stocked with food and water and covered with a sail spread on stanchions in order to protect the people from the sun. This was securely moored all ready for use should the schooner go to pieces. McMurdo would not allow the Kanakas aboard the schooner, but obliged them to sleep on the breakwater. On July 12 it was found that several men had slipped off to the schooner in order to plunder the stock of food. These were caught by the faithful boat's crew and punished by the stern McMurdo, who entered the punishment in the ship's log as follows:—

Two men had two dozen each; two younger six lashes; and youths one lash each; one man in undoing his bonds got an ugly mauling from me.

Soon after this all hands began to suffer with thrush, due to the stench of the decaying coral, and one boy died. The medicine chest soon began to run low, and on August 4 McMurdo wrote:—

My stock of castor oil, rhubarb, black draughts, nit. silver, and bluestone is nearly gone.

During the whole time that the shipwrecked people were on the reef McMurdo's chief trouble was in preventing the Kanakas from stealing ship's biscuit.

He seems to have attended to the disciplining of all hands single-handed, without help from either of the other two white men or from his faithful boat's crew. Some of his log entries make curious reading. One day he writes:—

Had to thrash only one man who was in the water and dared me.

A day or two later came the entry:—

In five minutes there were three robberies of food from one another; I pummelled two and thrashed a third. These men are really heartbreaking devils.

A week or so after this he caught six coolies stealing biscuits, and logs their punishment as follows:—

Ran amuck among the recruits to a proper tune. Thrashed the whole six, one after another, and laid it on well this time, not as before, as things are too serious. They can stand pain wonderfully and their skins are thick, only breaking a little.

He seems to have been afraid that his thrashings were little felt, for he next ordered the cook to make :—

A proper cat as there was no hold upon the other—three tails of spunyarn. He made one of five, done up hard, and with strips of lead let into the strands, and had just finished it when the man died! Horror!

McMurdo's last words referred to the death of one of the men he had lately punished called Mattabout. He continues in the log:—

He went off in about ten minutes. I must have greatly over-rated their powers of endurance, and it is a grave error and one for which I blame myself seriously; but I watched them narrowly during infliction, stopping now and again to see how they were, and saw no danger; God help me—none! They are all crying, and very quiet.

On August 21, the indomitable McMurdo wrote:—

The horrors of this wreck are beginning now.

The fact was that, owing to lack of rain, water was becoming very scarce, also most of the natives were ill. Some were delirious and one man was raving mad. However, at 8 a.m. on August 23 the *Venture* was sighted heading towards them from the northward. The ensign was immediately hoisted jack down and smoke set going. The rescuer made slow progress, and it was not until 4 p.m. that those on the reef knew that the vessel was the *Venture* with Captain Davies coming to their aid.

It took two days to get the 80 surviving Kanakas aboard the *Venture*. At the last moment, when the ship was about to square away for Queensland, a native named Johnny was found to be still on the reef. The weather was too rough to bring him off for about twenty-four hours, and when at last he was rescued he declared that he had heard the dead Kanakas talking all night.

The End of the " Bobtail Nag."

After leaving the *Stanley* Captain Wawn took command of the old Fiji brigantine *Bobtail Nag*, and he writes:—

The *Bobtail Nag* was a very indifferent vessel compared to my late command, the *Stanley*. Let it blow high or low, the latter shipped no more water than enough to keep her bilges sweet, whilst the poor old "Bob" leaked like a sieve in heavy weather, and even in fine she gave the watch a 15 minutes spell at the pumps every evening. We had to keep her "wee-gee" always rigged.

On January 7, 1878, Captain Wawn sailed from Havannah Harbour with 144 recruits on board. The glass was falling and the weather was squally and very threatening. At 5 p.m. he took refuge in Vila Harbour between the islets of Vila and Lelika. Early the following morning he went ashore in order to try to get some eggs from a white settler for one of his white men who was ill.

Whilst the skipper was ashore and breakfasting with the settler, John Roddin, a terrific squall struck the harbour and nearly shook the house down. At the first lull Captain Wawn dashed for his boat and pulled off to the *Bobtail Nag*. He had only just got aboard when another squall arrived and catching the schooner abeam laid her scuppers under. Captain Wawn found that the aneroid in his cabin had dropped two tenths during the time that he had been ashore. The wind was rapidly increasing from the east, and it was evident that the *Bobtail Nag* was in the direct path of a hurricane. The usual preparations were made as quickly as possible. The main topmast was housed; all the sails, besides being given an extra snug furl, were marled down to the masts, yards, and booms with close turns of new line. Captain Wawn also managed to moor his vessel in between the squalls, the chain being hove in and a second anchor dropped in 12 fathoms, the first being in 19. The cables were then paid out until only 5 fathoms remained on one and 20 on the other.

The brigantine lay about 50 yards from the Vila reef, but she was in smooth water, and if only the anchors and chain would hold Captain Wawn hoped to be able to ride out the storm. Whilst the vessel was straining at her cables during a violent squall the lead was dropped over her stern in 8 fathoms. The yards were next pointed to the wind; and the port boat got on deck, whilst the starboard boat was left in the davits with extra lashings, so as to be ready for lowering in case it was needed.

There was nothing more to do except stand by. At noon the aneroid had sunk to 29 and was still falling. By this time there was scarcely a lull between the squalls, presently there was no lull at all, and the cyclone screamed through the rigging of the *Bobtail Nag* with a fury which can only be realised by those who have experienced the "great wind." Soon after 1 o'clock, when the glass showed 28.40, the wind shifted   couple of points to the southward with a terrific howl. The blast was too much for the poor little *Bobtail Nag*. For perhaps half a minute she lay trembling all over as if terrified; then her starboard chain parted and she fell off broadside to the wind, which instantly laid her rail under with her lower yard in the water.

Captain Wawn at once realised that his vessel was adrift, and as she lay on her beam ends and he clung to the weather rail aft he noticed the colour of the water under the vessel's lee change to light green. The next moment the *Bobtail Nag* was grinding her port bilge on the reef.

The fear was that the ship would be blown over the reef into deep water, where she would at once sink. Captain Wawn immediately roared for axes to the foremast and the lanyards of the fore weather rigging. The mast fell clear to leeward. At the same moment the bumping and grinding ceased, and it was discovered that the schooner's forefoot was caught in the hollow of the reef. By this time the 'tween decks were almost full of water, and the recruits had to take refuge under the weather bulwark. Two of the Fijians jumped overboard with a lifebuoy and the end of a line in the hopes of being able to get ashore. They were soon hidden by the mist of spray which surrounded the vessel and it was thought that they were drowned. However, they made a landing all right. It is almost impossible to drown a South Sea Islander!

At 3.20 p.m., when the captain's aneroid showed 28.32, it suddenly fell a dead calm—the centre of the cyclone was passing over the wreck. Captain Wawn at once seized the opportunity to save his people. Both boats were got into the water, and most of the recruits were told to swim to the land which was 80 yards distant. Some of the bushmen were unable to swim, but they were supported by the others. The women recruits, about a dozen in number, were landed in the first boat. Captain Wawn knew that shipwrecked people received small mercy unless they could defend themselves, and he ordered the white men to buckle on their revolvers, and soon the second boat was loaded with guns, ammunition, the ship's papers and chronometer, and all the provisions that could be hastily collected. The captain, Government agent, and the Fijian boatman were still on the *Bobtail Nag* when a light puff from the south-west showed that the calm centre was passing. There was not a moment to lose. Indeed, the boat was not half way to the shore before the breath of the hurricane burst right in their teeth. By leaping into the water, which was up to their waists, they just managed to reach the beach and haul the boat above high water mark.

The island was covered with thick bush, and so the shipwrecked people were able to get shelter from the blast.

Not much remains to be told. The hurricane ceased blowing at midnight, after having made an end of the poor old *Bobtail Nag*, which was hopelessly bilged with her back broken.

Luckily for the shipwrecked people Havannah Harbour was within easy sail, and here a few days later Captain Wawn found the *Stanley* and *Sibyl*. The *Sibyl*, which was homeward bound, agreed to give the white crew of the *Bobtail Nag* a passage to Maryborough, whilst Captain Kilgour contracted to take the "Nag's" recruits to Fiji at £4 10s. a head; Captain Wawn, his Government agent and boatmen being given free passages.

The Schooner "Lucy and Adelaide."

Perhaps the smartest and handiest of the Blackbirders next to the *Stanley* was the schooner *Lucy and Adelaide*. As already noted, her captain, Anderson, was killed on St. Bartholomew Island, New Hebrides, whilst recruiting on June 25, 1876.

The *Lucy and Adelaide* was one of the many vessels commanded by Captain Wawn, who had her for two voyages in 1879.

The following account of the *Lucy and Adelaide* rounding Breaksea Spit, taken from Captain Wawn's log, is such a vivid sea picture that I cannot resist quoting it:—

It was a bright, sunshiny day when I drew near Breaksea Spit. The schooner was tearing along before the heaviest sea I have ever witnessed in these latitudes. She was under her lower topsail, fore trysail, inner jib and stay foresail, with the wind a little on the port quarter. Every now and then she rolled heavily as her stern rose to the seas, the port boat skimming the "comber," and once nearly filling. The horizon was all mist and drift; it was only from the main rigging that I could get a "sight," and that only now and then, to give me an approximate position as to latitude.

About 3 p.m. I sighted the sand hills on Sandy Cape, Fraser Island, a little forward of the port beam. At the same moment I saw a huge breaker bearing down on us, about three points on the port bow. The schooner was then close on to the end of the Spit. Suddenly a huge sea, with a roaring broken crest, swept past and ahead of her, followed by another and yet another. "Five fathoms!" sang out the bosun, who was handing in the lead amidships.

The next sea was a "boomer." A long, swiftly moving mountain of undulating blue water swept on. Its crest towered up like a ridge, threatening to break, but as yet only showing a sputter of foam here and there. For a few seconds I thought it would come right over us, but gradually the schooner's stern rose to it, then toppled down again behind the crest, which broke under the bows into a driving cloud of foam and mist.

The sea had taken hold of the schooner, however. In those few minutes I think the little craft travelled faster than she ever did since she was launched. She beat the wind. Her topsail was for a few seconds flat aback, and her fore-and-aft canvas swung amidships. But that sea had evidently taken her over the tail of the Spit. The next one broke astern of her, and gradually I got into smoother water and hauled up for the head of Hervey Bay.

Captain Wawn made one more recruiting voyage in the *Lucy and Adelaide*, and then, owing to a bad attack of fever, was obliged to hand her over to Captain Satini. On January 23 the little vessel was hurled ashore in Havannah Harbour during a hurricane, undergoing much the same experience as the *Bobtail Nag*. The *Lucy and Adelaide* was, however, not so badly damaged. She was afterwards got off, repaired, and was still afloat in the island trade during the nineties.

A Few Notes on the Queensland Labour Vessels.

The smallest vessel in the trade was the little iron schooner *Chance*, which had formerly been a yacht. Her best known commander was Captain McPhie. The *Chance* weathered out a hurricane off Lepers Island, New Hebrides, on December 8, 1881.

The schooner *Sibyl* of Maryborough, which took home the crew of the wrecked *Bobtail Nag*, was driven ashore and wrecked during a hurricane in 1887, being sunk in the lagoon at the head of South West Bay on the south coast of Mallicolo. She was one of the best known and most successful of the Queensland fleet.

The *Lizzie*, which belonged to Burns, Philp & Co., had the distinction of being the first ship to recruit the Louisiade Archipelago. She was a poor sailer, and in 1883 her owners attempted to improve her sailing powers by converting her from a barquentine to a brigantine, but this was not a success, although she was given a tremendous mainsail and towering gaff topsail on a mainmast 8 ft. longer than her old one.

The schooner *Forest King* was another early recruiter in the

Louisiade Archipelago. She was boarded whilst lying off Anchor Island by an officer from H.M.S. *Swinger,* who arrested her because he found that her recruits did not understand their agreement. The following night sixteen of them jumped overboard and swam ashore, frightened, so the Blackbirders declared, by the warship. The master and recruiter of the *Forest King* were tried for kidnapping in the Vice Admiralty Court at Brisbane on October 8, 1884, but they won their case, and the ship was restored to her owners with costs.

The brigantine *Ariel* was rather unlucky as regards her Government agents. One of these committed suicide in 1888, and the next one was killed by the treacherous natives of Manova. This latter, whose name was Armstrong, left his boat to take some medicine to a native who had once been a boatman in the *Fearless.* As the covering boat in charge of the mate pulled in to the beach, a horrible screech came from a village in the forest, which was about 100 yards from the boats, and the next moment a native boatman, who had been attending on Armstrong, appeared out of the trees running for dear life.

The mate and his boat's crew at once landed to rescue the Government agent, but were obliged to retreat amidst a shower of spears and arrows. According to the boatman, Armstrong had been suddenly seized from behind and his head half severed from his body with a tomahawk, whilst he, making play with his sheath knife, had only escaped by leaving his trousers and shirt in the hands of his attackers.

The head of the Government agent was afterwards taken to Sinnarango, whose chief was offering a reward for every white man's head brought to him.

In this way also the schooner *Young Dick* had her Government agent and several of her crew murdered.

I fear there are a number of the Blackbirding fleet about which I have no information beyond their names. Of such are:— *Dauntless — Flirt — Io — Helena — Magnet — Windward Ho — Meg Merrilies—Saucy Lass—Lord of the Isles—Surprise—Nautilus— Para—Roderick Dhu—Clansman—Ivanhoe—Lady Norman—Coquette —Vibilia.*

Most of these vessels were brigantines or topsail schooners, and bore a close resemblance to the British coasters whose photographs are shown, except that deckhouses were always more conspicuous on South Sea traders than on any other kind of small craft.

There were several brigs recruiting in the early days, and there was also one well-known brig in the Blackbirding fleet at the very last. This was the *Rio Loge*.

Captain Spence and the "Rio Loge."

Captain William Spence was a native of Garmouth, and brought the barquentine *Northern Belle* out to Australia about the middle of the eighties. The *Northern Belle* was then employed in the Samoa labour trade. She was lost in March, 1889, on a reef in the Navigator Group during the *Calliope* hurricane. After a terrible experience, during which four whites and twelve Kanakas of the crew were drowned, Captain Spence and the few other survivors of the *Northern Belle* were picked up by the brigantine *May* and taken back to Brisbane, where they all spent some time in hospital. As soon as he recovered Captain Spence was given charge of the *May*, which he sailed until he took over the brig *Rio Loge* in 1901.

The *Rio Loge*, which was built in the same year as the *Cutty Sark* by W. C. Miller & Sons at Garston, was first of all owned by C. W. Turner of Lyttelton, and it was under Captain Munro and C. W. Turner's ownership that she made the run from Mauritius to Lyttelton in 33 days in 1886. Shortly after this she was bought by J. E. Noakes of Maryborough, and, with Captain J. Patterson in command, became a Blackbirder.

Soon after Captain Spence became her master she was fitted with an oil engine and the yards were stripped off her mainmast.

After the Blackbirding trade was finished with and Queensland had deported all her Kanakas, Captain Spence, who by this time owned the *Rio Loge*, put his vessel into the Australian and New Zealand coasting trade.

The old brig went "missing" in 1909 on a passage from Kaipara to Dunedin. Captain Spence had his wife and two children on board—a boy of fourteen and a girl of sixteen. No trace of the

Rio Loge or any of her people was ever found.   She is supposed to have been lost, however, about the time that the ss. *Penguin* (Union S.S. Co.) came to grief outside Wellington.   Captain Schutze, in the *Mary Ysabel*, was bound down the New Zealand coast to Dunedin that same day, and, when just south of Cook Straits during the afternoon, passed a hull bottom up, which he was almost certain was that of the *Rio Loge*.

The illustration of the *Rio Loge* shows her in her Blackbirding war-paint.

She was, I think, the last South Sea labour recruiter in commission.

It is now time to bring this volume to a close with the hope that it may remind some old sea-cony of the time when

> He thought he heard the second mate say
> "Just one more drag and then belay!"

I further hope that it may incite some youthful landlubber to sing:

> I wish I was a bosun bold,
>   Or even a bombardier,
> I'd build a boat and away I'd float,
>   And straight to the ocean steer.
>
> And straight to the ocean steer, my boys,
>   Where the dancing dolphins play,
> And the whales and sharks are having their larks
>   Ten thousand miles away.

APPENDIX

APPENDIX A.

The Five-Masters.

Date built	Name	Tons	Length	Breadth	Depth	Builder	Where built
1890	*France (I.)* ..	3784	361	48·8	25·9	Henderson	Partick
1890	*Maria Rickmers* ..	3813	375	48	25	Russell	Port Glasgow
1895	*Potosi* ..	4026	366·3	49·7	28·5	**Tecklenborg**	Geestemunde
1902	*Preussen* ..	5081	407·8	53·6	27·1	**Tecklenborg**	Geestemunde
1906	*R. C. Rickmers* ..	5548	410·5	53·6	30·4	Rickmers	Bremerhaven
1912	*France (II.)* ..	5633	418·8	55·8	24·9	Ch. & Atel. de la Gironde	Bordeaux
1921	*Kobenhavn* ..	3901	368·9	49·3	26·9	Ramage & Ferguson	Leith

BB

APPENDIX B.

"The Caliph"—Number and Measurements of Sails and Spars.

	SAILS					SPARS	
No.	Name of Sail	No. of Canvas	No. of Yards	Lining		Name of Spar	Length in feet
1	Jib topsail	5	99	4½		Bowsprit	22
2	Flying jib	4	140	8		Jibboom	33½
2	Outer jib	3	165	8½		Foremast (extreme)	144½
2	Inner jib	2	181	8½		„ lower mast (doubling 14)	61
2	Fore topmast staysail	1	166	6		„ topmast (doubling 7½)	47
1	Stay foresail	1	120½	5½		„ topgallant mast	58
2	Jamie Green	6	142	—			
2	Foresail	1	455	63		Fore yard	80
2	Lower fore topsail	1	203	53		„ lower topsail yard	68
2	Upper fore topsail	2	215	41½		„ upper topsail yard	66
2	Fore topgallant sail	3	196	36½		„ topgallant yard	52
2	„ royal	4	102	11		„ royal yard	42
2	„ skysail	6	43	—		„ skysail yard	32
2	Square mainsail	2	568	72		Main mast (extreme)	148½
2	Lower main topsail	1	220	55½		„ lower mast (doubling 14)	64
2	Upper „	2	251	48		„ topmast (doubling 7½)	47
2	Main topgallant sail	3	225	38½		„ topgallant mast	58
2	„ royal	4	114½	12		Mainyard	80
2	„ skysail	6	51	—		Main lower topsail yard	68
1	„ staysail	1	167	6		„ upper „	66
2	„ topmast staysail	3	294	7		„ topgallant yard	52
2	„ topgallant staysail	4	206	5		„ royal yard	42
2	„ royal staysail	5	156½	4½		„ skysail yard	32
2	Crossjack	4	313	47		Mizen mast (extreme)	121
1	Lower mizen topsail	1	160	42		„ lowermast	56
2	Upper „ „	2	135	30		„ topmast	37
2	Mizen topgallant sail	4	141	21		Mizen topgallant mast	46
2	„ royal	5	69	10		Crossjack yard	66½
2	„ skysail	6	34	—		Mizen lower topsail yard	55
2	„ topmast staysail	4	168	5		„ upper topsail yard	52
2	„ topgallant staysail	5	116	5		„ topgallant yard	39
2	„ royal staysail	6	77	—		„ royal yard	30

"*The Caliph*"—*Number and Measurements of Sails and Spars.*—*Continued*

SAILS

No.	Name of Sail	No. of Canvas	No. of Yards	Lining
2	Spanker	2	242	16
1	Gaff topsail	5	105	10
1	Ringtail	5	163	—
2	Lower studding sail	4	330	—
2	Fore topmast studding sail	5	191	—
2	,, topgallant studding sail	6	96½	—
2	,, royal studding sail	4	55	—
2	Main topmast studding sail	5	214	—
2	,, topgallant studding sail	6	103	—
1	,, royal studding sail	6	60	—
2	,, skysail studding sail	8	25	—

SPARS

No.	Name of Spar	Length in feet.
	Main skysail yard	21½
	Spanker gaff	30
	,, boom	45½
	SPARE SPARS	
1	spare lower yard	
1	,, topmast	
1	,, topsail yard	
1	,, jibboom	
2	,, topgallant masts	
2	,, topgallant yards	
12	,, small spars assorted	

APPENDIX C.

The Building of "The Caliph."

On March 27 we launched the Japanese corvette, *Sho-Lho-Mane*, 1500 tons register, 280 H.P., and that day the keel, stem and sternpost of our new ship, No 263 (afterwards to be known as the *Caliph*), was lying alongside the corvette, ready to be laid down, which was done on the 29th, the intervening day being Sunday.   The keel is of peculiar construction, being a sort of double keel, composed of two American elm logs 17 ft. by 18 ft. one above the other.   The sternpost, composed entirely of teak, with rabbet cut on it to receive hood ends.   The stem in two parts: the lower of good British oak, the upper of teak, with knight-heads bolted on, is next hoisted up, planked, raked and shored.   The dead-woods of teak are next fitted on, and dressed from the boarding line to the rabbet. The keel-plate, 1 inch in thickness, and of a breadth to suit the shape of the bottom, is laid along the top of the keel, and kept up about 4 inches to allow for rivetting: the holes for securing the frames to it and for bolting the plate to the keel being all punched in it.

A wooden platform is now laid across the top of the keel, whereon to build the frames which consist of frame bars, floor plates, and reverse bars, with sundry cleats for securing keelsons and stringers.

When so many of the frames, say 20, are built and hoisted into their places, they are then rivetted to the keel plate which is then lowered down on top of the keel and bolted to it by $1\frac{1}{4}$ in. yellow-metal bolts through and clenched—one between each two frames; that is to say, one at every 18 ins., as that is the distance of the frames apart. The keelsons and stringers are now commenced and consist of main keelson, bilge keelsons, intercostal keelson, and hold stringers, which meet at the stem and sternpost, and so form breast hooks.   As the frames are hoisted up they are set fair and ribands put on them. The beams are hoisted along with the frames, and are composed of bulb iron with double angle iron on top and connected to the frame by knees or bracket-plates.

The ship being all framed, fore and aft, we now put on the sheer strake, a plate 3 ft. broad and extending along the top of the frames from stem to stern.   Then follow stringer plates, bilge plate and diagonal straps, etc.

The planking consists of American rock elm and mountain teak, the elm extending up to the 7 ft. water line; the planking on the bottom is 6 ins. thick, tapering to $4\frac{3}{4}$ ins. at gunwale.

It is secured to the iron frames by $1\frac{5}{16}$ and $1\frac{3}{16}$ yellow metal bolts, and nuts screwed up inside, the head of the bolt being covered over with teak dowel dipped in marine glue.   The two paint strakes or uppermost planks being put on, the stanchions, waterways and covering board are fitted, then the deck is laid, yellow pine 5 by 4 fastened with $\frac{5}{8}$ths galvanised iron bolts, the outside skin is now caulked, the oakum being driven back within $\frac{3}{4}$ of an inch of inside. . . . .

The windlass is Brown & Harfield's, according to the wish of the owner . . .   the deck-house is built of teak with iron frames, with accommodation for galley and engine room, with rooms for petty officers and midshipmen; attached to the cooking apparatus is a condenser, capable of distilling 50 gallons in 12 hours; besides this, the ship has two tanks holding 2000 gallons each.   In the after end of the house stands the steam engine, of 8 horse power, which works cargo, lifts the anchor, pumps the ship, and hoists sails and yards and warps ship.   This engine is made in such a way that it can be attached to a shaft for driving two small screws, one on each side of the vessel, worked by a bevelled wheel on end of shaft across the deck and a similar wheel on the end of the shaft which is along the ship's side at an angle, and can be lifted out of the water at pleasure; this machinery is expected to drive the ship about $2\frac{1}{2}$ knots per hour in a calm. . . .

The scuppers, three on each side, 6 by 3, are made of thick lead, with brass grating inside to prevent their getting stopped up with dirt and to keep Jack from poking holes in them with a broom handle.

The bulwarks are fitted with yellow pine, with four large ports of a side to clear the water off the decks. Sheaves are fitted in the bulwarks for fore and main sheets and studding sail sheets; belaying pins put in the rails with small metal heads for tacks and sheets.

The vessel's bottom is cemented with Portland cement over all bolt heads and iron plates, to prevent the action of water on bolts and rivets.

The ceiling is close up to the upper turn of the bilge, with every third strake left loose, so as to reach the frames for painting, etc.; from the bilge up to the main deck she is sparred with upright hard wood battens, put on as permanent dunnage. The forecastle is fitted below for thirty men, with scuttles inside for light and ventilation, and a small stove for cold weather. The chain locker is by the foremast and is all below the lower deck; the coal hole is down the fore peak; the sail cabin and store rooms alongside the main hatch. . . . The cut-water and figure-head are fitted along with stem knees, wing rail, sword rail, head board, trail boards, cross-knees, etc. The hawse-pipes, two on each side, 10 ins. in diameter, come through between the stem knees.

The rudder stock is English oak, $16\frac{1}{2}$ ins. diameter, and is what is known as a goose-neck or gunstock; rudder with four pairs of rudder-braces of brass.

The ship's bottom receives two coats of Archangel tar, and is ready for the copper sheathing, which is 26 and 28 oz. fastened with $1\frac{1}{8}$ nails and extends up to 22 ft. water line, . . . Owing to the extreme sharpness of her bottom, the (launching) sideways, were the whole weight to rest on them, would fly out beneath her. As it is we are obliged to put chains under the keel to hold in the sideways.

The Caliph moved away just when she ought to and made a capital launch on Monday, September 6, 1869.

APPENDIX D.

"Cambrian Hills"—Sail and Spar Plan.

Masts and Yards

	Feet
BOWSPRIT (outboard) ..	48
FOREMAST (masts and yards) ..	
Lowermast (from deck) ..	62½
Doubling ..	16½
Topmast ..	55
Doubling ..	11½
Fore yard ..	84½
Lower topsail yard	76
Upper topsail yard	68
Lower topgallant yard	60
Upper topgallant yard	55½
Royal yard ..	44
MAINMAST (masts and yards)	
Main lowermast ..	64½
Doubling ..	16½
Topmast ..	56
Doubling ..	11½
Topgallant mast ..	52½
Main yard ..	84½
Lower topsail yard	76
Upper topsail yard	68
Lower topgallant yard	60
Upper topgallant yard	55½
Royal yard ..	44
MIZENMAST (masts and yards)	
Lowermast ..	61
Doubling ..	14
Topmast ..	43½
Doubling ..	7½
Topgallant mast ..	45
Crossjack yard ..	66½
Lower topsail yard	58½
Upper topsail yard	52½
Topgallant yard	42
Royal yard ..	36
Spanker gaff ..	36
Spanker boom ..	54

Sails

	Sails Yds.	Sails No.	Linings Yds.	Linings No.
FOREMAST (sails)				
Flying jib ..	96	4	6	6
Outer jib ..	102	3	8	5
Inner jib ..	110	2	8	4
Fore topmast staysail	95	1	7	3
Foresail ..	441	1	75	3
Lower topsail ..	263	3	53	3
Upper topsail ..	273	2	40	4
Lower topgallant sail	160	3	28	5
Upper topgallant sail	135	3	21	5
Royal ..	158	4	8	6
MAINMAST (sails)				
Topmast staysail ..	181	2	12	4
Topgallant staysail	150	3	7	5
Royal staysail ..	104	4	5	6
Mainsail ..	542	2	85	4
Lower topsail ..	263	1	53	3
Upper topsail ..	273	2	40	4
Lower topgallant sail	160	3	28	5
Upper topgallant sail	135	3	21	5
Royal ..	158	4	8	6
MIZENMAST (sails)				
Mizen staysail ..	132	1	8	3
Topmast staysail ..	153	2	7	4
Topgallant staysail	104	4	5	6
Crossjack ..	352	3	59	5
Lower topsail ..	186	2	47	3
Upper topsail ..	155	1	22	4
Topgallant sail ..	186	4	34	6
Royal ..	108	5	6	6
Spanker ..	226	2	16	4
Storm spanker ..	196	1	12	3

APPENDIX E.

Potter's Spar Plans.

	Dunferm-line	*Forteviot*	*Wanderer*	*Dunstaff-nage*
	ft.	ft.	ft.	ft.
Stump bowsprit	45	45	45	45
Fore lowermast above deck	64	66	64	70
Doubling	14	14	14	16
Fore topmast	56	58	56	60
Doubling	12	12	10	12
Fore topgallant mast (telescopic)	59	61	65	63
Main lowermast above deck	67·3	70·6	70·6	75
Doubling	14	14	14	16
Main topmast	56	58	56	60
Doubling	12	12	10	12
Main topgallant mast (telescopic)	61	64	74	66
Mizen lowermast above deck	67·6	69·9	69·3	78
Doubling	14	14	14	16
Topmast	56	58	56	60
Doubling	12	12	10	12
Topgallant mast (telescopic)	59	61	56	63
Fore, main and mizen lower yards	92	92	92	94
Topsail yards	83·6	83·6	83·6	86
Upper topsail yards	74	74	74	75
Lower topgallant yards	66	67	63·6	67
Upper topgallant yards	58	59 }	single yard	59
Royal yards	48	50	55	50
Jiggermast main deck to top	54	52	52	65·6
Deck to truck	128	137	128	129·6
Spanker gaff	40	32	40	32
Spanker boom	54	54	53	54
Fore and main skysail yards	—	—	48	—
Depth of mainsail at bunt	—	—	35	50½

APPENDIX F.

Spar Plans of Shire Line Four-masters.

	Buteshire	Dumfries-shire	Ross shire	Kinross-shire
	ft.	ft.	ft.	ft.
Stump bowsprit	46	52½	63	45
Fore lowermast above deck	62	65½	} 108 in one	63½
Doubling	16	15½		16
Fore topmast	51½	53		65
Doubling	8½	9½	13	17
Fore topgallant mast	51½	68	59½	50
Main lowermast above deck	66	65½	} 112 in one	67
Doubling	16	15½		16
Main topmast	51½	53		65
Doubling	8½	9½	13	17
Main topgallant mast	51½	68	60	53
Mizen lowermast above deck	66½	69½	} 112 in one	67
Doubling	16	15½		16
Topmast	51½	53		65½
Doubling	8½	9½	13	17
Topgallant mast	51½	65	60	50
Fore, main and mizen lower yards	86	88	87	88
Lower topsail yards	73	77½	79½	80
Upper topsail yards	69	70½	74	75
Lower topgallant yards }	54	} 57	} 64	70
Upper topgallant yards)	single	single	60	60
Royal yards	40	45	50	—
Jiggermast, main deck to top	67	52	69½	65½
Deck to truck	118½	91	133	118½
Spanker gaff	32	35	36	31½
Spanker boom	46½	50	46	44
Fore, main and mizen skysail yards	—	34	—	—

APPENDIX G.

"Peleus"—Spar Plan.

		Feet
BOWSPRIT	.. ..	47
FOREMAST	(step to truck)	173
	(deck to truck)	148
	Lowermast (deck to cap)	64
	doubling	$17\frac{1}{2}$
	Topmast	59
	doubling	$14\frac{1}{2}$
	Topgallant mast	$56\frac{1}{2}$
MAINMAST	(step to truck)	177
	(deck to truck)	150
	Lowermast (deck to cap)	66
	doubling	$17\frac{1}{2}$
	Topmast	59
	doubling	$14\frac{1}{2}$
	Topgallant mast	$56\frac{1}{2}$
	Fore and main lower yards	90
FORE AND MAIN	Lower topsail yards	83
	Upper topsail yards	73
	Lower topgallant yards	65
	Upper topgallant yards	$57\frac{1}{2}$
	Royal yards	$45\frac{1}{2}$
MIZENMAST	(step to truck)	154
	(deck to truck)	129
	Lowermast (deck to cap)	59
	doubling	16
	Topmast	50
	doubling	10
	Topgallant mast	$46\frac{1}{2}$
	Crossjack yard	72
	Lower topsail yard	67
	Upper topsail yard	57
	Topgallant yard	45
	Royal yard	34
	Spanker gaff	28

APPENDIX H.

Shire Line Captains.

W. B. Anderson ..	..	*Linlithgowshire,* **Millwall.**
Andrew Baxter ..	..	*Dumbartonshire, Kirkcudbrightshire, Ross-shire.*
R. Blanche ..	..	*Berwickshire.*
Charles Bowden ..	..	*Agnes Oswald.*
A. Bowen ..	..	*Arctic Stream.*
H. Brabender ..	..	*Arctic Stream, Selkirkshire, Kirkcudbrightshire.*
J. R. Bremner ..	..	*Aspice.*
W. M. Caddell ..	..	*Fifeshire.*
William Couper ..	..	*Kincardineshire, Morayshire, Clackmannanshire, Kinross-shire, Ross-shire.*
C. C. Dixon ..	..	*Arctic Stream, Elginshire.*
C. Douglas ..	..	*Lanarkshire, Cromartyshire.*
J. Evans ..	..	*Banffshire.*
R. Evans ..	..	*Forfarshire.*
D. Ewing ..	..	*Nairnshire.*
R. W. Furneaux ..	..	*Largo Law, Dumfriesshire.*
R. Grant ..	..	**Peeblesshire.**
Robert Greig ..	..	*Elginshire, Duns Law.*
J. G. Hannah ..	..	*Elginshire.*
E. Hansen ..	..	*Stirlingshire.*
O. H. Henderson ..	..	*Cromartyshire, Largo Law* (steamer).
C. Hill ..	..	*Caithness-shire.*
J. Houghton ..	..	*Selkirkshire.*
J. N. Kennedy ..	..	*Jordan Hill.*
A. Kerbyson ..	..	*Gulf Stream, Clackmannanshire.*
W. Lane ..	..	*Kincardineshire.*
W. C. McGibbon ..	..	*Agnes Oswald, Dumfriesshire.*
Angus McKinnon ..	..	*Kinross-shire.*
John Nichol ..	..	*Duns Law, Glencairn, Fifeshire* (11).
D. Nicol ..	..	*Zuleika.*
David Nicoll ..	..	*Hannah Landles, Sutherlandshire, Gulf Stream. Cromartyshire.*
John Peattie ..	..	*Renfrewshire, Aberdeenshire, Nairnshire, Peeblesshire, Edinburghshire, Cowden Law, Sutherlandshire, Inverness-shire.*
T. K. Philip ..	..	*Lanarkshire, Agnes Oswald.*
R. Purdie ..	..	*Kirkcudbrightshire, Buteshire, Forfarshire.*
R. Purdy ..	..	*Forfarshire, Kinross-shire.*
John Reid ..	..	*Cromartyshire, Fifeshire.*
David Roberts ..	..	*Kirkcudbrightshire, Elginshire.*
—— Storm ..	..	*Morayshire.*
David Stott ..	..	*Linlithgowshire, Caithness-shire, Elginshire.*
W. W. Swinton ..	..	*Buteshire, Dumfriesshire.*
D. W. Thomson ..	..	*Clackmannanshire, Forfarshire, Falls of Halladale.*
E. L. Tindall ..	..	*Inverness-shire.*
H. G. Ward ..	..	*Berwickshire.*
William Wright ..	..	*Glencairn, Gulf Stream, Elginshire.*

APPENDIX I.

Abstract Log of "Queen Margaret."—Captain **D. F. Faulkner.**

Barry Dock to Nagasaki.

1897.   April 30.—6 p.m. Left Barry Dock in tow of tug *Flying Buzzard.*
Sunday, May 1.—8 a.m. Tug left Lundy Island abeam.
8 p.m. Off Newquay, Cornwall.

Date	Lat.	Long.	Course	Dist.	Winds
May 2	51 35 N.	6 27 W.	N. 66 W.	61 miles	West, S.W., mod. to fresh
3	48 40	8 10	S. 21 W.	186 ,,	W.S.W., W.N.W. ,,
4	46 35	10 10	S. 33 W.	150 ,,	W.N.W., N.W., fresh to light.
5	44 24	11 20	S. 20 W.	140 ,,	W. to W.N.W., light to mod.
6	41 36	12	S. 10 W.	171 ,,	N. to N.N.E., fresh to strong.
7	38 15	14 27	S. 29 W.	230 ,,	N.N.E. ,, ,,
8	34 44	16 20	S. 23 W.	230 ,,	N.N.E. to N.E., strong.

Remarks for week—All sail set every day except Sunday when royals and skysails were furled for a few hours. Passed two barques on Tuesday night and another going north on Wednesday. On Friday passed quite close to an Italian or Spanish barque. Sails being repaired most of week. Unbent spanker and set an older one on Friday. Rigged a studding sail on fore yard out of a mizen topgallant sail. The weather has been very fine and temperature gradually going up.

Total distance run, 1168 miles.   Daily average, 167 miles.

Date	Lat.	Long.	Course	Dist.	Winds.
May 9	32 41 N.	16 W.	S. 8 E.	125 miles	N.E. to S.W., light to fresh.
10	31 30	16 11	S. 7 W.	72 ,,	S.S.W. to S.W. & W., fresh.
11	29 4	17 22	S. 23 W.	159 ,,	W. to W. by N., mod. to fresh.
12	27 6	17 40	S. 8 W.	120 ,,	W., W.N.W., S.W. & N., light to mod.
13	25 13	18	S. 9 W.	115 ,,	N.N.E. to N.E., light Trades.
14	22 42	19 55	S. 35 W.	185 ,,	N.N.E. to N.E., mod. to fresh Trades.
15	20 25	22 42	S. 49 W.	207 ,,	N.N.E. to N.E., fresh Trades.

Remarks for Week—Passed **Porto Santo** 8 a.m. and Madeira on May 9. Tacked four times May 9 and 8. Palma Island, Canaries, abeam 2 p.m. May 11. Passed Ferro I. 8 a.m. May 12. Spoke a steamer going north 6 p.m. May 14.

Total Distance run, 983 miles.   Daily average, 141 miles.

Date	Lat.	Long.	Course	Dist.	Winds.
May 16	18 19 N.	25 20 W.	S. 50 W.	195 miles	N.N.E. to N.E., fresh to mod. Trades.
17	16 8	25 42	S. 9 W.	133 ,,	N.E. to E., mod to light.
18	13 52	26 11	S. 11 W.	140 ,,	N.E. to E. ,,
May 19-25 missing.					
26	0 17 N.	28 13	S. 48 W.	209 ,,	S.S.E. to S.E., fresh Trades.
27	3 20 S.	29 10	S. 15 W.	224 ,,	S.E. to E.S.E. ,, ,,
28	5 48	31 5	S. 38 W.	187 ,,	S.E. to S.S.E., fresh to mod.
29	8 6	31 11	S. 2 W.	138 ,,	S.E. to E.S.E., squally to mod.

Date	Lat.	Long.	Course	Dist.	Winds.
May 30	10 40	32 40	S. 30° W.	178 miles	S.E. to S.S.E. and S.E., fresh.
31	12	33	S. 15 W.	83 ,,	S.E. to E.S.E., light.
June 1	12 41	32 37	S. 28 E.	47 ,,	N.E., N. and W., variable, light very, to calm.
2	14 13	33 39	S. 33 W.	110 ,,	W., S.W. to S.S.E., light to fresh, squally
3	16 41	35 11	S. 31 W.	173 ,,	S.S.E. to S.E., squally to strong.
4	19 38	37 5	S. 31 W.	207 ,,	S.E. to S.S.E., strong.
5	21 34	38 42	S. 37 W.	146 ,,	S.S.E. to variable. Squally.

Remarks for Week.—Passed two barques May 30. Sighted two barques, one of which we passed yesterday. In company with barque *Strathisla*. Captain came on board May 31. *Strathisla* 10 miles astern June 1. Spoke steamer *Rangatira* bound north. Passed ship *Macedon* bound north 2nd. Heavy head sea. A large barque in company 4th. French barque *Canrobert* 37 days out kept neck and neck with us all Friday (4th), we passed through her lee to windward and tacked E. Saturday morning.

Total distance run, 944 miles. Daily average, 135.

Date	Lat.	Long.	Course	Dist.	Winds.
June 6	21 39	38 32	S. 64° E.	11 miles	Variable, light airs and calm.
7	22 20	37 26	S. 56 E.	74 ,,	Variable to E., light and calm to moderate.
8	24 40	37 11	S. 6 E.	141 ,,	E. to E.N.E., mod. to fresh
9	26 54	35 44	S. 30 E.	155 ,,	E. to E.N.E.
10	28 45	34 36	S. 28 E.	126 ,,	N.E. to N., moderate. ,, ,,
11	29 48	32 11	S. 64 E.	141 ,,	N.N.W. to S. ,, ,,
12	30 21	27 56	S. 81 E.	223 ,,	S. to S.S.W., strong.

Remarks for Week—Two barques in company 6th. Changing sails 7th. Passed a ship 6 a.m., 12th.

Distance for week, 871 miles. Daily average, 124 miles.

Date	Lat.	Long.	Course	Dist.	Winds.
June 13	31 42 S.	23 00 W.	S. 72° E.	266 miles.	S.S.W., strong to squally.
14	32 40	18 48	S. 75 E.	221 ,,	S.S.W., squally to moderate.
15	32 42	15 15	E.	179 ,,	S.S.W. to S.S.E., squally to mod.
16	31 44	12 21	N. 69 E.	160 ,,	S. to S.E., variable, moderate.
17	32 37	12 53	N. 27 W.	60 ,,	S. to S.E., variable, mod. to light.
18	32 16	11 5	N. 77 E.	94 ,,	S. to S.E., variable, light.
19	32 50	9 38	S. 65 E.	81 ,,	S. to S.S.W. and W., light to moderate.

Remarks for Week—Passed a four-masted barquentine, probably *Tacora* of Liverpool, on 13th. A barque in company, and another sighted from aloft 14th. A whirlwind passed very close to us at 10 a.m. on 14th, and we had to change our course from S.E., to E. to avoid it. Passed two barques, one of them *Duguesclin*, which were in company yesterday, 15th. In company with French barque *Duguesclin*, she sailed from Cardiff, May 2nd for Hongkong.

Total distance run, 1061 miles. Daily average, 151 miles.

Date	Lat.	Long.	Course	Dist.	Winds.
	° ′	° ′	°		
June 20	35 16	7	S. 52 E.	196 miles.	W. to N.W., fresh.
21	37 3	2 12 W.	S. 66 E.	255 ,,	N.W. to W.S.W., fresh to strong gale.
22	26 53	3 E.	N. 88 E.	250 ,,	W.S.W. to S.S.W., strong gale to moderate.
23	28 8	6 47	S. 68 E.	195 ,,	S.S.W. to N.N.W. and W., mod. to strong gale.
24	38 58	10 17	S. 73 E.	172 ,,	W. to N.W. and W., strong to light and fresh.
25	39 46	15 2	S. 79 W.	220 ,,	W. to N.W. and W., fresh to moderate and strong.
26	39 5	20 4	N. 84 E.	241 ,,	W.S.W. to W., strong gale to fresh.

Remarks for Week.—Passed French barque 20th. Lost a man overboard 10 p.m. on 20th.

Total distance for week, 1529 miles. Daily average, 218 miles.

Date	Lat.	Long.	Course	Dist.	Winds.
	° ′	° ′	°		
June 27	39 5	25 28	E.	251 miles.	W., moderate, fresh gale, mod.
28	39 26	30 43	S. 85 E.	245 ,,	W., fresh to strong gale.
29	39 35	36 23	S. 88 E.	264 ,,	W. to S.W., strong gale to mod.
30	39 35	41 40	E.	244 ,,	S.W. to W.S.W., fresh gale, hard squalls.
July 1	39 5	47 40	N. 84 E.	281 ,,	S.W., strong gale.
2	39 4	52	E.	203 ,,	S.W., W., W.N.W., and W., squally to moderate and light.
3	39 27	56 50	S. 84 E.	226 ,,	W., S.S.W. and S.W., fresh.

Remarks for Week—Heavy sea 27th, 28th, 29th and July 1st. All sail set 3rd.

Total distance for week, 1714 miles. Daily average, 245 miles=10¼ knots per hour (nearly).

Date	Lat.	Long.	Course	Dist.	Winds.
	° ′	° ′	°		
July 4	39 54	62 20	S. 84 E.	256 miles.	W. to W.S.W. and W., fresh.
5	39 23	67 54	N. 83 E.	262 ,,	W. and W.S.W., fresh to strong.
6	39	71 54	N. 83 E.	187 ,,	W. to W.N.W., mod. to fresh.
7	38 35	77 34	N. 85 E.	267 ,,	N.W., strong gale.
8	38	81 37	N. 80 E.	202 ,,	N.W. to W.S.W., strong gale to moderate.
9	36 15	85 22	N. 60 E.	209 ,,	W.S.W. to S.W., strong and squally to fresh.
10	35 31	87 40	N. 68 E.	120 ,,	S.W. to N.W., mod. to light.

Remarks for Week—Heavy sea from S.W. 5th and 6th. Passed St. Paul's Island 4 miles on the starboard beam at noon 7th.

Distance for week, 1503 miles. Daily average, 215 miles.

Date	Lat.	Long.	Course	Dist.	Winds.
	° ′	° ′	°		
July 11	34 58	89 26	N. 70 E.	92 miles.	N.W. to S.W., light and variable.
12	34 31	90 46	N. 68 E.	70 ,,	S.W., light.
13	34 14	91 30	N. 64 E.	40 ,,	S.W. to S.E. and N.E., light and calm.
14	33 53	94 40	N. 82 E.	158 ,,	N.E. to N.W., light to fresh.
15	32 24	99 22	N. 70 E.	252 ,,	N.W. to S.W., fresh to strong.
16	29 8	100 26	N. 16 E.	204 ,,	S.W., fresh to moderate.
17	25 55	101 42	N. 19 E.	204 ,,	S.W. to S., fresh.

Remarks for Week.—Distance for week, 1020 miles. Daily average, 145 miles.

Date	Lat.	Long.	Course	Dist.	Winds.
	° ′	° ′	°		
July 18	22 53	103 30	N. 28 E.	207 miles.	S., S.E. and E., fresh.
19	19 36	104 30	N. 16 E.	205 ,,	E.S.E. to E., squally to fresh Trades.
20	15 28	105 18	N. 10 E.	252 ,,	E. to S.E., strong Trades.
21	11 24	105 8	N. 2 W	245 ,,	S.E. to E.S.E. ,,
22	6 57	105 11	N.	267 ,,	S.E. ,,
23	5 54	105 55	Various	100 ,,	S.E., strong to light.
24	4 32	106 26	N. 22 E.	78 ,,	E. to E.N.E., light to fresh.

Remarks for Week.—Passed Christmas Island 5 p.m., July 21st. Sighted land 10 a.m 22nd. At noon Java Head 13 miles north. Passed Java Head 1 p.m., 2nd point 3 p.m. Total distance from Cardiff 13,956 miles. Daily average 168 miles=7 knots per hour. Arrived off Anjer at midnight 22nd, light airs, did not anchor. 6·30 a.m. 23rd went ashore. in boat with mate for 2½ hours. At noon 23rd off Button Isle. 12 ships in the Straits, including *Cromartyshire, Elginshire, Howard D. Troop, Eskasoni, Abner Coburn, Peru,* and *Glendoon.* Passed ships *Elginshire, Eskasoni, Peru, Glendoon* and a four-masted ship. *Cromartyshire* and *Howard D. Troop* in company.

Date	Lat.	Long.	Course.	Dist.	Winds.
	° ′	° ′	°		
July 25	1 53 S.	107 20	N. 19 E.	168 miles.	E., fresh to strong.
26	1 22 N.	108 27	N. 19 E.	207 ,,	S.E. to S. by E., fresh.
27	3 33	108 38	N. 5 E.	132 ,,	S. to S.S.W., fresh to moderate.
28	5 21	108 38	N.	108 ,,	S.S.W. to S., moderate to light.
29	6 28	109 2	N. 18 E.	71 ,,	S.S.W. to S., light.
30	8 38	109 33	N. 13 E.	134 ,,	S. to S.S.W., light to moderate.
31	10 48	111 47	N. 46 E.	187 ,,	S.W., fresh.

Remarks for Week—25th passed Gaspar Strait at 6 a.m. *Cromartyshire* and *Howard D. Troop* went Stolze. Passed *Cromartyshire* 26th. *Cromartyshire* gained abeam during night 26th. *Cromartyshire* about 3 miles abeam noon 28th, spoke her. *Cromartyshire* gained a few miles during night 28th. 3.30 p.m., 29th, squall brought us level with him and quarter of a mile apart. *Cromartyshire* hull down forward of beam noon 30th. Passed a P. & O. steamer going south 30th. *Cromartyshire* kept more to north and was out of sight morning 31st.

Distance for week, 1007 miles. Daily average, 144 miles.

Date	Lat.	Long.	Course	Dist.	Winds.
	° ′	° ′	°		
Aug. 1	13 10	114 33	N. 49 E.	216 miles	S.W. to S.S.W., fresh.
2	15 35	116 44	N. 41 E.	193 ,,	S.W. to S.S.W. ,,
3	17 36	118 8	N. 33 E.	142 ,,	S.S.W. to S., moderate to light.
4	18 6	118 34	N. 38 E.	40 ,,	E. to N.E., variable, light.
5	21 21	118 18	N. 4 E.	196 ,,	N.E., fresh to strong.
6	22 22	119 7	N. 36 E.	76 ,,	E., N.E. and N.N.W., moderate to light and calm.
7	22 58	119 55	N. 51 E.	57 ,,	N.N.W., light and calm.

Remarks for Week—Passed Pescadores Islands off Formosa coast 7th.
Total distance for week, 920 miles. Daily average, 131 miles.

Date	Lat.	Long.	Course	Dist.	Winds.
	° ′	° ′	°		
Aug. 8	23 48	118 53	N. 42 W.	75 miles.	N.N.E., strong.
9	25 10	120 15	N. 42 E.	111 ,,	N.N.E., N.N.W., W., and S.W., strong to fresh.
10	26 49	122 23	N. 49 E.	151 ,,	S.W. to S., strong and squally.
11	30 14	126	N. 43 E.	280 ,,	S. to S.S.W., strong.
12			various	250 ,,	S., strong.

(Arrived Nagasaki).

Remarks for Week—Working up Formosa coast. Tacked ship several times 8th. Arrived Nagasaki 12 o'clock (noon) on 12th.

Total distance to Nagasaki, 16,928 miles. Total days, 103½ days. Daily average, 164 miles.

APPENDIX I.—*Continued.*

Abstract Log of "Queen Margaret."

1897, September 13.—8 a.m. left Nagasaki.

10 a.m. threw off tow rope.   Wind very light.

Date		Lat.	Long.	Course	Dist.	Winds.
Sept.	14	31 14	129 45	S.	80 miles.	N. to variable, light.
	15	30 54	133	S. 83 E.	168 ,,	N.N.W., N. and N.E., fresh.
	16	30 29	134 5	S. 66 E.	61 ,,	N. to E.N.E. and variable, light.
	17	32	133 32	N. 15 W.	93 ,,	N.E., variable, light.
	18	30 17	136	S. 39 E.	160 ,,	N.E. to E.N.E., fresh.

Remarks for Week—Passed Van Diemen Strait at 8 p.m. 14th.   A dead beat **16th,** 17th, and 18th, tacked ship every four hours.

Date	Lat.	Long.	Course	Dist.	Winds.
Sept. 19	31 31	134	N. 54 W.	126 miles.	N.E. to N.E. by N., fresh to mod.
20	32	134 40	N. 50 E.	45 ,,	N.N.E. to E. and E.S.E., strong.
21	33 04	137 5	N. 62 E·	138 ,,	E.S.E., S.E., S. and S.W., fresh.
22	32 42	141 37	S. 84 E.	230 ,,	S.W., N.W. and N.E., fresh to moderate.
23	32 16	143 15	S. 73 E.	87 ,,	N.N.E. to N.E., mod. to fresh.
24	34 16	143 53	N. 15 E.	125 ,,	N.E., E. and S.E. ,,
25	37 55	147 53	N. 41 E.	294 ,,	S.E., S. and W.N.W., strong to fresh.

Remarks for Week—Passed islands south of Tokio Bay at midnight 21st.   Current **2 to 3 knots N.E. 21st.**

Total distance week ending 7th day out, 733 miles.   Daily average, 104$\frac{5}{7}$.

Date	Lat.	Long.	Course	Dist.	Winds.
Sept. 26	39 13	153 58	N. 75 E.	297 miles	W.N.W., N.W. and N., strong.
27	38 17	158 05	S. 74 E.	201 ,,	N. to N.E., strong to fresh.
28	38 2	158 51	S. 67 E.	40 ,,	N.E. to S.E., fresh to calm and light airs.
29	40 51	159 50	N. 15 E.	175 ,,	S.E. to E. and N.E., fresh gale.
30	41 15	164 22	N. 83 E.	207 ,,	N.E., N., N.W., strong to mod.
Oct. 1	43 16	166 40	N. 40 E.	158 ,,	N.W., S. and S.E., light to gale.
2	43 26	168 40	N. 83 E.	88 ,,	S.E., E. and N.W., strong gale to moderate.

Remarks for Week—

Total distance week ending September 27th, 1372 miles.   Daily average, 196 miles.

Date		Lat.	Long.	Course	Dist.	Winds.
		° ′	° ′	°		
Oct.	3	44 22	174 12	N. 77 E.	247 miles	N.W. to N.N.W., fresh to strong.
	4	45 15	179 25E.	N. 76 E.	226 ,,	N.W. to S.W., strong to mod.
	4	46	176 25W.	N. 75 E.	185 ,,	S.W., S. and S.S.E., light to fresh.
	5	46	172 54	E.	146 ,,	S.E., E., N.E., N. and N.W., moderate to heavy gale.
	6	45 53	168 5	S. 88 E.	202 ,,	N.W., W. and S.W., strong gale to fresh breeze.
	7	47 10	160 24	S. 76 E.	326 ,,	S.W., strong breeze.
	8	48 36	155	N. 68 E.	232 ,,	S.W., S., and S.E., strong gale.
	9	48 36	152 23	E.	105 ,,	S., S.W. and S.E., strong to light.

Remarks for Week—Foresail and cap jib blown to pieces and lost 5th. Royals set most of the time on 7th. Average for 23½ hours 13·87 knots. Were doing 14 knots most of the night.

Distance for week ending 4th October, 1141 miles. Daily average, 163 miles

---

Date		Lat.	Long.	Course	Dist.	Winds.
		° ′	° ′	°		
Oct.	10	48 20	151	S. 74 E.	58 miles.	Variable, light airs and calms.
	11	48 3	148 8	S. 82 E.	117 ,,	N.W. and N., light.
	12	47 41	145 18	S. 79 E.	116 ,,	N., N.W., and W., light.
	13	47	141	S. 77 E.	180 ,,	W. to N.W., moderate.
	14	47	135 47	E.	225 ,,	N.W. to W.N.W., fresh to mod
	15	46 30	131 07	S. 81 E.	200 ,,	W., S.W. and S.S.W., mod.
	16	46 16	127 54	S. 84 E.	129 ,,	S.S.W. to S.S.E., light.

Remarks for Week—
Total distance for week ending October 10th, 1254 miles. Daily average, 179·1 miles

---

Date		Lat.	Long.	Course	Dist.	Winds.
		° ′	° ′	°		
Oct.	17	46 7	126 45	S. 79 E.	49 miles.	S., light airs and calms.
	18	(Arrived Astoria noon)			118 ,,	
	19	Left Astoria 7 a.m., arrived 7 p.m., 6 miles below Portland and anchored for the night.				
	20	Arrived Portland 8 a.m. and made fast alongside Irving Docks.				

Remarks for Week—Sighted lightship 1 a.m. 18th and pilot came on board at 4 a.m. Tug came along at 9 a.m. and we reached Astoria about noon.

Total distance Nagasaki to Astoria, 5634 miles. Daily average, 156 miles = 6½ knot per hour.

APPENDIX J.

Register of Ships (in order of mention).

Date built	Name	Rig	Gross Tons	Length	Breadth	Depth	Builder	First Owners
1889	Liverpool	iron 4-m. ship	3396	333·2	47·9	26·5	Russell	Leyland
1889	Peter Rickmers	steel 4-m. ship	2926	332	44·4	25·4	Russell	Rickmers Reismuhlen
1868	Parsee	iron ship	1281	227·4	35·9	22·4	Steele	J. & W. Stewart
1877	Assaye	iron ship	1281	227·4	35·9	22·4	,,	J. & W. Stewart
1878	Mallsgate	iron barque	1073	215·3	34·1	21	Williamson	Sprott
1877	Selkirkshire	,,	1237	228·4	35·8	20·4	Birrell, Stenhouse	T. Law
1885	Countess of Derby	,,	775	186·8	31	18·6	,,	J. Allison & Son
1884	Forfarshire	,,	1354	239·6	36·0	21·5	Birrell, Stenhouse	T. Law
1877	Minerewa ex Vale Royal	iron ship	371	143·1	26·1	13·0	Murdoch & Murray	George Wood
1888	Dartford	steel barque	1327	221·5	36·0	21·9	Mounsey & Foster	D. Corsar
1888	Cupica	,,	1241	226	36·4	21·9	Bigger	Macvicar, Marshall
1888	Lorton	,,	1419	245·8	37·4	21·6	Workman	P. Iredale ; Porter
1889	Harold	,,	1376	240	36·5	21·3	Duncan	T. Stephens & Sons
1891	Camphill	,,	1240	226	36·4	21·9	Bigger	Squarey
1891	Craiglands	,,	1241	226	36·4	21·9	,,	
1897	Silverstream	steel ship	1242	226	36·4	21·9	,,	W. P. Herdman
1894	Acamas	steel barque	1860	262·4	38·9	22·9	Ritson	Ritson
1888	Ladas	,,	1395	233·3	36·9	22	,,	
1893	Tacora	iron 4-m. bkn.	911	204·7	35·6	18·3	Reid	Nicholson
1895	Oberon	steel 4-m. bkn.	1119	211·2	35·6	19·6	Russell	J. Fairlie
1895	Titania	steel 4-m. bkn.	1107	210	35·6	19·5	Russell	J. Fairlie
1896	Renfield	,,	1112	209·6	35·6	19·5	,,	J. A. Russell
1900	Sound of Jura	,,	1109	210·3	35·6	19·5	,,	C. A. Walker
1904	Alta	,,	1379	226	44	19·6	Duncan	A. P. Lorentzen
1866	Mozart	iron 4-m. ship	2003	262·9	40·1	24·2	Grangemouth	De Freitas
1887	Lancing ex Pereire	,,	2764	356	43·8	27·3	R. Napier	C. G. Trans-Atlantique
1888	Sindia	steel 4-m. bk.	3068	329·3	45·2	26·7	Harland	Brocklebank
1888	Holkar	,,	3073	329·3	45·2	26·7	,,	
1888	Muscoota ex Buckingham	steel 4-m. ship	2668	307·7	45·1	24·2	Royden	Macvicar, Marshall
1888	Galgate	,,	2356	293·5	42·8	24·2	Whitehaven	J. Joyce
1886	Lord Shaftesbury	,,	2341	293·3	42·8	24	,,	J. Herron
1888	Marion Lightbody	,,	2176	288·8	42·7	24·1	Henderson	Rogers
1886	Marion Inglis	steel ship	1587	250	38·1	22·7	McMillan	Lewis
1888	Pass of Balmaha	steel ship	1571	245·4	38·8	22·5	Duncan	Gibson & Clark
1889	Glaucus	steel 4-m. ship	2056	278·7	41·1	24·2	Barclay	Carmichael
1889	Carradale	,,	2085	285·7	41	23·7	A. Stephen	Roxburgh
1889	Ulidia	iron ship	2405	300	42·0	24	Richardson	P. Iredale & Porter

Register of Ships (in order of mention).—Continued.

Date built	Name	Rig	Gross Tons	Length	Br'dth	Depth	Builder	First Owner
1889	Andelana	steel 4-m. ship	2579	303·7	42·2	24·6	Williamson	Roberts
1890	Eusemere	„ „	2512	303·7	42·2	24·5	„	Fisher & Sprott
1891	Pendragon Castle	„ „	2510	303·9	42·2	24·6	„	Chambers
1892	Conishead	steel 4-m. bk.	2526	305·8	42·3	24·6	Williamson	Bourke & Huntrods
1891	Vortigern	„ „	2529	305·7	42·2	24·6	„	Brown, Jenkinson
1892	Caradoc	„ „	2531	305·8	42·3	24·6	„	Caradoc Co.
1889	Garthwray ex Wray Castle	steel ship	1891	264	39	23·6	„	J. Chambers
1889	Tamar	„	2115	286·8	42·5	24	Napier	Devitt & Moore
1889	Brablock	„	2062	278·7	41·1	24·2	Barclay	Aitken, Lilburn
1889	Neotsfield	iron ship	1894	269·6	40·1	22·7	McMillan	F. H. Dangar
1889	Grace Harwar	steel ship	1877	266·7	39·1	23·5	Hamilton	Montgomery
1889	Port Patrick	„	1740	260·2	38·2	23	Russell	Crawford
1889	Puritan	steel 4-m. bk.	2361	301·6	43·1	24·2	Reid	Cameron
1889	Glencaird	„ „	2614	312·8	41·9	24·5	Russell	Corsar
1889	Cairniehill	„ „	2524	312·9	41·9	24·6	„	
1889	Sir Robert Fernie	„ „	2528	312·7	41·9	24·5	Russell	W. J. Fernie
1889	Falkland	iron 4-m. bk.	2804	317·8	45·3	24·9	Potter	Macvicar, Marshall
1889	Hollinwood	steel 4-m. ship	2673	307·7	45·1	24·2	Royden	
1889	Alice A. Leigh	„ „	3003	309·6	46·1	25·2	Whitehaven	J. Joyce
1889	Lord Rosebery ex Windermere	„ „						
1888	Semantha	„ „	2833	304·1	46	25	„ Hamilton	J. Herron
1888	Buteshire	„ „	2280	296·7	43·2	23·8	Hamilton	Haws
1889	Elginshire	„ „	1910	266·5	40	23·7	Birrell	Law
1890	California	„ „	2160	285	40·5	24·7	„	Ismay
1891	Lord Templemore	steel 4-m. ship	3099	392·3	45·2	26·7	Harland	Dixon
1890	Simla	steel 4-m. bk.	3045	329·8	45·1	26·7	„	G. M. Steeves
1890	Swanhilda	„ „	2214	278·2	41·9	24·4	Russell	J. W. Carmichael
1890	Hinemoa	„ „	2150	273	42·3	24	McMillan	Leslie
1890	Dumfriesshire	„ „	2283	278·1	41·9	24·2	Russell	Law
1890	Mayhill	iron & steel 4-m. bk	2565	313·6	42·1	24·4	„	
1890	Strathgryffe	steel 4-m. bk.	2121	292	41	23·7	A. Stephen	G. W. Wood
1890	Cambrian King	steel ship	2276	279·4	41·9	24·4	Russell	McGillivray
1892	Cambrian Hills	„	1718	260·4	38·2	23·1	„	Roberts, Owen
1890	Cape York	steel 4-m. bk.	1760	260·7	38·1	23·1	Rodger	W. Thomas
1892	Cape Wrath	„ „	2128	276·5	41·2	24·3	Barclay	Lyle
1892	Cape Clear	„ „	2140	280·3	42·1	24·4	Duncan	„
1890	Pass of Brander	„ „	2129	279·6	42·1	24·4	„	„
			2127	280·5	42·1	24·4	„	Gibson & Clark

Register of Ships (in order of mention).—Continued.

Date built	Name	Rig	Gross Tons	Length	Br'dth	Depth	Builder	First Owners
1891	Pass of Melfort	steel 4-m. bk.	2346	298·8	44	24·5	Fairfields	Gibson & Clark
1893	Pass of Killiecrankie	steel barque	1746	252·6	39·1	22·5	Duncan	"
1890	Ainsdale	steel ship	1825	270	39·8	23·4	Bigger	P. Iredale & Porter
1890	Hawksdale	"	1824	270	39·7	23·3	"	"
1890	Dumbarton Rock	"	1716	260·7	38·2	23	Russell	Cornfoot & Co
1890	Andromeda	steel 4-m. bk.	1928	271·3	40	23·6	Duncan	G. F. Smith
1890	Drumalis	" "	2530	310	42·3	24·6	Pickersgill	P. Iredale & Porter
1891	Andrada	" "	2593	304·5	43·2	24	"	Roberts
1892	Andorinha	" "	3440	346·8	46·1	25·5	"	"
1890	Glenesk	steel barque	1369	231·8	36·1	21·7	Russell	Taylor
1890	Glencona	steel 4-m. bk.	2631	313·4	42·1	24·6	"	"
1893	Glencova	"	2369	283	43	24·5	Connell	Leyland
1891	Speke	steel ship	2875	310·3	42·2	25·6	Oswald	"
1891	Ditton	"	2901	311	42·3	25·7	Barclay	Carmichael
1891	Talus	"	2090	274·6	41·3	24	Connell	J. Hardie
1891	Vimeira	steel 4-m. bk.	2233	283·4	42·5	24·7	"	
1891	Pyrenees	" "	2243	284·5	42·5	24·7	"	J. D. Clink
1891	Thistle	" "	2284	284	42·5	24·7	"	
1892	Valkyrie	steel ship	2270	283·3	42·5	24·5	"	Law
1891	Ross-shire	steel 4-m. bk.	2257	289·1	41·2	24·4	Scott	Mahon
1891	Oweenee	" "	2432	309	42	24·6	Richardson	
1891	Muskoka	" "	2357	300·5	42	24·7	"	Ritson
1891	Auchencairn	" "	2040	287·7	40·2	23·4	Ritson	Haws
1891	Alcedo	" "	2470	301	43·1	23·7	Royden	Potter Bros.
1891	Dunsyre	steel ship	2149	277·8	41·8	24·4	Hamilton	Gillison & Chadwick
1891	Drumrock	steel 4-m. bk.	3182	329·2	45·4	25·7	Ramage	Leitch & Muir
1891	Robert Duncan	" "	2166	279·7	42·1	24·5	Duncan	Dixon
1891	Dundonald	" "	2205	284·2	42	24·4	Workman	Barrie
1891	Garthpool ex Juteopolis	" "	2842	310	45	25·1	W. B. Thompson	Soley
1891	Ancaios ex Lillian L.Robbins	steel ship	1826	257·1	39	22·7	Russell	Kelley
1892	Celtic Queen	"	1833	257·6	39	22·7	Pickersgill	Hughes-Jones
1891	Celtic Race	"	1874	263	38·2	23	"	
1891	Carnedd Llewelyn	"	1726	260	39·1	23·2	Russell	
1888	Banklands	steel barque	1239	225·7	38·2	23·1	Reid	Just
1891	Bankleigh ex Annie Speirs	"	1540	243	36·3	22	Stephen	Brownells & Co.
1890	Bankburn	steel barque	1427	261	37	21·6	Grangemouth	Just
1890	Ardnamurchan	steel ship	1718	259·4	37·6	21	Russell	Hogarth
1891	Earl of Dunmore	steel 4-m. bk.	2287	277·9	42·1	24·2	"	J. D. Thomson

Register of Ships (in order of mention).—Continued.

Date built	Name	Rig	Gross Tons	Length	Br'dth	Depth	Builder	First Owners
1892	Howard D. Troop	steel 4-m. bk.	2165	291·3	42·2	24	Duncan	Troop
1892	Dalgonar	steel ship	2665	296	42·3	25·2	Southampton	Gracie, Beazley
1892	Peleus	,,	2122	277·5	41·1	24·1	Barclay	Carmichael
1892	The Highfields	steel 4-m. bk.	2280	291·3	42	24·5	Richardson	Kellock
1892	Nal ex Lord Ripon	,,	2765	318	43·2	24·5	Grangemouth	Herron
1892	Hawaiian Isles	,,	2097	270	43·1	23·6	Connell	A. Nelson
1891	Dominion	,,	2539	294	43	24	Doxford	W. Thomas
1891	Trade Winds	,,	2859	315·3	45	25	Ramage	Gardiner
1892	Wiscombe Park	steel ship	2228	281	42·2	24	Blumer	Windram
1890	Orion	steel barque	2081	280	41·2	23·9	Ramage	W. S. Croudace
1892	Procyon	,,	2122	279·8	41·2	23·9	,,	
1892	Springburn	steel 4-m. bk.	2655	296	45·6	25·7	Barclay	Shankland
1892	Fort Stuart	steel ship	2433	302	42·3	24	Sunderland	Stuart & Douglas
1877	Forthbank ex Nebo	iron barque	1442	246·9	37·1	21·1	Dobie	Weir
1891	Collesse	steel barque	1465	236	36	21·9	Russell	,,
1892	Isle of Arran	steel ship	1918	263·3	39	23	,,	,,
1890	Comliebank	steel 4-m. bk.	2283	278·6	41·9	24·2	,,	,,
1891	Thistlebank	,,	2430	283·7	42·9	24·2	,,	,,
1891	Gowanbank	,,	2288	278	42	24·2	,,	,,
1892	Beechbank	,,	2288	277·5	42	24·2	,,	
1893	Levernbank	steel 4-m. bk.	2400	282·9	43	24·4	Russell	Weir
1896	Thornliebank	steel ship	2105	269·7	40·5	23·6	,,	,,
1894	Springbank	steel 4-m. bk.	2398	282·4	43	24·4	,,	,,
1892	Cedarbank	,,	2825	326	43	24·5	Mackie, T.	,,
1892	Olivebank	,,	2824	326	43·1	24·5	,,	,,
1894	Falklandbank	steel ship	1913	265	39·1	23·2	,,	,,
1892	Windermere	steel 4-m. bk.	3050	320·1	43·1	25·7	Oswald	Fisher
1892	Lyderhorn	,,	2914	311·2	42·4	25·5	,,	De Wolf
1891	Rathdown	steel ship	2145	279·5	41·7	24·4	Workman	Martin
1892	Howth	steel 4-m. bk.	2244	284·4	41·9	24·5	,,	,,
1892	Austrasia	,,	2718	305·1	44	24·7	Russell	Goffey
1892	Oranasia	,,	2706	305·1	44	24·7	,,	,,
1890	Dunfermline	,,	2902	308·6	45·2	25·1	Potter	Macvicar, Marshall
1891	Forteviot	,,	3145	317·3	46	25·2	,,	,,
1891	Wanderer	,,	2903	309	46	25·8	,,	Potter
1892	Osborne	iron 4-m. bk.	3166	325	46	25·2	,,	Macvicar, Marshall
1892	Balmoral	,,	2614	301·8	41·9	24·6	,,	,,
1892	Dunstaffnage	steel 4-m. bk.	3317	327·8	47·2	25·6	,,	,,
1892	Travancore	steel ship	1936	269	39·7	23·3	Hamilton	Crawford

Register of Ships (in order of mention).—Continued.

Date built	Name	Rig	Gross Tons	Length	Br'dth	Depth	Builder	First Owners
1892	Donna Francisca	steel 4-m. bk.	2277	277·5	42	24·5	Russell	Hayes
1892	Achnashie	" " "	2476	293·8	45·5	25·2	Duncan	Thom & Cameron
1888	Afghanistan	iron 4-m. bk.	2286	291·2	42·1	24·3	Richardson	J. Macdonald
1892	Arracan	steel 4-m. bk.	2282	291·3	42·1	24·5	"	"
1897	Deccan	steel ship	1985	266	40·1	23·4	Duncan	
1892	North Star	steel 4-m. bk.	2761	316·8	43·2	24·5	Grangemouth	Bilbrough
1892	Crocodile	steel 4-m. bk.	2555	288·4	41·2	24·6	Southampton	Peel
1892	Crown of Germany	" " "	2241	284·4	41·9	24·5	Workman, Clark	Crown S.S. Co.
1892	Sofala	" " "	2301	277·5	42	24·2	Russell	Steeves
1892	Somali	" " "	3537	329·9	47	27	"	"
1893	Saratoga	" " "	2297	277·1	41·9	24·2	"	"
1892	Birkdale	steel barque	1483	248·5	37·5	21·7	Bigger	Iredale & Porter
1879	Gantock Rock ex Macleod	iron ship	1611	255·5	38·3	22·5	McMillan	McMillan
1886	Inchcape Rock	" "	1599	250·5	38·3	23	Russell	Cornfoot
1892	Beacon Rock	steel ship	1917	265·5	40	23	Rodger	"
1892	Castle Rock	"	1912	268	40	23	Connell	"
1894	Red Rock	"	1719	249·8	37·7	22·5	Hamilton	Mackay
1892	Saint Mungo	"	1955	272	40	23·6	Connell	"
1892	Saint Enoch	"	1955	272	40	23·6	"	"
1892	Saint Mirren	"	1956	272	40	23·6	"	"
1892	Balasore	steel 4-m. bk.	2724	311	43·6	24·5	Barclay	Eyre, Evans
1892	Lawhill	steel ship	2942	317·4	45	25·1	W. B. Thompson	Barrie
1892	William Mitchell	"	2035	272·7	41	23·7	Bigger	Mitchell
1888	Madagascar	steel 4-m. bk.	2145	282	40·5	24·6	Russell	Boyd
1892	Mozambique	" " "	2433	283·3	43	24·2	"	"
1892	Manchester	" " "	3046	312·9	46·1	25·8	Doxford	J. Joyce
1893	Lydgate	" " "	2534	304·3	43·2	24·3	Palmer	"
1892	Alcides	" " "	2704	312·1	43·2	24·4	Grangemouth	Haws
1892	James Kerr	" " "	2420	293·9	41·2	24·5	Royden	Peel, McAllester
1892	Fannie Kerr	steel 4-m. bk.	2426	293·9	41·2	24·5	"	"
1892	Gifford	" " "	2245	281·6	42·3	24·6	Scott	Briggs
1892	Gunford	" " "	2261	281·6	42·3	24·6	"	"
1892	Chiltonford	" " "	2348	298·8	44	24·5	Fairfield	"
1893	Chelmsford	" " "	2347	299	44	24·5	"	"
1894	Belford	steel ship	1905	267	40·1	23·6	McMillan	"
1892	Tonawanda ex India ex Lita	"	1757	260·7	38·1	23·1	Russell	H. N. A. Meyer
1892	Durbridge	steel ship	2201	276·8	42	24·2	Hamilton	Potter Bros.
1892	Blackbraes	"	2207	277·1	42	24·2	"	"
1891	Bardowie	"	2146	277·3	41·8	24·4	"	Hamilton

Register of Ships (in order of mention).—Continued.

Date built	Name	Rig	Gross Tons	Length	Br'dth	Depth	Builder	First Owners
1892	Barfillan	steel ship	2197	275·9	41·9	24·3	Hamilton	Hamilton
1892	Hyderabad	,,	2195	276·2	41·9	24·3	,,	Crawford
1894	Riversdale	,,	2206	275·8	41·9	24·3		Leyland
1892	Samoena		1962	272	40	23·6	Connell	Clink
1892	Yavana		1965	272	40	23·6		,,
1894	Zinita	steel barque	1633	251·2	38·1	21·6	,,	Hardie
1893	Corunna	steel 4-m. bk.	2432	293	43	24·4	Henderson	Black
1893	Queen Margaret		2144	275	42·2	24	McMillan	Galbraith
1892	Lauriston	steel 4-m.ship	2301	284·6	42	24·4	Workman	Soley
1893	Ancona	steel 4-m. bk.	2852	280·2	44·8	22·9	Russell	Denniston
1893	Bermuda		2846	280·2	44·8	22·9		Dunlop
1893	Clan Graham	,,	2147	282·9	40·4	24·6	,,	
1893	Clan Galbraith	,,	2149	282·9	40·4	24·6	,,	Kerr, Newton
1894	Kilmallie	steel barque	1634	245·8	37·6	22·7	,,	Walker
1893	King David	steel ship	2240	279·4	42·1	24·2	Russell	,,
1894	King George		2242	278·4	42·1	24·2		,,
1894	King Alfred	iron barque	1319	228	36·5	21	Barclay	,,
1886	King Malcolm		1327	228	36·5	21	W. B. Thompson	,,
1885	King Arthur	iron ship	1647	257·6	38·2	23·2	,,	
1887	King Edward	steel ship	1734	260	38	23	Russell	Begg
1891	Norma	steel 4-m. bk.	2122	278	41·2	24·1	Barclay	J. Ferguson
1893	Royal Forth		3130	329·3	45·3	25·6	Ramage	Williamson
1893	Centesima	,,	2949	308	46·2	25·8	Williamson	
1895	Iranian	,,	2958	308·3	46·2	25·8	,,	Ruffer
1893	Marechal Suchet	steel ship	1920	267	40·1	23·6	McMillan	R. N. Smith
1894	Vincent		1904	267	40·1	23·6	,,	,,
1896	Conway		1899	267	40·1	23·6		Johnston, Sproule
1894	Lynton	steel 4-m. bk.	2531	299·8	43·7	24·5	Evans	Law
1893	Kinross-shire	,,	2299	282·2	42·5	24·7	Russell	Law
1894	Inverness-shire	,,	2307	282·9	42·8	24·7	Duncan	Aitken, Lilburn
1894	Loch Nevis	,,	2431	301·7	43·7	24·6	Reid	Denniston
1894	Grenada	steel ship	2268	278·4	42	24·1	Russell	Barrie
1894	Dudhope	steel ship	2087	271	41·1	23·6	Connell	Law
1894	Caithness-shire	steel barque	1641	247·3	37·6	22·6	Russell	Law
1896	Duns Law		1636	247	37·5	22·6		R. J. Swyny
1894	Aspice	steel ship	1909	265	39·1	23·2	Mackie & Thomson	Lang & Fulton
1894	East Indian	steel barque	1745	252·6	39·1	22·5	Duncan	
1895	East African		1731	252·5	39	22·5	,,	Lang & Fulton
1897	Australian	steel ship	2103	270·5	40·5	23·6	Russell	

Register of Ships (in order of mention).—Continued.

Date built	Name	Rig	Gross Tons	Length	Br'dth	Depth	Builder	First Owners
1893	Cambuskenneth	steel ship	1925	263·5	39·1	23	Russell	R. Russell
1895	Kynance	"	1964	265·5	40	23·5	Rodger	Cowan
1892	Largiemore		1938	262·8	39	23·6	Russell	Thomson, Dickie
1893	Arranmore	steel ship	1946	263·8	39	23·6	Russell	"
1895	Monkbarns		1911	267	40·1	23·6	McMillan	Corsar
1893	Almora	steel barque	1856	257·8	39·2	22·9	Hamilton	"
1896	Fairport	steel ship	1996	265·9	40	23·5	Russell	"
1896	Musselcrag	steel barque	1985	266·6	40	23·7	Hamilton	"
1896	Falkirk	"	1986	268	40	23·7	"	Potter Bros
1897	Wynford	"	1983	267·3	40·1	23·5	"	Hickie
1893	Glenbank		1481	240·1	37	21·7	Rodger	Sterling
1893	Glenard	steel ship	1937	265·5	40·1	22·9	"	"
1894	Glendoon	"	1981	266·3	40·1	23·1	"	"
1895	Glenelvan	"	1919	265·4	40·1	23·1	"	"
1895	Glenfinart	"	1963	265·2	40	23·5	"	"
1896	Glenholm	"	1968	265·2	40	23·5	"	"
1897	Glenpark	"	1959	265·8	40	23·6	"	"
1897	Nivelle	steel 4-m. bk.	2430	292·4	43·2	24·2	Scott	Hardie
1897	Hougomont	"	2428	292·4	43·2	24	"	"
1893	Ben Lee	steel ship	2341	284·5	42·2	24·5	Barclay	Watson Bros.
1894	Ben Dearg	"	2349	283	43	24·5	Connell	"
1901	Eva Montgomery	"	1944	267	40·1	23·6	Hamilton	Montgomery
1901	Ladye Doris	steel ship	1947	267·4	40·1	23·6	Hamilton	"
1902	Fitzjames	steel 4-m. bk.	1951	267·1	40·1	23·6	McMillan	Montgomery
1902	Medway ex Ama Begonakoa	"	2516	300	43·2	24·8	Reid	Sota y Aznar
1902	Colonial Empire	"	2436	302·1	43·2	24·7	McMillan	Duncan
1902	Speedonia ex Urania	"	3265	330	47	27	Dundee S.B.C.	B. Wencke
1902	Saragossa	"	2289	289·9	43·3	24·5	Rodger	Hardie
1902	Bay of Biscay	steel ship	1998	265·7	40·1	23·6	Rodger	Beynon
1903	Castleton	steel ship	1971	265·1	40·1	23·6	Russell	Beynon
1903	Ormsary	steel 4-m. bk.	2251	278·8	42·1	24·5	Ailsa S.B.Co.	Lang & Fulton
1889	Kildalton	steel barque	1784	261·4	39·2	22·7	Hall	Hardie
1890	Inverurie	"	1417	242·2	37·1	21·6	Russell	Milne
1890	Invermark	"	1436	235·8	36·1	21·8	Russell	"
1891	Invercauld	"	1416	237·5	36·2	21·7	McMillan	"
1891	Inveresk	"	1415	237·5	36·2	21·5	"	"
1891	Invergarry	"	1416	237·5	36·2	21·5	"	"
1891	Inveramsay	"	1438	236·6	36·1	21·7	Russell	"
1892	Invercoe	"	1421	238	36·2	21·7	McMillan	"

Register of Ships (in order of mention).—Continued.

Date built	Name	Rig	Gross Tons	Length	Br'dth	Depth	Builder	First Owners
1892	*Inversnaid*	steel barque	1418	238	36·2	21·7	McMillan	Milne
1893	*Inverlyon*	,,	1450	238·6	36·1	21·7	Russell	,,
1895	*Inverlochy*	,,	1471	238·5	36	21·7	,,	,,
1895	*Invermay*	,,	1471	238	36	21·7	,,	,,
1895	*Inverneill*	,,	1470	238	36	21·7	,,	,,
1898	*Inverclyde*	,,	1634	245·6	37·5	22·5	,,	,,
1902	*Inverness*	steel ship	1959	267·5	40·1	23·6	McMillan	**Mitchell**
1892	*Inveravon ex John Cooke*		1879	266·6	40·1	23·2	Bigger	
	Inverlogie ex Chelmsford	*see Chelmsford*						
1904	*Inverlyon ex Gostwyck*	steel barque	1827	262	39·2	23	McMillan	Nicol & Co.
1893	*Inverkip*	steel barque	1466	235·8	36	21·7	Russell	Walker
1882	*Inversnaid*	iron ship	1614	250·4	38·1	22·9	Steele	Thompson, Anderson & Co.
1905	*Archibald Russell*	steel 4-m. bk.	2385	291·4	43·2	24·1	Scott	Hardie
1904	*Bellpool ex Wellgunde*	steel ship	1909	264·8	40·1	22·9	Rodger	Folsch
1905	*Belico ex Pelikan ex Dione*	steel ship	2103	271	40	23	Rijkee	Wachmuth
1901	*Grossherzogin Elisabeth*	steel ship	1260	223·6	39·4	20·9	Tecklenborg	Deutscher Schulschiff Verein
1902	*Herzogin Cecilie*	steel 4-m. bk.	3242	324·1	46	23·8	Rickmers	Norddeutscher Lloyd
1894	*Herzogin Sophie Charlotte*	,, ,,	2591	276·3	43·1	25·4		,,
1916	*Richelieu ex Pola*	steel 4-m. bk.	3100	322·5	47·2	26·5	Blohm & Voss	F. Laeisz
1908	*L'Avenir*	,, ,,	2738	278·2	44·8	26·5	Rickmers	Ass. Maritime Belge
1902	*Fennia ex Goodrich*	steel 4-m. bk.	3230	312·1	45·1	23·9	Forges & Chantiers de la M.	J.A. des Longs Courriers Francais
1895	*Favell*	steel barque	1363	237·5	36·2	21·3	Hill	Hill
1907	*Viking*	steel 4-m. bk.	2952	293·8	45·9	23·8	Akties Burmeister & Wain	Danish School Ship Co.

APPENDIX K.

REGISTER OF SMALL FRY.

Fish Carriers.

Date built	Name	Rig	Tons	L'gth	Br'th	Depth	Where built	Owners
1859	Olinda	barque	251	124·3	24·2	13·8	Greenock (Steele)	J. Munn & Co.
1860	Islay	brigantine	134	94·6	22·8	12	Wallace, N.S.	„
1864	Atlanta	„	143	98·2	22·9	11·4	P. E. Island	A. Munden
1866	Fruit Girl	schooner	125	93·2	22·1	11·2	Ipswich	Prowse & Sons
1868	Sunbeam	„	133	93·2	20·3	11·8	Brixham	C. T. Bennett
1868	Coleridge	„	193	103·7	23·6	12·8	Topsham	
1869	Belle	brigantine	195	104·2	24·4	12·9	P. E. Island	Walters
1872	William	brig	207	114·5	24·2	12·9	Bridport (Cox)	J. Munn
1872	Trusty	brig	163	101·6	23·4	12·6		
1874	Kestrel	brigantine	158	102·6	22	11·9	Falmouth	„
1874	Carles W. Oulton	„	205	102	25·9	11	„	„
1874	Petunia ex Jane	3-mast barquentine	216	116·6	23·6	12·7	New Brunswick	P. & L. Tessier
1874	Violet	brigantine	170	107·8	23	11·1	Bideford (Cox)	C. T. Bennett
1874	Gratia	brigantine	164	97	21·8	12·5	Sunderland	
1875	Rose of Torridge	schooner	114	88·8	21·4	10·7	Scilly	J. Munn & Co.
1875	Sea Breeze	„	103	84·4	21·6	9·4	Cox of Bideford	C. T. Bennett
1876	Maud	„	149	97	23·5	11·7	Appledore	
1877	Scotswood	brigantine	252	114·6	25·8	12·9	P. E. Island	„
1877	Evelyn	brig	216	104·9	25·6	13·9	Portmadoc	Greaves & Co.
1878	Flora	barquentine	303	126	25·8	14·9	Newport	J. Munn & Co.
1878	Belle of the Exe	barquentine	233	120	25·5	12·8	Exmouth	H. J. Stabb
1878	Silver Sea	„	188	103·3	23·3	12·8	Brixham	Tessier
1878	C. E. Spooner	3-mast schooner	186	103·2	24	12·7	Portmadoc	J. Jones & Co.
1878	Telephone	schooner	114	90	22·1	11·1	Plymouth	J. Westcott
1878	Muriel	3-mast schooner	165	105	23	12·2	Barnstaple	C. T. Bennett
1878	Rosevear	brigantine	177	99·6	22·7	12·7	Scilly	
1881	Clutha	3-mast schooner	261	125	24·8	12·8	Ardrossan	J. Munn & Co.
1896	Olwen	„	153	96·7	22·4	11·2	Pembroke Dock	W. Francis
1897	Amy Louise (Stella)	brigantine	200	105	26	12	P. E. Island	J. E. McDonald
1898	Minto	schooner	143	102·2	25·4	10	Lunenburg, N.S.	D. Zinck
1900	Clara	„	132	98·8	25·3	10·7	Mahone Bay, N.S.	A. Ernst
1901	Harold	„	123	90·8	24·7	10	„	
1905	James O.Neill	schooner	119	91	22·4	9·7	Connah's Quay	Kinsale S. Co.
1902	Royal Lister	3-mast schooner	140	92·3	23	11·7	Portmadoc	L. G. Llewelyn

Bristol Traders.

Date built	Name	Rig	Tons	L'gth	Br'th	Depth	Where built	Owners
1842	Queen of England	wood ship	876	160	30·1	20·1	London	R. & W. King
1852	Burns	wood barque	385	123·5	25·8	17·2	Annan	"
1853	Dawstone	"	496	137·8	21·5	17·6	Arbroath	"
1854	Lord Raglan	"	725	169·2	31·5	20·1	Cardiff	"
1857	Bolivia	"	378	147·8	25·9	17·3	Whitehaven	"
1858	Laughing Water	"	223	119·7	23·2	13·8	Plymouth	"
1859	Mohican	"	326	130·6	26·6	16	Waterford	"
1860	La Zingara	"	276	123·6	23·5	14·1	Liverpool	"
1861	Ceara	"	293	127·5	23	14·9	Liverpool	"
1864	Sir Humphry Davy	"	307	123·3	24·5	15·4	Bristol	"
1865	Beatrice	"	461	143·7	27·2	15·4	Bideford	"
1865	Ribbllon (ex Manolo)	iron barque	402	138·7	25·3	17·6	Preston	"
1866	Mervyn	"	318	115·4	24·1	15	Sunderland	"
1867	Charlotte Young	"	302	133·3	24·2	13·9	Hartlepool	"
1868	Avonside	wood barque	254	114·8	25·4	15·1	Plymouth	"
1872	Elvira Camino ex Dona Juan	a composite barque	303	126·5	26·1	13·8	Glasgow	"
1873	Edmund Richardson	schooner	301	129	26·8	12·9	Sunderland	"
1875	Leonor Troncosa	iron bn.	330	136·7	25·1	14	Glasgow	"
1877	Gartmorn	wood barque	342	129·4	27·8	12·8	Alloa	Lucas Bros. & Co.
1847	Ann Hood	wood brig	199	95·4	22·2	14·1	Glasgow	"
1848	Watkins	wood snow	279	115·7	21·7	15·4	Newhaven	"
1850	Fanny Chapman	wood barque	266	119·5	23·3	14·6	Liverpool	"
1854	Cambrian	wood barque	231	116·7	24	14	Sunderland	"
1857	Frankby	wood barque	437	125·1	17·8	9·9	Liverpool	"
1858	Look-out	wood bn.	197	112·7	22·4	14·2	Workington	"
1859	Echo	wood barque	243	118	24	15	Sunderland	"
1861	Ibis	"	249	114	24	14·5	Liverpool	"
1862	Inca	"	440	132·6	26·6	18·3	Sunderland	"
1862	Daisy	wood snow	311	107·5	26·5	16·5	Liverpool	"
1864	Cavioca	wood barque	322	129·6	24·3	14·9	Jersey	Rider, Son & Andrew
1859	Amber Nymph	wood brig	254	129·5	25·6	12·8	Sunderland	Cummins & Co.
1866	Charmian	composite barque	575	150·4	28·8	18·7	"	"
1866	Jane Lamb	wood barque	303	117·5	26·1	15·8	London	"
1870	Gift	"	287	112·1	26·5	16·1	"	T. Daniel & Sons
1842	Sylph	wood barque	614	140·7	28·7	19·7	"	"
1842	Candidate	"	604	139·3	28·6	20·3	"	"
1842	Maria	"	373	107·2	24·4	18·6	Bristol	"
1853	Louisa	"	436	148·6	25·5	16·4	"	"
1854	Dora	"	216	114·6	19·5	12·6	"	"

Bristol Traders.—Continued.

Date built	Name	Rig	Tons	L'gth	Br'th	Depth	Where built	Owners
1858	Frances	wood barque	316	123	25·4	15·5	Bristol	T. Daniel & Sons
1861	Orchid	"	241	129	22·6	12·9	"	"
1866	Iduna	"	350	118·7	27·5	17·1	Sunderland	"
1868	Augusta	"	547	150·3	30·2	18·9	Bristol	"
1868	Maria Wakefield	Composite barque	362	121·6	26·1	16·6	Whitby	"
1869	Gwendoline	wood barque	356	128	25·9	16·1	"	"
1873	Mabel	"	465	144·6	27·9	17·6	"	"
1869	Okenbury	wood brig	247	112	24·5	14·9	Salcombe	W. W. Steer
1876	Beatrice	"	316	119	26·7	14·7	"	Yabsley & Co.
1871	Waterloo	"	264	113·8	25·8	14·8	Blyth	J. Manners
1861	Lady of the Lake	wood barque	348	118·8	25·4	16·3	Dundee	Turner, Edwards & Co.
1863	Light of the Age	"	472	133	28·5	18·2	S'wick	"
1867	Payta	iron barque	680	169·7	29·2	18·1	Sunderland	"
1886	Santa	"	979	205·8	33·6	19·6	"	"
1891	Lota	steel barque	1367	232	37	21·6	"	"

Sunderland Barques.

Date built	Name	Rig	Tons	L'gth	Br'th	Depth	Where built	Owner
1862	Claro Babuyan	wood barque	358	125	27	17	Sunderland	W. Adamson
1866	Sooloo	"	473	138·2	28·9	17·9	"	"
1866	Guam	3-mast schooner	291	112·8	25·7	16·7	"	"
1867	Bussorah	wood barque	395	122·7	28·9	17·6	"	"
1867	Loochoo	"	495	141	29·7	17·9	"	"
1868	Valkyrien	"	498	147·8	30	18·1	"	"
1868	Evangeline	"	352	116·2	27·2	16·5	"	"
1869	Fluelin	Composite barque	529	141·5	30·5	18	"	"
1869	Stanfield	Wood barque	595	153·1	30·7	18·3	"	"
1870	Ching-too	"	317	129	26·4	12·9	"	"
1859	Thomas Wood	"	520	125	28·6	18·9	"	F. & W. Ritson
1862	Alice Ritson	"	538	138	29	19	"	"
1863	Evelyn Wood	"	385	126	26·6	16·8	"	"
1867	T. B. Ord	brig	402	131·6	27·6	17·1	"	"
1867	Contest	composite barque	486	138	28·4	17·7	"	"
1868	John Ritson	brig	533	143·6	29·5	18·2	"	"
1868	Phaeton	composite barque	596	151·1	30·4	18	"	"

British Coasters.

Date built	Name	Rig	Tons	L'gth	Br'th	Depth	Where built	Owner
1854	Alice Williams	wood schooner	132	80.8	20.5	11.8	Llanelly	G. Sanders
1860	Elizabeth McLea	wood bn.	128	99.7	20.2	10.8	Greenock	J. Horan
1869	Resolute	3-mast schooner	229	116.6	24.6	13.2	Aberdeen	Whitstable S. Co.
1866	Margaret Sutton	iron bn.	197	104.5	23.7	12.8	Cork	F. Moses
1865	Iron Queen	barque	234	113	23.4	12.7	Newport	H. & E. Crundall
1890	Friendship	wood schooner	223	117	25.5	10.6	Sittingbourne	Smith Bros.
1884	Nellie Fleming ex Emily	3-mast schooner	119	94.1	22.4	9.5	Carrickfergus	M. J. Fleming
1879	Flying Foam	wood schooner	112	88.4	20.4	10.5	Jersey	P. Noel
1871	Waterwitch	barquentine	207	112	25.8	12.8	Poole	E. Stephens
1873	Lydia Cardell	3-mast schooner	241	118	24.8	13.6	Appledore	W. Geake
1874	Cumberland Lassie	,,	230	114.6	24	13.8	Almwych	T. H. Franks
1880	Coppename	wood barque	329	137.3	27.8	12.9	Sunderland	Sir W. Crundall
1857	James Simpson	wood schooner	173	91.5	23.2	13	Lynn	J. A. Beeching
1872	Kate	,,	129	91	22	11.3	Isle of Man	Mrs. C. Graves
1876	Pet	,,	113	89.4	21.2	10.4	Kingston	R. Jones
1868	Mary Ann Mandall	,,	112	84	20.6	10.9	Ulverston	A. Dilworth
1891	Elsa	steel 3-mast sch'r	128	97.1	21.9	11	Plymouth	W. H. Shilston
1885	Margaret Murray	wood schooner	184	107.2	23.7	11.7	Grangemouth	A. Tate & Co.
1846	Sapphire	,,	177	88.2	23.6	13.8	Greenock	McArthur Bros.
1847	Onyx	,,	208	91.7	22.8	14.5	,,	,,
1867	Jasper	iron schooner	268	129.1	24.5	13.8	,,	,,
1870	Flower of the Fal	wood schooner	149	98	23.3	12	Padstow	Captain J. Woolcock

Pacific Traders.

Date built	Name	Rig	Tons	L'gth	Br'th	Depth	Where built	Owners
1900	Ronga	wood schooner	143	98.7	23	7.1	Auckland	T. H. Ker
1878	Aratapu	wood bn.	122	95	23.7	9	,,	Union Sash Door Co.
1867	John Wesley	composite brig	238	118	23.9	13.5	Aberdeen	Wesleyan Mission
1874	Ysabel ex Southern Cross	wood 3-mast sch'r	148	107.1	21.2	11.8	Auckland	W. Ross
1869	George Noble	,, ,,	265	121.6	25.3	14	Fraserburgh	U. Chong
1878	Alexa	iron bkn.	441	144.3	26.8	15.6	Sunderland	D. H. McKenzie
1863	Stanley	wood schooner	115	92	20.1	10.5	Granton	W. A. Walpen

Pacific Traders.—Continued.

Date built	Name	Rig	Tons	L'gth	Br'th	Depth	Where built	Owners
1861	Sibyl	wood schooner	120	80	20·7	1	Milford	P. Graham
1868	Forest King	,,	172	98·2	22·3	13·1	Plymouth	S. Hodgson
1860	Alfred Vittery	,,	122	92	20·7	11	Brixham	
1834	Vibilia	,,	108	—	—	—	Plymouth	T. G. Kelly
1862	Para	wood brig	252	115·7	23·4	14·6	Alloa	J. MacMillan
1869	Rio Loge	iron brig	250	122·3	24·7	12·8	Garston	C. W. Turner
1869	May	wood bkn.	237	114·7	25·1	12·8	Sunderland	J. H. Cock
1881	Lord of the Isles	wood 3-mast s'chr	208	116·4	22·4	11·1	Sydney	H. Beattie
1876	Hopeful	wood bkn.	231	111·4	26·3	12·8	Padstow	Burns, Philp & Co.
1877	Northern Belle	wood schooner	214	114·6	25	13	Garmouth	W. Whyte & Co.
1878	Venture	wood bkn.	249	119·3	25·1	12·9	Garmouth	J. Geddie

INDEX

INDEX

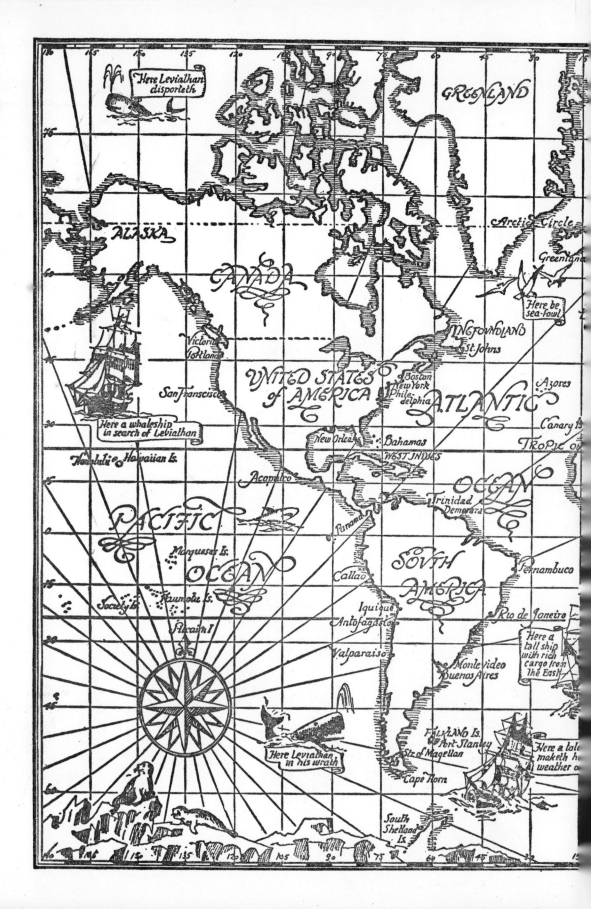